The BP exhibition

Troy
myth and reality

The BP exhibition

Troy
myth and reality

Alexandra Villing, J. Lesley Fitton,
Victoria Donnellan and Andrew Shapland

The BP exhibition *Troy: myth and reality*
Supported by BP

Captions with an asterisk * after the figure number indicate that the object is included in the exhibition.

Frontispiece: Red-figure jar (*stamnos*) showing Odysseus sailing past the Sirens. *c.* 480–470 BC. See Fig. 98.

Illustrations on chapter openers: Ralph Applebaum Associates.

This publication accompanies the BP exhibition *Troy: myth and reality* at the British Museum from 21 November 2019 to 8 March 2020.

This exhibition at the British Museum has been made possible by the provision of insurance through the Government Indemnity Scheme. The British Museum would like to thank the Department for Digital, Culture, Media and Sport and Arts Council England for providing and arranging this indemnity.

First published in the United Kingdom in 2019 by Thames & Hudson Ltd, in collaboration with the British Museum

British Library Cataloguing-in-Publication Data
A catalogue record for this book is available from the British Library

ISBN 978-0-500-48058-8

Printed and bound in Italy by Printer Trento SrL

Thames & Hudson Ltd, 181A High Holborn, London WC1V 7QX

To find out about all our publications, please visit **www.thamesandhudson.com**. There you can subscribe to our e-newsletter, browse or download our current catalogue, and buy any titles that are in print.

For more information about the Museum and its collection, please visit **britishmuseum.org.**

CONTENTS

SPONSOR'S FOREWORD

BOB DUDLEY
GROUP CHIEF EXECUTIVE, BP

For all the stories ever told, it is often said that there are just seven core plots. If so, then the story of Troy includes most of them: quests, voyages, fortune-seeking, rebirth, and, of course, tragedy. It is a story that has been told and retold numerous times over the centuries, and yet it maintains a strong grip on our imaginations.

This exhibition, the first on the subject of Troy in the UK in over 140 years, brings together recent finds and new thinking to untangle some of the myths from the historical truths, the two having become interwoven over the centuries. Through the skilful curation of remarkable artefacts such as the Felix Gem, a Roman marble sarcophagus lid, and the Greek Siren Vase, supported by archaeological evidence, we gain a fresh insight into the story of Troy and some of the best-known characters in Greek mythology, including Achilles, Hector, Helen and Odysseus.

At BP, we have our own stories that connect us with Troy and the British Museum. The modern homeland of ancient Troy is a country we know very well, having first established businesses in Turkey over 100 years ago. The thermal imaging that revealed new finds at the site of Homeric Troy is similar to the technology we use to discover oil and gas. And we share the commitment of the British Museum to bringing the very best of the arts and culture to a wide audience. So far, we have enabled nearly five million people to experience extraordinary exhibitions like this one, over a partnership that now spans more than 20 years.

We hope many thousands of people will enjoy this exhibition, and we look forward to supporting many more in years to come. I'd like to thank the British Museum for our continued partnership, and congratulate the team on creating a truly fascinating insight into Troy and its legend.

I do hope you enjoy the exhibition, and the information in this accompanying publication.

DIRECTOR'S FOREWORD

HARTWIG FISCHER
BRITISH MUSEUM

When Sultan Mehmed II captured Constantinople for the Ottoman Turks in 1453, he was said to have finally exacted revenge for the ancient Greek sack of Troy. Sympathies clearly lay with the Trojans in that period. Most of Europe's ruling houses, including the British, proudly claimed descent from Trojans who had fled the destruction of their homes at the hands of the Greeks. That a group of refugees from the East should be at the root of a shared European identity may come as a surprise to us today. Yet the story of Troy is full of unexpected twists and turns.

No other ancient Greek myth has had as influential a legacy as that of the Trojan War. Troy holds out for ten long years, but finally the Greeks are victorious and the city is destroyed. The war is won, but everyone suffers. In Homer, who gives us the most famous account of the story, there is no sense that either the Greeks or the Trojans have right on their side – both are equally heroic, and equally fallible. Their triumphs and tragedies are pictured with remarkable insight and humanity.

Countless artists have brought the story and its characters to life in sculptures, pottery and paintings, and in domestic interiors and jewellery. The British Museum collection includes some of the most striking ancient images of the Trojan War and this exhibition is an opportunity to place them beside other extraordinary works. The myth of Troy has also had a long life after antiquity, and the exhibition shows how artists up to the present have looked at it through fresh eyes.

Troy is not only a place of the imagination. It was a real city, its imposing remains first excavated in modern Turkey by Heinrich Schliemann in the late nineteenth century. The archaeology of Troy is presented here as it was understood by Schliemann and as it is viewed today by archaeology.

The exhibition has been made possible through generous loans from many museums, galleries and private collections, to whom we are extremely grateful. Special thanks are due to the Museum für Vor- und Frühgeschichte, Berlin, for its loan of nearly one hundred objects, enabling us to display many of Schliemann's finds.

Finally, I would like to express my gratitude to our long-term exhibition partner BP. Without their support it would be impossible to present such an ambitious exhibition to our visitors from the UK and abroad, allowing them to immerse themselves in the story of Troy.

INTRODUCTION
TROY: FALL OF A CITY, RISE OF A LEGEND

J. LESLEY FITTON, ALEXANDRA VILLING,
VICTORIA DONNELLAN AND ANDREW SHAPLAND

In Troy, there lies the scene.
Shakespeare, *Troilus and Cressida*, Act 1, prologue

The story of the Trojan War is one of the world's greatest stories, told and retold by generations for some 3,000 years. Its setting was the city of Troy – thought long lost, but rediscovered in modern Turkey in the nineteenth century. The archaeology of Troy continues to fascinate, not least because it holds out the hope of finding the historical truth behind the ancient myth: did the Trojan War actually happen? But perhaps more compelling truths can be found in the story itself and its characters. Beautiful Helen, swift Achilles and clever Odysseus who devised the fateful ruse of the Trojan Horse: they are as alive for us today as they were for the ancients, and have inspired poets and artists from Homer to Derek Walcott and from Rubens to Cy Twombly. The story of Troy, with its universal themes of violence and destruction, love, despair and hope, continues to speak to people across cultures and through time.

AN EPIC TALE

You tell so accurately what the Greeks
achieved, and what they suffered, there at Troy,
as if you had been there, or heard about it
from somebody who was. So sing the story
about the Wooden Horse, which Epeius
built with Athena's help.
Odyssey 8.489–93[1]

The ancient Greeks told an epic story about the heroes of a bygone age, who fought and won a long and bitter war against the powerful city of Troy. After a ten-year siege, a clever stratagem brought the Greeks victory. They built a huge wooden horse, large enough for armed warriors to hide inside, and tricked the Trojans into pulling it into their city. Troy fell, and its people were killed, enslaved or forced to flee.

To this day, the Trojan Horse is proverbial, having been used over the centuries as a metaphor for any clever deception successfully carried out. It has appeared in art from ancient times, when Greeks first told the story of Troy in images (Fig. 1), through the Middle Ages, when the city became a fantasy setting for knights and ladies, up to the present day, as artists and their audiences have made Troy their own in a dialogue of art and ideas. Thus in 1980, Scottish artist Eduardo Paolozzi created a lithograph entitled *After Biagio di Antonio* (Fig. 2), in which he incorporated a detail of a late fifteenth-century panel (Fig. 3; see also p. 248 and Fig. 252). The wooden horse is seen being pulled into Troy as though viewed through the windscreen of a car.[2] Ancient myth, Renaissance masterpiece and the modern world are strikingly captured together in this work, which evokes the way in which different visions and re-imaginings of the story of Troy have been layered over time.

Troy was important to the ancient Greeks because they claimed direct descent from the heroes who fought there. As they saw it, the age of heroes had directly preceded their own, and was a time when humanity was closer to the gods. Heroes, often of divine parentage, were extraordinarily strong, fast and bright, indeed larger than life in every way. But they were still human, and they were still Greeks. Their individual exploits were aspired to and admired, even if their transgressions were criticized, and what they had jointly achieved at Troy was breath-taking. After Helen, the wife of one of their kings, had been abducted by a Trojan prince, all the kingdoms across Greece had united to bring together the largest

OPPOSITE ABOVE
Fig. 2
After Biagio di Antonio

1980
Eduardo Paolozzi; printed
by Hans Kahler, Munich
Lithograph on paper
H. 152 mm | W. 254 mm
Tate
P07683

OPPOSITE BELOW
Fig. 3*
**Detail of *The Siege
of Troy – The Wooden
Horse***
The painting once
adorned a wedding
chest (*cassone*) (see
also Fig. 252).

c. 1490–95
Biagio d'Antonio
Tempera on panel
H. 470 mm | W. 1610 mm
Fitzwilliam Museum,
University of Cambridge
M.45

fighting force ever seen. A fleet of more than a thousand ships was launched to sail to Troy to bring Helen back.

The city of Troy was a noble adversary. Its high walls had been built by the gods and its warriors were heroes, like the Greeks themselves. Indeed, in this quintessentially Greek myth, the Trojans appear as if they were Greek, speaking the same language as their Greek opponents, living according to the same social norms and rules, and protected by the same gods. Nonetheless, Troy was a city on distant shores: it was located on the opposite side of the Mediterranean Sea, far from the Greeks' homelands (see Map, pp. 284–85). It dominated a coastal plain in what is now Turkey, near to the entrance to the Dardanelles strait (Fig. 4).

We know the story of Troy and the Trojan War because it was central to Greek thought and Greek art. Philosophers mused on it, dramatists brought it to the stage, historians considered how it fitted into the past, and poets found in it a source of inspiration. The story was depicted in sculpture, paintings and all the smaller media, particularly Greek painted pottery. The Greek inheritance was adapted and repurposed by the Etruscans in Italy and then the Romans, giving the story of Troy a long life in ancient art. The poet Homer was the dominant figure in the literary tradition, revered by the ancient world as the author of the *Iliad* and the *Odyssey*. These epic poems each tell a part of the story of Troy. Indeed, the word 'Iliad' means 'Troy story', and derives from Ilios or Ilion, the city's alternative name.

A CITY IN TIME

'Father', retorted I, 'if such walls once existed, they cannot possibly have been completely destroyed: vast ruins of them must still remain, but they are hidden away beneath the dust of ages'.
Heinrich Schliemann[3]

'Did the Trojan War really happen?' This is still the question most frequently asked by people thinking about the story of Troy today. It is deceptively simple to ask, but remains tantalizingly difficult to answer. Archaeology has not found anything as specifically linked to the myth as, say, the remains of the wooden horse at Troy. Only a discovery of that kind could really be viewed as hard evidence that the story is true. But archaeology has revealed the ancient city of Troy, located in modern Turkey exactly where the myth describes it. Its strategic position at the entrance to the Dardanelles explains its ancient importance.

The name of Heinrich Schliemann (1822–1890) will forever be linked with the discovery of Troy. He was not in fact the first to dig there, but he accomplished the first large-scale excavations, and so perhaps deserves the lion's share of the glory. He certainly told his own story in a heroic light, which has added to the lustre of what might be termed the Schliemann myth. After Troy, he went on to excavate at Mycenae, in Greece, famous in legend as the home of King Agamemnon, the leader of the Greeks in the Trojan War, and called by Homer 'rich in gold'. His claims to have found Priam's Palace and the Troy destroyed in the Trojan War, and indeed the tomb of Agamemnon at Mycenae, did not stand up to scrutiny. But he was certainly one of the first to uncover an early period of Greek (and Anatolian) history that had hitherto been virtually unknown, thus firmly putting the Greek Bronze Age (about 3000–1100 BC) on the map.

At both Troy and Mycenae, Schliemann's finds included extraordinary golden treasures. This has contributed to another myth, that of Schliemann as 'gold-seeker'. In fact he made no personal profit from his finds, and his true motivation was similar to that of the Homeric heroes: he sought fame and reputation above all. After Schliemann's lifetime, yet another tale has unfolded around the most famous of his finds: the so-called 'Priam's Treasure', which included what he thought were the 'Jewels of Helen'. The treasure, excavated by Schliemann at Troy and eventually taken to his native Germany, disappeared from Berlin at the end of the Second World War. Speculation about its fate was rife; many people suspected that it had been melted down and would never be seen again. It came as a surprise, therefore, when the Russian authorities revealed in the 1990s that the treasure had survived, because it had been removed from Berlin to Russia at the end of the war.[4]

Archaeologists continue to explore the site of Troy with modern techniques and add to our knowledge of its development over time. Schliemann's 'Priam's Troy' is now known to belong to the Early Bronze Age, about a thousand years too early to be a plausible background to the myth of the Trojan War. But the excavations of Late Bronze Age Troy have revealed a rich and powerful city with strongly built walls (Fig. 5) that was engaged in trade and contact with the Greek world. In Greece at this time, the city of Mycenae was equally flourishing. We know, then, that around the fourteenth and thirteenth centuries BC both Troy and Mycenae, the two main places in the myth, did exist and were aware of each other. They could certainly have entered into a conflict.

Further specifics, though, are lacking. We see Troy and Mycenae and their strength with our own eyes, but we can find no actual indication that a King Priam or a King Agamemnon once lived there. There is a feasible historical background for some sort of Trojan War, but for anything more concrete we can only look to future discoveries.

ABOVE LEFT
Fig. 4
An aerial view of the site of Troy and the Dardanelles, 2007

ABOVE RIGHT
Fig. 5
Reconstruction of the South Gate of Troy VI (1750–1300 BC)

A PLACE OF THE IMAGINATION

I too saw the wooden horse blocking the stars.
Derek Walcott, *The Odyssey: A Stage Version*[5]

It was from the rubble of a great city brought low that the legend of Troy took flight and began its long life. Scholars, writers, artists and musicians through the ages, all the way back to the ancient Greeks, have found their own truths within the story, discovering in it archetypes of human character and human experience closely related to their own, contemporary concerns. The richness of responses to the myth of Troy, at all times between antiquity and the present, shows the vitality of this long tradition.

In this book we explore some of the most compelling ways the story has been told, retold, used and imagined anew, drawing examples from medieval romance to Renaissance allegory, from Enlightenment scholarship to twentieth-century society and politics, and we follow the story through to the present day. There are recurring themes, such as Troy's role as cultural and political icon, linked to its position at the meeting point of Europe and Asia. Yet the story has proved almost infinitely versatile, inspiring a far wider variety of responses than can be summarized here. Much more could be said at every juncture. This becomes apparent if we briefly consider the Troy story in our own world today.

In Homer's *Odyssey*, the Greek hero Odysseus, at a feast, asks a bard to sing the story of the wooden horse and the fall of Troy. He weeps as he hears it. Already this retelling of the story provides a form of therapy for Odysseus, allowing him to express his grief. Those who have experienced war or suffered its consequences in modern times have found their experiences, too, echoed in the story.[6] In 2018 a staged reading of Alice Oswald's poem *Memorial* formed part of the commemorations of the centenary of the First World War.[7] Published in 2011, *Memorial* is a translation of the *Iliad* which strips away everything except the deaths of the fighters and the accompanying similes (see also pp. 207–8). It thus acts as a powerful memorial for all the dead, in every war. More immediate and personal are the experiences a group of female Syrian refugees in Amman in Jordan drew on for a production of Euripides' *The Trojan Women*, a fifth-century BC Athenian play. First staged in 2013, it later toured the UK as *Queens of Syria* (see p. 208 and Fig. 211).[8] In the words of one of the cast members, Maha: 'Troy's story is very similar to Syria's story, its women, its children, the country that was destroyed. So when they offered us this text and this play we were very keen to participate because we all lived the real experience.'[9]

The great versatility of the story is also apparent in the diversity of topical themes picked out in modern retellings. Madeline Miller's best-selling novel, *The Song of Achilles*, published in 2011, focuses on the relationship between Achilles and Patroclus that lies at the centre of the *Iliad*. Patroclus becomes the narrator, and Miller's exploration of his feelings towards Achilles softens the story for a modern audience in a way that contrasts with the unrelenting violence of the *Iliad*. Her *Circe* of 2018 provides a fresh perspective on the women in the *Odyssey*. In *The Silence of the Girls*, published in the same year, Pat Barker chooses Briseis, the captive woman awarded to Achilles as a trophy, as narrator and reflects on the experience of women in war. Most recently, in 2019, Natalie Haynes' *A Thousand Ships* gives voice to female characters, both Greek and Trojan, and shows this war belongs to the women just as much as it does to the men.

Other writers and artists have channelled the power of the *Iliad* and *Odyssey* towards cultures and circumstances far removed from their Greek origins. Derek Walcott relocated

the Troy story to his native St Lucia in order to create a Caribbean epic, *Omeros*, with some of the same characters, but with a memory of slave ships replacing Odysseus' homeward journey (see p. 225). The African-American artist Romare Bearden reimagined the return of Odysseus as part of the Black Diaspora in his collages (Fig. 6), which echo European paintings (Fig. 7) as well as incorporating African and Caribbean elements (see also pp. 225–26).[10] American artist Eleanor Antin's staged photographs similarly rework paintings by artists such as Rubens to reconsider the role of beautiful Helen (see p. 260). These subversive versions of the Troy story use familiar characters in order to re-evaluate traditional gender roles or colonial attitudes.

Twentieth-century artists have also invoked the battlefield of Troy. Between 1993 and 1994 sculptor Anthony Caro (1924–2013) made a group of forty sculptures called *The Trojan War* in a process that was almost archaeological (Fig. 8).[11] Lumps and rough chunks of clay, created in collaboration with his friend, ceramicist Hans Spinner, seemed to him to become the heads of gods and heroes. Fired into rugged stoneware, they were combined with wood and steel in a gradual process. Caro said: 'I worked very loosely, intuitively.'[12] Some of the works became human figures, others were buildings. The towers of Troy and the Scaean Gate became part of the group composition. This was a physical representation of the Trojan War on an epic scale that had in a sense been excavated from the sculptor's imagination. The work invited viewers to walk through the battlefield of Troy, experiencing the immediacy of the story, and reflecting on Troy as a place of myth as well as history.

ABOVE LEFT
Fig. 6
The Return of Odysseus (Homage to Pinturicchio and Benin)
Using Pintorrichio's fresco as the basis of his composition, Bearden appears to move the scene to the ancient African kingdom of Benin.

1977
Romare Bearden
Collage of cut-and-pasted papers, with graphite and touches of brush and black and grey wash on wood panel
H. 111.8 cm | W. 142.2 cm
Art Institute of Chicago
1977.127

ABOVE RIGHT
Fig. 7
Penelope with the Suitors
Odysseus' wife Penelope is seated at her loom as her son, Telemachus, announces Odysseus' homecoming, startling Penelope's suitors. Odysseus, dressed as a beggar, is seen in the doorframe.

1509
Pintoricchio,
Palazzo del Magnifico, Siena, Italy
Fresco, detached and mounted on canvas
H. 125.5 cm | W. 152 cm
The National Gallery, London
NG911

ABOVE
Fig. 8*
The Death of Hector,
King Priam and ***The***
Skaian Gate
From *The Trojan War*, a
series of forty sculptures
representing the Trojan
battlefield. The figure of
Priam recalls elements
of the Bronze Age
architecture of Mycenae.

1993–94
Anthony Caro
Ceramic, pine, steel
(left, centre); stoneware,
steel, jarrah wood (right)
H. 168 cm | W. 122 cm |
L. 135 cm; H. 137 cm |
W. 74 cm | L. 34.5 cm;
H. 229 cm | W. 305 cm |
L. 153 cm
Barford Sculptures

1 STORYTELLERS

J. LESLEY FITTON AND ALEXANDRA VILLING

Strangers, the ash of ages has devoured me, holy Ilion, the famous city once renowned for my towered walls, but in Homer I still exist, defended by brazen gates. The spears of the destroying Achaeans shall not again dig me up, but I shall be on the lips of all Greece.
Evenus of Ascalon, *The Greek Anthology* 9.62[1]

The fate of ancient Troy, or Ilion, destroyed by an army of Greek ('Achaean') warriors, is best known from the poems of Homer and Virgil and plays by Aeschylus, Sophocles and Euripides. Yet these are just some of the versions of the tale that existed in antiquity, many of which are lost today. Nor were all of these versions necessarily literary. The ancient Greeks and Romans knew of the Trojan War, and other events set in a mythical past, first of all through spoken words, from formal epic recitals to tales they heard as children. They also knew them from images – paintings on walls or on vases, stories woven into textiles, figures carved into gems or from stone, and from the art that decorated temples, houses or gardens. Plays in the theatre combined both visual and spoken elements, while informal performances such as mimetic dances or burlesques might be witnessed at religious festivals. This rich variety of narratives produced in different contexts and for different audiences, allowed for widely accepted stories to emerge but also for variations of them, often even existing in the same place at the same time. There was no one canonical version of the tale. Poets, visual artists and artisans would highlight different aspects, shaping, embellishing and continually modifying them for different audiences. This adaptability of the narrative is important to remember when we look at the selection of texts and artefacts that has come down to us from antiquity (and the even smaller selection included in this book). There can be no denying, though, that some realizations of the story were more powerful, and that some authors proved more influential than others.

HOMER AND BEYOND: TROY IN LITERATURE

The enigma of Homer

> The summit on which everyone's gaze should be fixed may rightly be named as Homer, 'the source whence all the rivers flow and all the seas and every fountain'.
> Dionysius of Halicarnassus, *On Literary Composition* 24[2]

These words of the ancient Greek historian Dionysius of Halicarnassus, writing in the first century BC, sum up the ancient Greek attitude to Homer, which was one of admiration bordering on reverence. The line 'the source whence all the rivers flow' is itself borrowed from the *Iliad* (21.196–97). As early as the fourth century BC, Aristotle had called Homer 'godlike', and ascribed to him pre-eminence and significance in many branches of study beyond the art of poetry. When Plato, around 380 BC, resolved that he must exclude all poets and poetry from his ideal republic, it was with palpable regret that Homer, too, must go, even though it was generally felt that he was 'the educator of Greece' (Plato, *Republic* 10.606e).[3]

Homer was, then, to the ancient Greeks the greatest poet of all time, and more. Although his epics were not viewed as holy scriptures, they came close. Homer invoked the divine Muse to inspire him, but made no claim to reveal the word of god; rather his works offered a wide-ranging survey of divine and mortal actions and their consequences from a human point of view. And, of course, they were compelling, action-packed stories. Aeschylus, one of the great fifth-century BC Athenian tragedians, allegedly described his own plays as 'slices from Homer's banquet'.[4] By this he meant the whole of the extensive Epic Cycle that circulated during antiquity and told the long and complex saga of Troy in its entirety.[5] Homer was loosely thought to be the towering figure who had originated all these stories, though in time his contribution was gradually narrowed down so that only the *Iliad*, which tells an episode from the tenth year of the Trojan War, and the *Odyssey*, which recounts Odysseus' long journey home after the War, were generally agreed to be his. These were the works that survived in their entirety, while the rest of the Epic Cycle has only been preserved in fragments (see p. 31).

The relief sculpture known as *The Apotheosis of Homer*, carved by the sculptor Archelaos of Priene in about 225–205 BC, sums up this reverence for Homer in visual form (Fig. 9).[6] The monument was commissioned as an offering to the gods by a contemporary poet who had won a poetic contest and who is himself represented as a simple draped statue on a plinth at the right, near the god Apollo, who is holding a lyre, and the Muses on Mount Helicon. Homer is shown enthroned at the bottom left, flanked by figures personifying the *Iliad* and the *Odyssey* and crowned by two figures representing Time and the Inhabited World. Inscriptions name all the figures, so we are in no doubt that what we are seeing here is Homer, revered as a god, being welcomed into the company of the gods and goddesses as he himself becomes divine. We know of numerous sanctuaries dedicated to Homer in cities during the Hellenistic period (323–31 BC), and in Roman times Homeric verses provided answers to oracular enquiries.[7]

In spite of this imagined ascent to divinity, Homer was certainly regarded as having been a real, living person, the inspired poet who had created two epic works of immense significance. Ancient scholarship enquired about when and where he had lived, weighing up the assertions of the different Greek cities that claimed to be his birthplace, and

Fig. 9*
*The Apotheosis
of Homer*

c. 225–205 BC
Said to be from Bovillae,
Italy, attributed to
Archelaos of Priene
Marble
H. 1230 mm | W. 812 mm |
D. 165 mm
British Museum
1819,0812.1

OPPOSITE ABOVE
Fig. 10*
**Manuscript of the
Odyssey, with
passages from
Book 3 annotated
by ancient scholars**

1st century AD
Soknopaiou Nesos, Egypt
Papyrus
H. 360 mm | W. 560 mm
(mounted)
The British Library
Papyrus 271

OPPOSITE BELOW
Fig. 11
**Silver coin (*didrachm*)
with head of Homer**
Minted on the Greek
island of Ios, this is
the earliest known
representation of
Homer on coins.

Mid-4th century BC
Ios, Greece
Silver
Diam. 12 mm
British Museum
1951,1007.8

speculating about the details of his life. Most of these cities were located in the eastern Aegean region, on the west coast of Anatolia (now Turkey) or on the islands off that coast (now mostly part of modern Greece), in the region scholars today call 'East Greece'. Above all, Greek scholars, particularly in the great library of Alexandria in Egypt in the third and second centuries BC, pored over the poems themselves. They wrote about them, sometimes adding detailed commentaries in the margins of the manuscripts that they studied and copied, and thus preserved (Fig. 10). Each line was subject to scrutiny, and various aspects of the poems were discussed, including the historical value of Homer's account of the Trojan War.[8]

Yet in all this extensive and detailed examination, it seems clear that no one ever questioned whether Homer had actually lived. It would have astonished the learned world of ancient Greece to know that the fact of his very existence would come to be doubted by scholars many centuries later. Indeed, so firm was the belief in an individual Homer that portraits of him were invented.[9] Some of the cities that claimed a particular association with Homer placed imaginary portraits of him on their coins (Fig. 11).[10] Wealthy patrons who valued learning wanted to display portraits of the great writers and thinkers of the past in their libraries and homes. Where none existed, the sculptors turned their hands to creating them to meet this demand. For Homer, some artists seem to have been influenced by the description of the blind bard Demodocus in the *Odyssey*, and created a portrait of a blind

Fig. 12*
**Bust of the 'blind'
poet Homer**

Roman copy (2nd century
AD) of a Hellenistic
original of the 2nd
century BC
Baiae, Italy
Marble
H. 572 mm | W. 325 mm |
D. 257 mm
British Museum
1805,0703.85

RIGHT
Fig. 13*
**Red-figure storage
jar (*amphora*)
depicting a performer
reciting a verse from
a poem: 'Once upon a
time in Tiryns'**

c. 500–480 BC
Made in Attica, Greece,
attributed to the
Kleophrades Painter;
said to be from Vulci, Italy
Pottery
H. 470 mm |
Diam. 249 mm
British Museum
1843,1103.34

poet with flowing locks and strong but weathered features (Fig. 12).[11] Very different in appearance from earlier images, which tended to take their inspiration from representations of the great god Zeus, Homer's face here seems etched with experience, and the sculptor perhaps intended him to look as though, driven by his relentless Muse, he had lived through the long battles on the plain of Troy and sailed with Odysseus on his wanderings. Yet this is also a face that would have seemed appropriate for a travelling bard. Bards, or *rhapsodes*, were familiar figures at public (and private) feasts and festivals in ancient Greece, including at all the major religious festivals of Greece in the Classical period, where they recited or sang poetry, especially the poems of Homer (Fig. 13).[12] This life naturally required long periods on the road, and presumably led to the weather-beaten appearance that we see in this sculpture. Whatever the inspiration, this portrait type for Homer was widely adopted, and was reproduced into the Roman period in multiple copies, a number of which have survived.

Despite the ancient belief in Homer as a historical person, he always remained something of an enigma. Traditional accounts of his origins and life existed, but there were no historical records that could substantiate the details in them, still less explain how he had composed the poems and how they had been put down in writing. Writing had been used in Bronze Age Greece, but lost after around 1200 BC, and we now know that it had only been reintroduced to the Greek world in the eighth century BC, with the adoption and adaptation of the Phoenician alphabet from the Middle East.[13] The dates many scholars today consider most likely for a living Homer, the eighth or early seventh century BC, would thus (see below) fall within the first century or two of the reappearance of writing in Greece after

LEFT
Fig. 14*
Small red-figure wine jug (*chous*) depicting a boy, seated, reading from a scroll
Another boy holds a lyre.

c. 440–430 BC
Made in Attica, Greece, attributed to the workshop of the Shuvalov Painter
Pottery
H. 154 mm | W. 132 mm | D. 122 mm
British Museum
1772,0320.221

it fell out of use in the so-called Dark Ages. This was therefore a period in which few historical records existed that could be expected to corroborate his existence.

In time the poems were indeed written down, disseminated and copied, and manuscripts of them were certainly circulating in the sixth century BC, which must have helped to formalize the versions performed in recitations. The first-century BC Roman author Cicero tells us that in the second half of the sixth century BC Peisistratus, tyrant of Athens, or perhaps his son, decreed that the works of Homer should be organized and recited in a set order. The *Iliad* and the *Odyssey* as we have them now are each arranged in twenty-four chapters or 'books', and their current order no doubt reflects something of this so-called 'Peisistratid recension', though some of the ordering may pre-date it and some may be later. In Homeric studies, nothing is entirely clear cut.

Whenever the poems were first written down, the *Iliad* and the *Odyssey* are the earliest major, complete works of poetry we have inherited from the ancient Greek world. To the Classical Greeks they would already have seemed old. They used a traditional metre – dactylic hexameter – and included some archaic forms of language and vocabulary. Listening to them in performance may have required some effort of concentration: this was not the Greek that was spoken in the streets. The poems were taught to pupils, who might be set the task of explaining some of the unusual words and constructions they contained (Fig. 14).[14] They also served for writing exercises: wooden tablets, which could be washed and rewritten or which were covered with wax, still to this day preserve some of the efforts of ancient schoolchildren (Fig. 15).[15] But although the poems would have seemed old, they would certainly also have appeared remarkably vivid and sophisticated. It is another

Homeric paradox that the earliest preserved works of Western literature are not faltering beginnings, but long, rich and accomplished poems.

After the end of antiquity, the Homeric poems were known and studied only in the Greek-speaking Byzantine Empire (and to a very limited extent in the Arab world).[16] The earliest extant manuscripts date from the ninth century AD onwards, the period of renewed interest in ancient Greek literature in Byzantium (Fig. 16). In the Western European world, it was only after they were reintroduced from Byzantium in the Renaissance that the poems again became subject to intense and continuous scholarly scrutiny.[17] Then during the Enlightenment period of the eighteenth century, that great age of scientific enquiry, new questions began to be asked. The ancient view that the *Iliad* and the *Odyssey* were coherent works of great brilliance certainly implied an individual genius as their creator, and subsequent scholarship would often agree. But it was questioned, particularly by the so-called 'Analysts', most notably the influential German scholar Friedrich August Wolf (1759–1824), who wondered whether the poems were unitary in composition or whether they revealed disparate material grouped together into a composite whole. Wolf published his *Prolegomena ad Homerum* in 1794, in which he concluded that the poems were indeed composite. He saw in them a group of traditional stories or lays that had been stitched together, perhaps in the 'recension' mentioned above in the Peisistratid period of sixth-century BC Athens.[18]

Wolf's view was radical, and was not accepted wholesale. A number of commentators felt (and still feel) that the poems had a coherent, overarching structure that implied one overall creative mind. It also seemed almost sacrilegious to doubt Homer. Wolf's contemporary, the German poet Johann Wolfgang von Goethe (1749–1832) teased him with a rhyming couplet that punned on his name:

The Wolfish Homer
Seven cities quarrelled over who claimed his birth-place,
Now the Wolf has torn him apart and each has a piece.[19]

Nonetheless, Wolf and the Analysts had asked what came to be known as the Homeric Question, and though not everyone felt that they had answered it convincingly, it was increasingly recognized that some passages and sections in the poems did not fit together entirely naturally. At the very least, it was clear that certain complexities remained. Intense textual criticism of the poems continued throughout the nineteenth century, and this went hand in hand with the textual study of the books of the Christian Bible, where some of the same problems of authorship applied. For example, the first five books of the Old Testament were traditionally attributed to Moses, but this was now questioned. From the middle of the century, a new Darwinian spirit would be added to the mix, bringing a sense that the Homeric poems might have evolved over time and that this evolution could potentially be charted within the shape and form in which the world had inherited them.

One issue that fell under the catch-all heading of the 'Homeric Question' was whether the *Iliad* and the *Odyssey* were by the same person, or whether the differences between them suggested two authors, which many scholars still believe to be the case. Pursuing this further, the author Samuel Butler published a book in 1897 in which he claimed the *Odyssey* was written by a woman, a theory that was, however, not widely accepted.[20]

A major breakthrough in modern understanding of the epics was achieved in the early part of the twentieth century with the work of the American scholar Milman

Parry (1902–1935). He and others were studying contemporary oral traditions of Serbo-Croat-speaking societies, with low levels of literacy, in what was then Yugoslavia. Listening to bards chanting long stories from memory, they realized that the resulting poems had significant aspects in common with the Homeric epics. These particularly related to the poets' use of 'formulae' – repeated scenes and descriptions expressed in the same order and sometimes the same words. Warriors put on their armour, for example, in much the same way throughout the *Iliad*, and combat between two individual warriors is described according to a set pattern. Housekeepers receive visitors in stock phrases, and dawn breaks in the same words repeatedly. At a detailed level, repeated metrical patterns are formed by the coupling of a proper name with an adjectival description. This is the famous 'Homeric epithet'. Achilles is 'fleet of foot', dawn is 'rosy-fingered' and the sea is 'wine-dark'. To our ears, these are poetic and atmospheric, but Parry and his colleagues demonstrated that they were also thoroughly practical, enabling the bard both to remember and to some extent to compose the poem during long performances. The long-lived nature of oral transmission is also evident from the Vedic oral tradition of India, stretching over three millennia.[21]

The significance of this new insight, known as the 'oral-formulaic theory', would be hard to overestimate. Immediately some of the elements of the poems that had puzzled the analytical critics could now be explained. In addition, the position of Homer on the cusp of the transition from a non-literate to a literate society in Greece came into better focus.

RIGHT
Fig. 16*
The 'Townley Homer'
One of the earliest known medieval codices, the manuscript preserves the text of the *Iliad* alongside an extensive commentary placed around the original text. It was acquired in 1773 by the British art collector Charles Townley from the Florentine Salviati family.

Probably written in 1059
Manuscript
H. 320 mm | W. 260 mm |
D. 85 mm
The British Library
Burney MS 86

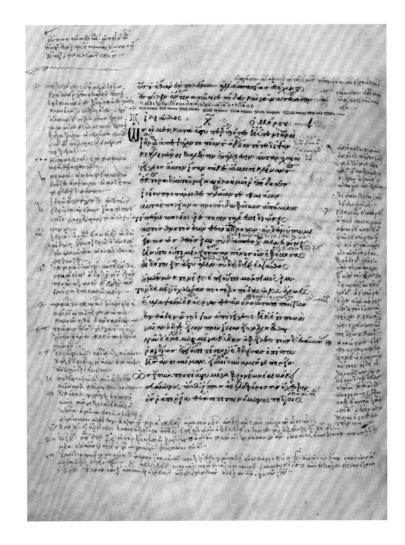

LEFT
Fig. 17
A bard playing the lyre and singing in the Mycenaean palace of Nestor at Pylos
This watercolour is a reconstruction of a fresco in the Throne Room dating to 1400–1200 BC.

1950s–1960s
Piet de Jong
Watercolour on block paper with pencil
H. 250 mm | W. 360 mm
Collections of the Department of Classics, University of Cincinnati
Painting no. 530

The poems had been viewed only as a literary phenomenon, but now it could be seen that this was not the whole story. They had become literature when they were captured in writing, but they had originated in the spoken word, in a tradition in which works were designed to be recited and listened to, not written down and read, and this remained part of their essential nature.

New ways of viewing the poems opened up, which had relevance not just to the date and nature of Homer himself, but also to the age of heroes he describes. There now seemed every possibility that memories of a Bronze Age past could be embedded in Homer's works, and a clear rationale for believing this to be the case. The poet himself makes it perfectly clear that the age his heroes lived in pre-dates his own, and, as we shall see (Chapter 3), some of the things he describes, such as bronze weaponry and boar's tusk helmets, are palpably descriptions of objects that were indeed in use in the Bronze Age and not later. It is in the nature of oral poetry, however, that it changes over time, reflecting the knowledge and experience of new audiences. Parry's work implied that Homeric poetry was a palimpsest, in which older features were joined by newer ones as the poems developed across generations. The poems became more fixed by virtue of being written down, though of course further changes could have been made even after they were part of a manuscript tradition. The *Iliad* and the *Odyssey* may well echo stories sung by the bards in Bronze Age Mycenaean palaces (Fig. 17), but there had also been plenty of time subsequently for them to develop and to change.[22]

As the twentieth century progressed, archaeology brought further understanding of not only the Bronze Age period in Greece, but also the succeeding Iron Age, the first possible period of Homer's own life. The centuries dividing the fall of the Mycenaean palaces in around 1200 BC and the eighth century BC were once known to scholars as the Dark Ages in Greece. It has become commonplace to remark that they no longer seem quite so dark, since archaeology has now thrown considerable light on them. Nonetheless, this was a period of relative poverty, depopulation and isolation in many parts of Greece, so to pursue the analogy and to describe the eighth century BC as a period of Greek renaissance still seems apt. It was a time of considerable change, when many elements that would become typical of later, classical Greece were formed or developed. These included the birth of the *polis* or city-state, the foundation of the great Panhellenic ('all-Greek') festivals at Olympia and elsewhere, the reintroduction of writing and the development of epic poetry. Perhaps it is precisely the break with earlier traditions that also inspired some of the great stories that formed the themes of the poems, including that of the Trojan War. Knowledge of actual Bronze Age history would have dwindled over the generations, yet the massive ruins of many Bronze Age cities still stood proud. Some of the burial mounds of this grand yet vanished age now became the focus of 'hero' cults, as people began to imagine the figures from the past who might have been associated with these imposing sites.[23]

Importantly it is also becoming increasingly clear that Greece was far from isolated in this period, and that contact with neighbouring cultures played a key role in its development. Just as the alphabet with which epic poetry was first written down originated in Phoenicia, and the papyrus upon which it was inscribed originated in Egypt, so many elements of epic itself, including themes, names and poetic forms, owed a debt to the Hittite (and other) peoples of Anatolia as well as the Near Eastern cultures of the Levant, northern Syria and Mesopotamia.[24] Texts such as the Epic of Gilgamesh are but the tip of the iceberg of the rich oral traditions that were shared by the ancient world, spread by traders, migrants and travelling bards. Later Greek epic may well have its origins, to some extent at least, in such inter-cultural exchange as much as in Bronze Age memory and tales inspired by ancient ruins.

All we can say for sure, though, is that epic poetry played an important part in the lives of the Greeks in this period, not just in Anatolia but also across all the regions in which they lived and traded. A small and relatively unimpressive cup is perhaps the most famous testimony (Fig. 18). It comes from the Greek colony at Pithekoussai (Pithecusae) on the

RIGHT
Fig. 18*
Geometric drinking cup (*skyphos*) from the early Greek settlement of Pithekoussai in southern Italy, inscribed with three lines of verse

c. 715 BC
Made in Teos, Turkey; found at Pithekoussai, Italy
Pottery
H. 103 mm | Diam. 151 mm
Museo Archeologico di Pithecusae
166788

island of Ischia, at the northern end of the bay of Naples, and so on the western fringes of the early Greek world. It bears a scratched inscription: three lines of verse, two of them in the dactylic hexameter typical of epic: 'I am the cup of Nestor, good to drink from; whoever drinks from this cup, immediately desire of fair-garlanded Aphrodite will strike him'.[25] The most famous Nestor is the Greek king who in the *Iliad* is described as drinking from a golden goblet that is too heavy for others to lift; describing an insignificant pottery vessel as Nestor's cup must have been humorous at the time, and certainly seems so today. But the inscription raises this cup far above the commonplace. It shows that the Greeks in Ischia knew, if not the *Iliad*, then at least the epic poetry that described Nestor. It also makes it clear that they were part of a wider network that included the East Greek world, the suggested home of Homer, as the cup was not made locally but produced in the city of Teos, not far from Smyrna and Chios, two main contenders for Homer's birthplace. When we add to that the fact that the inscription is among the earliest known examples of Greek writing anywhere, to modern scholars the cup is worth far more than its weight in gold.

Epic poetry, widely known and appreciated, played a fundamental role in the formation of Greek identity. Individual cities were often at war, so there is no doubt that fierce, local patriotism was widespread. But at the same time the Greeks were united by ties of a common language and religion, demonstrated when they met for the festivals at the great supra-regional sanctuaries. A shared knowledge of the epic poems and the role numerous local heroes from all over Greece played in them further fostered a sense of community. Later on, in the mid-fifth century BC, the Trojan War became important because it was felt to prefigure the Persian Wars of the period, representing the first occasion when Greeks had successfully united to face a common enemy from the East. The tales embodied in Homer and the epic tradition showed the Greeks that in the past they had been heroes, and no doubt made them feel they could be so in the future, too. Alexander the Great (356–323 BC) supposedly kept a copy of the *Iliad* under his pillow.[26]

How, then, can we sum up current thinking on Homer and his work? We now have both an understanding of the oral nature of the poems and constantly increasing knowledge based on archaeology of the progression from the Greek Bronze Age to the time of Homer's poems and beyond. Yet many uncertainties still remain. Some scholars maintain that the word 'Homer' can only be used as a sort of shorthand to represent the formation and eventual recording in writing of epic poetry. Others would acknowledge the difficulty of finding absolute proof that he existed as an individual, but would still argue that the poems required a single organizing mind to become the generally coherent works that we still read and admire. If indeed Homer lived and breathed, then the consensus would be that he probably came from the eastern part of the Greek world, and that he may have lived in the late eighth or seventh centuries BC. He composed orally, and may or may not have also used the relatively new technology of writing. If he did not, then his poems may have been written down by some sort of process of dictation. The ancient Greeks spoke of the 'Homeridae' or 'sons' of Homer, and perhaps they acted as his scribes.

Ultimately, we have the poems but not the poet. Whatever the truth of the matter, though, the modern world will continue to associate the name Homer with the *Iliad* and the *Odyssey*. In this we follow the Greek tradition. The ancient view of the single poet of great genius remains a tenable proposition, even though it cannot be proven.

The Epic Cycle and beyond: Troy in Greek and Roman literature

Troy the ill-omened, joint grave of Europe and Asia,
Troy, of men and all manliness most bitter ash.
Catullus, Poem 68, 89–90[27]

The *Iliad* and the *Odyssey* tell only two parts of the whole, long story of the Trojan War, but they were not the only epic poems that were in circulation. Six further poems, known collectively as the Epic (or the Trojan) Cycle, traced the story from the origins of the war to its aftermath. These other epics have survived today only in fragments, and are known to us from summaries and accounts of them in later Greek and Byzantine literature, along with some lines from each that were preserved as quotations. Their authorship was even then uncertain, despite names being traditionally attached to them, and the date of their composition was unknown, though vaguely felt to be early. It may be that they were more or less contemporary with the works of Homer, and were also products of the process of capturing the old and traditional heroic tales as epic poetry during the formative period of the eighth and seventh centuries BC in Greece. An alternative theory is that they were composed with knowledge of Homer's poems firmly in mind, with the specific intention of 'filling in the gaps' and telling the remainder of the story from beginning to end.

Certainly, if we list these poems in narrative order of the events they relate (though this is of course not necessarily the order of their composition) and include the *Iliad* and the *Odyssey* in the relevant positions, the resulting sequence of poems tells the complete story

RIGHT
Fig. 19
Black-figure storage jar (*amphora*) depicting the Ethiopian hero Memnon flanked by African attendants

c. 535 BC
Made in Attica, Greece,
attributed to Exekias
Pottery
H. 415 mm | W. 300 mm
British Museum
1849,0518.10

of the Trojan War, from its first causes to its consequences and the later fates of the Greek heroes. The order is as follows: the *Cypria*, the *Iliad*, the *Aethiopis*, the *Little Iliad*, the *Iliou Persis*, the *Nostoi*, the *Odyssey* and the *Telegony*. The ancient world did not generally consider the others to be as great as the works of Homer, which contributed to their later loss.

The *Cypria*, of which a summary and fifty lines survive, acted as a 'prequel' to the *Iliad*. It told of the decision by Zeus to reduce the population of the world by war, and covered the sequence of events from the marriage of Peleus and Thetis up to the situation at the beginning of the *Iliad*. The *Aethiopis*, of which few actual lines survive, picked up the tale after the funeral of Hector at the end of the *Iliad*, and tells of the Amazons and Memnon's Ethiopians joining in the war on the Trojan side (Fig. 19), and of the death of Achilles, including the dispute over his armour. It is not clear whether the resulting judgment in favour of Odysseus and the ensuing suicide of Ajax were told here or in the next poem of the cycle, known as the *Little Iliad*, which continues the story through to the building of the Trojan Horse and beyond.

Of the *Iliou Persis* or 'Sack of Troy' a summary and just ten lines survive. An important source for the Roman poet Virgil, this also covered the story of the Trojan Horse through to the sack of Troy. Only five and a half lines survive of the *Nostoi* or 'Returns', which narrates the return home of the Greek heroes and their various fates, apart from Odysseus. His story is, of course, told in the *Odyssey*, though fully completed only in the *Telegony*, of which just two lines survive. This covers the further adventures of Odysseus, including his death, as well as the story of Telegonus, son of Odysseus and the nymph Circe. The story somewhat surprisingly ends with Penelope marrying Telegonus, and Telemachus, the other son of Odysseus, marrying Circe.

As later Greek and Roman writers and artists were inspired by this rich narrative, the story of the Trojan War permeated all genres of literature.[28] Lyric poets such as Alcaeus and Sappho, both of the East Greek island of Lesbos and writing around 600 BC, or, some decades later, Ibycus of Rhegion (a city in southern Italy) and Pindar from Thebes in central Greece, all made reference to the story and its heroes and heroines. Helen was particularly popular with them. From the later seventh century BC onwards, the story of Troy was also taken up by the so-called Iambic poets such as Archilochus and his followers. Iambic metre was originally associated with bawdy poetry at certain festivals of Dionysus and Demeter, and these poets used insulting and obscene language for entertainment and for social criticism. They focused particularly on the anti-heroes in the Homeric story, for instance ugly Thersites. This and other poetry would have been performed at private gatherings such as the symposion (drinking party), but also at public feasts and festivals.

Historians such as Herodotus and Thucydides, both writing in the fifth century BC, placed the Trojan War at the beginning of their histories. As mentioned above, Herodotus paralleled the Trojan War with the Persian Wars of his own time, constructing a sharp divergence between Greek and Eastern values. Episodes from the Trojan War also proved popular with their contemporaries, the Classical Athenian playwrights. Nearly a quarter of all the tragic plays by Aeschylus, Sophocles and Euripides, over sixty in total, were based on Trojan myths.[29] Greek tragedians on the whole resisted stereotyping Trojans, and highlighted positive and negative aspects of both sides in the war. In part the plays were intended as a commentary on and criticism of the politics of the time. Thus Greek glory is often negated by the egotism of the heroes, internal strife or human suffering, and Greek claims of justice are revealed to mask darker motivations. *The Trojan Women* of Euripides (see also p. 208 and p. 262) is a powerful example of the political relevance of tragedy.

It presented the devastating effects of war on women and children to an Athenian audience that had itself been responsible for extreme and recent cruelty in the long Peloponnesian War (431–404 BC). In 416–415 BC the Athenians had attacked the island of Melos, killing all the adult male population and selling the women and children into slavery. This act was not unique in ancient warfare, but it was fresh in the minds of the Athenians when the play was first staged in 415 BC. Some audience members may have been uneasy about Athenian behaviour, others may themselves have been involved in the atrocity. Whatever their views, this is an extraordinary example of the immediacy with which tragedy, and the Troy story, could confront people with their own realities and responsibilities, and the conduct of a war in which their city was engaged.

No character in *The Trojan Women* could be more sympathetic than the Trojan queen Hecuba, about to be taken to Greece as a slave, yet in another play, *Hecuba*, Euripides shows her subject to further torments and responding differently. In this play, the queen suffers the sacrifice of her daughter Polyxena on the tomb of Achilles and must prepare her body for burial; she is then confronted with the corpse of her son Polydorus, treacherously killed by king Polymestor of Thrace, to whom he had been sent for safe-keeping. She takes revenge by blinding Polymestor and murdering his two young sons. The play questions whether such vengeance against innocents can ever be defensible, and whether Hecuba herself moves beyond our sympathy because of her actions. It makes harrowing viewing for modern audiences, as it must have done when it was originally performed.

Lighter notes, though again not without social criticism, were struck by comedy and satyr plays, burlesque tragicomedies in which the chorus was formed by mythical satyrs, creatures part-human and part-goat. Odysseus took centre stage in these as a popular hero, alongside Heracles.[30] One of the earliest attested comedies featuring Odysseus is *Odysseus and Friends* by Cratinus. The play, probably written around 439–437 BC, is a broad parody

RIGHT
Fig. 20
Red-figure wine-mixing bowl (*calyx-krater*) decorated with a scene of Odysseus and the Cyclops, inspired by Euripides' satyr play *Cyclops*

c. 420–410 BC
Made in Lucania,
Italy, attributed to
the Cyclops Painter
Pottery
H. 460 mm | Diam. 460 mm
British Museum
1947,0714.18

of the *Odyssey*, in which Odysseus and his companions travel in pursuit of good things to eat. A popular satyr play by Euripides, *Cyclops*, of 424 BC, may have inspired images on Greek vases, such as a scene of Odysseus and his companions preparing to blind the one-eyed giant Polyphemus, in which two satyrs make an appearance (Fig. 20).[31]

The most famous, if rather impenetrable, work of the Hellenistic period to rework the Trojan War story is probably the poem *Alexandra* by the third-century BC poet Lycophron, who worked in the library of Alexandria. Composed in the form of a prophecy by the Trojan princess Cassandra, it recounts the fate of Troy and of the Greek and Trojan heroes, and alludes to Alexander the Great uniting Asia and Europe in his empire.[32]

As early as the third century BC the *Odyssey* had been translated into Latin by Livius Andronicus, a Greek writer who had been brought to Rome as a prisoner of war. But most educated Romans knew Greek, so translation was not a necessary prerequisite for familiarity with the story. In the Roman period the story of the Trojan War, and associated myths, continued to be retold in both Latin and Greek, and indeed was as ubiquitous in Latin literature as it was in Greek, ranging from reworkings of particular episodes and new creations based around the theme, to the sort of passing references that assumed complete familiarity with the tale.[33]

New elements included, for example, an account of the Cyclops Polyphemus, pining for the love of the nymph Galatea. The theme had been introduced by the Hellenistic bucolic poet Theocritus in the third century BC and was picked up by Ovid in his *Metamorphoses*, completed at the very beginning of the first century AD. In these 'poems of transformations' Ovid frequently invokes characters from the Trojan myth, often giving voice to the more minor players in the story. His theme is their loves and losses, and of course the transformations of his title: thus when Acis, the mortal lover of Galatea, is killed by Polyphemus he is changed for eternity into a river. The focus here, as elsewhere in much of Latin literature, is on love and peace, in contrast to epic poetry's emphasis on heroism and war.

The longest work by the poet Catullus (his Poem 64), of the generation before Ovid in the first century BC, is written in the form of a 'little epic' that ostensibly takes the marriage of Peleus and Thetis as its subject, thus telling the story that stands at the very beginning of the Trojan myth, though it includes much else besides. Yet it is in the poem quoted at the head of this section, Poem 68 (p. 31), that Catullus' personal connection with Troy comes to the fore. His brother had died and was buried near Troy and the poem is filled with bitter lamentation. Catullus finds in the fate of Troy a suitable framing for his own grief.

Other poems consciously took Homer as their model and adopted epic form. One was the *Achilleid* of the Roman poet Statius, written around AD 94–96, which was intended to recount the whole life of Achilles, but remained unfinished at the time of the poet's death. The completed part describes Achilles' early life, including his education by the centaur Chiron. Another is the *Posthomerica* by Quintus of Smyrna, a Greek epic poet from the East Greek city of Smyrna (modern Izmir in Turkey). Composed at some time between the late second and the mid-fourth century AD and written in Homeric style, this draws on the earlier poems of the Epic Cycle and tells of the events following Hector's death. It thus covers the period from the end of Homer's *Iliad* to the end of the Trojan War.[34] By the time of its composition, the Trojan Aeneas had great significance for Rome. Quintus revisits the earlier tradition that Aeneas had to be preserved when Troy fell to reflect the significance the Trojan hero had gained for Rome by this period. In this account, Calchas the priest and seer shouts to the Greeks:

Stop making the head of mighty Aeneas the target
Of your deadly arrows and your murderous spears.
It is destined by the glorious will of the gods
That he shall go from the Xanthos to the broad-flowing Tiber
To found a sacred city, an object of awe to future
People. The rule of the line descended from him shall later
Extend to the rising sun and its eternal setting.
Quintus of Smyrna, *Posthomerica* 13.334–41[35]

The story of Aeneas himself was, of course, most famously told by Virgil, and it is to his *Aeneid* that we must now turn.

Virgil

The Roman poet Publius Vergilius Maro (70–19 BC) (Fig. 21), usually known simply as Virgil, gives the most detailed and dramatic description of the fall of Troy that survives from the ancient world.[36] The subject of his great epic poem the *Aeneid* is the Trojan hero Aeneas, who escapes from the burning city of Troy and goes on to lay the foundations for

RIGHT
Fig. 21
Roman mosaic showing Virgil seated between Clio, the Muse of History, and Melpomene, the Muse of Tragedy
Virgil holds a scroll inscribed with a line invoking the Muses from his *Aeneid* (1.8).

c. AD 210
Hadrumetum, Sousse, Tunisia
Mosaic
H. approx. 120 cm | W. approx. 120 cm
Bardo Museum, Tunis

the rise of Rome. The *Aeneid*, written in about the last ten years or so of the poet's life, was rapidly adopted as the Roman national epic, and Virgil, like Homer before him, was revered as a fount of knowledge and a source of great wisdom.[37]

In Homer's *Iliad*, Aeneas is a noble but relatively minor character, though he fights valiantly for the Trojan cause. He is the son of Aphrodite (Roman Venus), who saves him from death at the hands of Diomedes in Book 5 of the poem, while in Book 20 Poseidon saves him from Achilles, and explicitly says that he is fated to survive the Trojan War.[38] Greek artists showed Aeneas carrying his father Anchises away from the fallen city of Troy (see Fig. 87). His story was presumably brought to Italy by the Greeks, perhaps mediated by the Etruscans, whose art frequently represented episodes from the tale of Troy. It is not clear when Aeneas became specifically associated with the foundation of Rome, though the story seems certainly to have been known at least by the third century BC, and gained some importance from the late Republic, when Italian families gave themselves illustrious mythical ancestries by constructing genealogies linked to Greek myth.[39] In the period before Virgil, however, the Romans had focused on the figure of Romulus as Rome's legendary founder. It was only after Virgil had written the *Aeneid*, and as the story of Rome's Trojan ancestry was being promoted by the Roman emperors, that representations of Aeneas rescuing his father, his son Ascanius and usually some representation of the Trojan gods became popular in Roman art (Fig. 22).

Virgil's lifetime encompassed the momentous change in the Roman world from Republic to Empire after the battle of Actium in 31 BC, when Octavian defeated the forces of Mark

BELOW
Fig. 22
Figure of Aeneas escaping from Troy carrying his father Anchises and holding his son Ascanius by the hand

1st century AD
Pompeii, Italy
Terracotta
H. 170 mm | W. 126 mm
Museo Archeologico
Nazionale di Napoli
110338

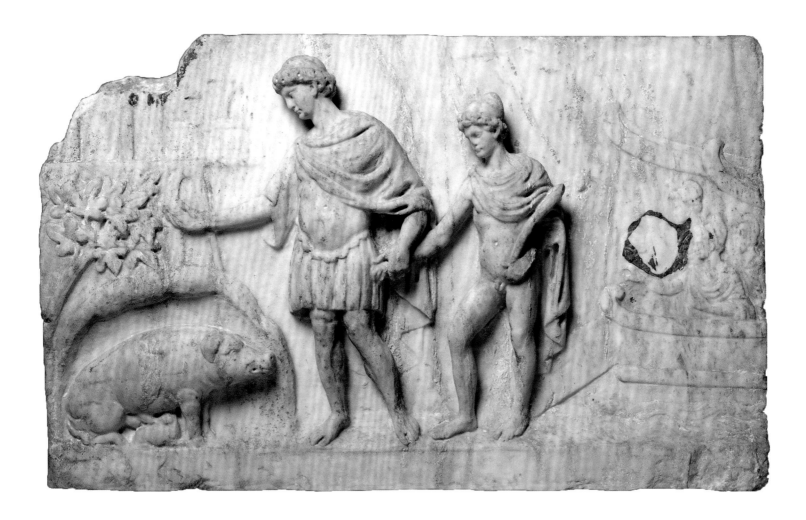

ABOVE
Fig. 23*
Relief depicting
Aeneas and Ascanius
in Italy
The discovery of a sow
shows them where
to found their new city.

c. AD 140–150
Rome, Italy
Marble
H. 370 mm | L. 610 mm
British Museum
1927,1212.1

Antony and Cleopatra and went on to assume power as Augustus, first emperor of Rome
(r. 27 BC – AD 14). Virgil was a friend and confidant of Augustus, and wrote the *Aeneid* during
the first decade of his reign. He was already an established poet, known particularly for
the *Eclogues* and the *Georgics*, before he turned to the composition of his great epic and
his enduring masterpiece. Augustus may not strictly have 'commissioned' the poem, but
tradition certainly attributed to him the fact of its survival. According to the story, Virgil
considered it unfinished and, on his deathbed, ordered that it should be burned, but
Augustus overruled him, thus saving the *Aeneid* from the flames. While scholars do indeed
point to some indications that the poem was not completely finished, these details pale
into insignificance against the monumental achievement of the poem as a whole. It was
immediately considered a great work that not only told the Romans of their origins in the
remote mythical past, but also foreshadowed their achievements, specifically the reign of
Augustus and Roman rule over Greece, from Achilles' homeland of Phthia in Thessaly to
great cities of the Peloponnese:

> The swift years will bring
> Anchises' clan as rulers into Phthia,
> And once-renowned Mycenae, and beaten Argos.
> *Aeneid* 1.283–85

The *Aeneid* would remain central to the sense of identity of Rome and its empire for the next five centuries, and went on to become a canonical work of Western literature.

Virgil's ambition was to create a Roman epic that would be the equal of the works of Homer. The *Aeneid* is written in the dactylic hexameters that are the traditional metre for epic poetry. Its twelve books loosely mirror first the *Odyssey* and then the *Iliad*, though with their own narrative purpose. The first six books tell of Aeneas escaping from Troy and his sea-borne wanderings and adventures, which echo those of Odysseus, before he eventually reaches the shores of Italy. The next six books recall the *Iliad* in telling of war. Aeneas leads the Trojans to settle in Latium, where they are welcomed by the king, Latinus. Here Aeneas and Turnus, ruler of a local people, the Rutuli, are rivals for the hand of the king's daughter Lavinia, leading to conflict between them. The poem ends with Aeneas defeating Turnus in single combat and killing him, echoing Achilles slaying Hector at the end of the *Iliad*. Aeneas would go on to found not Rome itself, but the city of Lavinium, named after Lavinia, whom he married (Fig. 23).[40] Where to found the city was foretold in a prophecy:

> But suddenly he saw the marvellous portent
> Through the forest: a white sow with her white offspring,
> Stretched on the grassy bank.
> *Aeneid* 8.81–83

Aeneas became king of the Latins on the death of Latinus, and his son Ascanius was his successor. Ascanius then founded the city of Alba Longa to relieve overcrowding in Lavinium. Unlike Lavinium, the site of Alba Longa is not now known, though tradition placed it in the Alban hills, near Rome. The royal dynasty of Alba Longa, descendants of Aeneas and Ascanius, ruled the Latins for some fifteen generations before the birth of Romulus and Remus to the then king's daughter, a priestess who was seduced by the god Mars. Romulus, who founded Rome itself, was thus a direct descendant of Aeneas. Moreover, because Aeneas was the son of Anchises and the goddess Venus, this bloodline had divine origins in two respects.

Both the *Odyssey* and the *Aeneid* describe episodes in which the hero descends into the Underworld. The *Aeneid* includes many portents and prophecies about Rome and its future, but it is in the Underworld that these are made most manifest. Aeneas is shown the great procession of his descendants up to the reign of Augustus and Virgil's own time. The Roman patrician family (*gens*) of the Iulii, of which both Julius Caesar and his adopted son Augustus were members, takes its name from Iulus. In Virgil this is an alternative name for Ascanius, though in some versions of the myth Iulus is Ascanius' son, and so the grandson of Aeneas. In either case, Augustus can claim heroic and divine descent in his role as re-founder of Rome. He is pointed out to Aeneas as 'the man so often promised you', of divine parentage and the bringer of a new golden age (6.791–94).

In a famous passage towards the end of the description of his descendants, Aeneas is reminded that all Romans are destined for greatness:

> But Romans, don't forget that world dominion
> Is your great craft: peace, and then peaceful customs;
> Sparing the conquered, striking down the haughty.
> *Aeneid* 6.851–53

The *Aeneid* was, then, the defining text of the age of Augustus. Under the emperor's patronage both the literary and the visual arts saw a great flowering. Yet while it is important to see the work in this context, it would be misleading to focus only on its praise of Augustus. Roman readers no doubt enjoyed the sense of Rome's inevitable glorious destiny as Aeneas took possession, by way of his love affair with Queen Dido, of Rome's old enemy Carthage, and as Roman rule over Greece was decreed by fate, as described in the passage quoted above (p. 37). Yet the poem rises far above mere propaganda, otherwise it would scarcely have occupied its exalted position in both the Roman and the later world's esteem. Interestingly, modern scholarship disputes whether the text truly offers as positive an account of Augustan history as on the surface it appears to do, or whether close reading actually reveals that Virgil sends a dark message about Augustan politics, his sympathies lying more with the old Republic than with the new order. Whatever the truth, Virgil succeeded in his ambition to create an epic that would match those of Homer, bringing the Greek myth of the Trojan War to Rome and using it as a springboard to present a new and potent Roman mythology. He is like Homer in that his work has been enduringly admired and revered, and indeed studied at all levels: the *Aeneid* was almost instantly introduced into the Roman school-room, just as the *Iliad* and the *Odyssey* had long been studied by young Greeks (Fig. 24).[41] Virgil's work has been described as completing an important stage in the process of the 'Hellenization of Rome'.[42] Its role in the transmission of the story of Troy through succeeding centuries to the present day will be discussed below (Chapter 4).

RIGHT
Fig. 24*
***Aeneid* school exercise papyrus**
A pupil has written seven times 'not for you the hated face of the Laconian woman, daughter of Tyndareus' (*non tibi Tyndaridis facies [inuisa Lacaenae]*), a line from Virgil's *Aeneid* (2.601), which refers to the role of Helen in the downfall of Troy.

1st century AD
Hawara, Egypt
Papyrus
H. 288 mm | W. 230 mm
University College London
P. Hawara 24

ARTISTS AND CRAFTSMEN: TROY IN IMAGES

Images in classical antiquity were far from being mere illustrations of texts. Of course, artists drew inspiration from words, and the Homeric epics or Classical theatre could not fail to have repercussions in imagery, as the pictorial world developed in dialogue with other arts. Visual renderings of the story of Troy, however, had their own dynamic, tradition and language, and thus made their own distinct contribution to shaping and interpreting the story through the centuries.[43]

The Greek world

From the beginning, the myth of Troy was prominent in narrative Greek art. Artists and craftsmen used the Trojan story to create emotional and artistically compelling images in a wide variety of media. Sculptors made complex, multi-figured scenes of Trojan battles to adorn temples such as that of Aphaia on the Greek island of Aegina (see p. 70, Fig. 52) or the Athenian Parthenon. Large-scale paintings of the sack of Troy and Odysseus' visit to the Underworld were created by the famous fifth-century BC painter Polygnotus for buildings at Athens and Delphi.[44] A multitude of representations is preserved from the so-called 'minor' arts, from armour, mirrors or funerary urns to figurines, gems or jewellery. Most prolific in the archaeological record, however, are images painted on pottery. This is not only because so many were produced, but also because the medium is exceptionally well suited to withstand the ravages of time. In antiquity, fine painted pottery served a variety of purposes from storing trinkets to being offered to the gods or to the dead, but in Greece and many neighbouring cultures it was used especially for dinners and drinking-parties. Painters chose themes that showed off their skill and appealed to buyers. The scenes on the vases could serve as conversation pieces for the leisured elite, offering them the opportunity to discuss the motivations of the characters, draw parallels to contemporary events, or discuss different versions of the story, thus displaying their own wit and knowledge.

The earliest images that might tell stories of the Trojan heroes go back to the later eighth century BC, the so-called Late Geometric period, when, after a time when purely geometric patterns were preferred, narrative imagery first developed in Greek art, including scenes relating to funerals, war and seafaring.[45] If this is the art of the age of Homer, as it could well be, then it is another Homeric paradox that highly sophisticated literary epics should be contemporary with much less developed storytelling in visual media. One of the oldest, and most impressive, examples is the large wine-mixing bowl decorated in the Geometric style in the British Museum (Fig. 25).[46] It shows a man ready to embark on a large ship with banks of oarsmen as he grasps the wrist of a woman standing on the shore. Could this be the Trojan prince Paris taking Greek Helen on to the ship that will carry them both to Troy? The hand-on-wrist gesture is characteristic of marriage scenes in Greek art, suggesting the control, even coercion, that the Greeks associated with the ritual. But we cannot certainly identify the scene. The figures are anonymous and only the context might give us clues. There is little to go on, but the ship with its two rows of oarsmen is impressive in scale. It does seem that mythical subjects are beginning to be shown in this period, and to interpret this as the first representation of the abduction of Helen – a scene frequently shown in later art – is tempting indeed.

Among the earliest clear references to the story, dating to around 680 BC, is the Trojan Horse with wheels and little windows engraved on a fibula, an ornate pin for fastening

BELOW
Fig. 25*
**Geometric wine-
mixing bowl (*krater*)
with a narrative scene
perhaps depicting
Paris and Helen**

c. 740–730 BC
Made in Attica, Greece;
said to be from Thebes,
Greece
Pottery
H. 300 mm | Diam. 560 mm
British Museum
1899,0219.1

dress, from Boeotia in central Greece (Fig. 26), followed soon after by the famous relief on a pottery storage jar from Mykonos (above, Fig. 1).[47] From around the mid-sixth century BC, it is Athenian pottery that becomes the most prominent setting for Trojan War images. From the beginning, attention focused on certain episodes. The repertoire changed and expanded over time, with some topics enjoying greater and longer-lasting popularity, while others remained marginal or short-lived.[48] Interestingly, in early imagery the focus firmly lies on stories from the wider Epic Cycle, not the *Iliad*, and often on rather unheroic aspects, such as the trick with the Trojan Horse or scenes of killing that clearly transgress social norms.[49] Some events that might be thought central to the story, such as the death of Hector or Achilles, are rare.[50] A remarkable Late Geometric small bronze figure (see Fig. 74) is perhaps our earliest image of the suicide of the Greek hero Ajax, 'bulwark of the Achaeans' (*Iliad* 3.229), following his disgrace after losing to Odysseus in the contest for dead Achilles' armour (see p. 92). This episode, although seemingly marginal, gained popularity in Archaic art, attesting to the interest of Greek artists in human psychology.[51]

A keen interest in a figure's state of mind is found also in fifth-century BC portraits of Penelope, Odysseus' faithful wife. Here the same type reappears over the centuries in a variety of media, from sculpture and reliefs (see Figs 104, 105) to vase-painting and finger-rings (Fig. 27), a long-lived stock figure that was not confined to Penelope but used also for

other female figures in distress or mourning.[52] Despite working within tight technical and spatial constraints, Greek vase-painters achieved images of great artistic and emotional accomplishment. One example is the striking scene of Achilles bandaging the wound of his comrade Patroclus (Fig. 28), which comes close to large-scale painting in quality and ambition.[53] The works by the Athenian Exekias are another example. His amphora of *c.* 530 BC showing the duel between Achilles and Penthesilea, queen of the Amazons (see Fig. 69), is a masterpiece of composition, execution and dramatic intensity, with the couple gazing into each other's eyes and falling in love at the very moment of her death.[54]

Episodes shown in art often differ to a greater or lesser degree from versions known in texts. An Athenian fifth-century BC image of Odysseus' encounter with the Sirens (see Fig. 98) is unusual in that it shows one Siren plunging to her death, having failed to charm the hero with her singing. In texts the idea of the despairing Siren only appears much later, yet the vase image shows that it must already have been familiar to Classical Greeks.[55] Just how differently individual artists might approach a scene becomes clear in many of the objects discussed throughout this book. Widely divergent renderings may be linked to differences in time, culture or context, but as a group of pottery drinking vessels all made in Athens in the early fifth century BC demonstrates, alternative versions of the story could also exist within a single time and place. They all depict a key scene in the narrative recounted in the *Iliad* (1.318–47), that of the captive girl Briseis being taken from

RIGHT
Fig. 27
Gold finger-ring depicting a seated woman, perhaps Penelope

c. 400–300 BC
Made in Sicily, Italy
Gold
Diam. 22 mm | L. 19 mm
(bezel)
British Museum
1867,0508.402

BELOW
Fig. 28
Red-figure drinking cup (*kylix*) depicting Achilles bandaging the wound of his friend Patroclus

c. 500 BC
Made in Attica, Greece, signed by Sosias as potter, attributed to the Sosias Painter; found in Vulci, Italy
Pottery
H. 100 mm | Diam. 320 mm
Antikensammlung, Berlin
F2278

Achilles to be given to Agamemnon.[56] On a cup in London (Fig. 30), Briseis is led away by two heralds, as in the *Iliad*, but contrary to the poem Achilles sits distraught in his tent rather than watching the scene outside. A vessel now in Paris (Fig. 29) shows Briseis being fetched by Agamemnon himself rather than by heralds, while in a third rendering, now in Rome, an angry Achilles jumps up and draws his sword as his friend Patroclus leads Briseis away, deviating both from the *Iliad* and from other images.[57] Even though Athenians in this period were undoubtedly familiar with the *Iliad* from recitals, an individual creative approach prevailed in relation to both the Homeric epic and possible iconographic traditions.

Some of the differences between images reflect the way different artists dealt with the challenge of visually condensing episodes of a complex drama into a single scene, rather than merely picking out a single climactic moment. The carefully choreographed sequence of events on the London cup is an example of a relatively extensive narrative distributed over the whole vessel: on the side shown here, Briseis is taken from Achilles' tent, while the other side (see Fig. 53) probably shows her arriving at Agamemnon's camp; in the cup's interior, Trojan elders may be seen debating the events.[58] More often, though, the narrative is more compressed. A particularly successful visual cipher is that of a figure clinging to the underside of a sheep's belly, denoting Odysseus' escape from the Cyclops Polyphemus. It concisely conveys a whole episode even if depicted in isolation and became firmly established in the artistic repertoire (see Figs 95 and 96).

For artists and their audiences, the images of the Trojan War were not just dramatic pictures in which to show off or admire artistry, but also a way to reflect on the great questions of their own lives and times. It is little surprise then that they frequently address issues of honour and power, gender roles and ethics. This is clear especially in the many sixth-century BC images that show Greek warriors displaying hubris and committing sacrilege by transgressing social and sacred norms in ways that are both fascinating and repulsive.[59] The decline of such violent imagery in the subsequent Classical period, in contrast, may reflect aristocratic warrior values becoming obsolete as larger groups of the population participated in political and military life.[60]

The traumatic Persian Wars, including the sack of Miletus and Athens in the early fifth century BC, also made their mark on art. In their wake, some especially moving images of the Greek destruction of Troy were created, including representations of a particularly Athenian episode.[61] This is the rescue by Acamas and Demophon, sons of the Athenian hero Theseus, of their grandmother Aethra from the burning city, where she had been brought as Helen's slave. The two warriors leading the old woman to safety on an Athenian vase of *c.* 490–480 BC (Fig. 31) were undoubtedly meant as positive role models that contrasted with earlier images of heroic duels or violent deeds.[62] Indeed, the Athenian heroes are the counterparts of the dutiful Trojan Aeneas, 'a son who is wonderfully kind to his aged father as well as a parent above reproach' (Quintus of Smyrna, *Posthomerica*, 13.348–49).[63] Drawing parallels with contemporary reality was fostered further through the blurring of boundaries between mythical and 'genre' scenes. Without additional identifying details, an image of a warrior and a woman with a child might represent the Trojan hero Hector bidding farewell to his wife Andromache, or it might show a contemporary Athenian couple (see Fig. 63), thus making the general point that all soldiers and their families share the same fate.

The way the Trojan War appears in Athenian art as a comment on the Persian Wars, as well as other wars of the fifth century BC, illustrates how the same story could be used to express even widely opposing views. On the Parthenon in Athens, sculptural images of the Trojan War are set alongside battles that pitch Greeks against various barbarian or semi-human creatures. The building celebrated the city's recovery from, and triumph over, the Persian assault some decades earlier, and in this context the images are a likely allusion to a long-term Greek–Asian divide and, perhaps, an early example of 'political propaganda'.[64] In contrast to this stands the work of the Athenian playwright Euripides, who was writing when Athens was embroiled in the Peloponnesian War, a bitter conflict with her former ally Sparta. His plays use the Trojan War story to critically highlight the moral dilemmas and

degradation resulting from war, including the suffering of women and children (see p. 33). When the revivals of Classical Athenian tragedies became popular in the Greek cities of Italy, we find some of the moving scenes in Euripides' tragedies, such as the cruel sacrifice of Iphigenia, also reflected in art (see Fig. 47).[65]

It is not until the later fourth century BC and the Hellenistic period, however, that imagery truly entered into a direct dialogue with written texts.[66] One example comes in the form of popular relief-decorated pottery bowls made in Greece in the second century BC, probably in imitation of silverware. Some carry continuous friezes showing episodes from the story of Troy, occasionally captioned with relevant quotations from epic or tragedy.[67] Similar cycles of episodes from the Trojan War and from the adventures of Odysseus were also popular in larger-scale and more high-profile art. The Syracusan ruler Hieron II (r. 269–215 BC) is reported to have installed mosaics on the floors of the officers' cabins of his royal barge showing the whole *Iliad*,[68] while around 300 BC, a series of panel paintings depicting the Trojan War is said to have been created by the painter Theon (or Theoros) of Samos, which were later taken to Rome.[69] Both of these, like so many other ancient works, are now lost, reminding us that those which do survive and are known to us provide but a small glimpse of a far richer reality.

Beyond Greece

Etruscans, Romans and other neighbours and successors of the Greeks in the Mediterranean world were intimately familiar with Greek myths. Many were avid consumers of Greek mythical imagery, with its dramatic, action-packed narratives and timeless human themes, importing richly decorated Greek pottery, producing copies of Greek sculptures, or adopting and adapting stories or imagery in their own works of art, sometimes kick-started by immigrant craftsmen from Greece.

After the Greek world expanded and was transformed with the conquests of Alexander the Great in the later fourth century BC, the story of the Trojan War could be found as far afield as in the ancient kingdom of Gandhara in what is now Pakistan and Afghanistan, where it was incorporated and re-interpreted in local Buddhist art (see Fig. 80). Even earlier, however, trade and human mobility had spread the story westwards. From the eighth century BC onwards, Etruscans and other Italic peoples in what is today Italy had close links with the Greek world, and it is here that Greek myth, including the Trojan cycle, featured especially prominently.[70] In Etruria, princely ceremonial chariots, tomb paintings, vessels, female toilet implements, funerary urns and other objects all carried Trojan imagery, which had been transformed, translated and made relevant for an Etruscan audience. Greek gods and heroes appear as their Etruscan equivalents, just as later on they are reshaped into Roman ones.[71] Often, Greek iconographic schemes are modified, while other scenes appear to be new creations by Etruscan artists. For example, Achilles' slaughter of the Trojan prisoners at Patroclus' tomb is a violent scene that is hardly ever shown in Greek art but was popular in Etruria, incised on bronze *cistae* (metal boxes, usually cylindrical in shape; see Fig. 64) and painted on the walls of tombs (Fig. 32).[72] Etruscan tombs are frequent settings for images of the Trojan War, and often the mythical images were adapted so as to carry a particular message for this purpose, as in the case of funerary urns (see below, Fig. 43 and Fig. 100).

The Romans had a special connection with the story of Troy through the figure of the Trojan prince Aeneas and his flight to Italy, as recounted in Virgil's *Aeneid*. As Classical

LEFT
Fig. 32
Detail of a fresco from an Etruscan tomb showing the killing of Trojan captives at the tomb of Patroclus

c. 330–300 BC
François tomb, Vulci, Italy
Wall-painting
Villa Albani, Rome

OPPOSITE
Fig. 33*
Fresco of Aeneas having an arrowhead removed from his thigh
The doctor, Iapyx, is assisted by Aeneas' mother Venus. Aeneas' young son Ascanius supports his father.

c. AD 45–79
House of P. Vedius Siricus, Pompeii, Italy
Painted plaster
H. 480 mm | W. 450 mm
Museo Archeologico Nazionale di Napoli
9009

Greek culture gained broad political and social currency, especially from the time of Emperor Augustus,[73] so the myth of Troy enjoyed widespread popularity. A wide range of scenes is found on Roman gems and silver vessels, lamps and terracotta reliefs, sculpture and wall-paintings.[74] Scenes of the life of Achilles on sarcophagi might allude to the 'heroic' qualities of the deceased and the ultimate mortality of even the best in society (below, pp. 74–75, Fig. 55), but in general Roman art was focused more on the 'secular' realm of the living, including the decoration and furnishing of private houses. Greek culture was part of the education of large sections of Roman society, and showing off knowledge and appreciation of it formed an element of social competition. Trojan stories are common among the myths represented in the fine wall-paintings that adorned Roman villas in the first century BC and first century AD, along with episodes of Odysseus' adventures, following

the Hellenistic fashion for Trojan cycles noted above.[75] Many images probably took inspiration from lost Greek panel paintings, which were highly esteemed by Romans, though some are also new creations, such as the image from Pompeii that depicts Aeneas wounded after a battle with local Italian king Turnus, as told in Virgil's *Aeneid* (12.389–508; and see p. 38) (Fig. 33).[76]

To audiences well versed in Greek and Latin literature and knowledgeable about Greek art, mythological scenes in paintings and on tableware would have served to stimulate learned conversation at dinner parties, encouraged by the complex interrelation between images and texts. The marble tablets known as Iliac Tablets (*Tabulae Iliacae*) may have been used as such conversation pieces. They appear in Roman Italy in the first century BC to first century AD and seem to have been kept primarily in private villas (Fig. 34).[77] Their relief decoration mostly consists of miniature images depicting episodes from the story of Troy, arranged like continuous comic-strips and, like the Hellenistic Greek pottery bowls mentioned earlier, captioned with quotations from texts drawn from the *Iliad*, the *Odyssey* or Greek tragedy. Playing with the idea of the miniaturization of big themes, they are the very opposite of the monumental sculptural decoration found in the grounds of imperial villas of the Julio-Claudian emperors, such as the groups detailing Odysseus' adventures, discussed below (see p. 113 and Fig. 92), or the sculptural group of Laocoön (see Fig. 193). The latter, from the house of the emperor Titus on the Esquiline Hill in Rome, shows the agonizing death of the Trojan Laocoön, uncle of Aeneas, in punishment for warning his fellow citizens against the Trojan Horse, as recounted by Virgil. One aspect that clearly shines through miniature and monumental images alike is a specifically Roman agenda, from the insertion of Aeneas into the imagery of the Iliac Tablets to the message of Laocoön: the old city of Troy is doomed, and the new era of Rome is beginning.[78] Yet works such as the Laocoön group, elevated to iconic status already by Roman writers and iconic once more in modern times after its rediscovery in the Renaissance (see p. 194), also stands for the enduring appeal of the story of Troy and its imagery across time.

OPPOSITE
Fig. 34
The 'Capitoline Tablet', the best preserved of all known Iliac Tablets
About two thirds of the original tablet survives, preserving over 250 carved figures and 108 lines of minute Greek text. The central scene shows the sack of Troy, with Aeneas escaping the city.

c. 5 BC – AD 15
Found near Bovillae, Italy
Calcite (palombino)
H. 250 mm | W. 300 mm
Musei Capitolini, Rome
MC 316/S

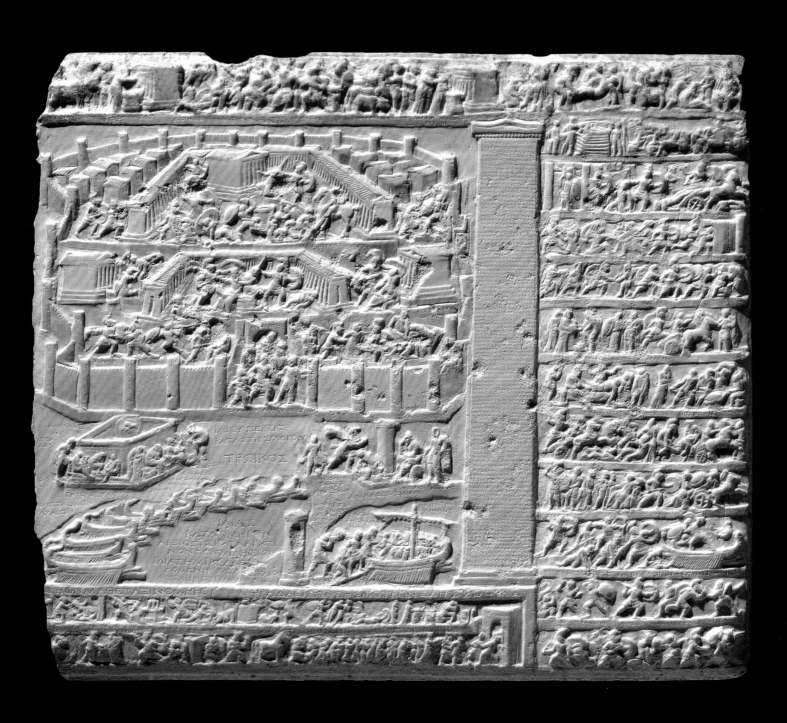

2 THE MYTH OF THE TROJAN WAR

VICTORIA DONNELLAN AND ALEXANDRA VILLING

An epic tale of heroism and emotion, triumph and tragedy, the story of the Trojan War involves a fateful chain of events in which a relatively minor cause has catastrophic effects, and in which not just mortals but also the gods are embroiled:[1]

> Give up your hatred of the lovely Helen
> And wicked Paris, since it is the gods
> Who are so cruel and topple wealthy Troy.
> *Aeneid* 2.601–3

It is epic also in scale, relating the downfall of the great city of Troy at the hands of a huge Greek army. From the sowing of the first seeds of war to the eventual return home of the surviving Greeks, the tale covers nearly half a century and draws in heroes and heroines from much of the then known world – Greece, Anatolia, the Black Sea and Africa. Its account of how kings and warriors from all over Greece united for a common cause reflects a nascent shared Greek identity in the period when it was composed. Yet its key message is not narrowly patriotic, but a universally human one: there is no glory without loss, and no such thing as victory in war, just a frail humanity shared by vanquisher and vanquished alike.

As one of the greatest Greek myths, the story of Troy was pervasive in the culture of ancient Greece, but also found its way into other civilizations in contact with it, first and foremost Etruria and Rome, but also non-classical cultures such as Buddhist Gandhara and Islamic Arabia. Set in Greece's mythical past, it evokes the twilight of a heroic age populated by gods and heroes who are larger than life, yet never other than human. On both sides there is courage and passion, but also weakness and deceit, and hardship is suffered equally. It is the Greeks who prevail in the end, but no moral judgment is passed: eternal themes of the human condition, fate and responsibility are explored through the actions and experiences of both Greeks and Trojans.

PROLOGUE: FROM ZEUS' PLAN TO THE ABDUCTION OF HELEN

Zeus plans the Trojan War

There was a time when the countless races [of men] roaming [constantly] over the land were weighing down the [deep-]breasted earth's expanse. Zeus took pity when he saw it, and in his complex mind he resolved to relieve the all-nurturing earth of mankind's weight by fanning the great conflict of the Trojan War, to void the burden through death. So the warriors at Troy kept being killed, and Zeus' plan was being fulfilled.
Cypria, fragment 1[2]

Long before the beginning of the Trojan War, a series of events sets the scene for the fateful conflict. According to one tradition, it was Zeus himself, the king of the gods, who instigated the war. His plan, according to the Athenian playwright Euripides, was not only 'to lighten mother earth of her crowded mass of mortals', but also to 'bring fame to the bravest man of Hellas' (*Helen*, 39–40).[3] The means is a great war – the greatest of all wars, one that also brings to an end an entire era: the Heroic Age. As the early Greek poet Hesiod described in his *Works and Days*, this was a time when 'a godlike generation of men who were heroes' (159–60)[4] lived, many of them descended from unions between gods and mortals. Thereafter follows the Iron Age, our own time, when humans lead a hard and miserable life, distant from the gods.

Zeus' plan is recorded in the *Cypria*, the epic poem which contains episodes that take place before those in Homer's *Iliad*.[5] It tells us that it was through two events in particular that Zeus set in motion his plan for fostering discord and pitching characters against one another: the marriage of a goddess to a mortal and the birth of a beautiful daughter of his own.

The Wedding of Peleus and Thetis and the Judgment of Paris

Thetis, a sea goddess, did not want to marry the mortal Peleus, who had fallen in love with her. To resist his pursuit, she transforms herself into a hissing snake, a roaring lion and even blazing fire and running water. But after a great struggle, Peleus finally wins Thetis for his wife. The wedding celebrations are attended by the gods.[6] Of the few images of this momentous event, one decorates a wine-mixing bowl, a masterpiece of Archaic Athenian vase-painting (Figs 35, 36a–d).[7] Perhaps carrying out a commission for an actual wedding, the vase-painter Sophilos here created a cleverly thought out image that hints at how the story will unfold in future. We see the divine wedding guests approaching the house of Peleus, to be received by the groom. Prominent in the procession are Eileithyia, goddess of childbirth, the wise centaur Chiron, who will become the teacher of the newlyweds' son, Achilles, and the lame god Hephaestus, who will later forge new armour for Achilles, who is destined to become a great hero in the Trojan War. Riding in different chariots are three goddesses: Hera, patron of marriage, Aphrodite, goddess of love, and Athena, goddess of war and wisdom. Their chariots are carefully separated, foreshadowing the fact that they are soon to become bitter rivals. The cause of this is Eris, the goddess of strife or discord (Fig. 37),[8] who, angered because she has not been invited to the festivities, throws a golden apple into the midst of the guests. It is inscribed 'to the most beautiful' and, as it is claimed by all three goddesses, a quarrel ensues.

ΘΕΑ

ΖΕΥΣ

ΝΥΦΑΙ

ΧΙΡΟΝ

ΗΒΕ

ΔΙΟΝΥΣΟΣ

ΔΕΜΕΤ

ΘΕΤΙΣ

ΛΕΡΕΝΣ

ΑΡΤΕΜΙ

ΝΥΦΑΙ

ΗΒΛΕΣ

ΑΘΑΝ

ΜΣΑΙ

As Zeus is unwilling to put himself in the crossfire, a young mortal is elected as arbiter of the dispute: Paris, also known as Alexandros, the son of Priam and Hecuba, king and queen of Troy. The prince is living in the mountains near Troy, where, according to some storytellers, he has been raised by shepherds after his parents had abandoned him because of a prophecy that he was destined to cause the destruction of Troy. Hermes, messenger of the gods, leads the three goddesses to the mountainside where Paris tends his sheep. The contending goddesses do not rely on their looks alone: in a bid to win over the youth, each offers him a bribe that lies within her divine competence.[9] Hera, queen of the gods, assures him rule over a wide empire, while Athena promises glory in battle. Yet it is Aphrodite's reward that proves most irresistible to the young man: the most beautiful woman in the world, Helen.

> Pallas [Athena] offered him command of all the Phrygians, and the destruction of Hellas; Hera promised he should spread his dominion over Asia, and the utmost bounds of Europe, if he would decide for her; but Cypris [Aphrodite] spoke in rapture of my loveliness, and promised him this gift, if she should have the preference over those two for beauty. Helen in Euripides, *The Trojan Women* 924–30[10]

In the image on an Athenian jar (see Fig. 39),[11] the goddesses' bribes are symbolized by their attributes: Hera's sceptre, Athena's spear and Aphrodite's bridal veil wrapped around her, an unusually demure attire for the goddess of love.

The Judgment of Paris was one of the most popular myths to be represented in Greek and Etruscan art, and the so-called Boccanera plaques are among the most splendid

renderings (Fig. 38).[12] Found in a tomb in the Etruscan city of Cerveteri in central Italy, they show Paris as a mature, bearded man at the far left. He is approached by Hermes, the messenger of the gods. Behind Hermes follow the three goddesses: Athena with a spear and wreath, and Hera and Aphrodite carrying pomegranate branches, symbols of fertility. Aphrodite, depicted in the centre, lifts her dress to show off her fashionable boots and a hint of leg, confident of victory. On the right, we most probably see what will follow next: Helen adjusts her snake-like girdle while three women bring perfume vessels and a box with adornments to prepare her for meeting Paris. With arms akimbo she strikes an unusually powerful pose, and the fact that she turns away may be a sign that she is not too pleased to be the prize in the divine scheme – though she could also once have faced a figure, now lost, further to the right. Etruscans often retold and reshaped Greek myths in local terms, including equating Greek gods with their own divinities. Here we are struck by the unusual bull-topped sceptre carried by Hermes (or rather his Etruscan equivalent Turms), the flirtatious pose of Aphrodite (Etruscan Turan), and the pointed boots worn by many figures, which reflect contemporary Etruscan fashion. Even though the panels' funerary context may be secondary (they may originally have adorned a different, unknown building), we may wonder if the tomb's owner and his wife saw themselves mirrored in prince Paris and charming Helen, while other elements such as the pomegranate branches could have been interpreted as alluding to the cycle of life and death.

ABOVE
Fig. 38*
The 'Boccanera plaques', painted Etruscan plaques that show scenes from the Judgment of Paris

c. 560–550 BC
From La Banditaccia cemetery, Cerveteri, Italy
Terracotta
H. 1025 mm | W. 1705 mm
(three panels)
British Museum
1889,0410.1, 2 & 4

GODS AND HUMANS

So the immortals spun our lives that we, we wretched men
live on to bear such torments – the gods live free of sorrows.
Iliad 24.525–26

In the story of the Trojan War, the gods are an integral part of the narrative.[13] They instigate the conflict, inspire love between Paris and Helen, and even physically appear before Paris (Fig. 39) or intervene in battles. And they are far from impartial: Aphrodite, Apollo and Ares take the Trojan side, while Athena, Hera and Poseidon support the Greeks. During his long journey after the war, Odysseus is frequently waylaid by Poseidon, but helped by Athena. Ancient Greeks imagined their gods as thoroughly anthropomorphic, even if free from the limitations of age or death. They also saw them as being subject to emotions. This 'human' quality is never more apparent than in the works of Greek poets; as the first-century AD Roman writer Longinus put it, 'in recording as he does the wounding of the gods, their quarrels, vengeance, tears, imprisonment, and all their manifold passions, Homer has done his best to make the men in the *Iliad* gods and gods men' (*On the Sublime* 9.7).[14]

For the Greeks, the role of the gods in the story crystallized a fundamental question of human existence, that of the role of free will (and responsibility) versus predetermined fate – a question that ultimately remained unresolved. In the narrative, as in ancient Greek belief, gods act to uphold order. They punish transgressions such as impiety, sacrilege and hubris, and enforce social rules. They also embody the unpredictability of human existence, shaping the course of the Trojan War through divine rivalries and partiality. Nonetheless, even the gods are not entirely free to decide, but are also subject to fate or necessity, while at the same time both gods and humans clearly have moral responsibility for their actions. Indeed, it has been argued that in the narrative the gods function as little more than projections of human qualities and feelings, such as erotic desire, reason, prowess in war or anger.[15] As many modern adaptations confirm, the story is remarkably easy to tell without any divine intervention at all, by focusing instead on the emotions and character of the human protagonists.

RIGHT
Fig. 39*
Red-figure water jar (*hydria*) depicting the Judgment of Paris
The three goddesses – Hera, who holds the golden apple, Athena and Aphrodite – advance towards Paris, who is playing a tortoise-shell lyre while tending sheep on Mount Ida.

c. 470 BC
Made in Attica, Greece; found in Capua, Italy
Pottery
H. 327 mm | Diam. 265 mm
British Museum
1873,0820.353

Helen is taken to Troy

Helen was a prize well worthy of a Trojan prince; she was not a mere mortal but the daughter of Zeus, and was in fact the second element in Zeus' supposed plan. Zeus had coupled with a mortal woman, Leda, queen of Sparta, and had done so in the form of a swan. The result was Helen, born from an egg (Fig. 40).[16] At least this is the version of the story that was popular in art. In other versions, including in the *Cypria*, Leda was merely Helen's foster mother; her actual mother was Nemesis, goddess of divine retribution.[17]

Aphrodite's promise of Helen to Paris has fateful consequences, for Helen is already married to Menelaus, king of Sparta, and mother of their child. It is Helen's abduction by Paris that sets in motion the Trojan War. As the poet of the *Iliad* notes, Helen was a woman of dangerous beauty:

> Ah, no wonder
> the men of Troy and Argives under arms have suffered
> years of agony all for her, for such a woman.
> Beauty, terrible beauty![18]

The story goes that Paris, having sailed to Greece from Troy, is welcomed according to custom as a guest at the Spartan court, yet one night, during Menelaus' absence, he runs off with Helen, taking her on his ship bound for Troy. The deed (which has probably been represented in Greek art since before 700 BC; see above, Fig. 25) was a grave violation of the rules of hospitality, some of the most fundamental principles of Greek society. But to what

BELOW LEFT
Fig. 40
Red-figure wine-mixing bowl (bell-*krater*) depicting the birth of Helen
Helen springs from the egg fully formed, watched by Leda and her stepfather Tyndareus.

c. 340 BC
Made in Campania, attributed to the Caivano Painter; found in Frigniano, Italy
Pottery
Museo Archeologico Nazionale di Napoli
147950

BELOW RIGHT
Fig. 41*
Neo-Attic relief depicting the meeting of Paris and Helen, assisted by the gods
Behind Helen and on a tall column sits Peitho, the personification of persuasion.

1st century BC – 1st century AD, based on 5th-century BC Greek models
From Rome
Marble
H. 670 mm | W. 670 mm
Museo Archeologico Nazionale di Napoli
6682

Fig. 42*
**Red-figure bucket
(*situla*) showing
Paris as a horseman,
arriving to take Helen
away**
Behind Helen stands
the goddess Aphrodite,
shown nude.

c. 350–340 BC
Made in Campania, Italy,
attributed to the Parrish
Painter
Pottery
H. 274 mm | Diam. 270 mm
British Museum
1928,0719.3

extent was a human culpable for an act committed at divine instigation, or prompted by
an overwhelming emotion? Was Paris a victim of fate and of Helen's charms, or a deceitful
traitor? Does Helen deserve our pity or our condemnation?[19]

Already in ancient Greece almost everything about Helen was contestable. In Euripides'
play *The Trojan Women*, Paris' mother, Queen Hecuba, sees Helen as driven by lewd impulse
and greed:

> My son was exceedingly handsome … so when you caught sight of him in gorgeous
> foreign clothes, ablaze with gold, your senses utterly forsook you … it was your hope
> to deluge by your lavish outlay Phrygia's town, that flowed with gold.[20]

Others placed much of the blame squarely on 'deceitful and murderous' Aphrodite, or
on Helen's 'most ill-fated beauty'.[21] In one version of the story Helen never goes to Troy at
all. Instead, she is whisked away by the gods to Egypt, and a 'phantom' Helen accompanies
Paris to Troy. The doppelgänger absolves 'real' Helen of blame, but at the same time
turns the war and all its sufferings into a cruel divine joke. The strangeness of this version,
which dates back at least to the time of the poet Stesichorus of the early sixth century BC
and was put on the Athenian stage by Euripides in his play *Helen* of 412 BC, already appears
to have puzzled the ancient Greeks. The Greek philosopher Socrates explained it as an
invention by Stesichorus, who came from Sparta where Helen was worshipped as a goddess,
after Helen had blinded him because his poems on the Trojan War had blackened
her reputation.[22]

Ancient artists often visualized the gods as the cause of the fatal attraction, either to underline divine input in human fate, or to signify the powerful emotions, embodied by the gods, that were at work. In a series of images going back to the fifth century BC it is Eros, the personification of sexual attraction, who incites desire for Helen in Paris. On a Roman relief based on Classical Greek models we see Eros talking to Paris, while Helen is seated opposite in a modest fashion, in turn being persuaded by Aphrodite to take notice of the attractive youth in front of her (Fig. 41).[23] A South Italian vase-painter shows Aphrodite standing directly behind Helen, who is lifting her veil for Paris for the first time (Fig. 42).[24] Below this scene, Eros playfully allows a dog to chase a goose, perhaps an allusion to infatuated humans being but a plaything of the gods. On an Athenian jar, Eros, flying above, almost physically links the pair, while a seated Helen admires herself in a mirror and Paris stands transfixed by her beauty (see Fig. 45).[25] In contrast, Etruscan funerary urns sometimes show a reluctant Helen, as if the love affair has turned into a cold-hearted abduction.[26] In one, a seemingly bored Paris is seated in front of his ship, while Helen is pushed along by his men, just another item among the treasures he is stealing from Menelaus (Fig. 43). One reason for emphasizing Helen's unwillingness here may be the urns' function, their decoration alluding to the deceased reluctantly parting from life. On a Roman wall-painting (Fig. 44) that once adorned a house at Pompeii, it is Helen's internal conflict that is foregrounded: she looks doubtful and hesitant as she steps on to the plank leading up to the ship, relying on a servant to steady her. She goes willingly, but with a sense of foreboding.[27]

LEFT
Fig. 43*
Funerary urn showing the embarkation of Helen
Paris, in Phrygian dress, sits on a folding-stool. Among his 'possessions' being loaded on to his ship are a vase and his bride, Helen.

c. 125–100 BC
Probably made at Volterra, Italy
Tufa limestone
H. 406 mm | L. 575 mm
British Museum
1849,1201.6

RIGHT
Fig. 44*
Wall-painting
showing Helen
leaving Sparta
for Troy
A servant leads Helen
on to the ship as a soldier
stands in the background.

AD 45–79
House of the Tragic Poet,
Pompeii, Italy
Painted plaster
H. 1160 mm | W. 580 mm
Museo Archeologico
Nazionale di Napoli
9108

GREEKS AND 'BARBARIANS'

From the mid-fifth century BC onwards, Greek (and Etruscan) images often show Paris dressed distinctly and differently from the Greeks, wearing patterned trousers, a patterned sleeved top and a soft cap with flaps (Fig. 45). In Greek art this 'exotic' dress is typical for both Persian and Anatolian peoples (it is based on the actual garments worn by Scythians and Persians), and thus designates Paris not as a Greek but as a foreigner from the East. Greeks had for some time called the Trojans 'Phrygians' (the Phrygians were a people of western central Anatolia, in what is now Turkey), but images that clearly differentiate Phrygians (Trojans) from Greeks only occur after the Persian Wars, when the Trojan War itself had come to be seen as a conflict between Greeks and 'barbarians', a term applied to non-Greek-speaking people, with increasingly pejorative connotations.[28] The two Persian invasions of the Greek mainland (490 BC and 480–478 BC) proved a traumatic experience for Greeks, despite the eventual Greek victory under the leadership of Athens and Sparta. For many Athenians in particular, the Trojan War became a paradigm of an unlikely victory of heroic, freedom-loving Greeks over a despotic, cowardly Eastern empire. This polarized construct was crucial in shaping modern perceptions of 'East and West'.[29]

In fact, however, ancient Greek attitudes were more complex. Greek heroes and their conquest of Troy were far from being viewed in wholly positive terms, and the excessive violence exhibited by some Greeks was highlighted as an example of how not to behave. Emotionally charged images of the atrocities inflicted by Greeks on Trojans during the sack of Troy may have had special meaning to Athenians following the Persian sack of their city in 480 BC, and the plight of any human being, be they Greek, Trojan or even Persian, was generally viewed with a degree of empathy.[30]

BELOW
Fig. 45*
Red-figure water jar (*hydria*) showing the encounter of Helen and Paris
Paris wears the floppy 'Phrygian' cap that in Classical Greek and later art characterized Phrygians and Persians.

c. 380–370 BC
Made in Attica, Greece; found at Kymissala, Rhodes, Greece
Pottery
H. 421 mm | W. 405 mm | D. 335 mm
Antikensammlung, Berlin
V. I. 3768

THE TROJAN WAR: THE FIRST NINE YEARS

The abduction of Helen and the violation of the sacred laws of marriage and hospitality require retribution. Helen's cheated husband, Menelaus of Sparta, calls upon his brother, Agamemnon, the powerful king of rich Mycenae (who also happens to be married to Helen's sister, Clytemnestra), to assemble a massive army. As noted by the sixth-century BC Greek poet Ibycus, 'a mere mortal' could never tell the details of the many ships that sailed 'to the horse-plains of Troy, and sailing in them the bronze-shielded sons of Greece'.[31] According to the *Iliad*'s 'Catalogue of Ships' (2.494–759) the fleet numbered over 1,000 ships, carrying perhaps 100,000 men – kings, heroes and ordinary soldiers from all over Greece (Fig. 46).[32]

One of the reasons why so many leaders agree to help recover a lost wife is that they had sworn an oath to do so. Helen's notorious beauty had attracted suitors from all over Greece. In order to prevent them from coming to blows, one of them, Odysseus, had suggested that they should all swear to defend possession of Helen by whomever she herself chose as husband. The suitors accepted and swore, and Helen chose Menelaus, king of Sparta. Many heroes undoubtedly now regretted their rash promise, even Odysseus, king of the small island of Ithaca, whose idea it had been and who now tries to evade the consequences by feigning madness. Yet all eventually rally round to form an alliance of the greatest

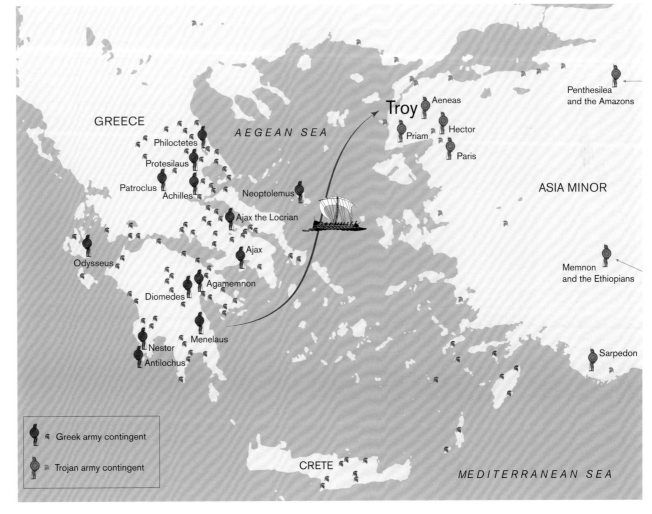

RIGHT
Fig. 46
Map showing the wide alliance of Greeks who participated in the Trojan War, as well as the Trojans and their allies
The Homeric epics call the Greeks fighting at Troy 'Achaeans', a term that goes back to 'Ahhiyawa', the name given to Mycenaean Greeks in 14th–13th-century BC Hittite sources (see p. 179).

heroes of the time. With them is Achilles, the son of Peleus and Thetis, leading the Myrmidons, people from his home country in Thessaly. Even though he had been too young to be among Helen's suitors (and even though his mother at first attempts to hide him on a remote island, disguised as a girl, since she knows he is going to his certain death; see p. 74), he is drafted in because he is the greatest of all Greek fighters.

As recounted in the *Cypria* and other ancient texts, the expedition gets off to a bad start. Having set sail, the fleet becomes lost and mistakenly lands in Mysia, south of Troy, engages in various battles and returns home only with some difficulty.[33] Reassembling at the port of Aulis, east of Boeotian Thebes, the ships are then detained by bad weather. This leads to one of the most brutal and horrifying episodes of the Trojan War even before it begins. A seer travelling with the Greek army, Calchas, tells the Greeks that to ensure favourable winds they must appease the goddess Artemis, who is angered because Agamemnon has killed one of her sacred deer. Agamemnon needs to sacrifice his own virgin daughter, Iphigenia.[34] While the sacrifice of animals to the gods was common in Greek religion, to demand a human life was considered outrageous. Nevertheless, Iphigenia is summoned from Mycenae under the pretence that she is to wed the hero Achilles.

LEFT
Fig. 47*
Red figure wine-mixing bowl (*krater*) depicting the sacrifice of Iphigenia
While Agamemnon pours a ritual libation over his daughter's head, Artemis, standing behind Iphigenia, initiates her rescue by replacing her with a deer.

c. 370–355 BC
Made in Apulia, Italy, attributed to a painter close to the Iliupersis Painter; found in Basilicata, Italy
Pottery
H. 695 mm | W. 434 mm
British Museum
1865,0103.21

The painting on a South Italian pottery vessel shows the moment of the sacrifice. Agamemnon himself holds the sacrificial knife (Fig. 47).[35] His is the classic, terrible dilemma of having to weigh individual feeling against communal objectives, and he is pressured by the needs of war into committing an unspeakable atrocity. His position as leader requires that he must sacrifice what is most dear to him, but his act is set to bring doom on his whole family until well beyond the end of the conflict. On the vase, Iphigenia stands docile beside the altar, having accepted her fate. She is not the piteous victim of earlier traditions, carried to the altar like an animal, but she is a heroine, ready to give her life for her country in the only form open to a female in ancient Greece.[36] She is rewarded for her patriotism when, at the last minute, she is whisked away to the divine realm by Artemis, who substitutes a deer in her place; on the vase we see its head and legs materializing behind the girl. This twist in the story, described already in the *Cypria*, was most famously told in the late fifth century BC in Euripides' *Iphigenia in Tauris*. Here and especially in his later tragedy *Iphigenia in Aulis*, Euripides reflects contemporary Athenian involvement in the catastrophic Peloponnesian War. The plays are likely to have provided inspiration also for this artist, who was looking for an appropriately heroic theme for a vase destined for a tomb.

The Greek heroes at Troy

> … the Greeks, leaping from their ships, filled the plain with bodies.
> And having shut up the Trojans, they besieged them …
> Apollodorus, *Library*, Epitome 3.31[37]

With the winds now in their favour, the Greeks sail to Troy. En route they abandon their seemingly incurably wounded comrade Philoctetes on an island (he will have an important role to play later on), and Calchas pronounces an alarming prophecy: it will take more than nine years to conquer Troy. The prophecy will prove to be true. As they land near Troy, the first Greek to set foot ashore, Protesilaus, is killed by Troy's crown prince, Hector (Fig. 48).[38] Initial fighting soon turns into a prolonged siege of the city. For the Greeks, their camp on the beach will become home for years to come, as raids and battles, as well as attempts at diplomacy, alternate with periods of inaction.[39]

Surviving texts tell us far less about these first years of the war than about the final, tenth year, which is the focus of the *Iliad* as well as the *Aeneid*, though some episodes were popular in art. An image on an Archaic Athenian black-figure amphora brilliantly captures the tediousness of the drawn-out siege. It juxtaposes two warriors, the great Achilles and his cousin Ajax, also a bold fighter, both wearing their full panoply. Yet they are not fighting, they are whiling away the time by playing a board game (Fig. 49).[40] We know of no literary references to such a game, but dozens of similar images survive on Archaic Athenian vases. As a character study of two heroes in a different, intellectual competition, it was probably a vase-painter's invention, eloquent testimony to how the visual arts formed an independently creative artistic form beside the textual tradition.

Another episode that apparently struck a chord with artists and their audiences was Achilles' killing of Troilus, a story that was also recounted in some now lost Athenian tragedies.[41] According to a prophecy, Troy could not fall if Troilus, a young son of King Priam, were to reach the age of twenty. Achilles therefore ambushes the boy at a

fountain-house just outside the city walls, where he had gone to fetch water, which was in short supply in the besieged city. An Archaic Athenian amphora (Fig. 50) shows armed Achilles pursuing the youth, who flees on his horse as his sister Polyxena runs before him, looking back in terror, her water jar dropped to the ground. On another jar (Fig. 51), Troilus has taken refuge in a nearby sanctuary of Apollo, but Achilles, relentless, murders him at the altar. As Troilus' dead body lies lifelessly on the altar, Achilles hurls the boy's severed head at two approaching Trojan warriors. The wider consequences of this pitiless deed will become clear only much later.[42] For by killing Troilus, Achilles may have eliminated an obstacle to Greek victory, yet he has also made two deadly enemies: the god Apollo, enraged at Achilles' violation of the sacred right of asylum, and Troilus' sister, Polyxena; both (at least in some versions of the story) are instrumental in bringing about Achilles' death.

According to the *Cypria*, as Troy itself holds strong, much of the fighting during this period takes place in the wider Trojan territory and the allied towns and cities that form Troy's support network. Here the Greeks, led by Achilles, capture another of Priam's many sons, Lycaon, and chase his nephew, Aeneas, from his hideout in the mountains. It is during such raids that women are also captured. Chryseis, daughter of Chryses, a Trojan priest, and Briseis, queen of a neighbouring city, are allotted to Agamemnon and Achilles as prizes of honour. They are to prove crucial in the unfolding story of the War, for it is a dispute over their possession that sets off the dramatic and emotional events recounted in the *Iliad*.

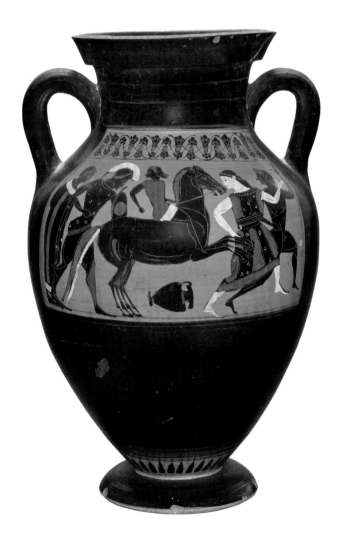

THE FIRST TROJAN WAR

The famous Trojan War, in which the Greek army was led by Agamemnon, was not the first conflict between Greeks and Trojans known to Greek myth. Already in the time when Laomedon, Priam's father, was king of Troy the great Greek hero Heracles had laid siege to and destroyed Troy with another army (*Iliad* 5.638–42).[43] This war, too, was motivated by revenge, since Laomedon had denied Heracles the reward he had been promised for rescuing Laomedon's daughter, Hesione, as well as having offended the gods Poseidon and Apollo, who had originally helped build the walls of Troy.

This earlier conflict between Greeks and Trojans is represented in the sculptures adorning one of the pediments of the temple of Aphaia on the Greek island of Aegina, built in the early fifth century BC (Fig. 52a); the other pediment shows the later, more famous Trojan War (Fig. 52b).[44] Some scholars have taken the story of two wars to reflect a long history of actual contact and conflict between Greece and Troy in the Bronze Age. In myth at least the two wars were not unconnected: Heracles had passed his bow, whose every shot with poison-tipped arrows was deadly, to Philoctetes, who participated in the second Trojan War, taking the famous bow with him.

A different version of an earlier destruction of Troy was ascribed to the Greek hero Jason and his Argonauts, who belong to the generation before the Trojan War heroes. It was part of their voyage to Colchis on the Black Sea, where they had gone to recover the celebrated Golden Fleece.[45]

BELOW

Fig. 52a, b
The first and second Trojan Wars on the pediments of the Temple of Aphaia on Aegina

The sculptures in the east pediment depict battles from the first war (top), the west pediment the later war described by Homer (bottom). Both prominently feature Aeginetan heroes: Telamon, who participated in the first war, and Ajax, son of Telamon, who fought in the second.

c. 490–480 BC (east),
c. 500–490 BC (west)
Aegina, Greece
Marble
Glyptothek, Munich

THE RAGE OF ACHILLES

Achilles and Agamemnon quarrel

> Rage – Goddess, sing the rage of Peleus' son Achilles,
> murderous, doomed, that cost the Achaeans countless losses,
> hurling down to the House of Death so many sturdy souls,
> great fighters' souls, but made their bodies carrion,
> feasts for the dogs and birds, and the will of Zeus was moving towards its end.
> *Iliad* 1.1–5

In the tenth year of the Trojan War, a series of dramatic events unfolds directly as a result of the rage of Achilles. This is the story told in the *Iliad*, beginning when Chryses, a priest of the god Apollo from an island near Troy, visits the Greek camp.[46] He comes to appeal for the return of his captive daughter, Chryseis, who has been given to the Greek king Agamemnon as a prize of honour. Despite the offer of an appropriate ransom, Agamemnon refuses to return her, provoking the anger of Apollo, who sends a deadly plague upon the Greek troops. Forced to recognize that he must give up Chryseis to pacify the god, Agamemnon demands another woman in exchange. This, however, would mean reallocating another hero's prize, as all the spoils from sacked cities have already been distributed. A quarrel between Achilles and Agamemnon ensues. Achilles threatens to withdraw his men and return home, yet Agamemnon insists on claiming Achilles' own prize woman, Briseis, for himself. Although the goddess Athena restrains him from physical violence against Agamemnon, Achilles swears a powerful and foreboding oath, predicting that Agamemnon's soldiers will suffer death at the hands of Hector, and Agamemnon himself will bitterly regret disgracing the 'best of the Achaeans' (*Iliad* 1.244), the term

RIGHT
Fig. 53*
Detail of a red-figure drinking cup (*kylix*) showing Briseis being taken to Agamemnon's camp by two heralds (see also Fig. 30)

c. 480 BC
Made in Attica, Greece, attributed to the Briseis Painter; found in Vulci, Italy
Pottery
H. 120 mm | W. 382 mm | Diam. 300 mm
British Museum
1843,1103.92

Fig. 54*
**Roman relief showing
two heralds seizing
Briseis**
Achilles sits with his head
turned away, as Patroclus
comforts Briseis.

c. 30 BC – AD 80,
reworked 1750–1850
Marble
H. 690 mm | L. 1321 mm
British Museum
1856,1226.1757

Homer uses for the Greeks. The girl Chryseis is duly put on board a ship for return to her homeland, bringing the plague to an end.

Agamemnon sends heralds to take Briseis from Achilles. For Classical artists, this key moment in the story provided a chance to explore the emotional drama of the separation. A red-figure cup (Fig. 53) shows Briseis being led to Agamemnon's camp by the two heralds, one of whom takes her by the hand, deliberately recalling the way brides were commonly depicted being led away by the groom on Greek vases.[47] On the other side, Achilles sits indoors in an attitude of mourning, wrapped in a heavy cloak, a pose that suggests his grief at the loss of Briseis and also his humiliation and angry withdrawal from battle (see Fig. 30).[48] In a relief representing the same scene (Fig. 54) the Roman sculptor has chosen a different approach to portray Achilles' outrage: the hero refuses to watch as Briseis, her head bowed, is led away, while his closest companion, Patroclus, appears to place a comforting hand on her shoulder.[49]

Dishonoured and disgruntled, Achilles appeals to Thetis, his mother, who tenderly tries to console him. He beseeches her to ask Zeus to bestow successes in battle on the Trojans, so that Agamemnon will realize his mistake in disrespecting Achilles. Zeus promises to grant her request and it becomes clear that the rage of Achilles will cause the death of so many Greeks, as described in the opening lines of the *Iliad* (quoted above, p. 71). Zeus' promise to Thetis provokes Hera, his goddess wife and supporter of the Greeks, to an argument. This divine quarrel, however, is resolved in laughter and feasting, unlike that of the mortal Achilles and Agamemnon.

Battles and duels

Greeks and Trojans prepare for war. A series of one-to-one combats and battles follows. The *Iliad* contains numerous vivid descriptions of the violence and cacophony of warfare:

> They slammed their shields together, pike scraped pike
> with the grappling strength of fighters armed in bronze
> and their round shields' bosses pounded hide to hide
> and the thunder of struggle roared and rocked the earth.
> Screams of men and cries of triumph breaking in one breath,
> fighters killing, fighters killed, and the ground streamed blood.
> *Iliad* 8.61–65

A key episode on this day of battle is the challenge to a duel issued by Paris, which is accepted by Menelaus. The wronged husband is dramatically pitted directly against his wife's abductor. The fight is watched by Helen from the walls of Troy. Menelaus is dominant and seems set for victory, but the goddess Aphrodite rescues Paris, carrying him off to the safety of his bedroom and the arms of the reluctant Helen. The gods debate whether to allow the conflict to end here, with victory declared for Menelaus and the Greeks, but decide to continue the war, making a Trojan break the truce which has been established by the duel.

Battle rages on, with many deaths on both sides, until an indecisive duel between Hector and Ajax concludes one day's fighting, with a respite to allow both sides to recover their dead. The Greeks build a defensive wall to protect their camp and ships. For the next day of combat, Zeus commands the other gods to refrain from intervening.

BIOGRAPHY OF A HERO: THE LIFE OF ACHILLES

The character of Achilles is central to the story of the *Iliad*. A wider set of myths describes his birth and upbringing.[50] Achilles is the son of Peleus, a Greek king, and Thetis, a sea goddess, and is sent to the centaur Chiron for his education and training (Fig. 55a). As a boy, he develops a close relationship with Patroclus, who joins Achilles' household as an exile, having accidentally killed another boy. They become friends and probably lovers: Patroclus is described by Achilles as 'the man I loved beyond all other comrades, loved as my own life' (*Iliad* 18.80–82).[51] Their intimate relationship, crucial to the plot of the *Iliad*, is eloquently evoked in the interior of a cup (see Fig. 28) that shows Achilles bandaging Patroclus' wounded arm, an episode that may have taken place during the mistaken expedition to Mysia (see p. 66).[52]

Achilles' parents attempt to prevent his participation in the expedition to Troy, as a prophecy has foretold he will die there. He is concealed on the island of Skyros, disguised as a maiden at the court of King Lycomedes among his numerous daughters. While there, Achilles has a child with the king's daughter, Deidamia: this child is Neoptolemus, who joins in the Trojan War later on. The Greek heroes Odysseus and Diomedes eventually trick Achilles into revealing himself. Visiting the island, they lay out gifts mostly intended to please the girls, but also include weapons and then sound a trumpet call to war. Achilles instinctively grabs the weapons and so is found out (Fig. 55c).

Events from the life of Achilles became very popular as decoration for Roman sarcophagi.[53] Their designers picked out disparate episodes to suit their desired message, rarely representing battle scenes and more often choosing ones that not only show off Achilles' powerful body but also highlight his emotions. Achilles' feminine disguise on Skyros – which appears on more than twenty sarcophagi – was an opportunity to draw attention to his youthful beauty as well as his virile nature, which causes him to betray himself. On the example illustrated, this features alongside his athletic education by Chiron and two episodes from the *Iliad*: Thetis presenting new armour to Achilles (Fig. 55b), and Achilles dragging the body of Hector (not shown).[54] Images of the deaths of young heroes – on this example Hector, but elsewhere also Patroclus (see Fig. 60) – had obvious relevance in a funerary context, providing a comforting sense of the universality of death, inevitable even for the brightest and best.

OPPOSITE ABOVE LEFT
Fig. 55a*
Roman sarcophagus depicting scenes from the life of Achilles
Here, the centaur Chiron trains the young Achilles.

AD 150–200
Made in Attica, Greece; found in Ierapetra, Crete
Marble
H. 151.5 cm | L. 271.3 cm | D. 123.3 cm
British Museum
1861,0220.1

OPPOSITE ABOVE RIGHT
Fig. 55b*
Thetis hands Achilles new armour while Hephaestus works on his shield.

OPPOSITE BELOW
Fig. 55c*
Achilles, holding a helmet, sits among the daughters of Lycomedes.

Zeus weighs out the fates of Trojans and Greeks against one another and a day of doom for the Greeks is foretold. The Greeks fall back before the Trojans, but rally in time to save their ships from destruction. By the time night falls, the Greeks have been driven back behind their defences, and the Trojans camp on the plain, confident of victory the following day.

Embassy to Achilles

Faced with this crisis, Agamemnon agrees to send an embassy to Achilles to try to persuade him to rejoin the fighting and win back Zeus' favour for the Greeks. Odysseus, Ajax and Phoenix, an old man who had been in charge of Achilles' upbringing, set off to Achilles' tent. Odysseus lists the many goods Agamemnon is promising Achilles in reparation if he relents and controls the anger that still consumes him: tripods, gold, cauldrons, horses and women, including the return of Briseis, together with further rewards if Troy is captured, and one of Agamemnon's own daughters in marriage, with an extravagant dowry. The embassy to Achilles became a popular subject for early fifth-century BC Athenian vase-painters, at a time when the Athenian playwright Aeschylus also wrote a tragedy (now lost) on the theme.[55] On a cup in the British Museum, Achilles is again shown heavily wrapped in his characteristic pose of mourning and withdrawal (Fig. 56).[56] It is likely that it was for this particular narrative context that the motif was first used, before being adopted for other scenes to convey the grief and anger of Achilles.[57] The figure shown speaking to him,

BELOW
Fig. 56*
The interior of a red-figure drinking cup (*kylix*) showing Odysseus appealing to an aggrieved Achilles, who refuses to fight

C. 470 BC
Made in Attica, Greece, attributed to Douris; found in Vulci, Italy
Pottery
H. 324 mm | W. 400 mm
British Museum
1843,1103.61

with his mouth slightly open, is Odysseus, appealing to Achilles to rejoin the fighting.[58] Achilles, however, remains unmoved, and declares his intention to load up his ships and sail home the following day.

The story of Patroclus

> Gazing down from his ridge on Ida, [Zeus] son of Kronos
> stretched the rope of battle tense and taut
> as the fighters kept on killing side-to-side.
> *Iliad* 11.336–37

The next morning, Agamemnon leads the Greeks into battle once more, and at first drives the Trojans back to the walls of their city, though after he is wounded he has to leave the battlefield. The Trojans under Hector try to seize the opportunity, but meet fierce resistance from the other Greek heroes, and fail to push the Greeks back to their ships. Among the many wounded on this day is the Greeks' doctor, Machaon. Achilles, watching the battle from the stern of his ship, sees Machaon being carried from the battle and sends his companion Patroclus to check what has happened. Patroclus finds Machaon with the aged hero Nestor. Alarmed at the many heroes wounded in the fierce fighting, Nestor urges Patroclus to persuade Achilles, even if he still will not fight in person, to allow Patroclus to lead his Myrmidon army into battle. If Patroclus wears the armour of Achilles, the Trojans will think that Achilles himself – the most fearsome Greek warrior – has rejoined the fighting.

Meanwhile the Greeks' situation is growing ever more desperate, as Hector and the Trojans succeed in breaking through their defensive wall. The gods on the Greek side become alarmed: Poseidon rallies the Greeks and Hera seduces Zeus and lulls him to sleep, so that the gods can defy his prohibition and aid the Greeks. As a consequence, the Greeks are able to resist for a time, Hector is wounded and the Trojans are pushed back behind the defences. But Zeus soon awakes and, furious at his wife's deceit, prophesies and sets in motion a terrible sequence of events.

Achilles grants Patroclus' request to lead his men into battle and wear his armour, but specifies that he should only force the Trojans away from the Greek ships, and not pursue them towards Troy. This, however, is not Zeus' plan: instead he urges Patroclus on to pursue the Trojans towards the city, killing many warriors – including Sarpedon, son of Zeus (Fig. 57). When Patroclus reaches the walls of Troy, Apollo confuses and disarms him and he is hit in the back by the spear of a Trojan called Euphorbus. It is Hector, however, who strikes the final blow. Homer characteristically employs a simile drawn from the natural world to describe the way Hector overpowers Patroclus:

> As when some lion overpowers a tireless wild boar
> up on a mountain summit, battling in all their fury
> over a little spring of water, both beasts craving
> to slake their thirst, but the lion beats him down
> with sheer brute force as the boar fights for breath
> *Iliad* 16.823–26

The East Greek artist who painted a plate found on the island of Rhodes (Fig. 58) chose to show the conflict over the fallen body of Euphorbus, the warrior who initially wounds

Patroclus, rather than the much more famous, and narratively pivotal, body of Patroclus. The reason for this may be because, according to one tradition, Menelaus dedicated Euphorbus' shield at the famous East Greek temple of Apollo at Didyma on his return journey from Troy, thus making Euphorbus a more prominent figure in that region.[59] On the plate, Menelaus and Hector are shown facing up to each other over the corpse, both dressed in the typical Greek foot soldier's armour – greaves, corselet, helmet and round shield – that was common in the time the plate was painted. Again, this deviated somewhat from the *Iliad*'s account, which describes how Menelaus kills Euphorbus and is about to strip his armour when the god Apollo sends Hector against him. The two do not actually contend over Euphorbus, however: Menelaus backs away, seeing that Hector has a god's support. He then fetches Ajax and together they fight to retrieve the body of Patroclus, from which Hector has stripped Achilles' armour. The fierce battle over the body is still raging when the news of Patroclus' death reaches Achilles. Grief overcomes him like a 'black cloud' and he lies fallen in the dust, clawing at the ground, tearing at and dirtying his hair (*Iliad* 18.22–27). There is a sense in Homer's poem that, with the loss of Patroclus, the life of Achilles has also ended.

BELOW
Fig. 57
Red-figure wine mixing bowl (*calyx-krater*) showing Sleep (Hypnos) and Death (Thanatos) carrying Sarpedon from the battlefield

c. 515 BC
Made in Attica, Greece, signed by Euxitheos as potter and Euphronios as painter; found in Cerveteri, Italy
Pottery
H. 460 mm | Diam. 550 mm
Archaeological Museum of Cerveteri

BELOW
Fig. 58*
East Greek plate
showing a duel
between Hector
(right) and Menelaus
(left) over the body
of Euphorbus
All names are inscribed.

c. 600 BC
Made on Kos, Greece;
found at Kamiros,
Rhodes, Greece
Pottery
Diam. 383 mm | D. 27 mm
British Museum
1860,0404.1

Once again, Achilles' divine mother, Thetis, consoles him. Achilles declares his intention to kill Hector and avenge the death of Patroclus, despite his weeping mother's revelation that it is fated that his own death will soon follow that of Hector. Thetis promises to bring Achilles new armour the next morning, made by the god Hephaestus. The making of the armour, described at length in the *Iliad* (see Epilogue), was a popular scene in art. On a fresco from Pompeii (Fig. 59), Thetis inspects the armour Hephaestus is making for Achilles. The helmet is still being worked on, while the shield is held up to Thetis, reflecting her own image. While this allows the painter to demonstrate his skill in capturing her reflection distorted by the curvature of the shield, its complex decorative friezes as described by Homer are not shown.[60]

After Thetis leaves, Achilles appears at the ditch between camp and battlefield, shouting his great war cry three times, while Athena sets a flame blazing from his head, high into the sky. The frightened Trojans fall back, and just before sunset the Greeks are able to retrieve the body of Patroclus. A scene on a Roman sarcophagus emphasizes the pathos of Achilles' loss, as Patroclus' body is brought to him lifelessly draped over the shoulder of a young Greek (Fig. 60). Another Greek standing behind the grief-stricken Achilles lays a hand on his shoulder.[61]

LEFT
Fig. 59*
**Roman fresco
showing Hephaestus
forging new armour
for Achilles**
A corselet (body armour)
and greaves (shin-guards)
are lying on the ground.

AD 45–79
House of Paccius
Alexander, Pompeii, Italy
Painted plaster
H. 159 cm | W. 113 cm
Museo Archeologico
Nazionale di Napoli
9529

THE RAGE OF ACHILLES

The anger or rage of Achilles – μῆνις (*menis*) in Greek – is a key theme of the *Iliad*, and is the first word of the entire poem. Achilles is consumed by two different kinds of anger during the course of the events related.[62] First, there is his angry reaction to Agamemnon's seizure of the captive woman Briseis. This makes sense in the context of ancient Greek social codes. The early Greek world was a highly competitive society, in which a hero's honour was vital to his sense of identity and position among his peers. By taking away the prize of honour that had been allocated to Achilles in recognition of his fighting prowess during the capture of a Trojan city, Agamemnon has dishonoured him. Achilles cannot submit to this without feeling unbearable shame and humiliation in the eyes of the other Greek leaders.

During the period of this anger, Achilles is inactive, withdrawn from battle, and he announces an end to it as he decides to re-engage with the war: 'Now, by god, I call a halt to all my anger – it's wrong to keep on raging, heart inflamed forever' (*Iliad* 19.67–68). By this point, however, Achilles is already in the grip of a powerful need for vengeance following the death of Patroclus. This is a very different kind of rage, a desperate emotion which is part of his grief for Patroclus. At first it manifests itself in the expected behaviour of a Greek hero: killing Hector to avenge the slaying of his comrade. But Achilles, consumed by his grief, surpasses the boundaries of accepted norms in desecrating the body of his enemy.

RIGHT
Fig. 60*
Relief from a Roman sarcophagus showing Achilles sitting grief-stricken as Patroclus' body is brought to him (see also Fig. 67)
The different sides of the sarcophagus had been re-used as decorative reliefs in one of the city gates of Ephesus.

c. AD 250–260
Made in Attica, Greece; from Ephesus, Turkey
Marble
H. 113 cm | W. 126 cm
Woburn Abbey and Gardens
5034

The death of Hector

As dawn breaks, Thetis arrives bringing the new armour to Achilles. On an Athenian vessel depicting this scene, Achilles is again seated and wrapped in his cloak, the motif now representing his grief for Patroclus (Fig. 61). Thetis' embrace of her son is rather awkwardly captured by the painter, but nonetheless conveys a deep sense of emotion, made tragic by the knowledge that Achilles' return to battle also means his imminent death. Thetis' sisters accompanied her in a now lost tragedy by Aeschylus, which this painter may have had in mind when he showed sea nymphs, or nereids, carrying the armour, flanking the central scene.[63] On a Roman sarcophagus (see Fig. 55b), the making of the armour is combined with its delivery to Achilles. The shield is still being worked on by Hephaestus, while Thetis presents greaves and a scabbard to Achilles.[64]

Determined to avenge Patroclus' death at any cost, Achilles calls an assembly and announces that he is ending his anger against Agamemnon. In return, Agamemnon provides the gifts he promised, including the return of Briseis, whom he swears he never touched. Sacrifice is offered, and Achilles arms himself. The two sides meet in battle once again, and with them are also the gods. A combat between Achilles and Aeneas is cut short when Poseidon carries Aeneas away to safety; Achilles repeatedly tries to attack Hector, but Apollo shrouds him in mist. Achilles nonetheless kills many men, including one of Priam's sons, Lycaon, who had been captured earlier (see p. 69) but found his way back to Troy. He then faces a supernatural battle with the River Scamander, which rises against him until Hera and Hephaestus come to his rescue. The gods themselves clash as the mortals fight on, until the Trojans flee and take shelter inside their city walls. Hector waits outside the gates, determined to fight Achilles. His father Priam and mother Hecuba fail in their appeals to him from the walls above to come back inside. Yet when Achilles approaches, Hector is seized by fear; he flees, with Achilles in pursuit. Three times they run around the walls of Troy.

> Past these they raced, one escaping, one in pursuit
> and the one who fled was great but the one pursuing
> greater, even greater – their pace mounting in speed
> since both men strove, not for a sacrificial beast
> or oxhide trophy, prizes runners fight for, no,
> they raced for the life of Hector breaker of horses.
> *Iliad*, 22.158–61

Ultimately the intervention of the gods is required to fulfil destiny: Zeus weighs the two men's fates in his golden scales, and Hector's side sinks down, causing Apollo to stop supporting him. Athena, disguised as Hector's brother Deiphobus, tricks him into facing Achilles in combat. Achilles plunges his spear into Hector's neck, where the armour leaves him vulnerable. Only a relatively small number of representations of this crucial scene survive in art. In his version of the confrontation (Fig. 62), the red-figure vase-painter known as the Berlin Painter did not follow the description in the *Iliad* – both heroes are nude, not clad in the armour Homer describes, and Hector holds a spear, rather than a sword – but he perfectly captured the poignancy of the conflict. Achilles lunges confidently forward towards Hector, who falls back, his wounded chest exposed. Athena stands to the left of Achilles, offering her support, while Apollo is forced to abandon Hector and walks away. The arrow held by Apollo foreshadows Achilles' own death.[65]

BELOW
Fig. 61*
Red-figure storage jar (*pelike*) showing Thetis embracing Achilles while sea nymphs bring him new armour

c. 470 BC
Made in Attica, Greece; found in Kamiros, Rhodes, Greece
Pottery
H. 362 mm | Diam. 265 mm
British Museum
1864,1007.126

OVERLEAF
Fig. 62*
Red-figure wine-mixing bowl (*krater*) showing the duel between Achilles (left) and Hector (right) (see also Fig. 68)

c. 490 BC
Made in Attica, Greece, attributed to the Berlin Painter; found in Cerveteri, Italy
Pottery
H. 635 mm | Diam. 460 mm
British Museum
1848,0801.1

Hector appeals to Achilles to return his body for cremation – a request that is heartlessly refused – and with his dying breath prophesies Achilles' own death at the hands of Paris and Apollo. Achilles, his lust for revenge still not satisfied, deliberately disrespects and sullies the body of Hector, tying it to his chariot by straps through the heels and dragging it behind in the dirt as he drives back to the Greek camp. Homer movingly describes Hector's body raising a cloud of dust, 'his dark hair swirling round that head so handsome once' (*Iliad* 22.401–3).[66] The gruesome episode was a favourite especially with Greek vase-painters of the sixth century BC, but also features on several Roman sarcophagi, a powerful reminder of the inescapability of human fate, and death, even for heroes (see Fig. 79).[67]

Book 22 of the *Iliad* ends with the laments of Hector's family: his father, mother and finally his wife, Andromache. The poem describes Andromache's domestic activities, weaving and preparing a hot bath ready for Hector's return, unaware of his death. When she hears the sounds of lamentation she rushes to see what has happened and collapses at the sight of her husband's body being dragged towards the Greek ships.

BELOW
Fig. 63a, b*
**The two sides of
a red-figure storage
jar (*amphora*)**
The woman and baby
shown on one side reach
out to the armed warrior
on the other, who is
departing for war.

c. 470–460 BC
Made in Attica, Greece;
probably from Vulci, Italy
Pottery
H. 486 mm | Diam. 295 mm
British Museum
1843,1103.33

ANDROMACHE AND HELEN

An amphora in the British Museum (Fig. 63a, b) has images of a helmeted warrior on one side and a woman and baby on the other, both seemingly reaching out to the man who has parted from them. There is nothing to identify the figures, but earlier scholars believed they represented Hector, Andromache and their child Astyanax.[68] Even if, as most scholars now think, the vase-painter did not intend them as such, the desire to see the Homeric characters in these figures reveals the enduring power and pathos of this story of a family broken apart by war, as told in the *Iliad*. A touching scene in Book 6 has Hector and Andromache speak of their fears for the future, but they also laugh together as their son Astyanax shrinks away from his father's plumed helmet, before being comforted in Hector's arms. In his portrayal of the women in the *Iliad*, Homer sets Andromache, the much-loved and dutiful wife of Troy's most dependable hero, in contrast with Helen, a much more complicated and enigmatic character. Helen is self-critical, constantly aware of her own role in the tragic events at Troy, and contemptuous towards Paris (see Chapter 4).

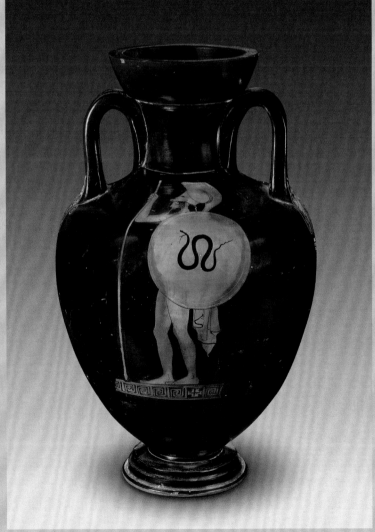

Funeral rites and resolution

Farewell, Patroclus, even there in the House of Death!
Look – all that I promised once I am performing now:
I've dragged Hector here for the dogs to rip him raw –
and here in front of your flaming pyre I'll cut the throats
of a dozen sons of Troy in all their shining glory,
venting my rage on them for your destruction.
Achilles to the dead Patroclus, *Iliad* 23.19–23

The Greeks return to the camp and, with Hector's body flung in the dust beside Patroclus' bier, Achilles provides a funeral feast. At dawn the next day, the Greeks build a funeral pyre for Patroclus and offer sacrifices, including twelve Trojans captured in the fighting the previous day. This scene of human sacrifice – which was not a normal practice among the ancient Greeks – only appears once in surviving Greek art, but was represented several times by Etruscan artists.[69] The engraving on a bronze container for toiletries (*cista*) (Fig. 64a, b) captures the brutality of this episode in the *Iliad*, as Achilles plunges his sword into the neck of a seated Trojan captive beside the funeral pyre, while other bound prisoners await the same terrible fate. The *Iliad* relates that, after cremation, Patroclus' bones are gathered and placed in a golden jar for burial in a mound to serve as his tomb, and the Greeks hold funeral games. According to ancient Greek beliefs, these funeral rites would enable Patroclus' spirit to pass peacefully into the afterlife. Achilles' refusal to hand over Hector's body denies this to Hector, profoundly contravening religious and social norms.

Following the funeral of Patroclus, Achilles' grief allows him no rest. For days, he repeatedly ties Hector's body to his chariot and drags it around the tomb of Patroclus in his furious need for retribution. But the gods preserve the body of Hector, keeping it fresh and undamaged despite Achilles' mistreatment. The painter of a black-figure vase (Fig. 65a, b) seems to merge the original dragging of the body from the battlefield, which takes place before the funeral of Patroclus, with Achilles repeating this act around the tomb – represented by a white mound – on the following days. The painter does not show Achilles driving the chariot himself, as the *Iliad* suggests he did, but follows the usual convention of battle scenes where the hero is accompanied by a chariot-driver, here dressed in the long white tunic traditionally worn by charioteers in athletic competitions. Achilles runs alongside, armed with helmet and shield, while Hector's body is dragged behind.[70]

BELOW
Fig. 64a, b*
An Etruscan container (*cista*) showing the sacrifice of Trojan prisoners at the hands of Achilles
The engraved scene is shown in the line drawing below.

350–250 BC
Palestrina, Italy
Bronze
H. 363 mm | Diam. 230 mm
British Museum
1859,0816.1

OPPOSITE
Fig. 65a, b*
Black-figure storage jar (neck-*amphora*) showing Achilles dragging Hector's body

520–500 BC
Made in Attica, Greece, attributed to the Leagros Group; found in Vulci, Italy
Pottery
H. 450 mm | W. 290 mm
British Museum
1842,0314.2

OPPOSITE
Fig. 66a, b*
Roman cup showing
Priam begging
Achilles to return
his son's body for
burial (above); on
the reverse, Greeks
are shown sleeping
while a Trojan guards
Priam's chariot
(below)

30 BC – AD 40
Found in Hoby, Denmark;
made and signed by
Cheirisophos
Silver
H. 109 mm | Diam. 135 mm
Nationalmuseet,
Denmark
DNF 10/20

BELOW
Fig. 67*
Scene from a Roman
sarcophagus showing
the weighing of
Hector's body
(see also Fig. 60)
The separate scene
on the far left
depicts Hector's wife
Andromache and son
Astyanax.

c. AD 250–260
Made in Attica, Greece;
from Ephesus, Turkey
Marble
H. 105 cm | L. 258 mm
Woburn Abbey and
Gardens
5034

On the twelfth day after Hector's death, the gods finally decide to intervene. Zeus sends Thetis to instruct Achilles to accept a ransom for Hector's body. The goddess Iris then encourages Priam to go alone to Achilles, taking gifts, to ask for the release of his son's corpse, under the protection of Hermes. Despite his wife Hecuba's fears, Priam decides to go and prepares fine gifts and has them loaded on to a mule-cart. The messenger-god Hermes guides Priam safely to Achilles' quarters in the Greek camp. The emotional encounter is powerfully evoked on a splendid silver cup (Fig. 66a, b), which shows Priam coming to Achilles as a supplicant, taking him by the knees and kissing his hands, just as described in the *Iliad*:[71]

I have endured what no one on earth has ever done before –
I put to my lips the hands of the man who killed my son.
Iliad 24.505–6

The two men weep together and share a meal. Achilles agrees to release Hector's body, in a moving transformation of character which restores humanity to the hero and a sense of order to the world. A Roman sarcophagus shows Hector's corpse being literally weighed to determine the ransom, with gold bars in the opposite pan (Fig. 67). This particular event is not described by Homer, but occurs in *Phrygians*, a lost play by Aeschylus.[72] Two Trojans wearing Phrygian caps are carrying other gifts, including a cuirass. Hector's mother Hecuba is shown on the left of the weighing scene. Priam would originally have appeared at the right, in the part that is now missing. In Homer's version, Achilles also agrees to cease the fighting for long enough for the Trojans to mourn and hold the funeral. As dawn breaks, Priam returns to Troy with Hector's body. The *Iliad* ends with the laments of Andromache, Hecuba and Helen, and the funeral of Hector: 'And so the Trojans buried Hector breaker of horses' (*Iliad* 24.804).

THE FALL OF TROY

An ancient world war

Hector's death does not bring about the immediate downfall of Troy.[73] First, the warrior Amazon women arrive to lend their support to the Trojans. The involvement of armies from beyond Troy's own territories makes this a conflict which affects the wider ancient world, not Greeks and Trojans alone.[74] The Greeks were fascinated by the idea of warrior women, so far removed from the norms of female behaviour in their own times. The same sense of exoticism continued in the Roman period, as exemplified by Virgil's description:

> Penthesilea, leader of the Amazons
> With their crescent shields, was storming through the throng,
> Her gold belt tied beneath her naked breast –
> This virgin warrior dared to fight with men.
> *Aeneid* 1.490–93

The Amazon queen faces Achilles in combat, in a scene that Greek artists frequently represented in sculpture and on vases.[75] It was the Athenian vase-painter Exekias who perhaps most powerfully captured the moment when Achilles kills Penthesilea (Fig. 69).[76] According to the most popular version of the story this is also the moment when their eyes meet and he falls in love with her. The Ethiopian king Memnon, too, brings an army to fight on Troy's behalf. In ancient Greek geography, Ethiopia was the region of Africa south

BELOW
Fig. 68*
Detail of a red-figure wine-mixing bowl (*krater*) showing Achilles fighting Ethiopian King Memnon (see also Fig. 62)

c. 490 BC
Made in Attica, Greece, attributed to the Berlin Painter; found in Cerveteri, Italy
Pottery
H. 635 mm | Diam. 460 mm
British Museum
1848,0801.1

OPPOSITE
Fig. 69*
Black-figure storage jar (*amphora*) showing Achilles killing Penthesilea

c. 530 BC
Made in Attica, Greece, signed by Exekias as potter and attributed to Exekias as painter; found in Vulci, Italy
Pottery
H. 410 mm | Diam. 308 mm
British Museum
1836,0224.127

of Egypt. Memnon succeeds in killing the Greek hero Antilochus, the son of Nestor, but is in turn killed by Achilles, a sequence of events mirroring Achilles' revenge on Hector. The two scenes are paired on a wine-mixing bowl by the Berlin Painter, which shows Achilles and Hector on one side (see Fig. 62) and Achilles and Memnon on the other (Fig. 68). As Memnon rushes forward on the right, the combat is watched by the heroes' divine mothers, Thetis and Eos, goddess of dawn, the latter raising one hand to her head in dismay.[77] Zeus makes the defeated Memnon immortal, at his mother's request.

Death of Achilles

After defeating Memnon, Achilles drives the Trojans right into the gates of Troy. There, at the Scaean Gate, Paris shoots him with an arrow. When his mother Thetis had made Achilles invulnerable to harm as a baby, according to the story by dipping him into the River Styx, she held him by the heel of one foot, which was not touched by the water. It was in this one vulnerable spot – the proverbial 'Achilles' heel' – that Paris' arrow hit him, unerringly guided by the god Apollo.[78] It is a relatively unheroic death for this most heroic of warriors. Roman poet Ovid scathingly refers to Paris as 'the cowardly thief of the wife of a Greek' (*Metamorphoses* 12.609),[79] and suggests that Achilles would rather have died at the hands of a female Amazon warrior than the womanish Paris. In another version of the story, the Trojan princess Polyxena plays a role: Achilles falls in love with her when she accompanies Priam to ransom Hector's body. Their marriage is arranged and Achilles duly comes to the temple of Apollo, where he is ambushed and killed by her brothers Paris and Deiphobus. An Etruscan scarab shows the wounded Achilles, the fatal arrow sticking from his foot (Fig. 70).[80] Ajax retrieves Achilles' body for burial in the same tomb as Patroclus. The moving image of Ajax carrying the dead Achilles was one of the great motifs especially of early Archaic Greek art (Fig. 71).[81]

Ajax and Odysseus then quarrel over the right to inherit Achilles' armour. In Ovid's account the debate is an orderly battle of words, each hero putting forward his case in turn, to be judged by the other Greek leaders. In Greek art, we see a more dramatic confrontation, as on a red-figure cup which shows the quarrelling heroes having to be

BELOW LEFT
Fig. 70*
Etruscan scarab showing the fatal arrow protruding from Achilles' heel

400–350 BC
Made in Italy
Carnelian
W. 12 mm | L. 17 mm
British Museum
1872,0604.1149

BELOW RIGHT
Fig. 71
Detail of the handle of a black-figure wine-mixing bowl (*volute krater*; the 'François vase') showing Ajax carrying the body of Achilles

c. 580 BC
Made in Attica, Greece; found in Chiusi, Italy
Pottery
H. 660 mm | Diam. 570 mm
Archaeological Museum, Florence
4209

OPPOSITE
Fig. 72a, b*
Both sides of a red-figure drinking cup (*kylix*) showing the confrontation over Achilles' armour (above), and a vote being held to decide the conflict peacefully (below)

490–480 BC
Made in Attica, Greece, attributed to the Brygos Painter; found in Vulci, Italy
Pottery
H. 138 mm | W. 415 mm
British Museum
1843,1103.11

physically separated (Fig. 72a).[82] There are numerous representations on Greek pottery which follow a similar scheme (Fig. 73).[83] In the absence of inscriptions or details such as the contested armour itself – seen under the handles of the red-figure cup – it is difficult to say for certain whether this specific dispute is intended, or whether its iconography was being borrowed for wider use.[84] The other side of the cup (Fig. 72b) shows the vote to decide the outcome, an episode that was popular in the arts of early fifth-century BC Athens as it provided a mythical precedent for the mechanisms of the nascent Athenian democracy. Odysseus is shown standing at the far left, leaning on his stick, while men are placing their

BELOW
Fig. 73*
Black-figure water jar (*hydria*) painted with a scene of quarrelling heroes, perhaps representing the fight between Ajax and Odysseus over Achilles' armour

c. 520 BC
Made in Attica, Greece; found in Vulci, Italy
Pottery
H. 508 mm | W. 335 mm
British Museum
1843,1103.2

Fig. 74
Figure of Ajax taking his own life

720–700 BC
Made in Greece
Bronze
H. 67 mm | W. 25 mm
British Museum
1865,1118.230

BELOW RIGHT
Fig. 75*
Detail of a red-figure wine-mixing bowl (*calyx-krater*) showing Ajax falling on his sword

c. 400–350 BC
Made in Etruria, Italy, attributed to the Turmuca Group; probably found in Vulci, Italy
Pottery
H. 394 mm | Diam. 272 mm
British Museum
1867,0508.1328

voting tokens on a block in the centre of the scene, presided over by the goddess Athena, a particular champion of Odysseus as well as of democratic Athens. The result is predicted by the mourning attitude of Ajax, standing on the far right wrapped in his cloak, as well as by the smaller pile of tokens on his side of the block.

The vote determines that the armour should be awarded to Odysseus, despite the fact that – as described in the *Iliad* – Ajax is the strongest and most courageous warrior after Achilles. Ajax is so outraged by this slight to his status that he plans to attack his fellow Greeks. Instead, he kills a flock of sheep after Athena strikes him with madness. Coming to his senses and deeply ashamed of his actions, he takes his own life. The story is dramatically told by the Athenian playwright Sophocles in the tragedy *Ajax*, which draws attention to the indifference of the gods and the cold-blooded actions of Athena, and movingly stages the title character's tragic death.

> He's firm in the ground, my Slayer. And his cut
> (If I have time even for this reflection)
> Should now be deadliest.
> [...]
> Here, too, it stands, lodged in this hostile ground
> Of Troy, its edge made new with iron-devouring stone.
> And, last, I've propped it, so, with careful handling,
> To help me soon and kindly to my death.
> Sophocles, *Ajax* 815–22[85]

Artists, too, were attracted by Ajax's desperation and the idea of his huge body being pierced by the sword (Fig. 74 and Fig. 75).[86]

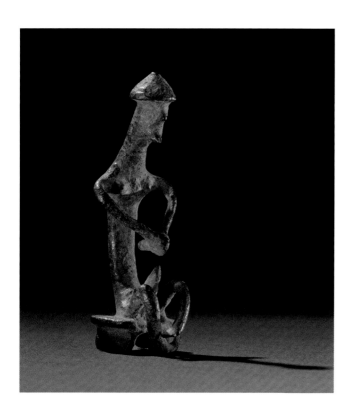

RIGHT AND BELOW
Fig. 76a, b*
Roman cup showing on one side Philoctetes having his wound washed (right) and on the other (below) Odysseus talking to an older Philoctetes, while Neoptolemus takes his bow

30 BC – AD 40
Found in Hoby, Denmark; made and signed by Cheirisophos
Silver
H. 106 mm | Diam. 135 mm
Nationalmuseet, Denmark
DNF 9/20

BELOW LEFT
Fig. 77*
Diomedes stealing the Palladium on a Greek coin (*drachm*)

c. 370–350 BC
Minted in Argos, Greece
Silver
Diam. 20 mm
British Museum
1880,0503.3

BELOW RIGHT
Fig. 78*
Roman gem (intaglio), known as the Felix Gem, showing Diomedes and Odysseus stealing the Palladium

c. 25 BC – AD 25
Made in Rome, signed by Felix
Sardonyx
W. 27 mm | L. 35 mm
The Ashmolean Museum, University of Oxford
AN1966.1808

Talismans protecting Troy

I have heard there were three fates which would bring destruction to Troy.
Plautus, *Bacchides* 953[87]

With the greatest heroes on each side now dead, the war is still not won. The Greeks learn of three prophesied conditions that must be fulfilled before victory is theirs: first, they must have possession of the famous bow and arrows which originally belonged to the hero Heracles; second, Neoptolemus, Achilles' son, must fight on the Greek side; third, the celebrated statue of Athena must be stolen from Troy.[88] A further prerequisite, that the Trojan prince Troilus must not live beyond the age of twenty, has already been taken care of by Achilles in the early years of the war (see p. 69). The Greeks now set about achieving the others.

Heracles had given his bow and arrows to Philoctetes, one of the Greeks who had set out on the original expedition to Troy (see p. 67). He had, however, been bitten by a snake during the journey and, when his wound would not heal, was left behind on the island of Lemnos.[89] On a Greek-inspired Roman silver cup, Philoctetes sits supported by a young man, while another washes his injury. His youthful appearance suggests that this image is intended to show the occasion when he was originally wounded (Fig. 76a).[90] On learning of Philoctetes' vital importance for the Greeks, Odysseus sails back to bring him and his bow to Troy, along with Neoptolemus. This story was dramatized in another play by Sophocles, *Philoctetes*.[91] On the other side of the same silver cup (Fig. 76b), Philoctetes, now bearded and with wild hair, sits with his foot bandaged, apparently in conversation with Odysseus. Behind Odysseus, Neoptolemus is removing Philoctetes' bow and quiver.[92] The cup and its twin (see Fig. 66a, b) are among the most exquisite examples of Roman metalworking, exemplifying the knowledge and appreciation of Greek culture under Emperor Augustus. Even more extraordinary is their findspot, the grave of a local chieftain in Denmark, who may have received the cups as a diplomatic gift from the governor of the Roman province of Germania Superior. Once his wound has been cured by the Greek doctor Machaon, Philoctetes goes on to kill Paris with his famous bow.

Athena's statue at Troy was the famous Palladium, the image of Pallas Athena, the war-like virgin goddess and daughter of Zeus, believed to have fallen from the sky. In Greek art it was generally portrayed as a rigid figure standing with spear and shield raised, ready for combat, the epitome of an ancient martial effigy. Emblematic of the city of Troy, it was later placed on coins of the city of Ilion (see p. 127 and p. 130), albeit in a slightly different guise influenced by local Anatolian traditions. Athena holds a distaff in one hand and carries a spear over her shoulder from which a knotted band dangles (see Fig. 108). The mission of Odysseus and Diomedes to steal the statue to remove its protection from Troy was popular in art and depicted in diverse media.[93] A coin minted in Argos, one of the cities that later claimed possession of the stolen Palladium, shows Diomedes carrying the statue in his hand (Fig. 77).[94] His pose wonderfully captures the sense that he is creeping away with stolen goods. Perhaps the most famous depiction of the scene, however, appears on a sardonyx gem beautifully carved by a craftsman called Felix, whose name is inscribed at the bottom (Fig. 78). Diomedes is on the right, holding the statue; Odysseus, facing him, appears to reproach him for killing the temple guard, whose feet can just be seen on the ground.[95] This act of sacrilege will be costly for the Greeks, as one of the deeds that provoke the gods' anger and lead to many of their deaths during or after their return home.

ABOVE
Fig. 79*
**Relief from a Roman
sarcophagus lid
depicting scenes
from the Trojan War**

C. AD 175–200
Probably found in Rome
Marble
L. 2120 mm | D. 100 mm
The Ashmolean Museum,
University of Oxford
ANMichaelis.111

The Trojan Horse

With all the talismans of success in place, the time seems ripe for the Greeks to take Troy.[96]
In Book 2 of Virgil's *Aeneid*, the Carthaginian queen Dido asks Aeneas, who has recently
washed up on her shores with his band of refugee Trojans, to tell his story. He recounts
the Greeks' clever plan: how they build a huge wooden horse from pine trees and hide their
best warriors inside it, leaving it behind as they pretend to sail away, in fact concealing their
ships behind the nearby island of Tenedos. The Trojans rejoice, thinking the Greeks have
given up and left, and begin to debate what to do with the horse. A Trojan priest, Laocoön,
warns that the wooden horse is a trick, full of Greeks or designed as a siege engine. Speaking
the famous words 'Even when they bring gifts, I fear the Greeks' (*Aeneid* 2.49), he throws
a spear at the horse. A captive Greek named Sinon is then dragged before King Priam.
This man has in fact been deliberately left behind to tell a convincing story to the Trojans
and encourage them to take the horse inside the city. Claiming that he is hated by Odysseus
and the Greeks, he says he has narrowly escaped being offered as a human sacrifice to ensure
them a safe journey. He explains to the Trojans that the Greeks, having upset the goddess
Athena when they took her image – the Palladium – from Troy, are required by her to sail
home and appease the gods before returning to Troy to continue their attack. The horse,
he says, has been set up as an offering to atone for the Greeks' sacrilege. He advises the
Trojans that ruin will befall them if they do not pay it due respect, while future victories
will be secured if they take it into the city.

Serpents suddenly appear from the ocean and seize Laocoön and his two young sons,
seemingly confirming that harming the horse will bring destruction, a scene dramatically
rendered in a famous and frequently copied Hellenistic sculptural group (see below, p. 194,
Fig. 193). This convinces the Trojans that they should bring the horse into Troy, even
though its huge size means having to breach their city walls.[97] Virgil's Aeneas describes its
ascent into the city, dramatically contrasting its ominous significance with the celebrations
of the still unsuspecting Trojans:

> The great catastrophe climbed to the fortress,
> Pregnant with arms. Young boys and girls around it
> Sang hymns and touched the cables in their joy.

It loomed into the middle of the town.
Aeneid 2.237–40

The Trojan Horse, the idea for which some ancient authors credited to Odysseus, was rarely represented in the earlier periods of Greek art, and such representations as there were tended to focus on the Greeks emerging from it (see below). It became more popular in Hellenistic and Roman imagery, the latter no doubt inspired by the account in Virgil's *Aeneid*.[98] Roman representations included the horse being wheeled into the city, as on a sarcophagus lid (Fig. 79), which also shows the attack that took place later on the feasting Trojans, as well as the dragging of Hector's body behind Achilles' chariot.[99] The splendid wheeled horse in this Roman representation – itself armed with helmet and shield – bears

BELOW
Fig. 80*
Gandharan relief panel, probably a stair-riser from a votive stupa

AD 100–200
Probably found near Hund, Pakistan
Schist
H. 162 mm | L. 323 mm
British Museum
1990,1013.1

ABOVE
Fig. 81*
**Roman fresco
showing the Trojans
pulling the wooden
horse into Troy**

AD 45–79
House of Cipius
Pamphilus Felix, Pompeii,
Italy
Painted plaster
H. 400 mm | W. 620 mm
Museo Archeologico
Nazionale di Napoli
9010

striking similarities to that in a Gandharan relief, probably found near Hund, in Pakistan, and also dating to the second century AD (Fig. 80). The relief may have been a stair-riser from a votive stupa (smaller-scale stupas presented at shrines by pilgrims in order to attain spiritual merit). It is part of the art of Gandhara, a region in northwestern South Asia (present-day Pakistan and Afghanistan), long a crossroads of cultures. The presence of an apparent Trojan War scene at a Buddhist site shows the reach and versatility of the myth. Here likely to have been reinvented in terms of a Buddhist mythological narrative, the figures shown, understood in classical terms, are probably Sinon pushing the horse towards the city, Priam behind it and Laocoön attempting to obstruct it. On the left, Cassandra, daughter of Priam, alone continuing to predict disaster, throws up her arms in dismay, but her words were fated never to be believed. Her dress is decidedly non-classical: she is wearing traditional Indian draped clothing and ornaments seen on *yakshi*, female nature or fertility spirits, in South Asian art. In the local context the 'Laocoön' figure may have represented a bodhisattva, a Buddha of the future, intervening to avert disaster.[100]

Cassandra is also probably the female figure kneeling near the statue of Athena on the left of a Roman fresco found at Pompeii, which also shows the Trojans pulling the wooden horse into the city (Fig. 81). The painter does not quite show the horse at a scale believably large enough to contain a band of hidden Greek soldiers (most ancient authors number them between twenty and a hundred), but the strong diagonal lines formed by the Trojans pulling the wheeled horse inject energy into the scene.[101]

The Greeks sack Troy

Ilium burned; the flames had not yet died down; Jove's altar was soaking up old Priam's meagre stream of blood; and Cassandra, the head priestess of Apollo, dragged along by her hair, stretched out her arms uselessly to the heavens.
Ovid, *Metamorphoses* 13.408–11[102]

When night falls, the Greek fleet sails quietly back to Troy. Sinon, the Greek captive now in the city, watches for their signal then unlatches the door of the wooden horse, allowing the concealed Greeks to emerge from inside. A fragment of an Archaic Athenian pot shows the Greeks climbing out. All that can be seen of the horse is one leg as two pairs of heroes descend, one on another's shoulders (Fig. 82).[103] This dramatic moment of the narrative was also chosen by the seventh-century BC maker of a *pithos*, or storage jar, found on the island of Mykonos, which showed the heads of warriors framed within windows in the horse's side, making explicit what was hidden within (see Fig. 1).[104] The band of elite warriors – including Odysseus, Neoptolemus and Menelaus – kills the Trojan guards and opens the gates of the city to let in the rest of the Greek army. In Virgil's *Aeneid*, Aeneas tells of a night of horror and confusion as the city begins to burn. There is fierce fighting as the Trojans desperately try to defend their homes, even tearing buildings apart for material to use as weapons against their attackers, and many atrocities are committed by the Greeks in their final hour of victory.

The 'lesser' Ajax, so-called to distinguish him from the more eminent hero who shared his name, drags Cassandra from the temple of Athena, where she has taken sanctuary and is desperately grasping the statue of the goddess.[105] Ajax's sacrilege is compounded in some versions by the rape of the young princess inside the temple.[106] Violence against women, and

RIGHT
Fig. 82*
A fragment of a black-figure wine-mixing bowl (column-*krater*) showing Greek warriors climbing out of the wooden horse
An inscription names one of the warriors as Phereus.

c. 550 BC
Made in Attica, Greece; found at Orbetello, Italy
Pottery
H. 97 mm | L. 78 mm
Antikensammlung, Berlin
F 1723

OPPOSITE
Fig. 83*
A water jar (*hydria*) showing Ajax attacking Cassandra

c. 340–320 BC
Made in Campania, Italy, attributed to the Danaid Group; found in Nola, Italy
Pottery
H. 337 mm | W. 205 mm
British Museum
1824,0501.35

BELOW LEFT
Fig. 84*
Red-figure water jar (*hydria*) showing Menelaus pursuing Helen

c. 480 BC
Made in Attica, Greece, attributed to the Syriskos Painter; found in Vulci, Italy
Pottery
H. 545 mm | W. 365 mm
British Museum
1843,1103.86

the capture and enslavement of the females of a defeated city, was not altogether unusual in ancient Greek warfare and to some extent accepted as a fact of war. It was the offence against the goddess that made the episode so shocking. On a South Italian vase (Fig. 83), Cassandra's half-naked body suggests the sexual violence committed against her, while the presence of the priestess of Athena, holding the temple key and looking back in horror as she flees, underlines the sacrilege.[107] The seated goddess who looks down on the scene may be Aphrodite, holding out the golden apple, as a reminder of the cause of the Trojan War.[108] She has also been interpreted as Athena herself,[109] who ultimately has her revenge on Ajax. Though he escapes the punishment of stoning by his fellow-Greeks, he drowns on his journey home. For Cassandra, though, the gods hold no respite in store: along with Queen Hecuba, Hector's widow Andromache and many other Trojan women, she is forcibly taken to Greece as a slave.

Helen is reclaimed by her Greek husband Menelaus, once he has killed her new husband. This is no longer Paris, who had already been killed by Philoctetes in the latter part of the war, but Paris' brother Deiphobus, to whom she had subsequently been married. The recovery of Helen, the woman whose abduction was the cause of the war, means the Greeks have finally achieved the goal of their expedition to Troy. It was often shown

RIGHT
Fig. 85
Engraved scene on an Etruscan mirror, with Menelaus seizing Helen (line drawing of the original)

330–300 BC
Found in Cerveteri, Italy
Bronze
H. 310 mm | Diam. 193 mm
British Museum
1865,0712.4

on Greek vases as a pursuit, with Menelaus running after Helen while she reaches back to him (Fig. 84).[110] This familiar iconographic scheme was used for many different instances of pursuit and rape in fifth-century BC Greek vase-painting, with varying implications as to power dynamics and erotic or violent intent.[111] Here, Menelaus' sword, levelled towards Helen, implies the threat of violence. The female figure into whose arms Helen seems to be fleeing may be Aphrodite, assisting her protégée in this moment of danger.[112] On an Etruscan mirror, Menelaus (here identified with his Etruscan name, Menle) again levels his sword towards an unnamed woman, almost certainly Helen, who clings semi-naked to a statue of Athena, in a visual conflation of Helen's recovery with the rape of Cassandra (Fig. 85).[113] The literary sources differ on exactly what happens next. Most agree that Menelaus intends to kill Helen, but takes pity on her once they are face to face. Certainly, in Book 4 of Homer's *Odyssey* they are reconciled and living together in Sparta.

While Troy's women are captured, the men of the city are not allowed to survive. King Priam takes refuge at the palace altar, where he is stabbed to death by Achilles' son Neoptolemus.[114] This is another key moment which recurs frequently in Archaic and Early Classical Greek art. The painter of a black-figure amphora (Fig. 86) has emphasized the horror by combining Neoptolemus' murder of Priam with the murder of Astyanax, Priam's young grandson and son of Hector and Andromache.[115] In the *Little Iliad*, Neoptolemus throws Astyanax from the walls of the city.[116] On this vase, he instead brutally uses the child's body as a weapon with which to attack Priam on the altar. The sacrilegious setting for this killing and the involvement of a young child both recall the murder of the young Troilus by Neoptolemus' father Achilles earlier in the war (see p. 69).[117] This horrific image of the atrocities of war was used on many Greek vases as an archetypal image of the sack of Troy.[118] With Troy's king and his male offspring now dead and the city ablaze, all is lost. Troy has fallen.

Escape of Aeneas

As the Greeks are infiltrating the city, Hector's ghost appears to Aeneas, urging him to escape and to establish a new city:

> run, escape these flames.
> […] If this right hand
> Could have defended Troy, you would be safe.
> Troy hands its rites, its household gods to you.
> *Aeneid* 2.289–93

Aeneas initially obeys his instinct to put on his armour and join the defence, witnessing the death of Priam and the devastation of Troy. His mother Aphrodite then visits him, revealing that the gods are actively destroying Troy and convincing him to seek out his family and flee. Rushing back home, he tries to persuade his father Anchises to abandon the city, who only agrees after the gods send an omen and set a flame burning on the head of Aeneas' son Ascanius. In the confusion of their escape, Creusa, Aeneas' wife, is left behind. Aeneas later describes to Dido how, distraught, he goes back to search for her, until her ghost appears and bids him continue with his journey. Returning to Anchises and Ascanius, he finds a band of Trojans gathered to join him. Aeneas lifts his old father on to his back and leaves Troy:

[…] The Greeks held every gate
To the city. There was nothing left to help us.
I picked my father up and sought the mountains.
Aeneas to Dido, *Aeneid* 2.802–4

This moment was already a popular image in the late sixth century BC: nearly one hundred Attic black-figure vases show the scene. Sometimes we clearly recognize Creusa among the accompanying characters, but on one black-figure amphora, two running women flank the central figures, along with an archer and an old man (Fig. 87).[119] Virgil's *Aeneid* increased the fame and popularity of this scene still further. In the many Roman representations on coins, lamps (Fig. 88) and as terracotta figurines, young Ascanius is usually also shown, holding his father's hand (see Fig. 22). Some of these images took their inspiration from a statue group which was set up in the Forum of Augustus at some point between 17 and 5 BC.[120] On this lamp Anchises holds the Palladium statue, whereas more often it is the sacred chest containing the household gods that is depicted in this context. Aeneas' piety, bravery and divine birth, as the son of Venus/Aphrodite, all served to glorify the emperors who claimed him as their ancestor.

BELOW LEFT
Fig. 87*
Black-figure storage jar (*amphora*) showing Aeneas carrying Anchises from Troy

c. 490–480 BC
Made in Attica, Greece; probably found in Vulci, Italy
Pottery
H. 245 mm | W. 151 mm
British Museum
1836,0224.138

BELOW RIGHT
Fig. 88*
Roman lamp depicting Aeneas fleeing Troy while carrying his father and holding the hand of his son

C. AD 25–75
Pottery
W. 83 mm | L. 115 mm
British Museum
1978,0603.1

BELOW

Fig. 89
Map of Aeneas'
travels in the
Mediterranean, based
on Virgil's *Aeneid*,
from the first modern
atlas of the world,
Ortelius' *Theatrum*
Orbis Terrarum*, first
published in 1570
Aeneae Troiani Navigatio.
Ad Virgilii sex priores
Aeneidos. Cum privilegio
Imperatorio, Regio, et
Cancellariae Brabantiae,
decennali.

1594
Antwerp; Abraham
Ortelius, Jan Baptista
Vrients, Jan Wierix
Map
H. 350 mm | W. 490 mm
David Rumsey Map
Collection at Stanford
University Libraries

AENEAS' DESTINY

Aeneas and his small group of refugees did not have an easy journey in their quest to find a new home. The *Iliad* (20.354–56) has him earmarked as king of the Trojans: as '[Zeus] has come to hate the generation of Priam', it is Aeneas and his descendants who will come to rule Troy. This seems to imply his return to the burnt city, yet Roman writers such as Sallust and Virgil, basing their stories on earlier Greek sources, located 'new Troy' in Italy. They also gave Aeneas many sea-borne adventures to overcome before he was finally to found Rome, or Lavinium, the city from which Rome would trace its history.[121] Virgil's *Aeneid* describes abandoned attempts to found cities on the Thracian coast and on Crete, near escapes from the monsters Polyphemus, Scylla and Charybdis, and a visit to the Underworld. Aeneas is also distracted by a love affair with the Carthaginian queen Dido, who tragically commits suicide when he leaves. Finally reaching Italy, he faces a long war against the Latins. Similar to the returns of the Greek heroes, these meandering voyages provided opportunities for many cities and regions to associate themselves with the great hero (and with the Roman Empire); unlike the *Odyssey* with its many fantastic destinations, however, the *Aeneid* made it much easier for later cartographers to chart the hero's journey (Fig. 89).

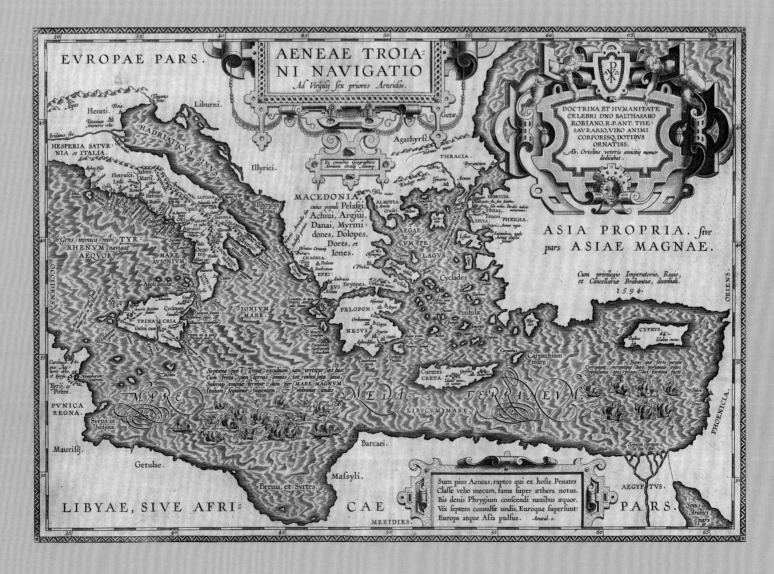

The Greeks depart

Victorious at last, it is time for the Greeks to sail home. Just as the expedition to Troy began with the sacrifice of Agamemnon's daughter Iphigenia (see p. 66), so it ends with the violent death of another royal maiden.[122] Achilles' ghost appears to the Greeks and demands the sacrifice of Polyxena, the youngest daughter of Priam and Hecuba, to ensure the winds they need to sail home.[123] In his play *Hecuba*, Euripides presents Polyxena as willingly choosing to be sacrificed rather than enduring life enslaved:

> Now I am a slave! That name first makes me long for death, so strange it sounds; and then perhaps my lot might give me to some savage master, one that would buy me for money – me the sister of Hector and many others – who would make me knead him bread within his halls, or sweep his house or set me working at the loom, leading a life of misery; while some slave, bought I know not where, will taint my bed, once deemed worthy of royalty. No, never! Here I close my eyes upon the light, free as yet, and dedicate myself to Hades.
> Euripides, *Hecuba* 357–68[124]

BELOW
Fig. 90*
Black-figure 'Tyrrhenian' storage jar (*amphora*) showing the sacrifice of Polyxena

c. 570–550 BC
Made in Attica, Greece, attributed to the Timiades Painter; said to be from Italy
Pottery
H. 380 mm | Diam. 240 mm
British Museum
1897,0727.2

RIGHT
Fig. 91
Sarcophagus showing the sacrifice of Polyxena
The sarcophagus was discovered in 1994.

c. 500 BC
From Kızöldün tumulus, Çanakkale, Turkey
Marble
L. 332 cm | W. 160 cm | H. 178 cm
Troy Museum, Çanakkale

The sacrifice is, nonetheless, a horrific act. There are relatively few scenes in art which certainly show Polyxena's death.[125] One on an Attic amphora shows her stiff and immobile as she is being carried to the altar by three Greeks (Fig. 90). She is being slaughtered in exactly the same way that a large animal might be killed as a sacrifice to the gods: the vein in the throat is cut by the priest – here by Neoptolemus – and the blood is allowed to run out on the altar.[126] A sarcophagus dating to around 500 BC found in the Troad has a similar representation, framing the sacrifice with Achilles' domed tomb and a group of female mourners (Fig. 91).[127] The actual killing of the sacrificial beast is only very rarely depicted, making the brutal image even more striking. The horror of this final act before the Greeks sail away from the shores of Troy, together with other sacrilegious deeds committed by them during the war, leave the gods angry and vengeful, and many of the departing Greek heroes are destined for a painful future.

HOMECOMINGS: ODYSSEUS' STORY

As for you [Poseidon], make the Aegean swell with high waves and eddies and fill the deep indentation of Euboea's coast with corpses so that henceforth the Greeks may learn to reverence my temple and show honour to the other Gods as well.
Athena in Euripides, *The Trojan Women* 82–86[128]

After ten exhausting years of war on foreign shores, all that the surviving heroes and their troops long for is home. Yet with divine wrath blighting their journeys, few Greeks reach their homes without difficulty, or live to enjoy their return. The Greek epic poem *Nostoi* or 'Returns', part of the Epic Cycle (see p. 32), told of their fates, as did other works by authors such as the early Greek poet Stesichorus or the Hellenistic writer Lycophron, whose poem *Alexandra* is written from the perspective of the Trojan prophetess Cassandra (see also p. 34).[129] A few heroes, such as Diomedes, return home unscathed. Menelaus, too, finally reaches Sparta safely with his recovered wife, Helen, after eight years of wanderings.

But many do not see their homes again. One of the main perpetrators of atrocities had been Ajax the Lesser, whom the Archaic Greek poet Alcaeus (fragment 298.5) called a man who did violence to the gods. Ajax's rape of Cassandra in Athena's temple amounted to an abuse of the goddess herself; he is killed in a storm at sea. The seer Calchas, too, perishes – according to some versions he dies of heartbreak and shame after losing to another seer in a contest of prophesying.[130] Others reach home, but meet their end there: Agamemnon returns to Mycenae, only to be murdered by his wife Clytemnestra and her lover in retaliation for the sacrifice of Iphigenia. The trilogy of plays known as the *Oresteia*, by Aeschylus, and many other ancient texts and images cover the tragic unfolding of this story. Clytemnestra is herself slain by her son Orestes in revenge for his father's murder, in a chain of events characteristic of Greek myth in which guilt breeds guilt, only to be resolved ultimately by the gods.

The key attraction of the stories about the various returns of the Greek heroes (and also of the diaspora of the Trojan refugees) was that these tales helped ancient Greeks to map and navigate their wider world both conceptually and literally, explaining, accommodating and setting others in relation to themselves. More specifically, they provided a welcome opportunity for cities and regions to construct their own, often competing, links with famous heroes or relics.[131] The Palladium statue, stolen from Troy by Odysseus and Diomedes, for example, was claimed variously by Argos (see Fig. 77), Athens or Lavinium, while the shield of Euphorbus was said to have been dedicated by Menelaus at Didyma (see p. 78).[132] The greatest popularity, and indeed the most adventurous journey, though, was reserved for Odysseus. His story is the topic of Homer's *Odyssey*, and with its happy ending provides a perfect counterpoint to Agamemnon's tragic tale.

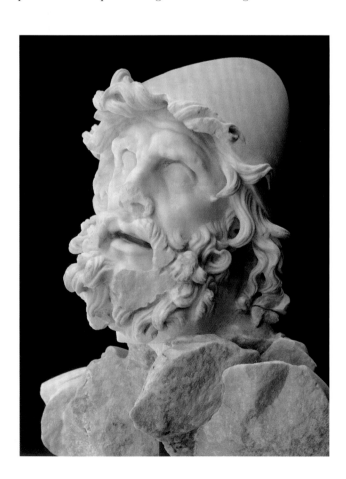

LEFT
Fig. 92
Head of Odysseus,
from a sculptural
group showing
the blinding of the
Cyclops

Early 1st century AD,
probably after a
Hellenistic bronze
sculpture of the mid-2nd
century BC
From the Villa of Tiberius,
Sperlonga, Italy
Marble
H. 635 mm
Museo Archeologico
Nazionale, Sperlonga
43

Odysseus, man of many ways

Tell me about a complicated man.
Muse, tell me how he wandered and was lost
when he had wrecked the holy town of Troy,
and where he went, and who he met, the pain
he suffered in the storms at sea, and how
he worked to save his life and bring his men
back home.
Odyssey 1.1–5

Odysseus, king of the small island of Ithaca in the Ionian Sea, is often considered the most human but also the most problematic of all the Greek heroes. Homer calls him *polytropos*, a Greek term notoriously difficult to translate. It literally means 'of many turns' and suggests an ambivalent character – ingenious and versatile, but also at times deceitful and untrustworthy, an ambiguity that is perfectly captured for today's audiences in Emily Wilson's translation: 'complicated'. Indeed, Odysseus' strength does not show so much in battle as in clever, strategic thinking: he is 'quick at every treachery under the sun' (*Iliad* 3.202). It is his craftiness and his cunning ways that also ensure his safe return, albeit not that of his men, after ten years of adventures at sea, guided by Athena.[133]

Though Odysseus' adventures proved a popular subject in Classical Greek comedy and burlesque satyr plays (see p. 33, Fig. 20),[134] their crucial, most influential literary treatment was their earliest description. Homer's *Odyssey* covers only the final forty days of Odysseus' long travels, yet from extended flashbacks, mostly in conversations, we learn the whole story, from the fall of Troy to the wanderings of Odysseus himself, the search for him by his son, Telemachus, and the fate of his faithful wife, Penelope.[135] As told by Homer, the siege of Troy reflects a Greek world of competing city-states and a society built on notions of honour and glory in battle. The world of Odysseus is one of travellers, traders and mercenaries roaming the Early Iron Age and Archaic Mediterranean world. It is full of encounters with different peoples, raiding and trading, enjoying the guest-friendship of foreign aristocrats, gaining profit and renown, yet also facing the dangers of sea travel in the form of the forces of nature as much as human, or part-human, adversaries.[136] In Odysseus' travels, these adversaries take the shape of a wide range of monstrous or bewitching beings, who either tempt or threaten the traveller – and both can be equally perilous.

The fantastic adventures of Odysseus are among the earliest mythical stories to be represented in Greek, as well as Western Greek and Etruscan narrative imagery, appearing from the early seventh century BC onwards.[137] Odysseus himself typically appears as a traveller, bearded and wearing the conical hat (*pilos*) of the wayfarer or craftsman (see also Fig. 198). His character as a fearless if weather-beaten adventurer is perfectly captured in an expressive sculpture that is probably the finest and most striking of all known Odysseus images (Fig. 92). This extraordinary work reflects a masterpiece of Hellenistic art perhaps from the sculptural centre of Pergamon, in Anatolia, one of the key cultural centres of the period, though copied or adapted by a Roman sculptor (see below).[138] A different aspect of the hero is expressed in the relief on the cheek-piece of a bronze helmet. Here Odysseus is seated, wearing a cape and his characteristic *pilos*. His sword and spear rest on the ground, while his hand is raised to his head, in a gesture of distress or mourning that expresses his unfailing yearning for home (Fig. 93).[139]

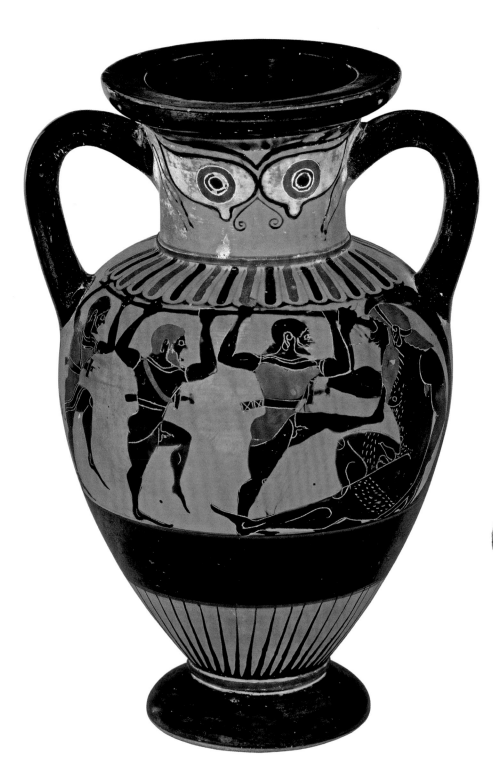

BELOW LEFT
Fig. 94*
Odysseus and his men blind the Cyclops Polyphemus on a 'Chalcidian' storage jar (*amphora*)

c. 520 BC
Made in southern Italy, attributed to the Polyphemos Group
Pottery
H. 300 mm | W. 210 mm | Diam. 180 mm
British Museum
1866,0805.3

BELOW RIGHT
Fig. 95*
Figure of a ram, with Odysseus clinging to its belly so as to escape from Polyphemus' cave

1st – 2nd century AD
From Paramythia, Greece
Bronze
H. 57 mm | L. 66 mm | D. 26 mm
British Museum
1824,0473.1

A narrow escape: Polyphemus

And as we were rounding Cape Malea, an east wind blew down on the ship and cast us to land near this crag of Aetna, where Neptune's one-eyed sons, the man-slaying Cyclopes, dwell in their remote caves.
Euripides, *Cyclops* 18–22[140]

After surviving storms, altercations with locals during coastal raids and the mind-altering powers of tasty lotus-flowers that make them sweetly oblivious to the desire to return home, Odysseus and his men encounter their first serious adversary in the giant Polyphemus, one of a tribe of one-eyed, man-eating, sheep-farming Cyclopes (the Greek name 'cyclops' meaning 'round eye').[141] Tempted to enter Polyphemus' cave because it is filled with delicious provisions, they find themselves trapped as the Cyclops returns home and, when inside, blocks the cave's entrance with a large stone. He proves to be a rather uncivilized host, eating six of Odysseus' companions before Odysseus can think of a plan for escape. He gets Polyphemus drunk and sleepy on strong wine, and, together with his remaining comrades, drives a wooden stake into the giant's single eye. Polyphemus calls for help, but because wily Odysseus has earlier given his name as 'Nobody', the other Cyclopes, puzzled at being summoned since 'nobody' has attacked Polyphemus, ignore his cries. When the next morning Polyphemus opens the cave door to let his sheep out to graze, Odysseus and his men tie themselves to the undersides of the animals, thus evading the blinded giant's searching touch and succeed in their escape.

For all its violence, the humorous story is a prime example of Odysseus' clever wit. Along with the episode of the Sirens (see below), it was the most popular of Odysseus' adventures in Archaic Greek, Western Greek and Etruscan art, especially vase-painting, from as early as the beginning of the seventh century BC. Both of the key moments of the story were represented: the communal effort of the line of men, led by Odysseus, to push the stick into the giant's eye as he is seated in his cave (Fig. 94), and the escape from the cave under the bellies of the sheep, which is immediately recognizable even when represented without any narrative context (Figs 95 and 96).[142]

Stories of Odysseus were also much appreciated in Rome. For the Roman philosopher Seneca, they epitomized triumph over all adversity, both that internal to human nature, and that in the world around us – and thus also perhaps also Roman domination of Italy.[143] One monumental sculptural rendering of the Polyphemus story stood in a nymphaeum in the villa of Emperor Domitian (r. AD 81–96) near Castel Gandolfo, southeast of Rome, a Roman version of a Hellenistic original.[144] Another large-scale group was set up in a seaside grotto of an imperial villa at Sperlonga, south of Rome, used by, among others, Emperor Tiberius (r. AD 14–37). The splendid head of Odysseus discussed above (see Fig. 92) belongs to this group. It formed part of a series of Odyssean (and other) deeds that also included representations of Odysseus and Scylla and the theft of the Palladium, which all probably took their inspiration from Virgil's *Aeneid* and were made by a sculptors' workshop on Rhodes that likely copied or adapted earlier Hellenistic Pergamene bronze sculptures during the reign of Tiberius or Claudius.[145]

Enchanted by love: Circe

The lucky escape from Polyphemus soon proves to have a downside: it has attracted the anger of the giant's father, Poseidon, god of the sea, so a quick return home to Ithaca looks increasingly unlikely. Encounters with yet more man-eating giants and the wind-god Aeolus ensue. The latter provides Odysseus with the right kind of wind for the return journey, while tying up the contrary ones in a bag. When they are already in sight of Ithaca, and as Odysseus sleeps, his greedy comrades open the bag, expecting it to be full of costly gifts. The winds are released and Odysseus' ships are propelled all the way back to where they started. Eventually, the sailors land on the island of Aeaea, the realm of the alluring sorceress Circe. Things do not get off to a good start when the 'beautiful, dreadful goddess' Circe (*Odyssey* 10.136) serves a drugged potion as a welcome drink that immediately turns twenty-two of Odysseus' comrades into pigs. Divine intervention in the shape of a herbal antidote supplied by the god Hermes, however, saves the day, and Odysseus happily succumbs to Circe's less worrisome erotic charms.[146]

Some of the most humorous among the different renderings of the scene in Archaic and Classical Greek art appear on a series of drinking cups produced specially for the sanctuary of the Cabiri at Thebes in Boeotia (Fig. 97a, b). On one cup Circe stirs the potion for Odysseus, who enters her house ready to fight, yet appears startled by the entirely respectable domestic setup, complete with a large loom. On the cup's other side we see Odysseus traversing the sea on a raft of wine amphorae, wielding Poseidon's trident and blown along by Boreas, the north wind. Highlighting the transformative power of alcohol

LEFT
Fig. 97a*
Black-figure cup (*skyphos*) depicting Odysseus with Circe
Circe stirs her potion in a large *skyphos*.

425–375 BC
Made in Boeotia, Greece, attributed to the workshop of the Mystae Painter; found in the sanctuary of the Cabiri at Thebes, Greece
Pottery
H. 154 mm
The Ashmolean Museum, University of Oxford
AN1896-1908 G.249

and (female) magic, while also grotesquely caricaturing the hero, the myth may have had a special meaning in the context of the coming of age rituals and dramatic performances that took place in the sanctuary's mystery cult, in which the drinking of wine, and perhaps also the countering of fear with laughter, played a central role.[147]

Odysseus stays with Circe for a year, until his comrades finally urge him on. Upon Circe's advice, Odysseus and his men travel to the Underworld.[148] The journey brings Odysseus face to face with many of his old comrades who fell in the Trojan War, but he also learns that his wife awaits him faithfully, and he receives instructions on how finally to get home – though further trials await him first.

The lure of music: the Sirens

The next danger encountered on the journey are the Sirens, whose sweet-sounding song full of age-old knowledge is known to lure sailors to their death. Greek artists rendered them as woman-headed, bird-bodied creatures. An Athenian Early Classical jar shows them perched high on the rocks on which mesmerized sailors are drawn to their destruction (Fig. 98).[149] As Odysseus' ship draws near, they begin to sing:

'Odysseus! Come here! You are well-known
from many stories! Glory of the Greeks!
Now stop your ship and listen to our voices.'
Odyssey 12.184–85

RIGHT
Fig. 97b*
The other side of the same cup depicts Odysseus at sea
Both Odysseus and Boreas are named in inscriptions.

Odysseus, though, has been forewarned by Circe and has taken precautions. He plugs the ears of his crew with wax to shield them from the enchanting sounds, while, eternally curious and thirsty for knowledge, he has himself bound to the mast so he can hear the song but is not able to yield to its enticement. In despair at being outwitted, one of the Sirens plunges into the sea below. It is episodes such as this that prompted Greek philosophers to see in Odysseus an example of intellectual and moral fortitude: he is willing to endure pain to acquire knowledge and able to resist erotic temptation.[150]

The story was popular also in Etruscan and Roman art. A Roman wall-painting from Pompeii (Fig. 99) shows the Sirens surrounded by the bones of earlier victims, while on Etruscan funerary urns they are turned into elegant female musicians playing the syrinx (pan pipes), lyre and flutes (Fig. 100); the imagery on the latter was probably meant to allude to the deceased's final journey from the pleasures of life.[151]

BELOW
Fig. 98*
Red-figure jar (*stamnos*) showing Odysseus sailing past the Sirens

c. 480–470 BC
Made in Attica, Greece, attributed to the Siren Painter; probably from Vulci, Italy
Pottery
H. 340 mm | W. 380 mm
British Museum
1843,1103.31

OPPOSITE ABOVE
Fig. 99*
Roman fresco showing Odysseus and the Sirens

c. AD 20–79
From Pompeii, Italy
Painted plaster
H. 480 mm | W. 480 mm | D. 30 mm
British Museum
1867,0508.1354

OPPOSITE BELOW
Fig. 100*
Etruscan funerary urn showing Odysseus and the Sirens

c. 150–100 BC
Probably made at Volterra
Alabaster
H. 450 mm | L. 785 mm | D. 265 mm
British Museum
1849,1201.2

From monsters to maidens: Scylla, Calypso and Nausicaa

Having escaped one danger, the next is just round the corner: a narrow strait flanked on one side by a cave inhabited by a multi-headed sea monster, Scylla, and on the other by a whirlpool, 'shining Charybdis', who 'with a dreadful gurgling noise sucked down the water' (*Odyssey* 12.235–36) and with it any ship. The situation is every mariner's worst nightmare. Difficult to visualize in its entirety, the episode proved most fertile in inspiring ancient artists to imagine Scylla as a terrifying hybrid monster, part-female, part-octopus, with a girdle of vicious dogs' heads, an iconography that became popular especially from the later fifth century BC onwards.[152] On an exquisitely carved Roman table support we see Odysseus' men seized by the coils of Scylla's tentacles and devoured by her dogs (Fig. 101).[153]

Six sailors are lost to ravenous Scylla, but Odysseus' ships make it through. Worse, however, is to come. Sitting out a calm on an island, Odysseus' men are driven by hunger to slaughter several cattle. Unfortunately, they are sacred cattle belonging to the sun god Helios, and Zeus unleashes his full anger: thunderbolts sink every ship and all the sailors drown. Odysseus alone, clinging to a mast, is beached on the island of Ogygia. Here again a beautiful female is only too happy to welcome a visitor, and for seven years the goddess Calypso keeps Odysseus on the island, captivating him with her song.[154] This is Odysseus' journey at its lowest ebb, as he weeps daily on the beach, longing both for home and to be once again the man in charge:

> If some god strikes me on the wine-dark sea,
> I will endure it. By now I am used
> to suffering – I have gone through so much,
> at sea and in the war. Let this come too.
> *Odyssey* 5.221–24

It is only through Athena's intervention that he is finally set free. Even so, his troubles are still not quite over: the raft he builds is caught in a storm sent by Poseidon (perhaps alluded to on the Cabiric drinking cup, Fig. 97b), and once more he eventually washes up ashore, this time on the island of Scheria in the land of the Phaeacians.

Shipwrecked, alone and devoid of any worldly possessions, even his clothes, Odysseus finds himself on the seashore at Scheria. Nothing but his wit and eloquence can save him now. He takes his chance as Nausicaa, the daughter of the local king, comes to the beach with her maidens to wash clothes. This is the moment depicted on a Classical Athenian cup (Fig. 102): naked and dishevelled, Odysseus emerges from the bushes 'like a mountain lion' (*Odyssey* 6.130), startling the girls. Only Nausicaa remains, for 'Athena made her legs stop trembling and gave her courage in her heart' (*Odyssey* 6.139–40).[155] Nausicaa provides Odysseus with clothes and directs him to her parents' court, where he is warmly received as a guest. The Phaeacians, finally, prove generous and trustworthy hosts, unlike nearly all the others whom Odysseus has encountered on his journeys. It is to them that he recounts the story of his adventures as they are reported in the *Odyssey*. They send him off with new ships, and at long last he safely reaches Ithaca.

OPPOSITE
Fig. 101*
A Roman table support on which the sea monster Scylla, part-woman, part-octopus, is juxtaposed with a centaur, part-man and part-horse, accompanied by Eros, god of love

c. AD 120–140
Made in Italy
Marble
H. 108 cm | W. 160 cm
Museo Archeologico
Nazionale di Napoli
6672

BELOW
**Fig. 102
Red-figure covered cup (*kantharos*) depicting Odysseus and Nausicaa**

c. 440–430 BC
Made in Attica, Greece; found in Nola, Italy
Pottery
H. 254 mm | Diam. 181 mm
British Museum
1867,0508.1132

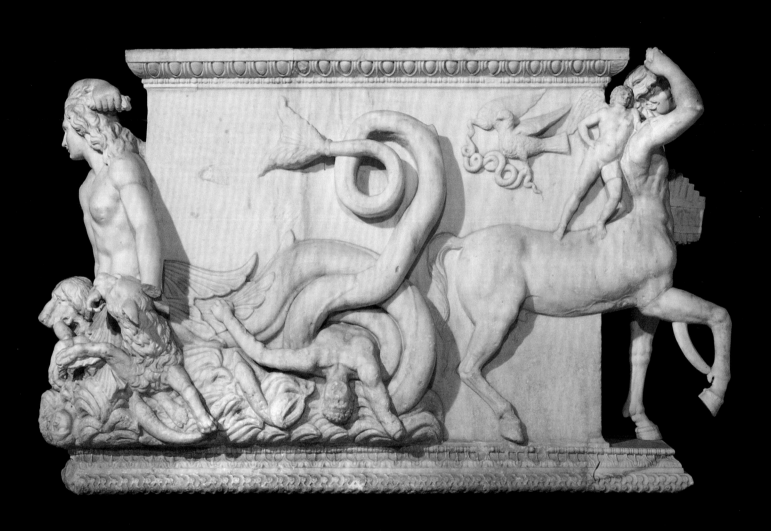

MAPPING ODYSSEUS' TRAVELS

[Odysseus], as some say, wandered about Libya, or, as some say, about Sicily,
or, as others say, about the ocean or about the Tyrrhenian Sea.
Apollodorus, *Library*, Epitome 7.1[156]

Many have tried to trace Odysseus' steps and map the fantastic locations of his journey
on to real places, through research in the library or by sailing the seas in Odysseus' wake.[157]
While most who have attempted this, from antiquity to the modern day, have focused on
the Mediterranean (Fig. 103), others have ranged as far afield as Norway, the Persian Gulf,
South Africa, China or Japan; some have even suggested a circumnavigation that also
touched on the Americas. The British Isles, too, have not been left out. The Roman writer
Plutarch located the island of Calypso west of Britain and in 1685 Roderic O'Flaherty
identified it with Ireland. In the early eighteenth century, the Norwegian Jonas Ramus,
arguing for a link between ancient Greek and Germanic myth, saw Albion – Britain – as the
home of the wind god Aeolus. In 1925 J. Rendel Harris placed Scylla and Charybdis in the
area of the Irish Skellig islands or the Scottish Hebrides, while in 1978 Hans Steuerwald
located the encounter of Odysseus and Nausicaa in Penzance, Cornwall.[158]

Yet already the ancient Greek geographer Eratosthenes, writing in the third century BC,
considered the search for reality behind the myth futile: 'You will find where Odysseus
wandered when you find the cobbler who sewed up the bag of the winds' (Strabo 1.2.15).
Modern scholarly consensus both agrees and disagrees. While fundamentally an account
of a fictional journey, the narrative still contains elements of real geography, in all likelihood
referring especially to locations around Sicily. Like tales of other mythical journeys such as
that of Jason and the Argonauts, it reflects the early Greek exploration of the Mediterranean
and the Black Sea, which was driven by trade, war and settlement. In this context, heroic
legends, including that of Odysseus' wanderings, provided useful instructions to travellers
for how to negotiate both the seas and its inhabitants, and served to integrate the newly
founded western Greek settlements in particular into a wider panhellenic community.[159]

BELOW
Fig. 103
**Hand-coloured
map with supposed
locations for the
various episodes of
Odysseus' travels,
from Ortelius' world
atlas, first published
in 1570**
*Ulyssis Errores ex
Conatib. Geographicis
Ab. Ortelij.*

1601
Antwerp; Abraham
Ortelius
Map
H. 279 mm | W. 356 mm
The Barry Lawrence
Ruderman Map
Collection

Return to Ithaca: Penelope and the suitors

On Ithaca, there is one final challenge to overcome. During Odysseus' absence, assuming he must be dead, a large crowd of suitors for the hand of his wife has taken over his house, frittering away his estate. Though forced by the laws of hospitality to entertain them, faithful Penelope, daughter of a Spartan king and cousin of beautiful Helen, has so far managed to avoid having to yield to any of them. Proving herself a worthy partner for wily Odysseus, she has devised a clever ruse of her own: having begged the suitors to let her choose a new husband only after she has woven a shroud for her father-in-law, Laertes, she spends all her days weaving and at night unpicks her work, thus postponing the choice indefinitely.[160]

> Lucky you,
> cunning Odysseus: you got yourself
> a wife of virtue – great Penelope.
> How principled she was, that she remembered
> her husband all those years!
> *Odyssey* 24.192–96

Penelope was a popular subject with Greek artists, especially from the early fifth century BC onwards, when she is often shown veiled in her mantle, sitting on a simple stool, legs crossed, her head resting in her hand (Fig. 104). Her mournful attitude is that of a devoted, loyal wife pining for her husband, while the wool basket under her stool hints not just at general homely dexterity, but also at the skilful tenacity with which she keeps the suitors at bay. As a study of human emotion, and also a powerful female role model, the type was popular especially in fifth-century BC Athens, where it was rendered as a life-size Early Classical

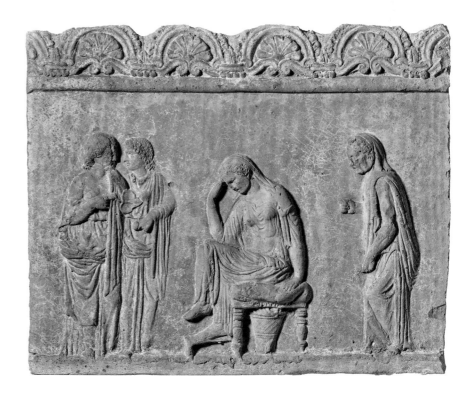

statue, perhaps originally part of a group that included also faithful Eurycleia, Odysseus' old wet-nurse. We find the type again in the Roman period, in terracotta reliefs that were probably once part of the interior decoration of Roman houses, now advertising female virtues to the women of Late Republican and Augustan Rome (Fig. 105).[161]

Forewarned of the trouble at home by Athena, Odysseus takes on the guise of a beggar as he approaches his house, and is recognized by no one apart from his old dog, Argos, and Eurycleia. Penelope, not yet realizing who he is, is encouraged by Athena to announce that the time has finally come for her to choose a new groom. An archery competition is arranged, with Penelope's hand in marriage as the prize. Still disguised, but having revealed himself to his son Telemachus and enlisted the help of his old slave, the swine-herd Eumaios, Odysseus, too, takes part. Each contestant must use Odysseus' old bow, but he alone is strong enough to string it and shoot an arrow through a dozen axes. An Athenian cup is one of several Classical renderings of the dramatic events that follow immediately

BELOW
Fig. 106a*
Red-figure cup (*skyphos*) showing Odysseus standing with his bow drawn next to two servants

c. 440 BC
Made in Attica, Greece; found in Tarquinia, Italy
Pottery
H. 197 mm | W. 337 mm | D. 232 mm
Antikensammlung, Berlin
F 2588

BELOW
Fig. 106b*
**The other side of the
same cup showing
Odysseus' targets,
the suitors, trying to
defend themselves
against his arrows**

afterwards (Fig. 106a, b).[162] Odysseus now turns the bow on the suitors, who are still reclining on couches at the feast and are thus entirely unprepared. One of them, wounded, turns in anguish, another rises in alarm from his couch, while a third uses a table to shield himself. Over one hundred men lose their lives that day, as well as a dozen servant girls, whom Odysseus has hanged for disloyalty (see also p. 223 and Fig. 227). Their fate is perhaps alluded to by the two women – characterized as house slaves by their short hair – who are shown standing behind the hero, watching with trepidation.

Now, finally, Odysseus reveals his true identity to Penelope – though clever and careful as she is, she puts him to one more test. She slyly asks him to move their marriage bed, and he confirms he is indeed Odysseus by knowing that this is not possible as it is carved from an olive tree still rooted in the ground. At long last the couple are reunited: the faithful wife, so different from deceitful Helen or revengeful Clytemnestra, with the steadfast husband, whose determination and wit have ultimately triumphed in the face of adversity.

3 ARCHAEOLOGICAL TROY

ANDREW SHAPLAND AND J. LESLEY FITTON

TROY LOST AND FOUND

I've stood upon Achilles' tomb,
And heard Troy doubted: time will doubt of Rome.
Lord Byron, *Don Juan*, Canto 4, 101

The ancient city of Troy, inhabited for thousands of years, was finally abandoned at the end of antiquity, soon after AD 600, and never substantially reoccupied.[1] It then became overgrown and absorbed into an area of farmland. Soon there was no memory of the fact that this place had once been Troy. Yet the name lived on in legend, and the story of the Trojan War continued to be told. Thus the quest to find the legendary city was born. Indeed, it became a major preoccupation in both scholarly and popular circles, particularly in the eighteenth and nineteenth centuries, when the study of Latin and Greek literature dominated European education and the works of Homer were held in high esteem. Travellers on the ground sought to walk in the footsteps of Homer's heroes, while scholars in their libraries pored over texts and maps in an attempt to solve the puzzle of the fabled city's location.

It was not a simple matter, even though Homer makes the general location of the city very clear. He describes geographical features – the Dardanelles, Mount Ida, the offshore islands of Tenedos and Imbros and the rivers of the Trojan plain. In fact, the northwest corner of Anatolia was always known as the Troad, so travellers and Troy-seekers were sure they were in the right general area. But it was also possible to doubt whether Troy had ever existed, and to argue that it was purely a product of the poet's imagination. And even 'realist' thinkers, however passionate in their conviction that Homer's account had a historical basis, had to contend with the fact that the story spoke of the city as having been totally destroyed when it fell and was burned. 'Etiam periere ruinae', as the Roman writer Lucan put it – 'Even its very ruins were destroyed.'[2] What, then, could anyone hope to find?

The plain of Troy, certainly, with its many tumuli or barrows that tradition said held the bones of heroes. But if total annihilation had really been the fate of Priam's Troy, then of the city itself there would be no trace.

Lucan was describing the supposed visit of Julius Caesar to the city of Ilion (or Ilium, as it was called in Latin). But here is another complication. Ilion/Ilium was a historical place, and throughout antiquity well known as the city that occupied the site of Homer's Troy – 'Troia' in Greek, but also called 'Ilios' by Homer. Lucan makes the point that no traces of Priam's citadel could be seen there, but he does not doubt that this was its location, and almost all other ancient commentators agreed. Julius Caesar was actually just one of a number of military leaders who visited, or are said to have visited, Ilion to pay their respects to the heroes of the Trojan War. Others include the Persian king Xerxes and Alexander the Great, king of Macedon and leader of all the Greeks, and after Julius Caesar's time a number of the emperors of Rome.[3] Indeed, in both the Greek and Roman periods the city would be given honours and privileges precisely because of its place in the mythical past, though this city, too, would be lost after antiquity.

However, considerable confusion was caused by the very influential geographer Strabo (*c.* 64 BC–*c.* AD 24). Contrary to the majority opinion, he stated that Homer's Troy did not lie beneath Ilion/Ilium, but was located some distance away, further inland and towards Mount Ida.[4] Strabo did not himself visit the Troad, but was following the work of Demetrius of Scepsis, a local geographer writing in about 180 BC, who said the legendary city was at a place called in his day Ilion Kome or 'the village of the Ilians'. It seems some local rivalry may have been behind Demetrius' attempt to undermine the position of Ilion in this regard: his own town of Scepsis claimed to be the home of Aeneas, and had reason to be jealous of the honours heaped on Ilion.

The notion that legendary Troy and ancient Ilion were at two different places may have been a minority view in the ancient world, but it would later cause endless problems for scholars and travellers in the eighteenth and nineteenth centuries who consulted Strabo's account to help them in their search for Troy.[5] They took his words at face value, and so in a way two searches became necessary. The site of Ilion/Ilium had also to be located, though this was felt to be of lesser importance. Homer's Troy was the real prize.

Success would only come to someone who ignored both Strabo's account and the ancient tradition that no ruins remained. Heinrich Schliemann tells the charming story of his own youthful conviction, formulated when he was only seven years old, that vast ruins of Troy must certainly have survived. The story may be pure invention, and is discussed in more detail below, but such a conviction was a prerequisite. Schliemann would succeed not so much because he had the *Iliad* in one hand, but because he had a spade in the other. His work would hit the headlines – but as so often in the history of great discoveries, others had prepared the ground that would allow him to gain the glory. Very particularly, others had done the research that informed his decision about where to dig. We must therefore now sketch in the background of the earlier search for Troy.

TRAVELLERS AND TOPOGRAPHERS

Throughout history, the strait of the Dardanelles has been a busy seaway, with travellers engaged in mercantile, military, diplomatic or private expeditions. Whatever their business, from ancient times onwards many would certainly have given a passing thought to the

Troad's heroic past and to the story of the city of Troy. With the Renaissance rekindling of interest in Homer and all things Greek and Roman, increasing numbers either broke their journey there to walk for a while by the ancient burial mounds in the footsteps of the heroes, or indeed made this the main object of their voyage.

Permanent embassies were established by western European nations at Constantinople (where the Ottoman sultanate was known as 'the Sublime Porte') in the middle of the sixteenth century.[6] Their existence encouraged and supported the journeys of merchants, in particular, but also made it easier for private travellers to visit the Troad. Helpful local guides would direct them to ancient ruins, though throughout the sixteenth and seventeenth centuries what they saw depended largely on where they landed from their ships. The extensive remains of the Hellenistic coastal city of Alexandria Troas, founded in the late fourth century BC, became a focus. The great arches of the Roman baths there were identified as Priam's Palace, at least by a process of wishful thinking. At the same time, visitors landing further north on the promontory of Sigeion could also see ancient remains, including those of the city that Constantine the Great began to build there in the fourth century AD, before changing his mind and moving on to Constantinople. The great attraction of Sigeion, though, were the two tumuli that were still clearly visible, said to be the burial mounds of Achilles and Patroclus. Some visitors viewed the ancient remains at both places, and saw no inconsistency in considering both to be Troy – presumably on the basis that a very large area of the Troad might well have been occupied by an ancient city of huge extent, its great size reflecting its legendary might.[7]

Enter the scholars

The eighteenth century saw the beginning of the intense scholarly controversy over the precise position of Troy that was to set the scene for Schliemann's activities. The Englishman Robert Wood (1717–1771) was among the first travellers to study the Troad in detail, on visits in 1742 and 1750–51. Although he did not identify the location of Homer's Troy or of Classical Ilion, his work was influential because he was the first topographer to study the area systematically and from a 'realist' point of view – in other words, he was convinced that the story of Troy was that of a historical place and historical events, even if Troy's very ruins had been lost.[8] Many aspects of the Trojan plain fitted well with the Homeric narrative, but Wood was ahead of his time in the realization that rivers had changed their courses and that the bay that had once provided Troy with a harbour had extensively silted up since antiquity, making the plain larger and leaving the site, whatever its exact location, a good deal further from the sea (see Fig. 172).

Wood believed that Homer had lived in the vicinity of Troy and had known the landscape personally, and indeed he thought that the poet might have heard the story of the Trojan War either from eye-witnesses, or at least from their children. Whether and to what extent Homer's works actually show first-hand local knowledge of the Troad was, though, a matter of dispute, and continues to be debated today.

Wood's studies were followed by two major steps forward in the search for Troy. The first was the extensive cartographic survey set up by the Comte de Choiseul-Gouffier (1752–1817), French ambassador to the Sublime Porte from 1784. He employed a large team of specialists to map the northeast Aegean, including the Troad (Fig. 107). Jean-Baptiste Chevalier (sometimes also called le Chevalier or Lechevalier; 1752–1836), who became the Comte's personal secretary, visited the region as part of the cartographic team in 1785 and 1786.

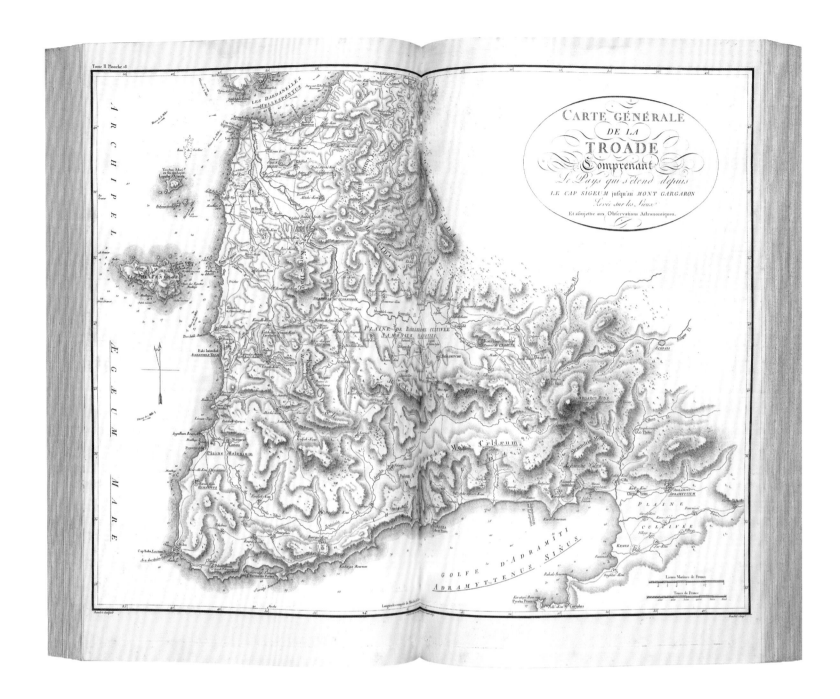

ABOVE
Fig. 107*
Map of the Troad

From Marie-Gabriel-
Florent-Auguste de
Choiseul-Gouffier,
*Voyage pittoresque de
la Grèce* (Picturesque
voyage in Greece), Vol. II
1809, Paris
H. 516 mm | W. 710 mm
(open)

LEFT
Fig. 108*
A coin (*tetradrachm*) minted in Ilium showing the head of Athena on the obverse and the statue of Athena on the reverse, inscribed 'Iliados' or 'of Ilion'

c. 95–87 BC
Found at Troy, Turkey
Silver
Diam. 16 mm
British Museum
RPK,p.130A.1.Ili

OPPOSITE
Fig. 109
Map of the Troad

From William Gell,
The Topography of Troy
1804, London
H. 216 mm | W. 170 mm
(image)

He came up with the new theory that Troy was to be sought near to the modern village of Pinarbaşı, or Bounarbashi as it was written by early travellers. This stood on the heights of a bluff named Ballı Dağ, some 14 kilometres or 9 miles from the Hellespont and close to a series of springs called in Turkish the Forty Eyes. Chevalier believed these springs to have been the source of the Scamander, a river frequently mentioned by Homer as running close to the walls of Troy. This proposal was widely accepted by 'realist' thinkers, and indeed prevailed for almost a hundred years, up until Schliemann's time. Yet the Bounarbashi theory relied on a rather idiosyncratic identification of the rivers in the Troad. The modern Menderes river is today generally recognized as the ancient Scamander, from which its name derives. For Chevalier, though, the Menderes had to be the ancient Simois, another of the rivers mentioned by Homer as flowing near Troy. Only with this identification would his theory work. Chevalier first made his findings and his ideas public in Edinburgh in 1791.[9]

The second major milestone was the recognition by the engineer Franz Kauffer, also employed by Choiseul-Gouffier, that the mound known as Hissarlik (Hisarlık) was an ancient site, as published in his map of 1793.[10] In 1801, the English traveller Edward Clarke (1769–1822) identified this site as Greek Ilion/Roman Ilium on the basis of coins and inscriptions. The coinage minted at the city bears its Greek name, and often shows the goddess Athena, its patron deity, as can be seen on two coins now in the British Museum that probably came from Clarke's collection (Fig. 108). By the time the second volume of Choiseul-Gouffier's *Voyage pittoresque de la Grèce* was published in 1809, both Bounarbashi and Hissarlik were marked on the map of the Troad.[11] The map does not label Hissarlik by name, though the contours show the mound, and 'Ilium Recens' (more commonly called Ilium Novum, that is, New Troy, by scholars) is placed at this location, with 'Ilium Vetus' (Old Troy) at Bounarbashi. Clarke did not claim to have found Ilium Vetus, Homer's Troy, but he nonetheless doubted the Bounarbashi theory, partly because of the problem with the rivers, and partly because the remains visible there were very scant and seemed to have 'no character of remote antiquity'.[12] Others would follow him, citing objections such as the hilly nature of Ballı Dağ when Homer says Troy was in a plain, the fact that Homer speaks of two springs – one hot, one cold – while at Bounarbashi there were forty, all of the same temperature, and also Bounarbashi's distance from the sea.

In spite of these reservations, no other idea seemed equally convincing, so the Bounarbashi theory held sway. It was accepted by William Gell (1777–1836), the celebrated classical

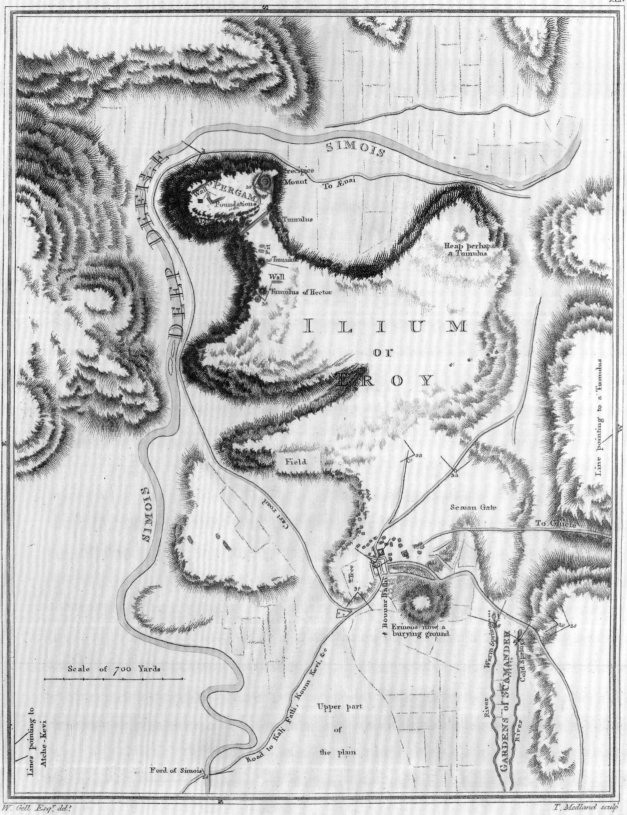

SIMOIS

DEEP DEFILE

SIMOIS

Precipice
Mount
To Ænai

Wall PERGAM___
Foundations

Tumulus

Heap perhaps
a Tumulus

Tumulus

Wall
Tumulus of Hector

I L I U M
or
T R O Y

Line pointing to a Tumulus

Field

Scæan Gate

To Gliucis

Carl road

Tree

Bounar Bashi

Erineos now a
burying ground

Scale of 700 Yards

River Warm Spring
Cold Spring

River

GARDENS of SCAMANDER

Lines pointing to
Atche-Kevi

Ford of Simois

Road to Kali Fatli, Koum Kevi, &c

Upper part

of

the plain

W. Gell Esq.ʳ del.ᵗ

T. Medland sculp

London, Pub. Jan.ʸ 1, 1804, by Mess.ʳˢ Longman & Rees, Patern. for Row

XXVIII

Bounarbashi

archaeologist, topographer and artist, who travelled and studied extensively in the Troad and published a detailed account in *The Topography of Troy* in 1804. Gell begins his work by saying, 'The voyage, of which the following pages are the result, had for its principal object, the examination of that part of the Troad, which is more particularly connected with the *Iliad* of Homer.' He was thus a firmly 'realist' thinker, and the general map that he includes in the publication follows Chevalier and unequivocally places Troy at Bounarbashi. He also has a more detailed map of the terrain and the visible remains at this site, which he confidently labels 'Ilium or Troy' (Fig. 109). Yet his real contribution to the study of the Troad lay not so much in the maps, interesting though these are, but in the series of very fine drawings of landscapes that he made during his travels. Bounarbashi was naturally a focus, featuring in many of the coloured plates included in the work (Fig. 110).[13]

Heated debates

Clarke's identification of the mound at Hissarlik as the site of Ilion/Ilium seems to us now to have been a breakthrough, but at the time it scarcely caused a stir. Under the influence of Strabo, no one felt it was relevant to the site of Homer's Troy. So as the nineteenth century progressed, controversy continued to rage, feelings ran remarkably high, endless books and pamphlets were published, and the debate around the topic often became positively vituperative. The argument essentially continued to be polarized between the 'realist' thinkers, among whom, as we have seen, most of the travellers and topographers were numbered, and those commentators and scholars who were equally firmly convinced that Homer wrote poetry, not history, and that the places, people and events in the poems were pure invention. In some ways this polarity is still evident in the debate today, though most scholars now take a position between these two extremes.

ABOVE
Fig. 110*
Bounarbashi

c. 1804
After William Gell
Hand-coloured engraving,
proof of plate 28 of *The Topography of Troy*
H. 179 mm | W. 387 mm
(sheet)
British Museum
1853,0307.180

A flavour of the earlier debate, and the heat it generated, is provided by the work of Jacob Bryant (1715–1804), a scholar who in 1796 published a monograph with a title so long it was scarcely necessary to read the work to understand his view. It was called *A Dissertation concerning the War of Troy, and the Expedition of the Grecians, as described by Homer; shewing that no such Expedition was ever undertaken, and that no such City of Phrygia existed*. The emphatic statement of the title underlines Bryant's passionate conviction. By way of equally passionate response we can quote the poet Byron. Both seasoned traveller and romantic believer, he had little patience with scholarly arguments formulated in libraries by those such as Bryant who had never been anywhere near the Troad. Byron himself spent time there in 1810, and later wrote in his diary:

> We do care about 'the authenticity of the tale of Troy'. I have stood upon that plain *daily*, for more than a month, in 1810; and if any thing diminished my pleasure, it was that the blackguard Bryant had impugned its veracity.… I still venerated the grand original as the truth of *history* … and of *place*. Otherwise, it would have given me no delight. Who will persuade me, when I reclined upon a mighty tomb, that it did not contain a hero? – its very magnitude proved this. Men do not labour over the ignoble and petty dead – and why should not the *dead* be *Homer's* dead?[14]

These exchanges give some sense of the war of words that raged, and consumed so much time and energy. Certainly, those such as Byron who had visited and walked the ground had a tendency to hold 'armchair scholars' in contempt. Yet it would not be one of the travellers and topographers who made the next big breakthrough, but rather a distinguished Scottish journalist, Charles Maclaren (1782–1866), who founded *The Scotsman* newspaper. Pondering from afar Clarke's evidence from Hissarlik, and also informed by an interest in geological processes, he published in 1822 his considered view that Strabo had been wrong, and that in fact Ilion/Ilium were one and the same place as Homer's Troy.

As had been the case with Clarke's rediscovery of Ilion/Ilium, this startling conclusion at first went relatively unnoticed. Maclaren continued to be interested in the subject, however, and in 1847 visited the Troad to see for himself the sites about which he had already written. Then in 1863, at the age of eighty, he published a revised version of his work. In 1822 it had simply been called *A Dissertation on the Topography of the Plain of Troy*, but this time he made sure the world could no longer ignore his conclusion by calling it *The Plain of Troy Described and the Identity of the Ilium of Homer with the New Ilium of Strabo Proved*. Here he writes with humorous insight: 'An inquiry into the site of Troy is often referred to as a typical example of purely idle and useless questions. Yet the number and price of the numerous volumes on the subject published in the present century tell a different tale; nor will the past history of the poems permit us to doubt that the question will possess an interest as long as men continue to read the *Iliad*, and this is a pleasure they will not in all probability deny themselves for some thousand years to come.'[15]

Maclaren was destined to remain a relatively unsung hero, even though he had hit upon the truth. He deserves more credit for his discoveries, as indeed does Frank Calvert, discussed below, whom he met while in the Troad and may have influenced to engage more deeply with the archaeological investigation of the mound of Hissarlik. By Calvert's time the world was changing. Travellers and topographers continued to have their place, as did scholars in their libraries, but they were joined by a new breed, that of excavators, as the discipline of archaeology began to come of age.

ARCHAEOLOGY AND TROY

Speculation about the location of Homer's Troy created favourable conditions for archaeological fieldwork. The local inhabitants had long been scouring ancient sites looking for either stone for building or treasure, and the arrival of Western travellers in search of Troy had also helped fuel a market for antiquities, which might be surface finds or dug from the various prominent mounds which dotted the Troad. One example is a statue base that arrived in the British Museum in 1857 and was said to be from the Troad (Fig. 111).[16] Appropriately enough, its poetic inscription shows it originally belonged to a statue of Hector:

> Bring forth, my Art, the splendid protector of the Trojan land,
> Just as Zeus aroused, just as Homer created.
> His eyes searing with the flame of tireless fire kindles (the Greeks) with terror,
> for his country.
> Tight in his grasp (his spear) still rages …

Early archaeological excavations in many ways resembled these previous activities, lacking the scientific rigour of modern fieldwork techniques, but they were increasingly driven by questions about the nature of topographical features, and the results were recorded and published. Unlike the more clandestine diggers, archaeologists also normally obtained the permission of the local landowner and the Ottoman authorities.

BELOW
Fig. 111*
Base of a statue of Hector with a Greek inscription

2nd century AD
Troad, Turkey
Marble
H. 457 mm | W. 800 mm | D. 165 mm
British Museum
1857,0220.2

RIGHT
Fig. 112
Tombeaux d'Achille
Drawing of the 'tomb of Achilles' from an album of 54 drawings.

1803
Possibly by Michel François Préaulx
Pen and ink with traces of graphite on paper
H. 480 mm | W. 680 mm
British Museum
2012,5004.1.9

BELOW
Fig. 113*
Funerary stele for Hierokle[i]a, with a Greek inscription

Probably 1st century AD
Found near the 'tomb of Achilles', near Sigeion, Turkey
Marble
H. 241 mm | W. 279 mm | D. 114 mm
British Museum
1816,0610.295

ABOVE
Fig. 114*
Objects excavated
by Frank Calvert at
Thymbra (clockwise
from top left): a small
lidded bowl (*lekanis*);
an Athenian cup
(*kylix*); a Corinthian
jug; a Rhodian figure
of a dove; a locally
made plate with
a Siren; a locally
made miniature
libation bowl (*phiale*);
a miniature cup
(*skyphos*)

600–475 BC
Thymbra, Turkey
Pottery
H. 59 mm | W. 163 mm |
L. 213 mm; H. 81 mm |
Diam. 215 mm; H. 147 mm;
H. 92 mm | W. 49 mm |
L. 100 mm; H. 20 mm |
Diam. 107 mm; H. 16 mm |
Diam. 126 mm
British Museum
1877,0930.22, 46, 7, 45, 20,
16, 25

The first archaeological excavation in the Troad was carried out as early as 1787 by Salomon Gormezano at the 'tumulus of Achilles', an artificial hill widely held to be the tomb of Achilles at the time (Fig. 112).[17] Gormezano was a member of a prominent Jewish merchant family based in Çanakkale, whose members also acted as dragomen (interpreters) and consuls for various European nations.[18] As with many early excavators, his archaeological career was essentially an extension of his consular service. In the tumulus he found the remains of a cremation burial and Classical pottery, which proved hard to reconcile with the burial of a Homeric hero. The excavation was instigated by Choiseul-Gouffier and later published.[19] One of the finds, a funerary inscription for a woman named Hierokleia or Hieroklea, was bought on behalf of Lord Elgin by Philip Hunt, his secretary and chaplain, and entered the British Museum as part of the famous Elgin Collection (Fig. 113).[20]

The Calverts were another family based in Çanakkale who were similarly involved in the consular service. They had an imposing house on the harbourside and had built up extensive landholdings in the Troad. Their main business interest was in growing Valonia oak, a Mediterranean species whose acorn cups were used in tanning leather. These were exported to Britain, where the Calvert family originated.[21] As consuls they often assisted foreign travellers who wished to explore the Homeric sites of the Troad. Both Frank Calvert (1828–1908) and his older brother Frederick (1818–1876) took an interest in this topic and conducted tours of sites, before themselves starting to excavate sites on their land.[22] Frederick was more heavily engaged in consular affairs than Frank, taking over the British consulship from their uncle. Nevertheless, Frank assisted him and another brother, James (1827–1896), and later became American consular agent. Frederick's diplomatic career ended in disgrace: after surviving accusations of profiteering from the Crimean War (1853–56) he was dismissed from the British consular service in 1862 for his involvement in an insurance fraud.[23] The resulting family shame and financial problems were to have serious implications for Frank Calvert's search for Troy.[24]

Frank Calvert's archaeological interests seem to have been stimulated and encouraged by some of the visitors entertained by his family. Charles Maclaren visited the Calverts in 1847 to tour the Homeric sites he had discussed in his earlier book.[25] He does not appear to have convinced either brother of his theory that Troy and Ilion were the same, however, since Frank continued to adhere to the Bounarbashi theory,[26] while Frederick believed that Troy was on family land known as Thymbra, just northeast of Bounarbashi. This was partly because the drainage of marshy land there had uncovered a hot and a cold spring, echoing Homer's description of the area of Troy.[27] Frank Calvert's first recorded excavation, in 1853, was at Thymbra, on the mound of Hanay Tepe. This excavation is mentioned by Sir Charles Newton (1816–1894) in an account of his travels in the region. Newton was British vice-consul at Mytilene on Lesbos, but had a keen interest in archaeology and a close association with the British Museum. He noted that Calvert had not dug deep enough to find anything in the mound, but he was present when Calvert excavated a number of large storage jars nearby containing skeletons and grave goods (Fig. 114).[28] It seems that Newton's advice led Calvert to return to Hanay Tepe in 1856, when he did dig deep enough to find a layer of ash and a skeleton at the base of the mound, published in an exemplary section drawing in the *Archaeological Journal* (Fig. 115). Calvert took a literal approach to Homer in the paper: 'The marvellous quantity of calcined bones contained therein induces the supposition that it was the funeral pile of a very great number of bodies, and is suggestive of that most probably

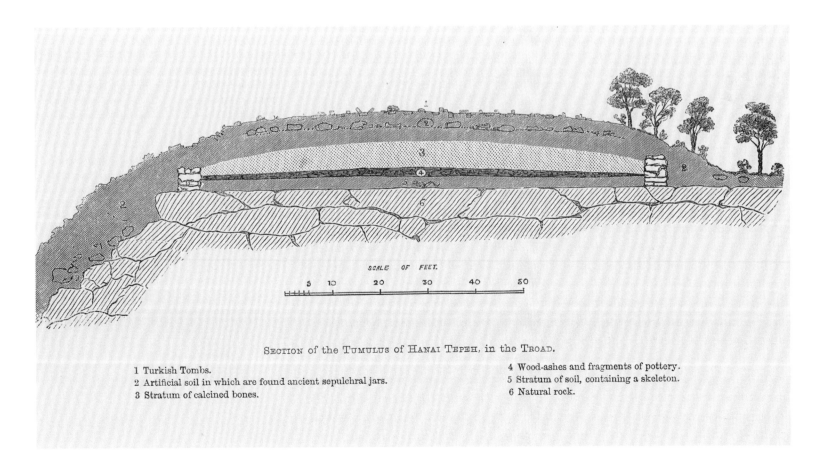

SECTION of the TUMULUS of HANAI TEPEH, in the TROAD.

1 Turkish Tombs.
2 Artificial soil in which are found ancient sepulchral jars.
3 Stratum of calcined bones.
4 Wood-ashes and fragments of pottery.
5 Stratum of soil, containing a skeleton.
6 Natural rock.

Painted fictilia and other relics, found in the tumulus of Hanai Tepeh.
* Small Vase of coloured glass.

raised by the Trojans after the first truce mentioned in the *Iliad*.'[29] He further argued that the proximity of the mound to Bounarbashi supported his theory. What distinguishes this paper is the high standard of archaeological recording, perhaps influenced by Newton. In addition to the section drawing, finds also were recorded (Fig. 116). In later papers Calvert was to adopt a more sceptical stance about Bounarbashi as he continued to explore sites in the Troad.

The outbreak of the Crimean War in late 1853 appears to have interrupted Frank Calvert's archaeological work as he helped his brothers deal with the increased activity in Çanakkale. The Dardanelles, as at many times in history, were of key strategic importance because they provided access to the Black Sea. The British built a hospital to the south of Çanakkale at Renkioi (Erenköy), an experimental prefabricated building designed by Isambard Kingdom Brunel.[30] Construction was overseen by one of Brunel's assistants, John Brunton, who was serving in the Army Works Corps. When the war ended in 1856 and there was no longer a need to extend the hospital, Brunton found himself with 150 men at his disposal and 'fearing they might get into mischief' he decided to put them to work digging archaeological sites instead. As he records: 'My men did not like this at first, but an extra pint of stout per day which I ordered for them partly reconciled them to it – and by & bye when we came on ancient tombs, sarcophagi, amphorae &c they got much interested and worked away with great zest.'[31] He describes the first site they worked at as 'the Necropolis', which was the area around Hanay Tepe where Frank Calvert had found jar burials before. It is not clear whether Frank Calvert was involved in these excavations or whether Frederick, whom Brunton had worked with, had simply pointed out sites on the family properties.[32] Brunton donated his finds to the British Museum, some of which are described in the register as coming from

ABOVE LEFT
Fig. 116
Drawing of artefacts found by Calvert in 1859 at Hanay Tepe (Thymbra)

From Frank Calvert, 'The Tumulus of Hanai Tepeh in the Troad', *Archaeological Journal*, vol. 16 (1859)

ABOVE RIGHT
Fig. 117
Objects excavated by John Brunton at Thymbra (left to right): a miniature cup (*skyphos*) decorated with birds; an oil flask (*lekythos*); a terracotta figure of a reclining man

c. 540–480 BC
Thymbra, Turkey
Pottery, terracotta
H. 53 mm; H. 146 mm;
H. 120 mm | L. 180 mm |
W. 65 mm
British Museum
1856,1208.24, 11, 6

'the cemetery near Troy' (Fig. 117). They include objects that are almost identical to Calvert's finds from Thymbra, helping to confirm that they were found in this location.

More importantly, Brunton also records that he despatched some of his men to dig at 'Illium Novum', where they found a huge Corinthian column, which they could not move, and a mosaic of a boar hunt.[33] Brunton was called away soon after the mosaic was discovered and so ordered the excavation to be backfilled. When he returned two weeks later he found that the boar hunt had been cut out and used as a floor in a local church. He consoled himself by removing some of the border, which he also subsequently donated to the British Museum along with his finds from elsewhere in the Troad (Fig. 118). At Ilium Novum Brunton had thus conducted the first recorded excavation at the site later recognized as Troy without realizing its significance. A very similar mosaic pavement of fourth-century AD date was found in recent excavations at Troy, suggesting that Brunton had been digging in the same area of the lower town.[34] Although Brunton gave an account of finding the mosaic in his memoirs, unfortunately no detailed records or drawings of this excavation are known. Brunton's assistant, William Eassie, appears to have explored the highest point of the entire site, the mound of Hissarlik itself, and found two Greek inscriptions.[35]

Calvert's excavations at Ilium Novum

Frank Calvert began excavating at Ilium Novum in 1863. He already owned one area of the site and around this time also purchased part of the mound of Hissarlik. It has been suggested that the publication in that year of Charles Maclaren's *The Plain of Troy Described* had persuaded Calvert that Homer's Troy was to be found at Ilium Novum.[36] Calvert also dug at Bounarbashi at around the same time, identifying the site with ancient Gergis rather than Ilium Vetus (Old Troy) and noting the absence of any early walls or pottery.[37] In the autumn of 1863 he wrote to Charles Newton, who was by now employed at the British Museum as Keeper of the newly formed Greek and Roman Department:

> You are aware of my proprietorship to a large portion of the site of Ilium (Novum) which contains many remains of antiquity buried below its surface. I have discovered that the site of the temple of Pallas occupied the prominent mound which rises out of the plain.... Now if anything could be managed with the British Museum to carry on excavations here (and elsewhere if they desired it) I would be very happy to offer my services. I would allow any part of my lands to be turned over, and all objects found to become the property of the British Museum (with the exception of any duplicates which the Turkish Govt would probably claim as their right in granting the firman of the excavation).[38]

Newton put Calvert's generous offer to the British Museum Trustees, recommending that they fund the excavation up to the sum of £100. The Trustees asked for more information from Newton before making a decision, but the matter was not discussed again.[39] Newton told Calvert that the Trustees had declined his offer, but it seems more likely that Newton had let the matter drop.[40] It is not recorded what information the Trustees had asked for and it is possible that the fraudulent activities of his older brother did not help Frank Calvert's

BELOW
Fig. 119*
Stemmed dish painted with a rosette and lotus frieze, excavated by Frank Calvert

590–570 BC (within the period of Troy VIII)
Made in East Greece; found in Troy, Turkey
Pottery
H. 103 mm | Diam. 280 mm
British Museum
1877,0930.10

case for receiving public money. Calvert did continue his excavations using his own resources, digging three trenches in his newly purchased eastern part of the mound in 1865 (Fig. 119). He appears only to have found Greek and Roman material, but the brackets around 'Novum' in his letter suggests that he was already of the opinion that New Ilium and Old Ilium were one and the same.[41] He did not publish his results, but a notice about his discovery of architectural and sculptural remains from the Athena temple was reported at a meeting of the Royal Archaeological Institute.[42] It is against this background that the claims of Heinrich Schliemann to have discovered Troy need to be assessed.

HEINRICH SCHLIEMANN

The story of Heinrich Schliemann's discovery of Troy is one of the most famous episodes in archaeology (Fig. 120). It is a story that he himself had a hand in crafting, since several of his books about his discoveries contained extensive autobiographies, which have contributed to the Schliemann myth. There is the gift of Georg Ludwig Jerrer's *Universal History for Children* one Christmas, whose picture of Aeneas escaping Troy (Fig. 121) inspired the following exchange: '"Father", retorted I, "if such walls once existed, they cannot possibly have been completely destroyed: vast ruins of them must still remain, but they are hidden away beneath the dust of ages". He maintained the contrary, whilst I remained firm in my opinion, and at last we both agreed that I should one day excavate Troy.'[43] There is the

drunken miller reciting Homer in a grocer's shop while Schliemann the apprentice spends his last pennies to keep his glass topped up despite not understanding a word, and vowing one day to learn Greek.[44] There is his wife Sophia, holding out her shawl to receive the gold of Priam, as her brave husband risks being buried under one of the toppling walls of Troy, in order to save the treasure for the benefit of archaeology.[45] He becomes the hero in his own myth, a morality tale that was held up as an example of the great life of someone who shapes his own destiny through hard work and perseverance.

Schliemann was a controversial figure in his lifetime, but following his death his life story tended to be retold uncritically, as his discoveries were being celebrated. A backlash has followed, in which many details of his autobiographical writings have been shown to be fabrications and even his discoveries questioned.[46] At the centre of the debate is whether someone who falsely claims in his diaries to have met the American President or experienced the San Francisco Fire can be trusted to record details of his archaeological finds truthfully.[47] For some, this is evidence that he was a compulsive liar, while others have argued that copying and reworking newspaper reports of these events in his diaries was merely part of Schliemann's technique for learning languages. Even his critics agree that Schliemann was a hard worker and a gifted linguist, who by the end of his life could speak as many as seventeen languages.[48] It was this talent that helped him in his business career: while working as a bookkeeper for the merchants B. H. Schröder & Co. in Amsterdam he taught himself Russian in order to become involved in the indigo trade. He was soon posted to St Petersburg to act as the company's agent and later made a huge profit trading in saltpetre, an ingredient of gunpowder, during the Crimean War. The California Gold Rush provided another business opportunity: there he acted as a banker for prospectors' gold dust until complaints grew about underweight consignments and he had to leave. His success as a businessman meant that by his late thirties he had already acquired a great fortune and he decided to travel around the world, visiting Egypt, India, China and Japan along the way, a trip he wrote up as his first book, *La Chine et le Japon au temps présent*, published in 1867. This was perhaps an odd topic for someone whose life's dream had been to excavate Troy.[49]

The route to Troy

By this time Schliemann was based in Paris, attending lectures at the Sorbonne and taking part in the intellectual life of the city. His eastern travelogue makes sense as a way to become part of the literary scene, converting his fortune into respectability. The same can be said of his next book, *Ithaque, le Péloponnèse, Troie, recherches archéologiques* (1869), which had its genesis in a journey through classical lands that followed in the footsteps of the eighteenth-century aristocrats' Grand Tour and earlier Homer scholars alike. The book was based on Schliemann's own diaries, themselves heavily indebted to John Murray's scholarly *Handbooks for Travellers*. The resulting publication diverges from the diaries in order to make it appear as though the archaeological research of the title was Schliemann's motivation for the journey, rather than mostly done on his return. There are also episodes which do not appear in the diaries and seem to have been entirely invented, with Schliemann casting himself as Odysseus in an encounter with ferocious dogs.[50] What distinguished Schliemann from earlier travellers was his readiness to hire local workers to excavate the sites he visited, often without the necessary permission. At Ithaca he claimed to have uncovered Odysseus' palace and decided that jars containing cremated remains were those of Odysseus, Penelope and their children.[51] Then he moved on to Mycenae, the site of his later excavations, before

TROIA'S ZERSTOERUNG.

ABOVE
Fig. 121*
Drawing of Aeneas escaping from Troy carrying his father on his back

From Georg Ludwig Jerrer, *Die Weltgeschichte für Kinder* (Universal History for Children) 1840 edition (first published 1819), Nuremberg

reaching the Troad and digging at Bounarbashi for a couple of days. The diaries give an indication that these digs were less intensive and more dilettante in character than the serious archaeological research they become in the later publication.

Schliemann visited Frank Calvert at Çanakkale at the end of his trip round the Troad, in August 1868. The Calvert archaeological collection was well known and a frequent stop for travellers to the region. Calvert later claimed that Schliemann was unaware when they met of the possibility that Troy could have been located at Hissarlik rather than Bounarbashi.[52] By contrast, in his book Schliemann presented his dig at Bounarbashi as his attempt to disprove the theory that it was Troy. He also claimed that he knew it could not have been Troy because it was too steep for Achilles and Hector to have run around it, as described in Book 22 of the *Iliad*.[53] Schliemann's diary from this period has been the subject of much scrutiny. Notably, he makes no reference whatsoever to Troy when describing his visit to Hissarlik (which he does not name) on 10 August 1868, whereas on passing it on his return from Bounarbashi four days later, he suddenly states his opinion that Hissarlik was the site of Homer's Troy. There can be little doubt that Schliemann wrote and backdated this entry after meeting Calvert, to make it look as if he had independently come to the same conclusion.[54] He describes Calvert in his diary as 'the famous archaeologist, who shares my opinion that Homer's Troy is none other than Hasserlik [sic]'. Schliemann made a similar comment in his book, crediting Calvert for exploring the site but not for introducing him to it.[55] The two remained in correspondence when Schliemann returned to Paris, with Calvert supplying him with a reading list including Maclaren's work and patiently answering Schliemann's questions about Hissarlik. Schliemann finished writing his book by the end of the year, by which time he had absorbed enough of the scholarship on Homeric geography to reshape his travels as a scholarly contribution to the subject.

Excavations at Hissarlik

On 9 April 1870 Schliemann began excavating at Hissarlik, as Frank Calvert had encouraged him to do since their first meeting. By then the British Museum had turned down Calvert's offer to dig at the site and his family was in financial difficulties as a result of his brother's conviction for fraud. Until Schliemann turned up, Calvert must have had little hope of fulfilling his desire to begin large-scale excavations at the site. It would have soon become apparent, however, that Schliemann was going to prove a difficult collaborator, since he decided to start his excavations on the half of the mound that Calvert did not own. Calvert himself was absent, lying in bed with a fever. It seems that Schliemann preferred the look of the mound's higher, western end, and dug there despite the opposition of the Turkish landowners. At first Schliemann was disappointed with what he found, expecting walls like those he had seen at Mycenae, but when he unearthed a substantial building he declared it to be Priam's Palace and sent off an article to a German newspaper to announce his discovery. After only eleven days he departed for Greece, his first season's excavation over, leaving Calvert to sort out the problems in his wake. Because of the newspaper article the Ottoman authorities had become aware of both the illicit dig and Frank Calvert's involvement in it. They responded by buying the western half of the mound, not necessarily to prevent excavation, but to give them a stronger hand in negotiations for a permit to dig and to ensure ownership of the finds. A recent law in response to the removal of antiquities by foreign visitors meant that important finds must now go to the newly founded Imperial Museum in the capital.[56]

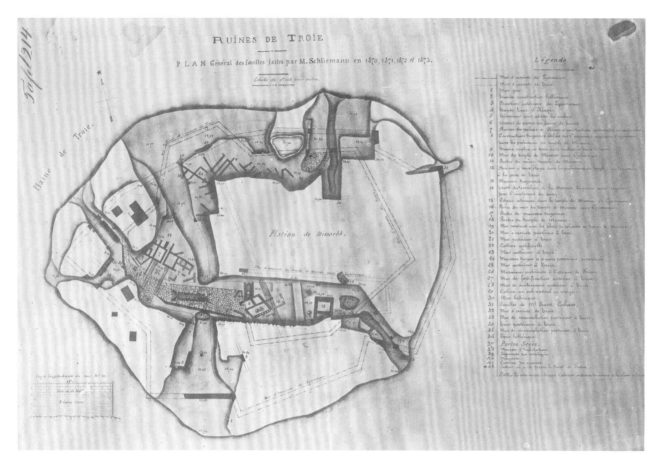

LEFT

**Fig. 122
Schliemann's plan
of his 1870–73
excavations**

From Heinrich
Schliemann, *Atlas
Trojanischer Alterthümer:
photographische
Abbildungen zu dem
Berichte über die
Ausgrabungen in Troja*
(Atlas of Trojan
Antiquities: photographic
records accompanying
the reports of excavations
at Troy)
1874, Leipzig

Schliemann's excavations at Hissarlik began in earnest in the autumn of 1871. With the help of the American embassy he had been issued with a firman by the Ottoman government, giving him permission to dig, provided that his work was overseen by an official. The protracted negotiations meant that he could only start on 11 October, and he continued, despite worsening weather, until 24 November. He began at the north of the mound and, with around eighty workers, expanded one of his trenches from the year before (Fig. 122). As he put it: 'The simple object of my excavations from the beginning was to find Troy, whose site has been discussed by a hundred scholars in a hundred books, but which as yet no one has ever sought to bring to light by excavation.'[57] In practice this meant digging down to the earliest level, 'on the primary soil', where he presumed he would find Homer's Troy.[58] Once he thought he had reached it, at around 14 metres (46 feet) below the surface, he then proceeded to open out this level by removing everything above it. When he recommenced work in April 1872, he broadened the previous year's trench significantly, so that it was 79 metres (260 feet) wide at the top. In doing so he finally began to excavate Calvert's share of the land. Instead of digging down he then started to attack the vertical side of this trench, essentially quarrying into the mound. In this way he maintained the level of the 'platform', as he termed the base of his excavations, at this depth of 14 metres (46 feet).[59] He soon started a similar trench at the south, with the aim of meeting the excavation from the north. This huge cut through the mound has become known as the 'Schliemann Trench' (Fig. 123) and can still be seen today. New trenches to the east and west were dug in 1873, converging on the building he now identified as Priam's Palace instead. By this time he had decided that Homer's Troy was at a slightly higher level, based

**Fig. 123
A photograph
showing the view
across the plain
of Troy through
the trench that
Schliemann dug
through the centre
of the mound of
Hissarlik**

The trench revealed that
the mound was made
up of many layers of
successive settlements.

From Heinrich
Schliemann, *Atlas
Trojanischer Alterthümer*
1874, Leipzig

on its more spectacular finds. In the 1872 and 1873 seasons, each lasting around 4½ months, he had up to 180 workers at his disposal, with railway engineers as foremen because they were experienced in moving such large quantities of soil.

In these first seasons of 1870 to 1873, Schliemann largely supervised the excavations himself. Subsequent archaeologists have tried to piece together this work from his notebooks and publications,[60] but it has proved difficult for a number of reasons. First, the scale of the dig meant that it was impossible for one person to record everything effectively. Although Schliemann cast his young, second wife, Sophia, as a constant collaborator, in fact she was often not present. Secondly, as his excavations increased in scale and Schliemann began to quarry into the mound, his workers were often digging into several different layers of the site at the same time. This meant that his recording of the depths at which objects were found became less accurate. Rather than identifying different archaeological strata, Schliemann tended to rely on the depth from the top of the mound to give an idea of the relative age of a building or object. Although it is generally true that the earliest finds came from the deepest part of the mound, Schliemann was unable to grasp the complexities of a site where rubbish pits or the foundations of buildings cut into

earlier layers below. Finally, Schliemann's fieldwork was pioneering: as one of the first excavations of a prehistoric site in the Aegean, the finds it yielded were largely unfamiliar. For these reasons, Schliemann's published accounts of his excavations are often difficult to reconcile with a modern understanding of the site. Instead, they offer an insight into how he sought to make sense of what he encountered, using Homer's *Iliad* as his guide.

The distinctive pottery from the lower levels of the site provided fertile grounds for speculation. Among the different vessel types are 'face pots', with eyes and nose modelled in relief on the neck of the jar, handles like arms, and breasts or navel applied to the body (Fig. 124). In these Schliemann saw Athena, 'the owl-faced tutelary goddess of Ilium'.[61] As he explained, most scholars translated the Homeric epithet for Athena, *glaukopis*, metaphorically as 'bright-eyed', whereas he preferred a more literal translation of 'owl-faced'. From this he reasoned that the site must be Troy because he had found so many images of its patron deity. The most famous image of Athena in Greek myth was the Palladium, housed in the goddess's temple at Troy until Odysseus and Diomedes stole it (see p. 97). Schliemann regarded these pots, and also stone idols of a similar shape, as representations of this ancient cult statue (Fig. 125). With apparently unassailable logic he declared: 'According to legend, the feet of this Palladium were joined together, and they

BELOW LEFT
Fig. 124*
An owl-like 'face pot'

2550–1750 BC (Troy II–V)
Troy, Turkey
Pottery
H. 280 mm | W. 110 mm
Museum für Vor- und
Frühgeschichte, Berlin
Sch 1070

BELOW RIGHT
Fig. 125*
Stone figurine

2550–1750 BC (Troy II–V)
Troy, Turkey
Marble
L. 85 mm | W. 49 mm |
D. 13 mm
Museum für Vor- und
Frühgeschichte, Berlin
Sch 7361

could not possibly be more joined than on these idols, on which the whole inferior part of the body is represented as a hemispherical lump.'[62] Over time, he suggested, these primitive images of the goddess had evolved into the owl, which accompanied Athena in later Greek representations.[63] There was an element of one-upmanship in this because Schliemann refused to admit that Calvert had already found the later Temple of Athena in his share of the land. Schliemann was claiming to have discovered much earlier evidence linking the site to Athena, and hence Homer's Troy.

Further evidence for Homeric associations came in the form of cups and jars. In the *Iliad*, heroes drink out of a vessel described as a *depas amphikypellon*, meaning something like 'double cup'. Schliemann translated this as 'double-handled cup' and applied the Homeric term to a distinctive two-handled goblet with a tapering base (Figs 126, 127).[64] Another common type of vessel was a jar with three legs, which for Schliemann called to mind the bronze tripod offered as a prize at Patroclus' funeral games, though he puzzled over the fact that he only found ceramic tripod vessels at Troy, and none of bronze (Figs 128–30).[65] Accepting that Homer did not provide a contemporary account of the Trojan War, Schliemann nonetheless assumed that there was continuity in certain object types across the ages, and that Homer in this case must have been describing a version of a tripod more familiar from his own time. Bronze tripods are known from many later Greek sites.

Although Schliemann initially looked for Homer's Troy at the lowest level of the site, he decided that the pottery of the level above was more appropriate as it was more sophisticated. Most of it is made without the use of a potter's wheel, but it is often carefully burnished and sometimes has plastic decoration, whether abstract spirals or human or animal features (Figs 131, 132). This layer also contained objects made of bronze, the metal used to make weapons in the *Iliad*, as well as the moulds for making them (Fig. 133). Significantly, given the fate of Homer's Troy, this level was topped by a red layer of earth from a burnt destruction. In 1873, in the layer that Schliemann termed the 'Burnt City', the excavations revealed a large building, fortifications and a paved ramp that he vividly identified with Priam's Palace, the Great Tower of Ilium and the Scaean Gate (Fig. 134).[66] Although evocative, these identifications nonetheless caused some trouble for Schliemann. Locating the Scaean Gate within the mound of Hissarlik, close to Priam's Palace, meant that Homer's Troy became a much smaller city than he had hoped for, or Homer had described:

> Now as Homer never saw Ilium's Great Tower, nor the Scaean Gate, and could not imagine that these buildings lay buried deep beneath his feet, and as he probably imagined Troy to have been very large – according to the then existing poetical legends – and perhaps wished to describe it as still larger, we cannot be surprised that he makes Hector descend from the palace in the Pergamus and hurry through the town in order to arrive at the Scaean Gate; whereas that gate and Ilium's Great Tower, in which it stands, are in reality directly in front of the royal house.[67]

Here the gap in time between Homer and the Trojan War gave Schliemann room to manoeuvre when his finds stubbornly refused to fit Homer's descriptions.

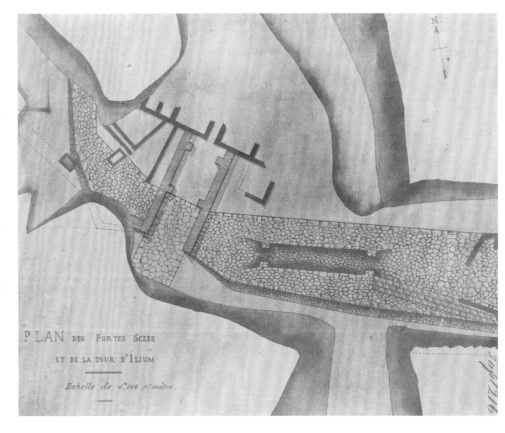

PLAN DES PORTES SCEES
ET DE LA TOUR D'ILIUM

Echelle de 0,003 p. mètre.

Priam's Treasure

It was in the area of the Scaean Gate, in the western part of the mound, that Schliemann made his most famous discovery at Hissarlik. It has since been the source of much controversy, because of both the circumstances of its discovery and its later fate. According to Schliemann, while digging just within the Gate he found a large copper object. A glimpse of gold within made him cautious and so he dismissed his workmen for an early breakfast and set about extracting the object with a knife. As he relates:

> This required great exertion and involved great risk, since the wall of fortification, beneath which I had to dig, threatened every moment to fall down upon me. But the sight of so many objects, every one of which is of inestimable value to archaeology, made me reckless, and I never thought of any danger. It would, however, have been impossible for me to have removed the treasure without the help of my dear wife, who stood at my side, ready to pack the things I cut out in her shawl, and to carry them away.[68]

Priam's Treasure, as Schliemann inevitably named it, was a hoard of metal objects of varying types. In all there were 137 metal objects and 8,750 gold beads.[69] The most recognizable of these objects are the gold diadem and earrings known as the 'Jewels of Helen', which Sophia Schliemann wore in a widely circulated photograph (Fig. 135). As can be seen in another photograph published by Schliemann (Fig. 136), there were a large number of vessels, including one two-handled cup made of solid gold. Packed inside one of the large silver vessels (Figs 137–39) was the collection of gold jewellery, including diadems, necklaces and earrings. Among the copper or bronze objects were tools and weapons (Figs 140–43), and the large copper vessels which first caught Schliemann's eye.

Schliemann's report of the discovery is problematic because, as he later admitted to Charles Newton, Sophia Schliemann was in Athens in May 1873, when the find was made.[70] His rather unlikely explanation was that he was trying to foster her interest in archaeology. It seems more probable that he was trying to embellish the story of the discovery by having his steadfast wife help him on his dangerous quest. This lie has often been seen as an indication that the entire story of the discovery of Priam's Treasure was fabricated. Some have suggested that Schliemann may have assembled various finds from the 1873 season, perhaps even including some bought elsewhere, and turned them into one spectacular find.[71] The evidence for this is a number of inconsistencies in the published account of the objects identified as being part of Priam's Treasure. But some of the inconsistencies could have resulted from Schliemann's decision to pack up the Treasure in secret, and have Frederick Calvert smuggle it to Athens before the Ottoman authorities could claim it.[72] As a result, Schliemann only had the chance to study the objects upon his return to that city. Schliemann's conflicting accounts of the findspot are also problematic. At first he was keen to associate the objects with Priam's Palace, before deciding that they must have been put in a chest and carried out of the burning building, in order to explain where he actually found them.

Controversy has continued to surround Schliemann's finds to the present day. He gave his Trojan collection to his native Germany, and it went on display in Berlin in 1881. During the Second World War, some of Priam's Treasure, including the gold, along with other valuable artefacts from Troy, were moved to a heavily fortified flak tower in Berlin Zoo for safety. This proved a sensible decision, since many of the other items from the site

Trésor de Priam découvert à 8½ mètres de profondeur

were destroyed during the Allied bombing of Berlin in 1945. When the Martin Gropius Bau, home of the Museum für Vor- und Frühgeschichte, suffered a direct hit, some objects survived but were burnt black (Fig. 144).[73] The fate of the objects in the flak tower was unknown until the 1990s, when it was revealed that they had been removed to Russia during the fall of Berlin and divided between the Pushkin Museum in Moscow and the Hermitage in St Petersburg.[74] They went back on display at the Pushkin in 1996, but their ownership remains contested, one of many unresolved cases involving the theft or destruction of cultural property during the Second World War. In 2013 Germany lent some of the other objects from Priam's Treasure to an exhibition in Russia, 'Bronze Age: Europe Without Borders', but this act of cultural diplomacy resulted in a public disagreement between Angela Merkel and Vladimir Putin about the objects' repatriation.[75] The opening of a new museum in Çanakkale in 2018, near the site of Troy, has led to renewed Turkish claims for the same objects.[76] A few pieces of gold jewellery from Priam's Treasure remain in Athens, donated by Sophia Schliemann to the National Archaeological Museum.[77] Even if Priam's Treasure was all found together, as Schliemann claimed, it is unlikely ever to be fully reunited again.

Schliemann and London

The discovery of Priam's Treasure only became publicly known after the end of the 1873 excavations, when Schliemann had returned to Athens. There he put it on display in his house, and as news of the sensational discovery spread, he announced it in the German press.[78] As it became clear that he had exported finds from Troy without permission, Schliemann was asked to explain himself to the Turkish authorities. Finding Schliemann unwilling to make amends, they launched legal action against him in the Greek courts. This merely prompted Schliemann to hide the Treasure at the French School at Athens, beyond Greek jurisdiction. The lawsuit was only dropped a year later, after Schliemann had agreed to pay reparations of more than the equivalent of £200,000 in today's money to the Ottoman government.[79] This allowed him to keep all his finds from Troy rather than forfeit a share. Meanwhile, Schliemann rapidly published an account of his discoveries, *Trojanische Alterthümer: Bericht über die Ausgrabungen in Troja* (1874). This was accompanied by a two-volume *Atlas* of photographs of the finds and the excavations, which showed that Schliemann was willing to embrace the latest technology, though this proved expensive to produce.[80] An English version, published by John Murray, with engravings and lithographs rather than photographic plates, appeared as *Troy and Its Remains* in 1875.[81] Soon after, Schliemann visited London and met with a favourable reaction to his work at Troy and the resulting publications. His supporters included Charles Newton and the prime minister, William Gladstone, a noted Homer scholar. Although there was some scepticism about Schliemann's attempts to associate his finds with the *Iliad*, there was a general consensus that he had made an important archaeological discovery.

Schliemann's legal problems with the Ottoman authorities forced him to look elsewhere for a new site to excavate. Continuing his search for Homeric heroes, he returned to Mycenae, which he had first visited as part of the itinerary which led him to Troy. Typically, he began to excavate in 1874 without the permission of the Greek government and was forced to stop after a week. Two years later he returned, this time under the auspices of the Greek Archaeological Society, with the work supervised by one of its officers, Panagiotis Stamatakis. At Mycenae, once more, Schliemann's faith in ancient Greek texts proved fruitful. Pausanias, in his *Description of Greece* from the second century AD, had recorded the legend that Agamemnon had been given a hero's burial within the walls of Mycenae following his murder upon his return from Troy. Whereas later tradition had located Agamemnon's tomb elsewhere, in the so-called Treasury of Atreus, Schliemann decided to dig within the citadel walls, just inside the famous Lion Gate. There he found a circular enclosure, and sunk into it a number of shafts with rich burials at the bottom. Each proved wealthier than the last, the skeletons adorned with golden jewellery and accompanied by metal vessels and elaborately decorated weapons. Some of the skeletons in the last two shaft graves discovered by Schliemann, Graves IV and V, were adorned with gold face masks. On 28 November 1876, Schliemann sent a telegram to King George I of Greece to announce his discovery of the graves of Agamemnon and his followers. From this comes the apocryphal story that Schliemann said 'I have gazed upon the face of Agamemnon'. The finest mask was soon called the 'Mask of Agamemnon', despite Schliemann never identifying it as such (Fig. 145).[82] As at Troy, doubts have been expressed about the authenticity of Schliemann's discoveries: suggestions were made at the time, and have never entirely gone away, that some objects were made by Athenian goldsmiths and planted.[83] The recently surfaced excavation notebooks of Stamatakis largely support

RIGHT
**Fig. 145
Photograph of
the 'Mask of
Agamemnon',
a funeral mask
discovered by
Schliemann in Shaft
Grave V, Mycenae,
Greece**

1878
Romaïdes Frères; Athens,
Greece

BELOW
**Fig. 146*
Stirrup jar excavated
from the cemetery of
Ialysus on the Greek
island of Rhodes**

1375–1300 BC
Made in Greece; found in
Tomb 31, Ialysus, Rhodes,
Greece
Pottery
H. 108 mm | Diam. 103 mm
British Museum
1978,0707.17

Schliemann's account, as well as revealing new details of the placement of finds.[84] Once again, Schliemann had dug at a site with Homeric associations and made spectacular discoveries that were to have a lasting impact on both scholarship and the public imagination.

In 1877 Schliemann spent an extended period of time in London and gave a triumphant lecture about his finds at Mycenae at the Society of Antiquaries. Such was his celebrity that a picture of him addressing the Society appeared in the *Illustrated London News* (Fig. 147). He spent his time in London overseeing the publication by John Murray of his excavations at Mycenae, again lavishly illustrated. He even persuaded a reluctant William Gladstone to write the foreword. Charles Newton also made an important contribution to the book, gratefully acknowledged by Schliemann. Newton pointed out that the pottery from the citadel at Mycenae was similar to that recently found on the island of Rhodes,[85] where the chamber tomb cemetery of Ialysus had been excavated by Sir Alfred Biliotti between 1868 and 1872, with the finds now on display in the British Museum. In particular, a distinctive type of vessel, known as a stirrup jar because of the shape of its handle, was found at both sites. As Newton pointed out, at Ialysus stirrup jars were found in association with Egyptian scarabs from the reign of Pharaoh Amenhotep III, around 1400 BC (Figs 146 and 148). This provided an important fixed point in the dating of Schliemann's finds from the citadel at Mycenae and was later to prove important in the dating of Troy.

Pleased with the reception he had been given by the scholarly community of London, Schliemann decided to put his finds from Troy on display there in 1877 (Fig. 149). After being turned down by the British Museum, which did not at that time put on temporary exhibitions and also lacked room for them, he was provided with a space in the South Kensington Museum (now the Victoria and Albert Museum). The Trojan material, including Priam's Treasure, was arranged in a series of glass showcases, with handwritten labels provided by Schliemann, which helped to advance his claims about the links between

LEFT
Fig. 147
Heinrich Schliemann's
address to the
Society of Antiquaries
at Burlington House,
London, in 1877

Published in the
Illustrated London News,
31 March 1877
Engraving

BELOW
Fig. 148*
An Egyptian scarab
from the reign of
Pharaoh Amenhotep
III discovered in the
cemetery of Ialysus

1390–1352 BC
Made in Egypt; found in
Tomb 9, Ialysus, Rhodes,
Greece
Faience
H. 38 mm | W. 25 mm |
D. 15 mm
British Museum
1870,1008.130

descriptions of objects in the *Iliad* and his finds. The first object visitors encountered
was a large face pot, establishing the connection between the site and owl-faced Athena.[86]
The display was also supplemented by photographs of the excavation, probably the first
archaeological exhibition to do so. It appears to have left many visitors with a sense
of disappointment: the archaeological reality of the site did not live up to their Homer-
inspired expectations. Failing to provide a compelling alternative vision of Troy to that
already familiar from classical art, it did not have the same effect on contemporary visual
culture as comparable exhibitions of Egyptian material had done. The exhibition continued
until 1880, when Schliemann removed the material to a permanent display in Berlin,
donating his Trojan collection to Germany in the process. The British Museum made
an offer to buy the collection instead, but it seems Schliemann preferred to gain recognition
in his native country through this generous act.[87]

The British Museum did acquire other Trojan objects from the auction house
Sotheby's earlier in 1877. Frank Calvert had decided to sell part of the family collection
of material excavated in the Troad, as well as his share of the finds from Schliemann's
excavation in his part of the mound at Hissarlik. The British Museum was most interested
in two objects which weren't from Troy: an inscribed Achaemenid Persian bronze weight
in the shape of a lion (Fig. 150), which was tentatively associated with Xerxes' visit to the

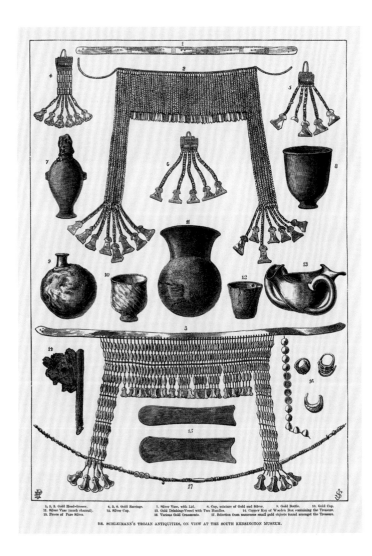

1. 2. 3. Gold Head-dresses.   4. 5. 6. Gold Earrings.   7. Silver Vase, with Lid.   8. Cup, mixture of Gold and Silver.   9. Gold Bottle.   10. Gold Cup.
11. Silver Vase (much charred).   12. Silver Cup.   13. Gold Drinking-Vessel with Two Handles.   14. Copper Key of Wooden Box containing the Treasure.
15. Pieces of Pure Silver.   16. Various Gold Ornaments.   17. Selection from numerous small gold objects found amongst the Treasure.

DR. SCHLIEMANN'S TROJAN ANTIQUITIES, ON VIEW AT THE SOUTH KENSINGTON MUSEUM.

Troad in 480 BC on his way to attack Greece, and a long inscription from the site of Sestus in Thrace.[88] These two objects were acquired for £75 and £20 respectively through the firm of Rollin & Feuardent, which often acted as an intermediary for the Museum. In addition, the same firm bought a lot described as 'an interesting collection of upwards of 300 Trojan Antiquities and Prehistoric remains discovered by Mr. Calvert at Hissarlik', together with 91 Greek painted vases from elsewhere in the Troad. These fetched only £8 10 shillings and were not bought at the Museum's direction. Even so, some of them appear to have become part of the collection following their purchase from Rollin & Feuardent by Augustus Wollaston Franks, an independently wealthy British Museum curator who often bought objects for the Museum. The Greek pottery entered the collection of the Greek and Roman Department in 1877, but the other prehistoric material appears not to have been registered until 1937, by which time its origin had been forgotten and it was recorded only as having come from Schliemann's excavations. The history of this material is symptomatic of the way in which Frank Calvert's contribution to the discovery of Troy was continually eclipsed by his collaborator Heinrich Schliemann. It also highlights the fact that prehistoric material was not valued in the same way as inscribed objects. Perhaps Calvert's Trojan material might have fetched more if he had sold it some months later, at the time of the exhibition.

Frank Calvert's collaboration with Heinrich Schliemann was fraught with difficulties. It never broke down entirely, but relations were generally volatile. Schliemann was unwilling to give Calvert credit for telling him that Hissarlik was Troy, and also downplayed Calvert's discovery of the Temple of Athena. When Schliemann found one of the metopes from this temple in Calvert's part of the mound he haggled over the amount of compensation due, buying it off Calvert at a fraction of its value. The metope (Fig. 151), showing Helios as the sun god in his chariot, was a spectacular find, as Schliemann acknowledged after the deal had been done.[89] Unsurprisingly, Calvert was upset when Schliemann subsequently boasted of its true worth, feeling that Schliemann had violated a gentlemen's agreement to value any finds fairly. Characteristically, Schliemann refused to make amends, regarding it merely as a successful business deal. At various times Calvert had articles published in the press aimed at setting the record straight about his part in the discovery of Troy, and also to put forward his own interpretation of Schliemann's finds. These in turn were often met with a furious response from Schliemann, further straining their collaboration. Such public spats raised the profile of Calvert's contribution among at least some of his contemporaries. Overall, though, Calvert firmly remained in Schliemann's shadow, as the latter's ability to tour Europe to present his discoveries and disseminate them in lavish publications assured him much greater prominence.

As early as 1873 Calvert had argued that beneath the Greek levels of Hissarlik, the remains appeared to be of a very early date, since bronze was rare and stone tools frequent. Schliemann had tried to connect certain types of pottery with Homer – the owl-faced vases, 'depas' cups and tripod vessels (see p. 147) – but in Calvert's mind these levels were too early, while the Homeric levels were not immediately apparent. The subsequent discovery of Priam's Treasure showed that Hissarlik was an important site, but it did not fully address the problems of chronology. Others, too, expressed their doubts. In 1877 William 'Crimean' Simpson, a war correspondent as his nickname suggests, had visited Hissarlik and noted how unimpressive the remains were (Fig. 152). In an article in the *Illustrated London News*, for which he also supplied the drawings, he described the palace as 'Priam's pigsty'. This touched a nerve, since privately Schliemann had voiced his concern that the city he had identified as Priam's Troy was little bigger than Trafalgar Square.[90] The excavations at Mycenae had complicated the issue because the putative Homeric remains here were very different, with an impressive citadel and few similarities in finds. Schliemann solved this problem by arguing, correctly, that the Shaft Graves at Mycenae were earlier than the citadel and so at both sites there was a long gap in time between the remains Homer might

BELOW
Fig. 151
Marble metope depicting Helios in his chariot being pulled across the sky by four horses

250–100 BC
Temple of Athena, Troy, Turkey
Marble
H. 858 mm | W. 2012 mm | D. 580 mm
Antikensammlung, Berlin
LV 21, 1 (LG)

ABOVE
Fig. 152*
Excavations at
Hissarlik, Mount
Ida in the distance

1877
William Simpson
Watercolour touched with
bodycolour, over graphite
on paper
H. 372 mm | W. 551 mm
British Museum
1900,0411.40

have seen and the levels associated with Priam or Agamemnon. Consequently, he asserted that the traditional date of the Trojan War of 1174 BC must be incorrect, since his finds at both Troy and Mycenae proved that it occurred at a much earlier date.[91]

Schliemann's return to Troy from 1878 can be seen as a way of seeking to address some of these criticisms, and perhaps also to settle his private doubts. His legal problems with the Ottoman authorities settled, he continued the work of extending what he still regarded as the Homeric levels at the bottom of the mound. There he found more hoards of gold jewellery, but nothing on the scale of Priam's Treasure. His approach now was more collaborative: over time he had gathered a team of specialists to work with him. Rudolf Virchow (1821–1902), a distinguished anthropologist and archaeologist, joined him in 1879 and undertook a survey of the Trojan Plain. Émile Burnouf (1821–1907), Director of the French School at Athens, who had allowed Priam's Treasure to be deposited there during the court case, also worked with him. Another member of the team was Frank Calvert, who returned to dig at Hanay Tepe, with funding from Schliemann. This proved to be a mutually beneficial arrangement, with Calvert contributing to Schliemann's latest publication of the excavations at Troy, *Ilios: The City and Country of the Trojans*, in 1880. The book did not mark a significant change in Schliemann's opinions, and included a

LEFT
Fig. 153
Pottery drinking
cups known as
'Grey Minyan Ware'

2000–1600 BC
From Dimini, Greece
(left); from Mycenae,
Greece (centre); from
Aspis, Greece (right)
Pottery
H. 112 mm | Diam. 247 mm;
H. 186 mm | Diam. 252 mm;
H. 80 mm | Diam. 167 mm
British Museum
1912,0626.307, 35, 55

restatement of his views about owl-headed Athena, two-handled cups and so on. Also familiar from previous works was the author's autobiography, running for over sixty pages at the start. But in contrast with earlier publications, which had read as expanded excavation diaries, the tone was more scientific. Each of the successive levels or 'cities' Schliemann had identified at Troy, from one to seven, was discussed in turn, and the finds examined typologically. There were also appendices from Virchow, Calvert and others on their contributions to the project.

In 1880 Schliemann recruited a young architect named Wilhelm Dörpfeld (1853–1940), who had been a member of the German excavations at Olympia, to be his assistant. The two men had worked together first at the Greek site of Orchomenos, the home of the mythical King Minyas. Excavations at the so-called Treasury of Minyas there had failed to find any treasure, but did uncover a ceiling decorated with spirals, reminiscent of finds from Mycenae. The pottery from both sites was also very similar. In the deeper levels a number of distinctive grey wheel-made vessels were found, which looked like they were based on metal prototypes. Pottery of this type is still known as Grey Minyan Ware in reference to the site where it was first identified (Fig. 153).[92] In his publication of the excavation Schliemann noted the similarity of some of this pottery to that of the sixth city at Troy,[93] which he described as 'Lydian' and regarded as the level immediately below his seventh, the Greek city of Homer's time. This was only a passing observation, but was more significant than Schliemann realized.

Schliemann had also found painted pottery like that from Mycenae and Orchomenos at Troy, tending to assign it to the Greek city. The most complete example is an unusual

figurine in the form of a pig, discovered in the 1872 season (Fig. 154), illustrated without further comment in *Troy and Its Remains*.[94] Schliemann later associated the figurine with similarly decorated sherds, including a fragment he described as 'exactly like a vase found by me at Mycenae'.[95] In *Troja*, the publication of the 1882 excavations at Troy, he reported finding more of this pottery in the upper levels, 'as well as other pieces with a spiral ornamentation similar to that on the Mycenean [sic] pottery'.[96] As before, the implications of these observations were not explored, and did not affect Schliemann's identification of the Troy of the Trojan War at a much lower level. The only modification of this view, as a result of Dörpfeld's work on the stratigraphy, was Schliemann's recognition that the 'Burnt City' was the destruction layer of the second city from the bottom rather than a distinct third city as he had reported in *Ilios*.[97] The 1882 season did not, however, radically change Schliemann's views and he concluded *Troja* with the assertion: 'My work at Troy is now ended for ever, after extending over more than the period of *ten years*, which has a fated connection with the legend of the city. How many tens of years a new controversy may range around it, I leave to the critics: *that* is their work; *mine* is done.'[98]

But Schliemann was notoriously short-tempered with his critics and found it hard to ignore one in particular. Ernst Bötticher (1842–1930) published a number of articles suggesting that Hissarlik was not a settlement but a vast cremation ground, a theory that can only be described as half-baked. When a paper of Bötticher's was read at a conference in Paris attended by Schliemann, perhaps as a deliberate provocation, he challenged his opponent to pay a visit to the site with him.[99] This Bötticher did in late 1889, along with a number of neutral witnesses to adjudicate which interpretation best fitted the archaeological remains. According to Schliemann's account, Bötticher accepted that Hissarlik was indeed a settlement, but refused to apologize for maligning the accuracy of Schliemann's published works. Early the next year Schliemann decided to press home his victory by inviting a number of international delegates to Troy, who duly agreed on a statement endorsing Schliemann's findings, which was published in *The Times*.[100]

At the same time as organizing these conferences, Schliemann had sought permission to dig again at Troy, with excavations recommencing in March 1890, despite his earlier statement. One of his main aims now was to find a cemetery, which would prove beyond doubt that Troy itself was not a burial ground. As a result, Schliemann and Dörpfeld began to dig around the edges of the mound. In an area to the west, not far from where Schliemann had first excavated in 1870, they uncovered buildings made of large stone blocks. Here they came across a mixture of the grey pottery that was similar to that found at Orchomenos, and pottery identical to that found at Mycenae, including a complete stirrup jar (Fig. 155). In his report Schliemann was equivocal about their significance: 'I cannot feel certain whether these ancient types of vases were imported from Greece or not', before suggesting that the pottery might be later than it seemed, in an attempt to maintain his dating of this level.[101] His report was published posthumously. Heinrich Schliemann died on 26 December 1890 in Naples of complications from an operation on a longstanding ear problem.

It was left to Dörpfeld in his part of the report to point out the problematic gap between the 'Burnt City' of the second level, which Schliemann regarded as Homer's Troy, and the sixth 'Lydian' city which seemed to have a great deal in common with Mycenae. As Dörpfeld put it, 'the second stratum, the citadel of which we have described, must be older than this stratum with the Mycenaean vases. How much older it is impossible to say, but the interval cannot have been a short one, as between the two lie three other strata of poor settlements.'[102] This was further evidence, as Schliemann had perhaps already realized, that his Homeric level at Troy was far earlier than his Homeric level at Mycenae; for them both to be associated with the Trojan War they needed to be contemporary. Ironically, Schliemann's own discoveries at Mycenae and elsewhere in Greece had helped to disprove his theories about Troy. It is also testament to the significance of his work at Mycenae that by the time of his death 'Mycenaean' was the term used to describe a previously unknown period in Greek history and its characteristic pottery.

LEFT
Fig. 156
Photograph of Gate IV of Troy from the south

From Wilhelm Dörpfeld, *Troja und Ilion: Ergebnisse der Ausgrabungen in den vorhistorischen und historischen Schichten von Ilion 1870–1894* (Troy and Ilion: Results of the excavations in the prehistoric and historic levels of Ilion, 1870–1894) 1902, Athens

ABOVE
Fig. 155*
Stirrup jar found at Troy, identical in shape to others found at Mycenae

1400–1200 BC (within the period of Troy VI–VIIa)
Troy, Turkey
Pottery
H. 130 mm | Diam. 112 mm
Museum für Vor- und Frühgeschichte, Berlin
Sch 3386

TROY AFTER SCHLIEMANN

Dörpfeld returned to excavate at Troy in 1893 and 1894, with the financial support first of Sophia Schliemann and then of the German state. He continued to explore the buildings associated with Mycenaean pottery, finding that they stood next to a large defensive wall. As he uncovered more of this wall, he realized that he had found a much more substantial fortification that ringed the area on which Schliemann had focused. Dörpfeld identified this large circuit wall as belonging to the sixth city. With its impressive battlements, particularly to the east of the site (Figs 156, 157), he had no hesitation in pronouncing it the Troy of Homer's poems. Given that the Mycenaean pottery associated with this sixth city meant that it was contemporary with the heavily defended sites in Greece at Mycenae and Tiryns, this walled city was a more likely candidate for Homer's Troy than Schliemann's much smaller (and earlier) version. Both Calvert and Schliemann had missed the importance of this later wall, despite starting their excavations at the edge of the mound: Calvert had almost certainly found part of it, but no associated finds.[103] Schliemann, too, appears to have dug through the wall of the sixth city and associated buildings.[104]

Dörpfeld also spent time trying to understand the stratigraphy of Troy, excavating the mound layer by layer. By splitting Schliemann's 'Lydian' city and the Greek city above it into four separate cities, he now identified nine levels instead of seven. Dörpfeld's publication of his findings, *Troja und Ilion*, in 1902, finally explained how the site had formed and why Mycenaean pottery only appeared in any quantity at the edges of the mound. As his section drawing shows, Hissarlik is a tell site, built up from the debris of different layers of occupation, ringed by fortification walls (Fig. 158). At various times the site was levelled and retaining walls built, as can also be seen in the drawing. Crucially, the levelling operation for building the later Temple of Athena had removed the upper layers of the ancient mound in the third century BC. In digging a huge trench through the centre of the mound, Schliemann would have found little evidence for cities VI, VII and VIII, which helps explain why these layers were

RIGHT
Fig. 157
Gate IV of Troy today

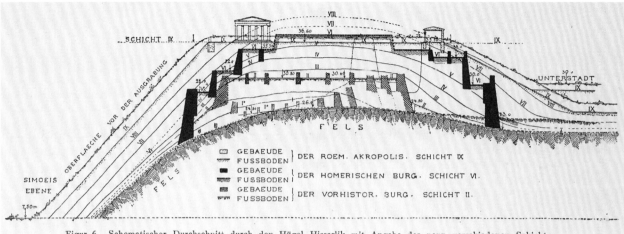

Figur 6. Schematischer Durchschnitt durch den Hügel Hissarlik mit Angabe der neun verschiedenen Schichten.

poorly defined in his work. Dörpfeld incorporated Schliemann's cities into his new dating system, which was based on a better understanding of the architectural history of the site. The resulting classification of nine levels (I–IX) continues in use today (see p. 171).

As a result of Dörpfeld's focus on architecture, the levels of Troy are defined primarily by identifiable phases of destruction and rebuilding. The end of Troy II, for instance, is defined by the burnt destruction layer identified by Schliemann. It was left to one of Dörpfeld's collaborators, Hubert Schmidt (1864–1933), to publish the pottery, though he was mostly unable to identify particular types of pottery that were characteristic of each layer. The black, burnished pottery of Troy I could be isolated, but he grouped the pottery from layers II–V together. This highlights the problems Schliemann would have faced in trying to distinguish different layers by pottery alone. The pottery of Troy VI, including its characteristic wheelmade grey wares and Mycenaean vessels proved easier to define. It was succeeded by a handmade type of pottery decorated with distinctive projections which belonged to Troy VII. The succeeding Greek and Roman pottery of Troy VIII and IX was already well known from comparison with other sites. Schmidt also turned his attention to the Schliemann collection in Berlin, which included material from up to the 1890 season, and published a valuable catalogue of almost 10,000 objects there (Figs 159–65).[105]

Pottery and dating Troy

The importance of pottery as a dating tool for the prehistoric Aegean had been apparent ever since Newton pointed out to Schliemann that the pottery from Mycenae could be dated with reference to finds from Ialysus on Rhodes (p. 155). In the decades after that, the excavations of W. M. F. Petrie (1853–1942) in Egypt produced more dating evidence: his finds of Mycenaean pottery at the short-lived site of el-Amarna, the capital city of Pharaoh Akhenaten (1353–1336 BC), provided an important fixed point. Petrie's other contribution was to establish a relative means of dating pottery, termed seriation, which traced the development of particular forms and decorative styles over time. In the early twentieth century this technique contributed to the development of pottery chronologies for what was now called the Aegean Bronze Age, spanning the third and second millennia BC. Following the system established by Sir Arthur Evans (1851–1941) for dating the site of Knossos on

ABOVE
Fig. 158
Section plan of Troy showing the layers of occupation

From Wilhelm Dörpfeld,
Troja und Ilion
1902, Athens

OPPOSITE: TOP LEFT
Fig. 159*
Bowl

3000–2550 BC (Troy I)
Troy, Turkey
Pottery
H. 125 mm | W. 150 mm
Museum für Vor- und Frühgeschichte, Berlin
Sch 96, 99

MIDDLE LEFT
Fig. 160*
'Depas' cup

2550–2300 BC (Troy II)
Troy, Turkey
Pottery
H. 114 mm | W. 120 mm
Museum für Vor- und Frühgeschichte, Berlin
Sch 534

BOTTOM LEFT
Fig. 161*
Drinking cup (kantharos)

2200–1750 BC (Troy IV–V)
Troy, Turkey
Pottery
H. 95 mm | W. 140 mm
Museum für Vor- und Frühgeschichte, Berlin
Sch 715

TOP RIGHT
Fig. 162*
Bowl with two handles

1750–1180 BC (Troy VI–VIIa)
Troy, Turkey
Pottery
H. 55 mm | W. 205 mm
Museum für Vor- und Frühgeschichte, Berlin
Sch 3068

UPPER MIDDLE RIGHT
Fig. 163*
Drinking cup (kantharos)

1180–900 BC (Troy VIIb)
Troy, Turkey
Pottery
H. 90 mm | W. 190 mm
Museum für Vor- und Frühgeschichte, Berlin
Sch 3565

LOWER MIDDLE RIGHT
Fig. 164*
Black-glazed Greek-style bowl

3rd century BC (within the period of Troy VIII)
Troy, Turkey
Pottery
H. 60 mm | Diam. 120 mm
Museum für Vor- und Frühgeschichte, Berlin
Sch 3870

BOTTOM RIGHT
Fig. 165*
Roman bowl

AD 75–225 (within the period of Troy IX)
Troy, Turkey
Pottery
H. 32 mm | W. 62 mm
Museum für Vor- und Frühgeschichte, Berlin
Sch 4025

Crete, the Aegean Bronze Age was divided into Early, Middle and Late periods and subdivided into phases, anchored at various points with the Egyptian chronology. One of the people who had played a role in establishing the pottery sequence for mainland Greece was Carl Blegen (1887–1971), who had excavated a number of prehistoric sites in the early part of the twentieth century. In 1932 he began excavations at Troy, organized by the University of Cincinnati and with the blessing of Dörpfeld. The aim was to locate Troy within the chronological framework of the Aegean Bronze Age, and in doing so understand more about the development of the site and its relations with the wider Aegean.

The Cincinnati team excavated Troy over seven seasons, from 1932 to 1938.[106] As Blegen noted, 'From the start the excavations at Troy were planned as a work of sober, serious research, and there was no compulsion to recover objects of startling or sensational character with high publicity value.'[107] Instead, the team focused particularly on excavating undisturbed deposits from the various different levels of the site in order to better understand the pottery sequence. As part of this the archaeologists collected plant remains and animal bones which could give an insight into the site's economy. They also searched for tombs, and a small cremation cemetery associated with Troy VI was discovered outside the walls in 1934. In some ways this was a continuation of Schliemann and Dörpfeld's work, as was an interest in the surrounding sites of the Troad. The resulting four-volume publication, with extensive illustrations, for the first time established a pottery typology for Troy, with nearly 300 vessel shapes identified as well as different 'wares' which related to different methods of manufacture and decoration (Fig. 166). Although Blegen retained Dörpfeld's

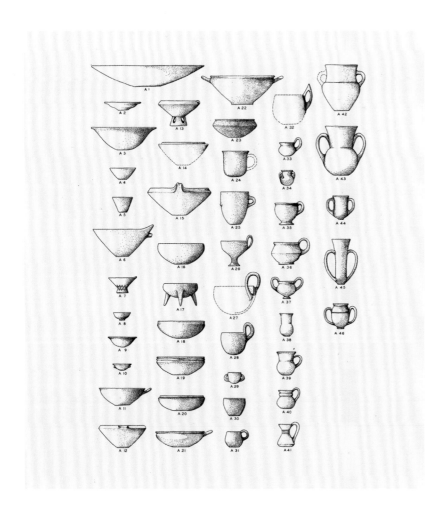

LEFT
Fig. 166
Typology of drinking vessels found at Troy

From Carl Blegen, *Troy: General Introduction, the First and Second Settlements* 1950, Princeton

nine levels, he divided each major 'settlement', the term preferred to 'city', into phases, of which 46 were identified. The pottery and other finds in each phase were noted, providing a much more detailed account of the site's history, which could now be compared with other sites in the Aegean. Fortunately, Schliemann and Dörpfeld had left a 'pinnacle' of earth in the middle of the mound unexcavated and this allowed Blegen to excavate intact deposits there (Fig. 167). Since there was little else left to dig in this area, Blegen mostly worked around the edges of the mound, uncovering areas outside the fortification walls that Dörpfeld had found. He also spent time excavating the 'Lower City' to the south of the citadel, with remains of Roman housing and civic buildings.

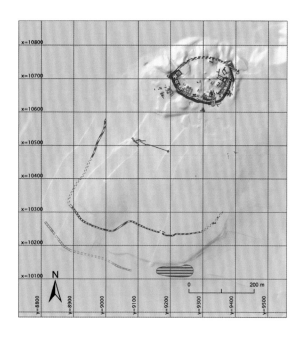

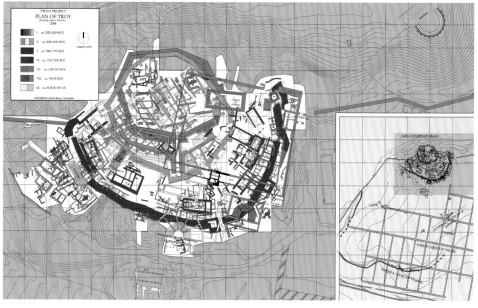

Later investigations

Blegen deliberately left some areas unexcavated for future archaeologists, and this opportunity was grasped by a joint project of the universities of Cincinnati and Tübingen from 1988 to 2012.[108] It was led by Manfred Korfmann from Tübingen, who was responsible for Bronze Age Troy, and Brian Rose, who focused on Greek and Roman Troy. Rose continued Blegen's excavations in the part of the site called the West Sanctuary, a cult area established up against the Late Bronze Age walls.[109] Here Blegen had thought he had found evidence for destruction and abandonment at the end of the Bronze Age. Instead, Rose showed that the site had not been abandoned, and a cult area had emerged almost immediately after the destruction that marked the end of the seventh settlement. As with other Iron Age sites associated with Greek myths, it seems that visitors from across the Aegean came to Troy to pay homage to its mythical heroes. This means that the city was already an important place at the time Homer composed the *Iliad*, around the eighth century BC. In turn the *Iliad* reinforced Troy's importance as a place of pilgrimage (Fig. 168).

The joint Cincinnati–Tübingen team surveyed the entire site using various geophysical techniques that allowed them to detect archaeological features below the surface (Figs 169, 170). This revealed that the layout of the Roman city of Ilium spread out to the south of the mound of Hissarlik. The area where Brunton had found mosaic floors in 1856 (p. 139) could now be understood in the context of the Late Roman city plan. Schliemann and Dörpfeld had already discovered the important civic buildings of Greek and Roman Troy – the Theatre to the east and the Bouleuterion (council house) and Odeion (theatre) to the south of the Temple of Athena. All of these were comparatively late in the site's history, since it was only after the visit of Alexander the Great in 334 BC that the architecture of the city began to live up to its prestigious mythical past. It was at this time that the Greek city of Ilion was declared a polis and started to issue its own coins. The Theatre was built soon after, and in the third to second centuries BC the mound was levelled and the Temple of Athena rebuilt. Lucan's description of Troy, mentioned at the beginning of this chapter, suggests that the civic buildings were dilapidated by the time Julius Caesar visited in 48 BC.

ABOVE LEFT
Fig. 169
Plan of the site of Troy showing Late Bronze Age ditches

Part of the recent work by the Cincinnati-Tübingen Troy Excavation Project (1988–)

ABOVE RIGHT
Fig. 170
Plan of the citadel mound at the site of Troy by the Cincinnati-Tübingen project

Fig. 171*
Roundel carved with depictions of Romulus and Remus

AD 150–250 (within the period of Troy IX)
Theatre A, Troy, Turkey
Stone
H. 1270 mm | W. 1200 mm | D. 320 mm
Museum für Vor- und Frühgeschichte, Berlin
Sch 9586

In the following centuries a number of Roman emperors supported building projects at Troy, partly in order to celebrate Aeneas' role in Rome's foundation. One example of this is a roundel found in the Theatre, which shows Romulus and Remus (Fig. 171).[110] Although the outline of the development of Greek Ilion and Roman Ilium was known from ancient sources and earlier excavators, Rose was able to combine this with modern technology and targeted excavation to provide a complete account of this period in the site's history.[111] He suggests that the site was finally abandoned in the early seventh century AD, with limited reoccupation in the thirteenth century, after which it was turned over to farmland, by which time its mythical associations had been forgotten.

The geophysical survey was also important for Korfmann's part of the project, which investigated the Bronze Age site. It revealed two ditches far to the south of the mound, which, when excavated, proved to have been cut into the bedrock in the Late Bronze Age (see Fig. 169). This discovery dramatically increased the size of the site, showing that the fortifications of Troy VI, which probably consisted of a wooden palisade as well as the ditch, enclosed some 25 to 35 hectares (62 to 86 acres). Several thousand people could have lived within these defences, making Troy a city of significant size. The defences also enclosed an underground water supply, known as the 'Spring Cave', which would have enabled the city to withstand a siege. Korfmann's team also had other scientific methods at their disposal, including radiocarbon dating, which gave them an independent means of dating the various levels of Troy without having to rely on Blegen's pottery sequence. Another scientific technique, neutron activation analysis (NAA), was used to examine the chemical composition of potsherds to trace their origins, showing that some of the Mycenaean-style pottery was made locally.[112] Used alongside traditional methods of excavation in the increasingly small areas of the mound that had not already been dug, these scientific techniques enriched the archaeologists' understanding of Troy. Today, work is still ongoing, with new excavations begun by a Turkish team led by Rüstem Aslan. But even though the history of occupation of Hissarlik and its surrounding area, from the Early Bronze Age to the Byzantine period, is now very well understood, one question remains that is more difficult to answer archaeologically.

TROY THROUGH THE AGES

Troy is a tell site, an artificial mound built up over centuries of occupation. From the time of its first occupation at the start of the Bronze Age, around 3000 BC, its buildings were a mixture of mud brick and stone, surrounded by impressive fortification walls. As these structures came to the end of their lives, or were destroyed by fire (accidentally or otherwise), they were levelled. As a result, the mound grew upwards and outwards, and it is these episodes of levelling and rebuilding that archaeologists use to divide the mound into periods and phases. The largest-scale building project occurred in Troy VIII, when the top of the mound was levelled in order to form a precinct for the Temple of Athena. This probably removed the Late Bronze Age buildings here, and with them any evidence for written administration, but still left 14 metres (46 feet) of occupation levels intact when Calvert and Schliemann began to excavate. By their time in the nineteenth century, the landscape around Troy was much changed from what it had been in antiquity. Over the millennia, silt carried by the rivers Scamander and Simois had settled between Troy and the Sigeion peninsula, creating a large alluvial plain where there was once a large bay (Fig. 172).[113]

The first five levels of Troy (I–V) belong to the Early and Middle Bronze Ages. Archaeologists now group Troy I–III as the 'Trojan Maritime Culture', pointing to connections across the Aegean Sea. Marble figurines are found at Troy and across the Aegean at this time and gold jewellery from Troy II is paralleled on a nearby island (Lemnos). Troy was one of many fortified sites in a wider Aegean exchange network in this period, and was perhaps distinguished by its strategic position at the entrance to the Black Sea. In the following 'Trojan Anatolian Culture' of Troy IV–V, changes in architecture and pottery instead point inland.

Troy VI and VIIa span the Middle and Late Bronze Ages, the period of palaces and empires in the Aegean and Eastern Mediterranean. Evidence for relations between Troy and its neighbours comes in the form of Mycenaean pottery, which was also imitated locally, and Hittite texts. Much of the evidence for day-to-day trade is missing. The spindle whorls found in every layer at Troy hint at the production of textiles for export (see Fig. 173). Horse bones become abundant in Troy VI, perhaps an indication of the horse-breeding for which Troy was famous in myth. Horses and chariots were used in Late Bronze Age warfare: this might be the reason for a defensive ditch dug around the lower town in this period, which enclosed an area of around 30 hectares (74 acres).

The wider collapse seen across the Eastern Mediterranean at the end of the Bronze Age coincides with the apparently violent end of Troy VIIa. It is not clear whether a new type of burnished black pottery present in Troy VIIb and termed 'Barbarian Ware' reflects an incoming group. Nevertheless, the impressive fortifications of Troy VI still stood and increasingly became a ceremonial focus, particularly in the form of the cult activity associated with the 'West Sanctuary'. Greek and Roman Troy (Ilion and Ilium) traded on these mythical associations, attracting tax breaks, festivals and building projects. These were instigated by illustrious visitors including Alexander the Great and Hadrian, who wanted to make their mark on this famous city.

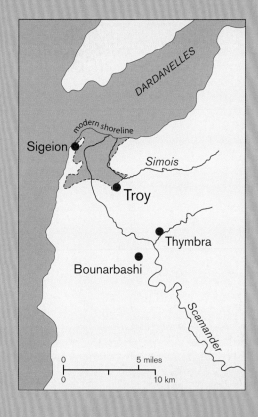

ABOVE
**Fig. 172
Map of the Troad
showing the coastline
during the 3rd
millennium** BC

RIGHT
**Table 1
Timeline of
occupation at
the tell site of Troy**

ABSOLUTE DATES	TROY LEVELS	CULTURAL LABELS	BROADER DATING SCHEME	TIMELINE EVENTS
3000–2550 BC	Troy I	Trojan Maritime Culture	Early Bronze Age (3000–2000 BC)	First settlement at Troy [3000 BC]
2550–2300 BC	Troy II			Introduction of wheel to make pottery [c. 2500 BC] Metal treasures (including Priam's Treasure) preserved by destruction of Troy II [2300 BC]
2300–2200 BC	Troy III			
2200–2000 BC	Troy IV	Trojan Anatolian Culture		
2000–1750 BC	Troy V		Middle Bronze Age (2000–1600 BC)	Contact with Minoan Crete
1750–1300 BC	Troy VI		Late Bronze Age (1600–1180 BC)	Arrival of horse [1750 BC] Mycenaean pottery Earthquake [1300 BC]
1300–1180 BC	Troy VIIa	Wilusa		Contact with Hittites: Alaksandu Treaty [1280 BC]
1180–900 BC	Troy VIIb		Iron Age (1180–900 BC)	'Barbarian Ware'
900–85 BC	Troy VIII	Greek Troy (Ilion)	Geometric (900–650 BC)	Cult activity at the West Sanctuary [c. 800 BC]
			Archaic (650–500 BC)	Temple of Athena built
			Classical (500–334 BC)	Xerxes visits [480 BC]
			Hellenistic (334–85 BC)	Alexander the Great visits and declares Ilion a polis [334 BC] Mound levelled and new Temple of Athena built [after c. 250 BC] Fimbrian sack [85 BC]
85 BC – AD 600	Troy IX	Roman Troy (Ilium)	Roman period (85 BC – AD 395)	Julius Caesar visits [48 BC] Emperor Hadrian visits [AD 124] Emperor Julian visits [AD 354] Abandoned [c. AD 600]
			Byzantine Empire (AD 395–1453)	
AD 600 – today			Ottoman Empire (AD 1453–1922)	Sporadic small-scale reoccupations, especially in the 13th century, no significant finds thereafter[114]
			Republic of Turkey (1923–	

DID THE TROJAN WAR HAPPEN?

In 2001, like Schliemann before him, Manfred Korfmann put his finds from Troy on display to a wider public. The exhibition, *Troia: Traum und Wirklichkeit* (Troy: Dream and Reality), was shown at three venues in Germany and attracted large visitor numbers and widespread press coverage.[115] It also attracted the criticism of one of Korfmann's colleagues at the University of Tübingen, Frank Kolb, who accused him of misleading the public. One specific charge was that a model at the exhibition had reconstructed dense housing within the newly discovered fortifications. This, Kolb suggested, made the site seem much larger and with a greater population than the evidence permitted. The implication was that the excavator was trying to claim that the settlement was much more significant in order to justify its identification with the city described by Homer. An international conference was convened in 2002 to hear both sides of the debate, and most observers sided with Korfmann.[116] What this conference demonstrated, apart from providing an insight into the nature of academic politics, was that over a century after Schliemann had gathered experts at Hissarlik to defend his theories, the debate still raged. Even such fundamental questions as whether Hissarlik was the site of Troy described by Homer were still under discussion. And even if most archaeologists today are convinced that Hissarlik is Troy, the question of whether any evidence for the Trojan War has been found there is far more contentious. Ultimately the problem is that archaeological evidence is not always easy to reconcile with historical, let alone mythical, events.

Written records at Troy

The Trojan War became a historical event with the Greek historian Herodotus' statement that it had occurred 800 years before his own time, that is around 1250 BC. A later Greek scholar, Eratosthenes, calculated the date precisely by working back through the list of Spartan kings, a genealogy which began with Heracles. By estimating the lengths of their reigns he came up with a date equivalent to 1183 BC. This date (or 1184 BC) became widely accepted in the medieval period, when the Fall of Troy was regarded as a significant event in human history. By the time Schliemann began his excavations at Troy, the decipherment of Egyptian hieroglyphs and the Near Eastern cuneiform script had opened the possibility that contemporary written sources about Trojan history might be found that could date the site, rather than relying on a chronology based on mythical people's lifespans. This helps to explain the great care that Schliemann took in publishing spindle whorls incised with what looked like written characters (Fig. 173). Spindle whorls are small weights used in spinning thread, but Schliemann regarded them as inscribed offerings. The first sixteen plates in his photographic album consisted of drawings of these supposed inscriptions, in the hope that they would be deciphered. In an appendix to *Ilios*, the linguist A. H. Sayce proposed readings of some of them, and other apparently inscribed objects, derived from the newly deciphered Cypriot syllabary. This effort came to nothing and no written records were identified by Schliemann in the early levels of Troy.[117]

One symbol found inscribed on a number of different objects at Troy, including spindle whorls, attracted a great deal of scholarly attention. The swastika was already known elsewhere as a sun symbol, so its appearance at Troy opened the possibility of a different sort of history, of the migration of peoples. Schliemann was not the main proponent of this theory, but gave space in *Ilios* to philologist Max Müller's account of the swastika as a

BELOW LEFT
Fig. 173
**Illustration of spindle
whorls with incised
designs**

From Heinrich
Schliemann, *Ilios:
The City and Country
of the Trojans*
1880, London

BELOW RIGHT
Fig. 174
**Seal with Luwian
hieroglyphic
inscription found
at Troy in 1995**

symbol used by the Aryan peoples of India, and also Rudolf Virchow's description of skulls from Troy as indicating an Aryan race. As Virchow wrote of Troy's position between Europe and Asia, 'It is probable even that our own ancestors, the Aryan immigrants, came by this passage on their victorious career into Europe, long before the *Iliad* was composed, and still longer before the history of mankind began to be written.'[118] As the term Aryan became mixed up in now discredited debates about racial superiority, other scholars located the origin of the Aryan people in northern Europe, to Virchow's disapproval. Nevertheless, Schliemann's discoveries at Troy popularized the idea that the swastika was an Aryan symbol, although the associated theory about tracing a movement of people from India was forgotten by the time it became the emblem of the Nazi party. The popularization of the swastika is the only remnant of Schliemann's attempts to find writing at Troy to be remembered today.

Despite Schliemann's best efforts, only one Bronze Age object with a readable inscription has been found to date at Troy. This is a bronze disc, just over 2 centimetres (almost 1 inch) in diameter, found by the German team in 1995 (Fig. 174).[119] It was inscribed on both sides in a hieroglyphic script used in Bronze Age Anatolia and has been partially deciphered: one side has the name of a man, identified as a scribe, and the other a woman's name. It is likely that they were a married couple. The object is a seal, used to make an impression in wet clay, which acted as the signature of the person using it. Seals, often made of stone, but sometimes of metal, were used widely across the Eastern Mediterranean in the Bronze Age in conjunction with written documents. The documents that tend to survive are clay tablets because these were baked hard, either deliberately or when buildings were accidentally destroyed by fire, although other media such as wood were also used. Seal impressions could authenticate documents or act as receipts for transactions. The owner of this seal was a scribe, and so belonged to the restricted group of people who could write. Scribes seem to have been associated with centres of administration, where written records were kept. Troy

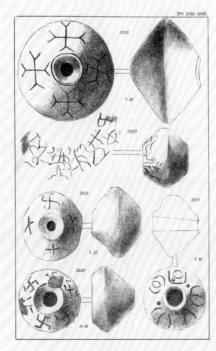

SPECIMENS OF WHORLS, &c. DUG UP AT TROY.

ABOVE
Fig. 175*
Linear B tablet listing swords

c. 1375 BC
Knossos, Crete
Clay
L. 165 mm | W. 30 mm
The Ashmolean Museum,
University of Oxford
AN1910.213

LEFT
Fig. 176*
Mycenaean sealstone depicting a chariot being pulled by two horses

1450–1375 BC
Knossos, Crete
Carnelian
W. 20 mm | L. 33 mm |
D. 10 mm
British Museum
1880,0428.1

appears to have been one of these centres, controlling the area of the Troad, but unfortunately no such documents survive, only the seal of one of the people who might have written them. It is likely that there was a central archive at Troy, but any remaining traces of it would have been destroyed when the mound was levelled to build the Temple of Athena.

Linear B and Hittite records

In the Late Bronze Age there were a number of literate societies interacting with one another in the Eastern Mediterranean. The writing system used across the southern Aegean was Linear B, and clay tablets inscribed with it have been found at a number of settlements on mainland Greece and Crete. The largest concentrations were found by Sir Arthur Evans at Knossos and by Carl Blegen at Pylos, the Mycenaean site in the Peloponnese he went on to excavate after Troy. The large central buildings at Knossos and Pylos where the tablets were found are called palaces, and both have throne rooms decorated with colourful frescoes (see Fig. 17). Their architecture, with large courts and storage spaces for agricultural produce, suggests that the palaces were primarily locations for hosting great gatherings of people. When the first Linear B tablets were found at Knossos in 1900, there was hope that some might contain historical records. However, their general appearance of consisting of lists of people, animals, goods and agricultural produce turned out to be a true reflection of what they in fact are. The Linear B script was finally deciphered in 1952 by Michael Ventris and the language it recorded was shown to be a form of Greek. Although the tablets give some hints about social organization and religion, they largely provide a snapshot of the economy of the palaces in the year they were destroyed and the tablets were thus accidentally preserved. The person at the head of society is known as the 'wanax' but is not named, and no lists of rulers survive. But tablets preserved from an earlier destruction at Knossos list weapons and chariots, showing that these palaces were centres of military power (Fig. 175). Some Mycenaean seals and gold rings also show scenes of warriors fighting and chariots, helping to give a picture of the society that used them (Fig. 176).

Fortunately, Hittite and Egyptian records do provide material for a history of this period, with tantalizing clues about Troy's involvement. Since excavations began at the site of

RIGHT
Fig. 177*
Papyrus with hieratic script recording the Battle of Kadesh, Syria, in 1274 BC

19th Dynasty,
c. 1270–1190 BC
Egypt
Papyrus
H. 258 mm | W. 332 mm
British Museum
EA10181.4

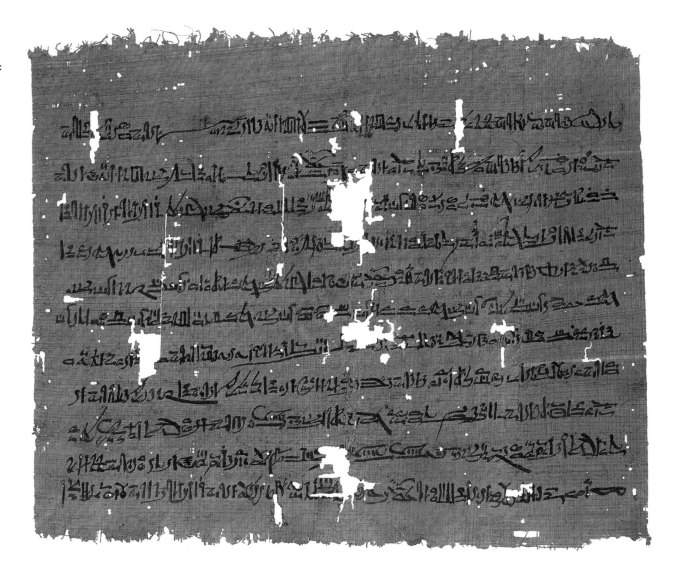

Boğazköy (Boğazkale) in central Anatolia in 1906, over 14,000 tablets written in cuneiform script have been found. These tablets, in a mixture of Akkadian (used for foreign correspondence) and Hittite (for internal affairs), showed that this was the city of Hattusa, the Hittite capital. The Hittite Empire came to cover most of Anatolia and what is now Syria, rivalling the Egyptian Empire in size and power. In 1274 BC the forces of Pharaoh Ramesses II met those of Hittite King Muwatalli II at the Battle of Kadesh, an event recorded in detail in contemporary Egyptian sources (Fig. 177). A standard account of the battle, claiming a glorious victory for the Pharaoh, was carved on the walls of a number of temples in Egypt, and also recorded on papyrus. It lists the allies of the Hittites, including a group known as the Dardani. In the *Iliad* the Dardanians, led by Aeneas, appear as allies of the Trojans, but the Egyptians might well be referring to the whole of northwest Anatolia, including Troy. The Hittite records also provide evidence for the relationship between the Hittite kings and the people of northwest Anatolia, although not specifically referring to this alliance. Two texts appear to have particular relevance to the question of the Trojan War: the 'Alaksandu Treaty' and the 'Tawagalawa Letter'.

The Alaksandu Treaty, the earlier of the two, was made between King Muwatalli II (ruled *c.* 1295–1272 BC) and a ruler called Alaksandu of Wilusa. Part of the treaty records the history of Wilusa's alliance with the Hittites in relation to the neighbouring land of Arzawa (Fig. 178). Scholars have long pointed out the similarities between the name Alaksandu and the alternative name for Paris in the *Iliad*, Alexandros or Alexander.[120] It was also suggested that Wilusa could be the Hittite form of the Greek Ilios, the name Homer uses for Troy. The problem, however, was that there was no way of independently proving this

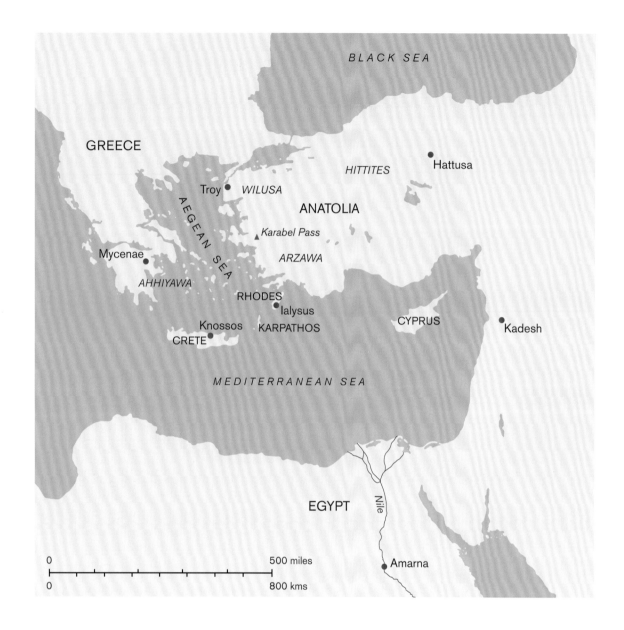

LEFT
Fig. 181
Map of the Bronze Age Eastern Mediterranean

identification of Wilusa with Ilios, because the geographical location of many of the places mentioned in the Hittite archives was unknown, until recently. The breakthrough came in 1998 when a distinguished Hittitologist, David Hawkins, published a decipherment of a hieroglyphic inscription carved on the rock face of a pass near Izmir in Turkey called the Karabel relief (Fig. 179).[121] This inscription had been known since the nineteenth century, but the hieroglyphs, of the same type as those on the seal from Troy described above, could not be read until Hawkins' decipherment. Another seal, of which a copy exists in the British Museum, provided the key, since it has a bilingual inscription in cuneiform and hieroglyphs (Fig. 180).[122] These hieroglyphs are now known to represent a language called Luwian, and Hawkins showed that the Karabel inscription was made by a ruler called Tarkasnawa (who, Hawkins realized, is also named on the bilingual seal) to demarcate the boundary between two of the territories that made up Arzawa. This gave the fixed point that allowed Arzawa and the cities within it to be located on the ground. The capital of Arzawa, Apasa, had long been associated with Ephesus, and now there was independent proof. Once this mapping was done, the only possible area that remained for Wilusa to be located was the

Troad (Fig. 181). And the only site known in the Troad large enough to have been its administrative centre in the Bronze Age is Hissarlik. Wilusa and Ilios are thus one and the same.

The Tawagalawa letter, of which only one tablet survives, preserves correspondence between an unnamed Hittite king and the king of another land called Ahhiyawa; this king's brother, Tawagalawa, is mentioned in the text. The letter concerns a rebel named Piyamaradu, whom the Hittite king is keen to capture. Of particular interest is a statement that the two kings had once fought over Wilusa, but were now at peace. Ahhiyawa is generally agreed to refer to some part of Mycenaean Greece and again there is a Homeric parallel: in the *Iliad* the Greeks are referred to as Achaeans. No further record of the conflict between the Hittites and Ahhiyawa over Wilusa has been found and so it is not clear what form it took. The author of the letter is probably King Hattusili III (ruled *c.* 1267–1237 BC), thus placing the conflict in the thirteenth century BC. The name of the recipient is unknown, but the Hittite king refers to him as 'my brother', showing that, in the diplomatic language of the day, he recognizes him as an equal. In fact the Ahhiyawans seem to be peripheral to the diplomatic relations of the Eastern Mediterranean, and appear only rarely in the Hittite archives. A later letter from the Hittite king Tudhaliya IV to Tarkasnawa, the ruler whose boundary marker assumed such later importance, showed that Wilusa was now firmly back under the control of the Hittites, who had reinstated a deposed ruler named Walmu to the throne.[123] Unlike his predecessor, Alaksandu, Walmu's name does not seem to relate to any of the Trojans in the *Iliad*. The frustration of the Hittite archives for scholars in search of the Trojan War is that they give detailed information about the movements of the rebel named Piyamaradu, but almost no hint of any of the events preserved in Greek legend. This is partly because the random survival of tablets has made them incomplete, but also because Wilusa was on the fringes of the Hittite Empire. Nevertheless, the archives do provide evidence that, at least at some periods, the Hittite Empire and Mycenaean Greece were in conflict, and somewhere in the middle was Wilusa.

Texts and archaeology: evidence for the Trojan War

The Bronze Age textual evidence offers a useful background for assessing the archaeology of Troy. The Troy VI and VII ditches make sense as a defensive measure during a turbulent period, particularly at a time when the chariot was the latest military technology. The events described in the Hittite archives took place in the thirteenth century BC, which equates to the earliest level of Troy VII. The impressive walls of the Troy VI citadel were destroyed in around 1300 BC, but the scattered blocks indicate that this was the result of an earthquake. The inhabitants of Troy rebuilt their city as well as they could, but it now had a less orderly arrangement and the houses in the citadel were often packed with storage jars sunk into the floor. This settlement, termed Troy VIIa by Blegen, came to an end amid signs of burning and violence indicated by spears and arrowheads (Fig. 182). For Blegen this was clear evidence for the siege and destruction associated with the Trojan War, but later scholars have disagreed. Whereas Blegen dated the end of Troy VIIa to around 1240 BC, which would have fitted with the period of the Hittite–Ahhiyawa conflict, archaeologists now place its destruction as late as 1180 BC. This was a time of widespread destruction across the Aegean and wider Eastern Mediterranean, sometimes blamed on marauding attackers called the 'Sea Peoples' in contemporary sources.[124] Crucially, this was also the time that the Mycenaean palaces on the mainland were destroyed, making it difficult to argue that the Mycenaeans sacked Troy. The archaeological evidence does not provide

any clues about the identity of the attackers and so can neither confirm nor deny that this destruction was indeed the event that came to be described as the Trojan War.

There is a final problem with identifying a Trojan War level at Troy, which goes back to the fierce debates about Homer in the nineteenth century: the only source for the events of the Trojan War comes from the society that emerged in the Aegean hundreds of years after the end of the Bronze Age, primarily in the form of its poetry. With the destruction of the Mycenaean palaces and Hittite Empire in around 1180 BC, writing disappeared from the Aegean. The story of the Trojan War was transmitted in the medium of oral poetry until the *Iliad* and the *Odyssey* (and other poems now lost) were composed around the eighth century BC and written down soon after. It is now generally accepted that Homer was the last in a chain of oral poets who inherited and recycled material going back to the Bronze Age (see Chapter 1). Some descriptions in Homer appear to relate directly to Bronze Age buildings or objects: in *Iliad* Book 10 he describes a helmet given to Odysseus as being made of leather and covered in boars' tusks. Such boar's tusk helmets are known from Mycenaean graves (Fig. 183) and even appear in an Egyptian papyrus that shows Mycenaean mercenaries (Fig. 184).[125] City sieges are depicted in various media, the most

LEFT
Fig. 183
Mycenaean boar's tusk helmet

c. 1500–1300 BC
Chamber Tomb 518, Mycenae, Greece
Boar's tusk
H. 290 mm | Diam. 210 mm (rim)
National Archaeological Museum, Athens
6568

famous of which is the silver 'Siege Rhyton' found by Schliemann in one of the Shaft Graves at Mycenae, which dates to around 1600 BC. This makes it clear that stories about the sieges of cities go back much earlier than the assumed date of the Trojan War, and are likely to have been the stuff of oral poetry from at least the beginning of the Late Bronze Age.[126] Imports of Mycenaean pottery to Troy VI show that there was contact between Troy and mainland Greece for at least 250 years, as trading partners and perhaps sometime adversaries, and a tale of a conflict could have grown in the telling. Some episodes could even have been borrowed from a more general stock of epic poetry about sieges.

As a result, the precise relationship between the *Iliad* and events at Bronze Age Wilusa remains unclear. Archaeologists have found and excavated the different levels of Troy, but there are also accumulated layers in the Greek sources that are just as difficult to understand. There is no direct way of relating archaeology and poetry, but it is increasingly clear that Homer's epic tale of the Trojan War relates to the much earlier world of the Bronze Age Aegean, and a long history of contact and conflict in which the great city of Troy did indeed play a central role. To some extent, at least, Schliemann's belief in the veracity of Homer has been vindicated.

RIGHT
Fig. 184*
Fragmentary papyrus showing warriors wearing helmets apparently of 'boar's tusk' type

18th dynasty,
c. 1350–1300 BC
el-Amarna, Egypt
Painted papyrus
H. 205 mm | W. 540 mm
(multiple fragments)
British Museum
1992,0725.1

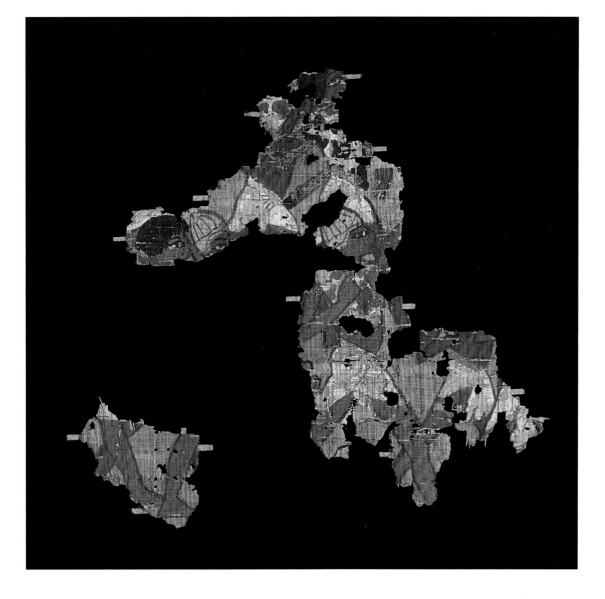

4 TROY ENDURING STORIES

J. LESLEY FITTON, ALEXANDRA VILLING AND VICTORIA DONNELLAN

TROY REINVENTED: THE MYTH OF THE TROJAN WAR AFTER THE END OF ANTIQUITY

With the end of antiquity and the rise of Christianity, the story of Troy was in some ways fundamentally transformed. The broad outline remained the same – the Greeks still win, Troy still falls and many of the main protagonists are still present. Yet new characters and episodes emerged, while others were downplayed or disappeared.[1] This was in large part due to the fact that the story was being re-told in and for a Christian world. The pagan gods came to play a much less significant role and the narrative was either secularized or transformed into Christian allegory. Indeed, during the Middle Ages the Fall of Troy emerged as a kind of parallel to the fall from grace of Adam and Eve. Just as their expulsion from the Garden of Eden began biblical history, so the destruction of Troy and subsequent migrations of the Trojan heroes began ancient history. Many of the nascent states of the European West claimed a Trojan hero as their founder, as Rome had done from antiquity. The effect of this was that the Trojans, though vanquished, came to be seen as very much the 'good' side in the conflict and the Greeks as 'bad'.

This chapter traces the major reinventions of the story of Troy through the Middle Ages, the Renaissance and Enlightenment up to the present. Later sections focus on the story's central figures, exploring how they, and the human dilemmas they stand for, have been rediscovered by successive generations, and the different ways in which their thoughts and actions have been reinterpreted and reimagined through changing times.

Preserving the story of Troy in late antiquity

The Roman world was divided in the third century AD into the empire of the East, Greek-speaking and centred on Constantinople, and that of the West, Latin-speaking and centred

Fig. 185*
P. VIRGILII MARONIS
Opera, viz. Bucolica
Medieval manuscript
of Virgil's *Aeneid*, copied
in Rome for a church
official. The miniature
at the beginning of
Book 2, in which Aeneas
describes the fall of Troy,
depicts the Trojan Horse.
In the initial, Aeneas
carries his father and
leads his son away
from the city.

1483–85
Rome, Italy
Manuscript
H. 300 mm | W. 200 mm
The British Library
Kings MS 24

on Rome. In the East, familiarity with the works of Homer and with Greek literature allowed a continuum of knowledge, even while Christian values prevailed.[2] In the West, however, knowledge of Greek and access to Greek texts gradually dwindled as Latin became the dominant language of literature, scholarship and administration.

Virgil's *Aeneid*, the Roman national epic since the reign of Emperor Augustus (see pp. 37–39), was therefore extremely influential in the transmission of the Troy story in the Latin West, as it continued to be known and read throughout the Middle Ages (Fig. 185). This was in part because Virgil was felt to be a precursor or even prophet of Christianity. In the Middle Ages his *Fourth Eclogue*, which described the birth of a boy who would rule the world and become divine, was viewed as a prophecy of the birth of Christ. Aeneas' journey into the Underworld in the *Aeneid* also suited a Christian interpretation, as the spirits of the dead are rewarded for virtue and punished for sin. The *Aeneid* did not tell the whole story of the Trojan War, but focused on those elements that were crucial for ancient Rome's claim to Trojan ancestry: the westward journey of Aeneas after he fled the burning city with his father, son and images of the Trojan gods, and his eventual arrival in Italy. Medieval writers were particularly interested in this episode, too, but they had to look elsewhere to find the full account of events leading up to Troy's fall.

The poems of Homer were accessible to readers of Latin only via a brief synopsis of the *Iliad*. In fact Homer was seen as an unreliable source, because he made no claim to have been an eye-witness to the events he described. This assertion was, however, made by Dares of Phrygia and Dictys of Crete. These two authors became extraordinarily important in the transmission of the Troy story, influencing both literary responses and the representation of early history.[3]

Dictys, allegedly a companion of the Cretan hero Idomeneus, recounted the Trojan War from the Greek point of view. An elaborate and dramatic explanation was given for the preservation of his work: it had been written in Phoenician characters on bark tablets and subsequently buried, but came to light after an earthquake during the reign of the Emperor Nero (r. AD 54–68). In reality, his pseudo-eye-witness account seems originally to have been written in Greek in the first or second century AD, and was perhaps created for the amusement of a sophisticated audience rather than being intended as an outright deception. It was then translated into Latin in the fourth century AD and was widely read, and widely taken at face value.

Dares, by contrast, was supposed to have been a Trojan priest of Hephaestus (and indeed he is mentioned as a minor character in the *Iliad*) and as such his account was more admired. Writers in European states with proud claims to Trojan heroes as their founders (see below) naturally thought that the Trojans were the morally superior force in the war that began their history. The work of Dares is much more likely than that of Dictys to be a conscious literary fraud. It is not clear if it was originally written in Greek, but the Latin version, thought by its medieval readers to have been translated by the Roman author Cornelius Nepos in the first century BC, may well have been written as late as the fifth or sixth century AD.

Both Dictys and Dares largely remove the gods from their accounts and explain the events of the Trojan War entirely in terms of human motivations. Dictys, though nominally pro-Greek, sees both Greeks and Trojans as more or less completely ignoble and corrupt, motivated by greed and lust. For him, the fall of Troy happens because Aeneas and Antenor, Trojans both, open the gates of their city to let the Greeks in. There is no Trojan Horse, though the image of a horse's head is said to decorate the Scaean Gate of Troy. A treacherous Aeneas was difficult to reconcile with the heroic figure who founded Rome, but Dares also agrees that this is how Troy fell. Antenor would become a powerful symbol of treachery in the Middle Ages. Indeed, in Dante's *Inferno* the Antenora is a section of the ninth circle of hell reserved for those guilty of acts of betrayal. A further great departure from the Homeric tradition is found in Dares' account, which creates a love interest between Achilles and Polyxena, the Trojan princess.[4] Major elements of Homer's *Iliad* are absent, and far different human motivations are in play.

Troy as identity: our ancestors the Trojans

> For noble Britons sprang from Trojans bold,
> And Troynovant was built of old Troy's ashes cold.
> Edmund Spenser, *The Faerie Queene*, Book III, Canto IX

Classical Greek historians such as Thucydides in his *History of the Peloponnesian War*, Byzantine chroniclers including John Malalas (*c.* AD 491–578) and medieval Western annals all recorded the Trojan War as an actual historical event. Using genealogies and dynastic successions, Hellenistic Greeks and Romans had variously calculated it to have taken place

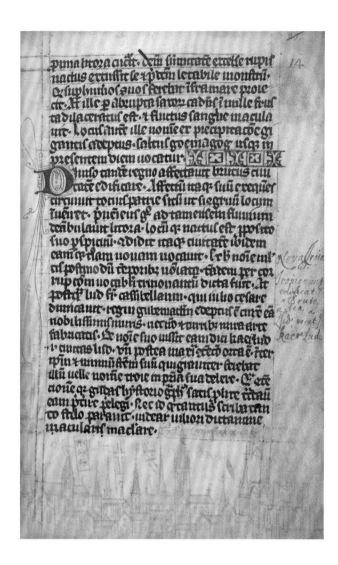

LEFT
Fig. 187*
***Historia regum
Britanniae***
The association of
'Troynovant' with London
is underlined by a sketch
of the city's skyline in this
copy, which shows the
Tower of London (right),
Old St Paul's (middle
and left margin), and
Westminster (left).

c. 1300–25
England; Geoffrey
of Monmouth
Manuscript
H. 195 mm | W. 135 mm
The British Library
Royal 13 A III

sometime between 1334 and 1135 BC, with 1184/3 BC the most popular date for the fall of Troy.[5] Medieval authors instead anchored the War in terms of biblical chronology. They commonly placed it in the third of the six ages of the world in the time of biblical King David, preceding the foundation of Rome.[6]

From as early as the seventh century AD, quasi-historical narratives appropriated the Troy story primarily in the shape of genealogies. These traced the foundation of European ruling dynasties back to Trojan heroes, some of whom were previously unknown and thus essentially 'invented' for the purpose.[7] Hartmann Schedel's *Liber chronicarum*, or 'Nuremberg Chronicle', a 'world history' printed in both German and Latin in 1493 (Fig. 186a, b),[8] features 'Franco', a son of Hector, along with 'Turcus', a son of Troilus, as founders of the kingdoms of France and Turkey respectively. Both are portrayed in the Chronicle's elaborate woodcuts as medieval dignitaries, while Troy itself appears as a standard European town of the day – albeit with some Turkish touches. Many major European cities, including Venice, Padua and Paris, are said to be foundations by Trojan refugees (Padua's thirteenth-century tomb monument to Trojan Antenor is still a central feature of that city). The text accompanying Schedel's entry on Troy reminds the reader that this once most famous among all cities is now no more, and hardly a 'footprint' remains of it: 'thus all human endeavour ends' – a moral that was often associated with Troy in the period.[9]

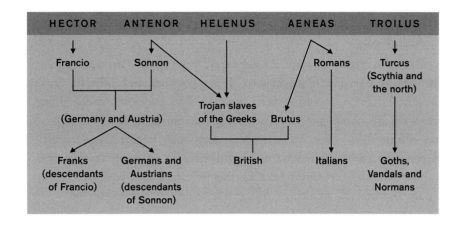

HECTOR	ANTENOR	HELENUS	AENEAS	TROILUS
↓	↘	↓	↗	↓
Francio	Sonnon		Romans	Turcus (Scythia and the north)
		Trojan slaves of the Greeks Brutus		
(Germany and Austria)				
Franks (descendants of Francio)	Germans and Austrians (descendants of Sonnon)	British	Italians	Goths, Vandals and Normans

RIGHT
Table 2
Genealogy of Trojan descendants as described by Rigord, *Gesta Philippi Augusti* **(Deeds of Philippe Augustus), 1196**
Rigord's genealogy, created for King Philip II of France (*r.* 1180–1223) is one of many such competing genealogies.

BELOW
Fig. 188
Portrait of Sultan Mehmed II

1480
Gentile Bellini
Oil on canvas, perhaps transferred from wood
H. 699 mm | W. 521 mm
National Gallery, London
NG 3099

Britons, too, considered themselves Trojans. They identified their founding figure in a grandson of Aeneas named Brutus (or Brute), as recorded, among others, by Geoffrey of Monmouth in his *History of the Kings of Britain*, written in the twelfth century. According to Monmouth, Brute also founded a city by the Thames called 'Troy Novant' (or 'Troynovant'). That this was London is underlined by the detailed sketch of the London skyline in a fourteenth-century copy of Monmouth's *History* (Fig. 187).[10] The name, found in early chronicles, was presumed to mean 'New (or 'renewing') Troy', though it may actually derive from the name of the Celtic tribe called the Trinovantes by the Romans, whose territory bordered London. The association with Troy is also found in Elizabethan literature. In the passage from Edmund Spenser's *The Faerie Queene*, written in 1590–96, that is quoted above, 'Troynovant' is described as 'built of old Troy's ashes cold'.

To a remarkable degree, ruling elites and their chroniclers all felt that the ancient and noble lineage offered by origins in Troy was immensely desirable (Table 2). The Viking Normans were sometimes considered descendants of the Trojan Antenor, while in tenth- and eleventh-century German traditions the Trojans were regarded as the founders of both the Saxons and the Teutons. According to the Icelandic poet Snorri Sturluson, writing in the prologue to the *Edda* (early thirteenth century), Trojan warriors even migrated to the far north, where they were transformed into the Norse gods. The astonishing result is that the roots of a shared European identity are to be found in a mass movement of refugees from the East, fleeing the catastrophic destruction of their homeland.[11] Interestingly, this movement could be seen to complete a circle: according to Virgil (*Aeneid* 3.167–68) the Trojans' founding ancestor, Dardanus, came from Italy, while in some Greek sources he was Greek.

It might be questioned to what extent, if at all, the general populace in these areas felt particularly Trojan. Elements of the legend of Troy were undoubtedly present in popular consciousness in much of Europe, whether through secular storytelling, allegorical sermons, plays or poetry, including the songs of bards. Variations of the phrase 'Troy town' entered the lexicon in both Britain and Scandinavia and were used to refer to mazes and labyrinths, suggesting an awareness of Troy as a city with complex defensive walls. Popular stories often picked up strangely garbled elements of the myth. In the Easter 'Pace Egg' play traditional in Lancashire, Hector appears as a great warrior, but he fights at the command of the King of Egypt against British knights and is finally defeated by St George.[12] This is clearly a folk echo of the Crusades, with a stray Trojan hero added to the mix.

The Crusades certainly encouraged associations with the story of Troy. The ancient city was known to have been near Constantinople, and its legends seemed consonant with the exotic splendours that the Crusaders encountered in the East. The story of the Trojan War came to be seen as a mythical and mystic rationale for the subjugation of the East and a westward transfer of sovereignty.

From the time of the first crusade in 1096, disputes arose between the Crusaders and the Byzantine Christians of Constantinople, in spite of their common faith. In 1204, during the Fourth Crusade, the Crusaders brutally sacked Constantinople. They saw this as righting an old wrong and restoring to them goods and lands that were rightfully theirs through their identification with the Trojan line. Apparent in contemporary English, French and German accounts, this attitude certainly seems a most questionable and contorted justification of an aggressive and ruthless act. Yet Orthodox Christian writers in the Greek East also sometimes refer to the fact that the attacking Crusaders were descendants of Aeneas. The equation of Constantinople with old Troy was a persistent trope.[13]

When Sultan Mehmed II captured Constantinople for the Ottoman Turks in 1453, contemporary writers represented him as having ancient precedents very much in mind (Fig. 188).[14] His models included historical military leaders such as Julius Caesar and, above all, Alexander the Great. The latter no doubt appealed to him particularly because of his youthful successes: Mehmed himself was only twenty-two when Constantinople fell to him. But he also admired the work of Homer. He could read ancient Greek, and the library at Topkapı Palace still holds the manuscript copy of the *Iliad* made for him in 1463. We are told that a year earlier, in 1462, he visited the ruins of ancient Troy, and that he followed Alexander in paying respects to Achilles and the heroic dead. According to his own Greek court-historian, Michael Kristoboulos, whose version of these events should probably be taken with a pinch of salt, he said:

> God has reserved to me, through so long a period of years, the right to avenge this city and its inhabitants.… It was the Greeks and Macedonians and Thessalians and Peloponnesians who ravaged this place in the past, and whose descendants have now through my efforts paid the just penalty, after a long period of years, for their injustice to us Asiatics at that time and so often in subsequent times.[15]

A letter said to be from Mehmed to Pope Nicholas V in which he seems to claim that he shares common ancestry from Aeneas with the Italians and the papacy is widely viewed as spurious.[16] But there is no doubt that the equation of the Trojans and the Turks gained considerable traction. Indeed, by the fifteenth century a confusion (or even a fusion) between the words Turci (or Turchi = Turks) and Teucri (the Latin name for the Trojans, used by Virgil) was very much accepted. The two were used more or less interchangeably in Western writings, and the confusion is found also in the works of Byzantine chroniclers. Western writers such as Hartmann Schedel had not helped by suggesting Trojan lineage for the Turks, probably in an attempt to bring them into the European 'family'.

The linguistic confusion between the two names had, however, largely faded away by the end of the sixteenth century. It was not until the twentieth century, and the reforms of Kemal Atatürk, founder of the Turkish republic in 1923, that an argument was made suggesting that Turkic peoples had migrated into Anatolia in successive waves from prehistory on, and that the modern Turks were therefore indeed of 'Trojan' descent – or rather, were connected to the earliest past of the region by a historical and archaeological continuum. This belief has become firmly embedded in the modern Turkish sense of identity, with the notion of Anatolia as the cradle of European civilization gaining significance especially in recent political discourse.[17]

BELOW
Fig. 189
Illumination showing Hector bidding farewell to his wife Andromache and their son Astyanax before heading off to war

c. 1410–14
From *The Book of the Queen* by Christine de Pizan; attributed to the Master of the Cité des Dames and workshop
Manuscript
H. 365 mm | W. 285 mm
The British Library
Harley 4431

Troy as medieval romance and exemplar

In medieval Europe, the works of Dares and Dictys, although not great literature, also served as the inspiration for romantic and courtly tales.[18] With the rise of the notion of romantic love, the Trojan story, known as 'the matter of Troy', now became peopled with fair maidens and noble though often ill-fated knights (Fig. 189). In both literature and the visual arts, these tales were very much set in medieval reality. Just as artists of the ancient world had seen the story of Troy through largely contemporary eyes, the feudal and courtly scenes of illuminated manuscripts, castle wall paintings or decorated marriage chests (see p. 231) gave the story a contemporary relevance: the pennants flying from the towers of Troy could have been modelled on those of any number of real-life medieval towns.[19]

The writers of the romances were often clerics who knew the classical legends, and used them to create works intended for the entertainment of courts and ruling elites. Their plots included deeds of heroic warriors and also dwelled on mysteries and enchantment, but love stories dominated. Indeed, while the old gods had largely disappeared, the force of love was still represented by Venus, with her attendants Eros, Cupid or Amors. Amors was a new, medieval personification, but he is instantly recognizable as a Cupid-like figure, who shoots arrows that arouse love. Romantic love, too, was a new concept, arguably closer to modern ideals than to ancient models because it was both all-consuming and transformative to the lover. It was felt to be ennobling as well as potentially destructive. The arrows of love could

RIGHT
Fig. 190*
Two pages from a manuscript based in part on the *Roman de Troie* by Benoît de Sainte-Maure showing the Greeks attacking Troy from the sea
King Priam and Queen Hecuba watch from their palace in the city, which is a medieval-looking town complete with a large cathedral.

c. 1400–25
From the *Histoire ancienne jusqu'à César*
Manuscript
H. 375 mm | W. 260 mm
(closed)
The British Library
Stowe 54

strike both male and female hearts, always resulting in an enduring passion, though with varying outcomes. In the chivalric tradition, it also became important that lovers conducted themselves with the refinement of feeling and action appropriate to their noble birth.

One of the major romances that survives intact is a long poem called *Le Roman de Troie* (The Romance of Troy), written in rhyming couplets by the French cleric and poet Benoît de Sainte-Maure in the twelfth century (Fig. 190). Benoît was probably attached to the court of Henry II Plantagenet, king of England, and Eleanor of Aquitaine. The *Roman de Troie* is, naturally, a story about war and its consequences, but the events of the Trojan War provide the back-drop for four ill-fated love affairs: the story of Jason and Medea as part of the voyage of the Argonauts (whose journey had led to the very first destruction of Troy at the hands of Greeks, pre-dating the Trojan War[20]), followed by Paris and Helen, Troilus and Briseida, and Achilles and Polyxena.

The *Roman* was soon translated from French into a number of other European languages as well as into Latin. It was widely accessible and very popular and was key to establishing 'the matter of Troy' as one of the major literary themes of the day. It was also the starting point for a rich tradition of Troy literature in medieval Germany, including the influential *Trojanerkrieg* (*c.* 1281–87) by Konrad von Würzburg.[21] An edited translation of Benoît's poem into Greek proved popular even in the fourteenth-century Byzantine world, where a local tradition of Trojan War poetry written in Greek included Late Byzantine romances such as the *Tale of Achilles* (or *Achilleid*) and the *Tale of Troy*. Greeks in Constantinople and beyond had kept alive and reinvented the story of Troy, just as the Latin West had done, underlining the East's rival claim as true successor to the Roman Empire.[22]

In Italy, the story of Troilus and Briseida as told by Benoît inspired the fourteenth-century Italian poet Giovanni Boccaccio (1313–1375) to write his poem *Il Filostrato*. Composed for the entertainment of the elite of Naples, this relatively short poem was the first to tell the story of the lovers as an independent entity, written, moreover, in accessible Italian not Latin. The title refers to Troilus as 'the one laid low by love', and Boccaccio introduces new characters and original elements that would in turn inspire both Chaucer and Shakespeare. Briseida has now become Criseyde/Cressida, all the more confusing because both names also derive from the ancient Briseis and Chryseis (see p. 69 and p. 71). In fact, although the Trojan prince Troilus also played a part in the ancient version of the myth, both he and Cressida are now essentially new characters in a fresh story, with only the haziest of links to the earlier Greek tradition.

The great English poet Geoffrey Chaucer (*c.* 1340–1400) also told this tale in his *Troilus and Criseyde*, which not only relates the tragic love story, but also ends with a musing on earthly and divine love. The spirit of Troilus, who has died at the hands of Achilles, concludes that human love is ultimately fallible and is transcended by love for the Saviour, Jesus Christ, whose own divine love offered redemption to mankind. As this love was not possible for the pre-Christian characters in the tale, there is a sense that tragedy was an inevitable part of their lot.

Chaucer is frequently referred to as an example and a master by John Lydgate (*c.* 1370–1449/50?), a monk of the Abbey of Bury St Edmunds in Suffolk. He wrote his *Troy Book* between 1412 and 1420 (Fig. 192) based on his own translation into vernacular Middle English poetry of the very influential Latin prose work *Historia Destructionis Troiae* by Guido delle Colonne (*c.* 1210–1287) in 1287. Like Benoît, whose *Roman* was in turn the major source for delle Colonne, Lydgate told the story of Troy from the earliest mythological times to the return of the heroes after the Trojan War, concluding with the lives of the next generation. Lydgate was commissioned to write the *Troy Book* by Henry, Prince of Wales, later Henry V,

BELOW
Fig. 191
Illumination showing Circe receiving Odysseus and his companions, some already transformed into swine

c. 1410–14
From *L'Épistre d'Othéa à Hector* in *The Book of the Queen* by Christine de Pizan; attributed to the Master of the Cité des Dames and workshop
Manuscript
H. 365 mm | W. 285 mm
The British Library
Harley 4431

so it is perhaps not surprising to find that it offers both moral and political lessons aimed at an aristocratic audience; among its concerns is how best to rule.[23]

The popular songs, poems and dramas composed by the German shoemaker and 'mastersinger' Hans Sachs of Nuremberg (1494–1576) demonstrate that the reach of Troy's story went well beyond the aristocracy. Sachs chose the Trojan War for the moral instruction of his audience of fellow burghers, to encourage them to trust in god, reject war or violent conflict, and be wary of the dangers of love.[24]

A female perspective was introduced in the work of Christine de Pizan (1364–*c*. 1430). Her *Le Livre de la Cité des Dames* (The Book of the City of Ladies) of 1405, written in vernacular French, was intended as a defence of the good character, intelligence and social importance of women against their portrayal in popular romances. Its allegorical 'city' included characters from the Troy story, such as Circe, Cassandra, Penelope, Polyxena and Helen. A similar agenda and an even stronger Trojan theme are apparent in Pizan's earlier work, the didactic *L'Épistre d'Othéa à Hector* (Epistle of Othea to Hector) of 1399, which proved the most popular of her literary creations. An intriguing section of the *Epistle* is devoted to Circe changing Odysseus and his companions into swine. It features an illustration of Circe as a stately queen seemingly guarding a walled city, shown behind her, against the arriving Greeks (Fig. 191).[25] Where the great Trojan warriors have failed, she, a woman, succeeds.

A Trojan Renaissance

Though forgotten in the West, the works of Homer in the original Greek had continued to be studied in the Byzantine world.[26] Indeed, they were so revered that they escaped the neglect or destruction that affected so many ancient texts in the early centuries of Christianity. Their reintroduction to the West began as early as the fourteenth century. We know for example that the poet Petrarch (1304–1374), a key figure in the rediscovery of classical antiquity in Renaissance Italy, received a manuscript of the *Iliad* from a Byzantine scholar in 1354.[27] While he expressed enthusiasm for the gift, he regretfully acknowledged that he was not able to read it. He then took pains to find scholars to help and instruct him. This set the pattern for a renewed engagement with ancient Greek works, as both texts and the scholars who could read them began to move to the West, with a particular influx after the fall of Constantinople in 1453.

The collecting of such original texts and their study became one of the major elements in Renaissance humanism. In addition, examples of Greek and Roman visual art were being discovered in Italy around that time, particularly in Rome, fuelling the rise of a new aesthetic and profoundly affecting the way the story of Troy was understood and represented. Sculptors and painters found inspiration in ancient works and many of the Europeans who now gravitated towards Italy took home with them not just new ideas but also works of ancient art. Their great collections of classical antiquities would transform European art and taste.

Some of the works artists and collectors most passionately admired represented Trojan themes and came to light by accident, during building works on the estates of the noble families of Italy. The Vatican's collection became particularly rich in such works. One of its most famous pieces, rediscovered in 1506, is the ancient sculpture group of Laocoön, which was set up in

ABOVE
Fig. 194*
Opera omnia, Vol. 1
This is the first printed
edition of Homer
in Greek, edited by
Demetrius Chalcondylas
of Crete

1488
Florence, Italy; Printer
of Vergilius
Book
H. 325 mm
Royal Collection Trust
RCIN 1057927

the Vatican's Belvedere courtyard. A Roman-period marble copy of a Hellenistic original, probably of the second century BC, it illustrates the story of the priest Laocoön, who, as he tries to warn the Trojans against bringing the wooden horse into their city, is strangled by sea serpents, along with his sons (see p. 98). The sculpture immediately became famous and remained a cornerstone of art history. It inspired debates about art and poetry and was a popular subject for small-scale, table-top copies into the eighteenth century (Fig. 193).[28]

It is easy to see why artists were fascinated by the Laocoön group, a compositional tour de force of writhing bodies and serpents. A key reason for Renaissance interest in ancient sculpture was the way it depicted the human body, notably the nude body. A sculptural group discovered shortly before 1570, often thought to represent Menelaus carrying the dead body of Patroclus,[29] exerted a direct influence on the work of Michelangelo (1475–1564). In two-dimensional art, Raphael's frescoes in the papal apartments included a figural group based on ancient representations of Aeneas fleeing burning Troy with his son and father (see below, Fig. 219). For the discerning clientele of Raphael or Michelangelo, the meaning of the iconography mattered just as much as the prestige or aesthetics of the classical style. Virgil's story of Aeneas, with its Roman significance and high moral connotations, remained popular, but increased familiarity with Greek texts also encouraged the development of new themes, such as a whole new repertoire based on episodes of the *Odyssey*. In the sixteenth and seventeenth centuries a canon of images of Greek (rather than Trojan) heroes, often instructed by gods, enjoyed particular popularity in baroque art as models for royalty and the elite, exemplified by Rubens' tapestries of the life of Achilles (see below, p. 243 and Fig. 248). Moralistic interpretations increasingly focused on social and political rather than spiritual Christian values, as cities and private individuals began to patronise artists, as in the wealthy trading centres of Germany or the Netherlands.[30]

In the European world of letters, one of the most fundamental transformations in this period was the invention of the printing press. It was in 1487/8 that the first edition of Homer's works appeared as a printed book, in Florence, edited by Demetrius Chalcondylas of Crete (Fig. 194). Surprisingly, perhaps, the first book ever to be printed in English was the *Recuyell of the historyes of Troye*, published by William Caxton in about 1474. This was a translation by Caxton of the work composed some ten years earlier by Raoul Lefèvre (or Le Fèvre). Closely following Dares, Lefèvre frames the 'abduction' of Helen as a mutual attraction, paints Aeneas and Antenor as traitors, and, like Chaucer, ends with an invocation to the Christian god, this time praying for an end to war and for peace for humankind. Lefèvre scarcely breaks new ground, as one in a great chain of retellings of the Troy story, but the importance of his text lies in Caxton's decision to translate and print it. From this point on, such works could not only be written in accessible languages but could also be printed and disseminated much more readily.

Caxton's *Recuyell* was available to William Shakespeare, and, along with Boccaccio, Chaucer and Lydgate, may have been one of the sources for his *Troilus and Cressida*, probably written in 1602.[31] This somewhat bleak play was apparently not performed in Shakespeare's lifetime. It was perhaps slow to gain an audience because it seems cynical and pessimistic rather than tragic, portraying the protagonists of the story in a more or less uniformly unheroic light. Hector is the most sympathetic, and Shakespeare gives to Ulysses (the Latin form of the name Odysseus) some of the play's most interesting philosophical musings, but commentators have argued that the war story and the love story are not quite satisfactorily integrated. It is true that the tone of the work varies between tragedy and broad humour in a rather difficult way, but it has also been said that it is among Shakespeare's most 'modern' plays precisely because of its cynicism. During the twentieth century its popularity grew, not least because its criticism of military leaders struck a note after the horrors of the First World War.[32]

Shakespeare was only one example – though the dominant one – of the many playwrights who put Troy, and classical myth in general, on the stage in this period. In the Middle Ages, episodes such as the Judgment of Paris might be staged as comical burlesques during carnival, in a tradition of secular drama that drew on material from Dares and Dictys,[33] but it was only from about the fifteenth century that surviving ancient plays, and contemporary works inspired by them, started to form the staples of Renaissance theatre from which modern theatre and opera developed.

Especially in England and Italy, stories relating to Troy enthralled audiences drawn from a wide social spectrum. Although not a tale of Troy, Christopher Marlowe's play *Doctor Faustus*, first performed in 1592 or 1593, included an apparition of Helen as the paradigm of female beauty. The speech that Faustus makes to Helen shows complete familiarity with Trojan myths. It also gave the world its most memorable description of Helen's face as the one that 'launched a thousand ships'. Neoclassical theatre in France included Racine's hugely popular *Andromaque* (1667). Some of the earliest operas were also inspired by the Troy story, from Monteverdi's *Il ritorno d'Ulisse in patria* (The Return of Ulysses to his Homeland) first staged in 1639/40 to Purcell's *Dido and Aeneas* (1688–90).[34]

Spreading the word: English translations of Homer and Virgil

Ben Jonson famously described Shakespeare as having 'small Latin and less Greek',[35] but in his day they were already less essential for reading the classics. Translations of the works of Homer were increasingly made available in a range of modern languages, and it is possible that Shakespeare already had access to the first complete English translation of the *Iliad*.[36] This was the magisterial work of playwright George Chapman (*c.* 1559–1634), which would reign supreme for almost a century.

Chapman's *Iliad* was published in parts from 1598, and his *Whole Works of Homer*, with both the *Iliad* and the *Odyssey*, was published in 1616 (Fig. 195). Chapman's approach was to capture the essence of the original in his own poetic style, resulting in a fine piece of seventeenth-century writing that was and remains much admired. Its profound impact on the young John Keats was famously captured by him in his 1816 sonnet 'On first looking into Chapman's Homer':

> Oft of one wide expanse had I been told
> That deep-brow'd Homer ruled as his demesne;
> Yet did I never breathe its pure serene
> Till I heard Chapman speak out loud and bold[37]

Chapman's magnificent achievement was gradually joined by other versions, and around the beginning of the eighteenth century a number of English translations were available. The next literary landmark, though, was the translation by Alexander Pope (1688–1744). Pope's *Iliad* was published between 1715 and 1720 (see also p. 277), followed by his *Odyssey* in 1726. As with Chapman, Pope's own voice is clearly heard in these widely acclaimed poems, which he writes in a style of English that is much influenced by classical models. His translation of the *Iliad* was described by Samuel Johnson as 'the greatest version of

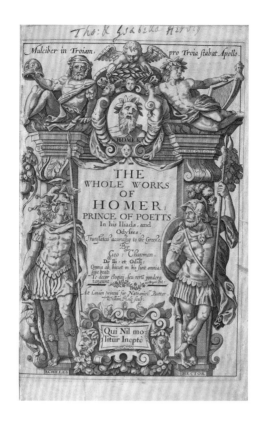

ABOVE
Fig. 195*
***The Whole Works of Homer; Prince of Poetts*, translated by George Chapman**

c. 1616, engraved title page inserted later, after 1634
London
Book
H. 295 mm | D. 75 mm
Royal Collection Trust
RCIN 1058130

Fig. 196*
***The Works of Virgil: containing his Pastorals, Georgics and Aeneis** translated*
by John Dryden

The illustration facing the beginning of Book 1 shows Aeneas' ships caught in a violent storm as described by Virgil. Below it is a dedication 'To his Royal Highness Prince George of Denmark'. Dryden's work had been funded in advance by private subscribers, who are named at the bottom of the illustrations throughout the book.

1697
London
Book
H. 455 mm | D. 60 mm
Royal Collection Trust
RCIN 1054105

poetry which the world has ever seen' – though not all of Pope's contemporaries shared this view. Classics scholar Richard Bentley complained: 'It is a pretty poem, Mr Pope, but you must not call it Homer.'[38]

Virgil had never disappeared from medieval Europe the way Homer (and the Greek language) had, and, consequently, translations of his works into English are earlier. In fact, William Caxton can in a way be credited with the earliest translation of the *Aeneid*, in his *Eneydos* of 1490, though this was actually a translation of a French version of the work. Gavin Douglas in 1513 translated the *Aeneid* into a Scots dialect of English, while the English translation by Thomas Phaer, unfinished on his death, was completed by Thomas Twyne and published in 1573. Henry Howard, Earl of Surrey, deserves mention because although he translated only Books 2 and 4 and not the whole *Aeneid*, he was the first writer in English to use blank verse (unrhymed iambic pentameters) and thus introduced a whole new world for English poetry. He probably worked on his translation when he was confined at Windsor Castle between 1537 and 1539, having become entangled in the politics of the court of Henry VIII, but it was not published until 1547, ten years after he was executed.[39]

The first English translation of the *Aeneid* that was truly a landmark was that of John Dryden (1631–1700), which was published in 1697 (Fig. 196). Dryden was the pre-eminent literary figure of Restoration England, known for his stage plays, poetry and translations. He explained something of his approach to translation in the Dedication to the first edition of his *Aeneid*, saying that he had made additions and changes to the Latin text as he saw fit, but that these were always done very thoughtfully and with immense respect for Virgil. He therefore hoped they would seem 'not stuck into him, but growing out of him'. Dryden's translation stood at the beginning of an ever-proliferating number of renderings of Virgil into English.

The rediscovery of Greece in the Age of Enlightenment

With the eighteenth century, the traditional focus on Rome shifted further eastward, towards Greece. For the likes of Byron or Shelley, Goethe or Schiller, ancient Greek culture embodied the immortal values and ideals of freedom, truth and friendship.[40] Such ideals became a potent force in the Age of Enlightenment, a time that saw revolution first in America and then France, and would have particular resonance during Greece's own War of Independence from 1821 to 1832. It was in the Classics, notably the works of Homer, by now translated into all major European languages, that European thinkers found these ideals most profoundly expressed.

The new enthusiasm for the world of ancient Greece can be charted in the steep increase in the popularity of Greek myth, poetry, architecture and the visual arts. The German art historian Johann Joachim Winckelmann (1717–1768) was the towering influence behind the rise of the neoclassical movement in art in the late eighteenth century.[41] In his influential *Geschichte der Kunst des Altertums* (History of Ancient Art), published in 1764 and widely read throughout Europe, he classified ancient works and tried systematically to distinguish Roman from Greek ones, based on close observation. Above all, he felt the goal of art was beauty, and that artists could achieve this by imitating Greek art – not in the sense of slavishly copying it, but in following the Greek approach of selecting from nature to create the ideal form. For the first time, the story of Troy self-consciously became 'ancient' and 'other', at least in visual terms, rather than being instinctively translated into a contemporary visual idiom.

BELOW
Fig. 197*
The Heads of the Seven Main Heroes of the Iliad
The engraving shows, from left to right: Menelaus, Paris, Diomedes, Odysseus, Nestor, Achilles and Agamemnon.

c. 1796
Johann Heinrich Wilhelm Tischbein
Etching and engraving
H. 260 mm | W. 465 mm
British Museum
1873,0809.150

OPPOSITE ABOVE
Fig. 198*
Head of Odysseus

Roman, late 1st to early 2nd century AD
Marble
H. 495 mm | W. 220 mm
Musée d'Art Classique de Mougins
MMoCA176

OPPOSITE BELOW
Fig. 199*
A Wedgwood plaque showing King Priam begging Achilles for the return of Hector's body

c. 1788–1800
Josiah Wedgwood & Sons; designed by Camillo Pacetti
Ceramic, Jasper ware
H. 158 mm | W. 386 mm
British Museum
1909,1201.206

Artists could find inspiration in books such as the *Tableaux tirés de l'Iliade, de l'Odyssée d'Homère, et de l'Eneide de Virgile*, published in 1757 by the Comte de Caylus (1692–1765).[42] This series of text vignettes drawn from the *Iliad*, *Odyssey* and *Aeneid* was specifically designed to serve as a model for artists. Visual references were available in the collections of antiquities formed by wealthy individuals, often with diplomatic positions in Mediterranean lands, and soon also in public museums such as the British Museum, founded in 1753. Sculpture collections in particular flourished, with statues or busts much in demand for gardens, libraries or mantlepieces in the houses of the social elite in Britain and elsewhere.[43] In addition to the frequently chosen Roman emperors and Greek philosophers there were also the great heroes of Troy. A print by the artist Johann Heinrich Wilhelm Tischbein (1751–1829), a German painter and friend of Goethe, strikingly lines them up in profile (Fig. 197). The head of Odysseus, wearing his characteristic *pilos*, a conical hat, was based on a Roman 'portrait' of the hero then in a private collection in Rome (Fig. 198).[44]

The most influential British artist to heed Winckelmann's advice to imitate the Greeks was sculptor and draughtsman John Flaxman (1755–1826).[45] Flaxman travelled to Rome in 1787, where he began to make drawings for the line engravings illustrating the works of Homer that would establish him as a leading exponent of neoclassical art and gain him considerable fame. His drawings, which have great clarity of form and purity of line, are not copies. Rather, following Winckelmann's ideas, they are original creations using the ancient visual language. Later in life, back in London, he worked on designs for *The Shield of Achilles* between 1810 and 1817, a work widely considered a masterpiece (see Epilogue). He achieved his broadest appeal, however, early on in his career, when he worked for the pottery manufacturer Josiah Wedgwood. He and other artists, including Camillo Pacetti, designed and modelled reliefs on classical themes to serve as decoration for fine tablewares and architectural interiors, which were popular with a wide clientele (Fig. 199, and see also p. 245).

In the first half of the nineteenth century the works of neoclassical sculptors, frequently featuring Homeric subjects, were in high demand for public and civic display, often with

LEFT
Fig. 200
A View in Hyde Park
The Duke of Wellington
rides past the statue of
Achilles dedicated to him.
Richard Westmacott's
statue originally caused
outrage because of its
nudity and a fig leaf was
subsequently added.

1852
John Harris the Younger,
after Henry de Daubrawa
Etching and aquatint with
hand-colouring
H. 388 mm | W. 426 mm
British Museum
1880,1113.1895

the idea of promoting patriotic heroism.[46] Antonio Canova (1757–1822), by 1800 a highly renowned sculptor, created statues of Greek and Trojan heroes, including his famous Hector (see also p. 262), while Richard Westmacott (1775–1856), whom Canova both influenced and helped, created an Achilles in 1822 that now stands at Hyde Park Corner in commemoration of the Duke of Wellington's victory over Napoleon (Fig. 200).[47] The statue is based on the two ancient Roman 'Horse Tamer' statues on Rome's Quirinal Hill.

Between romance and history: Troy in the nineteenth century

The pursuit of beauty and heroism in an ideal human form was not the only inspiration that artists and writers of the eighteenth and early nineteenth centuries drew from the Greek world. Increasing emphasis was placed on the humanity of the ancients and their perceived 'natural nobility'. They were felt to have lived in a simpler time, one of true feelings and their pure expression. This Romantic view found much to respond to particularly in the range of emotions evident in Homer's texts. In 1800, for example, Goethe set the grouping of Hector and Andromache as a subject for an artists' competition.[48]

Among the many versions of the Troy story in romantic poetry, one of the best-known is 'Ulysses' by Alfred, Lord Tennyson (1809–1892), published in 1842. Taking as its theme the archetype of Odysseus as the perennial traveller, the last line of the poem, 'To strive, to seek, to find and not to yield', can be seen as a rallying-cry for Victorian values in a time of empire and exploration. Poetics, history and politics, of course, were often intertwined. In particular the notion of the Trojan War as a 'battle of civilizations' that pitched Europe against the 'East' and that harked back to Classical Greek ideas remained a prominent

undercurrent. Thus British politician and scholar William Gladstone (1809–1898) saw
in the Trojan War, as in the medieval Crusades (and indeed the conflicts of his own times),
a recurrent theme of the West pursuing 'the recovery of that which the East had
unrighteously acquired', each time proving the 'superior prowess of the former'.[49]

Not all engagements with the Troy story were so serious, as can be seen in a poster
advertising an equine spectacle at Astley's Amphitheatre in London in April 1833 (Fig. 201).
Philip Astley (1742–1814) is regarded as the father of modern circus and was the first to
adopt the circular riding arena that would become established as the circus ring. After his
death, Astley's Amphitheatre continued to specialize in shows based around horses and
trick riding, so it is not surprising to find the Trojan Horse featuring on the programme.
This example was among the earliest pictorial posters illustrated with large woodcut
images. They were either positioned in prominent locations or drawn through the streets
on carts. To advertise this performance 'The Giant Horse of Sinon' is shown at an
extraordinary scale compared with the Greek warrior climbing on to its hoof.[50]

As in earlier periods, operas were also inspired by Trojan themes. Nineteenth-century
France would see the production of two operas based on myths associated with Troy.
The first was *Les Troyens* (The Trojans) by Hector Berlioz (1803–1869), conceived on so
grand a scale that theatres struggled to achieve a complete performance of it.[51] Singers
were daunted by the demands it made; it had an unusual number of soloists and also
required a huge orchestra of about eighty players, a chorus one hundred strong, a
children's chorus, dancers and all kinds of extras. Further resources were needed to
realize its elaborate stage settings, including a Trojan Horse (Fig. 202). It is perhaps
understandable that its premiere in Paris in 1863 included only three of the five acts.

LEFT
Fig. 203*
Set model for a
staging of *Helen!*
at the Adelphi
Theatre, London

1932
Oliver Hilary Sambourne
Messel
Wood, fabric, paper
and paint
H. 715 mm | W. 635 mm |
D. 580 mm
Victoria and Albert
Museum
E.184-1934

OPPOSITE ABOVE
Fig. 204
A Reading from
Homer
Homer's name, written
in Greek, is just visible
at the top right corner,
engraved in the marble
back of the chair on
which the reader, unfolding
a scroll, is seated.

1885
Lawrence Alma-Tadema
Oil on canvas
H. 91.8 cm | W. 183.5 cm
Philadelphia Museum of
Art
E1924-4-1

OPPOSITE BELOW
Fig. 205
Captive Andromache

c. 1888
Frederic Leighton
Oil on canvas
H. 197 cm | W. 407 cm
Manchester Art Gallery
1889.2

Berlioz had long admired the *Aeneid*, and based the opera on two episodes from Books 2 and 4. Cassandra becomes the heroine of the first part, given a love story in Berlioz' libretto, and ultimately dies by her own hand. The second part of the opera faithfully follows Virgil's account of the ill-fated love affair between Dido and Aeneas, again ending with the self-destruction of the heroine.

There could be no greater contrast with this than the comic opera that premiered in the same city the following year, in 1864. This was *La Belle Hélène* (The Beautiful Helen) by Jacques Offenbach (1819–1880), a light-hearted work set in an improbable ancient Greece and filled with frivolous humour. The plot scarcely stands up to detailed scrutiny, but essentially tells of Helen's elopement with Paris. Here the prophet Calchas becomes a comedy high priest, much fun is poked at the idiotic duo formed by the greater and the lesser Ajax, and Helen blames Menelaus for his lack of tact in discovering her and Paris in each other's arms. The operetta was an instant success and has remained a firm favourite ever since. An English-language production, retitled *Helen!*, was shown at the Adelphi Theatre in London in 1932. The sets and costumes were designed by Oliver Messel (Fig. 203) and were startlingly innovative in their use of the colour white, which had not previously been deployed in the theatre and gave this production an exciting and fresh feeling that audiences loved.[52]

Colourful historical or mythical narrative and genre scenes were a particular favourite of Victorian artists and their clientele.[53] Lawrence Alma-Tadema (1836–1912) in 1885 beautifully captured the popular appeal of Homer's poems in the enraptured and diverse ancient audience he presented in his *A Reading from Homer* (Fig. 204).[54] Paintings were often executed on an impressively large scale. *Captive Andromache* by Frederic Leighton (1830–1896), painted around 1888, is more than 4 metres (13 feet) in width (Fig. 205).[55] It nonetheless remains an intimate portrait of Andromache, enslaved and draped in black, a figure filled with pathos as she waits to fill her jar with water at the fountain. The foreground figures of a man, a woman and a little boy in a happy family group heart-wrenchingly invoke all that she has lost.

The Pre-Raphaelites saw the tale of Troy through their characteristically medieval lens, offering quite a different response to the pressures of industrialized urban life from mainstream nineteenth-century romanticism and historicism. The women of the story, from Helen to Circe, were their particular concern. In 1858 William Morris (1834–1896) wrote a long poem, 'Scenes from the Fall of Troy', that he based on Benoît (see p. 192) and medieval romances, and in which the love between Paris and Helen takes centre stage. Destined to be retrieved by her husband against her will at the poem's end, Helen paints a bleak picture of a war that knows no victors:

> I shudder when I think of those fell men
> Who stand around about Troy Town
> And every night wipe the rust off their spears …
> They know themselves to be but ruined men
> Whatever happens – Doubt not they will win
> Their dreadful slow revenge at last, Paris

BELOW LEFT
Fig. 206*
Britannia between Scylla and Charybdis
Here, Odysseus' encounter with Scylla and Charybdis is transformed into political criticism. Britain is shown caught between the 'rock of democracy' and the 'whirlpool of arbitrary power'.

8 April 1793
James Gillray; published by Hannah Humphrey
Satirical print; hand-coloured etching
H. 296 mm | W. 359 mm
British Museum
1868,0808.6288

BELOW RIGHT
Fig. 207
Le baptême d'Achille
Baby Achilles cries as a crayfish pinches his nose.

1842
Honoré Daumier; printed by Aubert & Cie; published by Bauger et Cie in *Le Charivari*
Lithograph
H. 249 mm | W. 194 mm
British Museum
1918,0511.165

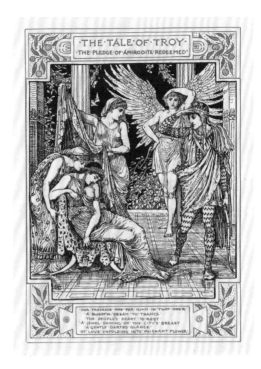

Fig. 208*
Echoes of Hellas:
The Tale of Troy

Helen, collapsed on a
chair as Paris approaches,
wears a copy of the
golden diadem excavated
by Schliemann at Troy;
Paris is dressed in the
patterned garb typical
of 'Easterners' in the arts
of classical Greece.

1887
George C. Warr;
illustrations by Walter
Crane
Printed book with
lithographic illustrations
H. 378 mm | W. 292 mm
British Museum

Yet another, different perspective on the story emerges in political and social satire. During the second half of the eighteenth century, caricaturists such as James Gillray (1756–1815) utilized classical, and sometimes Homeric, motifs to create biting satirical images that mocked the political elite who were so well versed in those stories (Fig. 206).[56] In France, in the work of Honoré Daumier (1808–1879), the classical itself became the target. Daumier produced fifty satirical prints in a series called *Histoire ancienne* in 1841–43, seventeen of which satirized the *Iliad* and the *Odyssey*. Reacting against neoclassical sculpture and what he saw as the limitations of its white marble perfection, Daumier shows mythological figures with caricatured features and the dress and manners of the French bourgeoisie (Fig. 207).[57] This spirit of broad humour also permeates the doggerel verse that captions the images, often in the form of a comic 'translation' of Homer.

Underlying the artistic and poetic engagement with the Classics in the nineteenth century was a growing understanding of, and wider fascination with, antiquity: an immense leap of knowledge, driven by popular interest and fuelled by economic growth. The study of the Classics became firmly embedded in middle-class education, while archaeology was developing as a discipline. All this also transformed the way Troy was viewed.[58] From antiquity on, the Trojan War had more or less been regarded as a historical fact. As we have seen (p. 132), however, doubters became more vocal through the eighteenth century into the nineteenth century, and controversy raged. By the time George Grote (1794–1871) wrote his great *History of Greece* in twelve volumes, published between 1846 and 1856, many arguments on both sides of the question had been advanced and then refuted and much ink spilled to little effect. Small wonder, then, that when Grote surveyed the literature, both ancient and modern, he took the entirely rational and pragmatic decision that continuously recorded Greek history could at most extend back to 776 BC, the year given by ancient sources for the first Olympic festival and the beginning of the dating system that the ancient Greek world used. Prior to that, all was too vague for inclusion: he described the tales told of earlier events as belonging to 'a past which never was present – a region essentially mythical, neither approachable by the critic nor measurable by the chronologer'.[59]

The latter part of the nineteenth century, though, saw the 'coming of age' of archaeology, and the establishment of major archaeological campaigns in Greece and the Middle East. It was not long after Grote's pronouncement that Schliemann began excavating Troy, and a whole new type of evidence was brought into play. A small but early example of its impact on the arts is the performance, staged in 1883 in a private house in London, of a series of artistic tableaux telling the story of Troy with words and music. The scenery was modelled on the plain of Troy, and Helen wore a copy of the diadem found by Schliemann, part of the 'Jewels of Helen' (Fig. 208). Professor George C. Warr was the main author, but he worked with distinguished collaborators including British painters Frederic Leighton, G. F. Watts and Edward Poynter, as well as the British Museum's then Keeper of Greek and Roman Antiquities, Charles Newton.[60]

Troy in the twentieth and twenty-first centuries

By the twentieth century, the role of classical culture as setting a moral standard had been broken. With the advent of modernism, the quest for ideal beauty lost its hold, while the trauma of modern warfare would soon transform notions of heroism. Homeric themes no longer appealed in the same way. In addition, the discovery of historical Troy introduced a new complexity – a dilemma of how to reconcile 'myth' with 'reality', as well as a change

LEFT
Fig. 209*
Troops Landing on C Beach, Suvla Bay, Later in the Day, 7th August 1915

1915
Norman Wilkinson
Oil on canvas
H. 609 mm | W. 914 mm
Imperial War Museum
Art.IWM ART 2452

BELOW
Fig. 210
Identification Disk
The soldier, carrying an upside-down rifle and wearing an identity disc around his neck, has his missing left leg replaced with an angled stump. The image recalls mutilated soldiers returning from war but also ancient statues with missing limbs propped up in museums.

20 November 1957
Sidney Nolan
Coloured crayon with textile dye on coated paper
l l. 304 mm | W. 254 mm
Australian War Memorial
ART91209

of focus in questions of national identity away from mythical genealogies and on to archaeological remains.[61] Despite all this, engagement with the timeless Trojan story continued unabated as novel ways of looking at it began to spring up.[62] In the modern, post-Freudian world a new emphasis was placed on the individual, on identity and on the personal quest – hence the popularity of Odysseus as a subject. Thinking about the Trojans raised existential questions about human tenacity and futile endeavours, as expressed in the 1905 poem 'Trojans' by Alexandrian Greek poet Constantine Cavafy (1863–1933):

> Our efforts are those of ill-fated men;
> our efforts are like those of the Trojans.[63]

But the mirror of Troy also reflected more specific contemporary historical turbulence: political repression and social unease, gender inequality and racism, displacement and war. In a century that saw two devastating world wars and countless other conflicts, it is not surprising that it was such themes in particular that took centre stage.[64] With the ancient site of Troy now placed firmly on the map, Homer was very much in the minds of the public-school educated British officers sailing towards Gallipoli in the First World War (see also p. 253). En route to battle, Rupert Brooke (1887–1915) scribbled fragments of poetry including:[65]

> And Priam and his fifty sons
> Wake all amazed, and hear the guns,
> And shake for Troy again.[66]

The horrors of the War, however, confronted high ideals of heroism with brutal reality. Homer's visceral descriptions of the deaths of heroes, with their details of blood and gore, torn bodies and bubbling breaths, became all too real (Fig. 209). Awareness of reliving an

ancient mythical conflict was rife not just among the British, but also among Australians and New Zealanders, French, Germans and Turks, on both sides of the battle lines. We see this expressed even long after the event in the *Gallipoli* series by Australian artist Sidney Nolan (1917–1992), which explores the connections between Gallipoli and the story of Troy, inspired in part by his reading of Homer (Fig. 210).[67]

Among those who served at Gallipoli was the young French author and playwright Jean Giraudoux (1882–1944). Severely wounded at Suvla Bay, he was deeply affected by the carnage he witnessed and went on to write *La Guerre de Troie n'aura pas lieu* (The Trojan War Will Not Take Place). This anti-war play, first performed in Paris in 1935, when the Second World War was a dire probablility, is set in Troy on the day before the war begins. Hector tries desperately to persuade the Trojans that Paris should return Helen and war should be avoided. But too many Trojans want to fight for glory. The play lost nothing of its power in the latter half of the twentieth century, its performances still lending a voice to protests against the Vietnam War in the 1970s, the Falklands War in the 1980s and the 1990s Balkan conflicts.[68]

Countless other works of fiction and poetry, and studies of history or psychology have used the Trojan War as a universal parable to question the reasoning behind war and highlight its consequences. The poet and diplomat George Seferis (1900–1971), a Greek exile from Anatolia who lived through the two world wars, perhaps sums up despair at war's futility most concisely in his poem 'Helen' of 1953:

> so much suffering, so much life
> went into the abyss
> all for an empty tunic, all for a Helen.[69]

Christopher Logue's *War Music*, an English translation of part of the *Iliad* published in five volumes from 1959, is a vivid modernist poem that he preferred to call 'an account' of Homer's *Iliad*. Although initially reluctant to take on the commission from BBC radio because he did not know ancient Greek, Logue made the poem his life's work and it remained unfinished at his death in 2011.[70] It ends at the point when Achilles, grieving for the dead Patroclus, hurls himself back into the battle in a vengeful fury. Logue adopts a filmic point of view that echoes the effect already apparent in Homer, with the action seen both from a wide, aerial view and then zooming in on individual conflict. His swift lines essentially force the reader to experience war at first hand, and his use of striking anachronisms and modern, casual language makes the Trojan War contemporary. Indeed it becomes all wars at all times, in a grim and inevitable progression that will see no end.

> And here it comes:
> That unpremeditated joy as you
> — The Uzi shuddering warm against your hip
> Happy in danger in a dangerous place
> Yourself another self you found at Troy —
> Squeeze nickel through that rush of Greekoid scum![71]

That the tragedy of war is first and foremost an individual tragedy is beautifully captured in Alice Oswald's 2011 poem, *Memorial*. It begins with a list, in capital letters, of the names of all two hundred heroes mentioned by Homer as dying at Troy. The effect is that of

names carved on a war memorial. The second part of the poem then sketches in something of their individual histories and personalities. Powerful personal connections are made also in Ellen McLaughlin's 2008 play *Ajax in Iraq* about the experiences of modern female American soldiers in Iraq, and in Michael Hughes' novel *Country* (2018) which relocates the story of the *Iliad* to Northern Ireland.[72]

A recent production by a group of Syrian women refugees of a version of Euripides' *The Trojan Women*, a tragedy first performed in Athens in 415 BC, shows how the story resonates with the experience of civilians as well as soldiers in times of war (Fig. 211). In Euripides' play, the women of Troy, defeated and powerless, await their fate at the hands of the Greeks, who are mostly an off-stage presence; the tragedy is unusual in its female focus. The Trojan queen Hecuba, whom we first meet prostrated by grief, is the central character, though she is joined by her daughter Cassandra and daughter-in-law Andromache. The play delivers blow after miserable blow. Not only are the women facing their individual humiliations at the hands of the brutal Greeks, but they are faced, too, with the terrible fate of Astyanax, which is a central part of the drama. The baby son of Hector and Andromache is torn from his mother's arms and murdered, and his body is then returned to the women on his father's shield. As they mourn, the women learn that the city of Troy itself is being torn down. They suffer the annihilation of their whole world, both place and people, and they are left with no hope, only the prospect of endurance and bitter survival. The Syrian women had never acted before, but their performances in their version of the play, *Queens of Syria*, were powerful, and deeply informed by their own experiences (see p. 13). In speaking of the

(see p. 13)

ABOVE
Fig. 211*
Queens of Syria
The play by women refugees from Syria interweaves elements of Euripides' *The Trojan Women* with testimonies of the women's own experiences.

Trojan Woman Project, UK
Still from a 2016 Developing Artists/ Refuge Productions/ Young Vic production, staged at the Young Vic, London, directed by Zoe Lafferty, costumes by Farah Karouta, lighting by Howard Hudson
Film director/ cinematographer: Charlotte Ginsborg

production, they explained their desire to find a voice to articulate the pain of those who are powerless against the effects of brutal human conflict – and their hope that the world would listen.[73]

The fact that many of these recent engagements with the story of Troy involve women is hardly coincidence. It highlights another trend of the last decades: the female appropriation of the story of Troy, which can be witnessed both in creative and scholarly works. An early example is *Cassandra*, a dramatic monologue written by East German author Christa Wolf in 1983, narrated from the perspective of a figure who is marginalized both because she is a woman and because, as a prophetess, she pronounces unwelcome truths (though she is fated not to be believed). Written at the height of the Cold War, the work casts a wide social and political net as it paints a picture of a male-dominated society that distorts truth and suppresses and violates women, while blindly heading towards self-destruction.[74] More recently, Margaret Atwood's 2005 novel *The Penelopiad* (see below, p. 224), Colm Tóibín's *House of Names* (2016), Madeline Miller's *Circe* (2018), Pat Barker's *The Silence of the Girls* (2018) and Natalie Haynes' *A Thousand Ships* (2019) are all works in which women in the story are given the role of narrators. Other 'outsiders', such as the figure of Philoctetes, have been used to give a voice to those stigmatized on grounds of illness.[75]

Modern works open up new perspectives which also affect our reading of the ancient works on which they draw. Not surprisingly, perhaps, topics of gender, violence and rape have begun to be given due weight in the curriculum of classical scholarship, as have serious considerations of issues of racism, class conflict or political propaganda.[76] The concept of 'the hero' is challenged, and classical archetypes are no longer given unquestioning respect. This does not mean, however, that we no longer need heroes, or rather, characters we can identify with: we have merely discovered new heroes for a new age. Ultimately what matters to any audience is that they can see themselves in the story, whether they battle alongside Brad Pitt's Achilles, are mesmerised with Doctor Faustus by the beauty of Elizabeth Taylor's Helen (see Fig. 215), set off with Kirk Douglas' Odysseus for adventures on the high seas, or feel the plight of the war victims with the *Queens of Syria*. The heroes and heroines of the Troy story are its heart.

TROY IN FILM AND POPULAR CULTURE

In modern times, the Trojan War myth remains a hugely popular theme and its global reach is demonstrated by its appearance in art forms such as Japanese manga. In these graphic novels, the ancient story can be depicted in a heady mix of international comic-strip conventions, elements of archaeology and Japanese traditions of depicting, for example, mythical creatures (Figs 212, 213).[77] Nowhere does its appeal show more strongly, however, than in globally successful Hollywood movies. Films about Troy go back to the very beginnings of the medium.[78] Several early French and Italian films made between 1905 and 1911 cover the adventures of Odysseus, including an ambitious, 45-minute-long rendering of the entire *Odyssey*. The first significant film on the Trojan War, 35 minutes long, was the Italian *La Caduta di Troia* (The Fall of Troy) of 1911. This silent film included early use of photography to allow Aphrodite's veil to conceal Paris and Helen's embrace and a remarkable sequence in which the lovers are wafted from Sparta to Troy on a giant shell. The wooden horse is impressive, though suspiciously two-dimensional, and flame effects are put to good use as Troy burns.

In 1924, German film director Manfred Noa (1893–1930) made *Helena*, a silent movie in two parts (Fig. 214). This astonishing film deserves to be better-known: conceived on an extraordinarily grand scale, it involved huge sets and an enormous cast, and largely fulfilled the promise of its truly heroic ambition. It was not a commercial success, however, and fell into obscurity partly because it was overshadowed by other products of the golden age of German silent film production. A recently rediscovered and restored copy runs for nearly four hours and still has considerable power. The visual world of Noa's film interestingly adopts elements from the Bronze Age archaeology of Mycenae, particularly the Lion Gate, and from Knossos on Crete. The costumes make use of Aegean-looking decorative motifs, and the jewellery nods vaguely towards Schliemann's discoveries at Troy.

BELOW
Figs 212*, 213*
The story of Troy in Japanese manga
The cover of one graphic novel (left) shows Helen against a backdrop of Bronze Age and classical Greek buildings and beside the wooden horse that today stands at Hissarlik. Another novel illustrates the episode of Odysseus caught between Scylla and Charybdis.

Cover of *Trojan Horse: The Greek Myths 7* and inside pages of *Voyage of Odysseus: The Greek Myths 8*
2004
Tokyo; Satonaka Machiko; Chūōkōron-shinsha Inc.
Books
H. 150 mm | W. 105 mm
British Museum

It was of course the discoveries of Schliemann at Troy and Mycenae in the late nineteenth century, and the results of excavations in Greece and Crete as the twentieth century progressed, that made such borrowing possible, and that encouraged retellings of the myth to be held up to scrutiny against some understanding of ancient reality. Excavations at the site of Troy had revealed the strongly sloping walls with square bastions that protected the Late Bronze Age city, and Troy's walls on film always to a greater or lesser extent resemble these, but the site did not offer much evidence for the built environment inside the citadel. This gap was filled by the remains of the Minoan palace of Knossos, restored to great dramatic effect with downward-tapering red-painted columns, which could scarcely fail to appeal to set designers; if historical justification were needed, the links between Crete and Troy in the Bronze Age could be invoked. The use of ancient, particularly Minoan Cretan, architectural styles to build Troy in films is a persistent trope, found in both Robert Wise's *Helen of Troy* in 1956 and Wolfgang Petersen's *Troy* of 2004. Another challenge for directors has been casting; notably for the role of beautiful Helen. The choices made reveal much about contemporary notions of beauty (Fig. 215).

The debates such films engender regarding their archaeological accuracy are testimony to today's popular quest for historical truth even in a quintessentially fictional medium. An example of an explicitly 'historical' rendering of the story is American graphic artist Eric Shanower's painstakingly researched Age of Bronze series, based only on prehistoric artefacts. It was created by the artist to demonstrate that the stories of Troy can be told in full and with all dramatic effect, within a coherent and chronologically plausible visual setting.[79]

JOURNEYS: ODYSSEUS AND AENEAS

The ten-years war is finished.
Helen's hair, a grey cloud.
Troy, a white ashpit
by the drizzling sea.
Derek Walcott, 'Map of the New World'[80]

For James Joyce, there was but one hero worth writing about: 'After Troy there is no further talk of Achilles, Menelaus, Agamemnon. Only one man is not done with; his heroic career has hardly begun: Ulysses.'[81] Joyce (1882–1941) was right, up to a point. There is one other hero, not a Greek but a Trojan, whose story, too, only begins once the war ends: Aeneas. But by the time Joyce was writing, Trojan Aeneas was no longer at the forefront of everyone's minds, the way he had been for centuries past. It was a Greek who had become the hero of the modern age, the hero who, for Joyce, was 'the most human in world literature'.[82]

From one perspective, Odysseus and Aeneas could not be more different: one Greek, one Trojan, they fought on opposite sides. One is the victor who helped destroy a city and now returns to his home and family. The other is the defeated, who has lost virtually

LEFT
Fig. 216
***Odysseus und Nausikaa* (Odysseus and Nausicaa)**

1918
Lovis Corinth
Lithograph
H. 375 mm | W. 500 mm
British Museum
1920,0712.109

everything and becomes a refugee. Yet now the war is over they share a parallel fate, each experiencing a long, difficult journey to reach their destination, where further trials await before peace and prosperity are theirs once more.

The two journeys were immortalized in two great epics: Homer's *Odyssey* and Virgil's *Aeneid*. Odysseus' journey is one of endurance: after ten years of war it will be another ten years before he finally reaches home. It is a tale of adventure, but also of longing, loss and hardship, as he is the only one of his comrades to survive; a restless, complicated man, he is unable, perhaps, ever to settle again. Aeneas' journey is that of a refugee who needs to find a new home, a new identity. It is also the tale of a virtuous hero on a divinely ordained mission of foundation. In many ways, their fortunes run counter to expectations. It is Odysseus who sets out as a king and returns as a beggar, lacking even clothes, as in the lithograph by Lovis Corinth (1858–1925) of a shipwrecked Odysseus startling the princess Nausicaa (Fig. 216). Aeneas, in contrast, appears like a king already in his new home in Italy in the painting by Claude Lorrain (1600 or 1604/5–1682), *The Arrival of Aeneas at Pallanteum* (Fig. 217). The background architecture foreshadows the city he is later to help found on the banks of the River Tiber: Rome.[83]

Both heroes and their fates have spoken to people across millennia, offering blueprints to all those who journey, whether to escape, to explore, to discover or to conquer.

New horizons and old empires

Speak no more about the wise Greek and the Trojan,
And the great sea voyages they made;
Enough of Alexander and Trajan
And of the fame of their victories;
I sing of the illustrious Portuguese
Whom both Neptune and Mars obeyed.
Luís Vaz de Camões, *Lusiads* Canto 1.3[84]

The Classics were never far from the minds of the early European explorers and colonizers as they sailed to far-flung destinations. When in 1768 Louis Antoine de Bougainville (1729–1811) reached Tahiti, it seemed to him a Garden of Eden ruled by the goddess Venus, where Tahitian beauties received French sailors just as the mythical Carthaginian queen Dido had once received Aeneas.[85] Like Odysseus, early travellers were not sure what awaited them in strange lands. Beyond the borders of the known world anything seemed possible. People with unfamiliar ways, not to mention the dangers of the natural world, were easily interpreted as inhuman or supernatural, and reassurance was sought by linking them with classical travellers' tales.[86] Often the voice of colonial superiority was unmistakable.

BELOW
Fig. 218
Dido and Aeneas
Dido and Aeneas stand towards the right, separate from their large hunting party. The imaginary buildings of Carthage rise in the background.

Exhibited 1814
J. M. W. Turner
Oil on canvas
H. 146 cm | W. 237.2 cm
Tate
N00494

In his epic *Columbeis* of 1585/9, the poet Giulio Cesare Stella (1564–1624) mapped the *Aeneid* on to the travels of Christopher Columbus, who is seen as bringing civilization and Christianity to the 'New World' in the same way that Aeneas had brought his virtues and the gods of his Trojan homeland to Italy. A decade earlier, in 1572, Luís Vaz de Camões (*c.*1524/5–1580) drew on both the *Aeneid* and the *Odyssey* when composing the Portuguese national epic *Os Lusíadas* (*Lusiads*) to celebrate the Portuguese as a nation of seafarers. The *Aeneid* played a special role also in the history of the United States. While seventeenth-century Protestant settlers in North America saw their experiences as the 'chosen people' fighting native resistance reflected in Virgilian and biblical narrative, Joel Barlow's (1754–1812) North American take on the *Aeneid*, the *Columbiad* (1807), discovers the rather different ideals of the Enlightenment in the same poem, making it a call for peace and harmony among races.[87]

British artist J. M. W. Turner (1775–1851) used themes from the *Aeneid* in a dozen of his canvases, several of which focus on the episode of Aeneas' visit to the Carthaginian queen Dido. Their tragic love story had long captured artists' and audiences' hearts and imaginations.[88] As recounted in Virgil, after Dido seduces Aeneas, Hermes (Roman Mercury) has to be despatched by the gods to make him resume his divine mission; Aeneas sets sail without Dido's knowledge and Dido kills herself, abandoned and betrayed. The episode was popular with artists for the opportunities Dido's tragic fate offered for a heady mix of moral dilemma, emotional drama and erotic allure. Yet already in Roman times it also had political undertones, justifying Roman domination of North Africa, and Turner's paintings, too, are often seen as alluding to Britain's imperial might.

In his *Dido and Aeneas* (Fig. 218), the couple are standing together on a bridge as they gaze at the city of Carthage.[89] As so often in Turner's work, similar to that of Claude Lorrain, from whom Turner drew much inspiration, it is the landscape that takes centre stage. This is not North Africa, however, but the riverscape of the Thames near London. Turner drew inspiration from the Thames landscape for many of his paintings, including other scenes of Dido at Carthage, but also other mythical port scenes set in distant lands. Not too much should perhaps therefore be made of the fact that Carthage here appears to be set near Richmond Hill.[90] Elsewhere in Turner's work, however, a deeper symbolism clearly underpins his view of Carthage as a city doomed to be conquered and obliterated by its Mediterranean rival, Rome. Carthage's fate seems symbolic of the rise and fall of all empires, and thus arguably it is a portent of the eventual decline of Britain's imperial power.[91]

Aeneas the refugee

One difference in the way that Aeneas and Odysseus were conceived after antiquity was that while Odysseus was the archetypal traveller, Aeneas' importance lay more in his arrival:

> Arms and a man I sing, the first from Troy,
> A fated exile to Lavinian shores
> In Italy.
> *Aeneid*, 1.1–3

It was Aeneas' role as the ancestor of a new people that ultimately gave significance to his travels. As the mythical founding father of ancient Rome and much of medieval and

Renaissance Europe (see pp. 188–89), his image was that of a pious, brave and responsible hero. Long after any notions of the veracity of these stories had been abandoned, allusions to Aeneas as an illustrious ancestor remained popular among noble families. In Claude Lorrain's *The Arrival of Aeneas at Pallanteum* (above, Fig. 217), one of several paintings depicting scenes from the *Aeneid* painted by the artist in the final decade of his career, the scene is as described in Virgil's *Aeneid*, Book 8. Aeneas stands at the prow of his ship, offering an olive branch of peace to the local king, Evander, and his son, Pallas. A second ship flies a flag with the coat of arms of the venerable Roman Altieri family, who traced their lineage back to Aeneas and who commissioned the picture.[92]

It is hardly surprising that among the diverse episodes of Aeneas' adventures represented in art, especially between the Renaissance and the eighteenth century, the most popular was the one that reflected Aeneas' qualities most obviously: his flight from Troy.[93] It was the great Renaissance artist Raphael (1483–1520) who gave it its definitive form, in a fresco in the papal apartments in the Vatican. The *Fire in the Borgo* (Fig. 219) was executed between 1514 and 1517 by Raphael and his workshop for Pope Julius II and his successor Leo X. Part of a cycle of paintings depicting historical events, the image showed Pope Leo IV in 847 miraculously extinguishing a fire that threatened St Peter's by making the sign of the cross. Among the figures fleeing the fire, Raphael included a youthful male figure carrying an old man on his shoulders, accompanied by a young boy, clearly an allusion to Aeneas' flight from burning Troy with his father Anchises and his son Ascanius, as described in Virgil's *Aeneid* and depicted in Greek and Roman art (see p. 106, Fig. 22 and Fig. 87). Its implied message here is that just as Aeneas saved his family (and the Trojan ancestral gods) and founded Rome, so a succession of popes protected ancestral religion, the Christian congregation and the Church of Rome.[94]

Surprisingly, perhaps, there appears to have been little perceived conflict between the pagan story and its new Christian context. From at least the fifth century the Church

LEFT
Fig. 219
Fire in the Borgo
The figures in the bottom left corner allude to the group of Aeneas with his father and son as they flee burning Troy.

c. 1514–17
Raphael and Giulio Romano
Fresco from the 'Stanza dell'Incendio' (Hall of Fire)
W. 670 cm
Apostolic Palace, Vatican City

fathers had taken Aeneas as an allegory of a virtuous life and an exemplar of Christian duty and piety, *pietas*. It was a small step only to see him as the founder of a spiritual empire. Already Dante (1265–1321) in his *Divine Comedy* had alluded to Aeneas' flight as part of a divine plan to establish Rome as the centre of the Christian church, and in the seventeenth century Aeneas could still prefigure the pope in Pietro da Cortona's frescoes for Pope Innocent X in the Palazzo Pamphili in Rome (1651–54).[95]

Allegorical or political allusions were just one element in the popularity of classical motifs in Renaissance art. As mentioned above, another was the artistic appeal of the (nude) body as represented in ancient art. In his portrayal of the naked man climbing down the wall Raphael shows himself equal to his rival Michelangelo in depicting a heroic male nude in strenuous action, while in the Aeneas group he artfully combined varied expressions of fear, determination and hope with the three ages of man. Roman sarcophagi, with their multiple figures and vigorous battle scenes, were one of the main sources of inspiration for Renaissance artists. This is also evident in the dramatic image showing the battle for Troy made in the 1540s by Italian Mannerist Giorgio Ghisi (1520–1582), one of the foremost Italian engravers of his day, after designs by Giovanni Battista Scultori (Fig. 221).[96] Amidst the tumultuous melee outside the walls of Troy as the Greek warriors rush towards the opened gate, Aeneas succeeds in escaping unseen. He is helped by his mother, the goddess Venus, who floats above him, with Cupid beside her, shielding the hero with a large cloud. Unlike in Raphael's composition, here old Anchises descends from the wall, while Aeneas carries his son Ascanius, almost a baby. But what Ghisi's engraving shares with Raphael is a fascination with the human body and with the human drama the story offers, from the soldiers' brutality to the old man's anguish.

It was Raphael's rendering of the Aeneas group that proved the most influential in art. The colourful scene on a maiolica plate of 1531 clearly shows its debt (Fig. 220). It was painted by Francesco Xanto Avelli (*c.* 1487–*c.* 1542), one of the outstanding figures in the history of Renaissance maiolica, which was centred on Urbino in central Italy.[97] Maiolica was a revolutionary new form of ceramic that combined technical finesse with brightly coloured decoration often depicting historical narratives.[98] Made for an educated humanist clientele, much of the subject matter consisted of classical tales from ancient authors such as Livy, Ovid and Virgil, with occasional explanatory quotations on the back. In this case, the plate features a line based on the poem 'Triumph of Love' by Italian fourteenth-century poet and 'father of humanism' Petrarch: 'Quest è colui che piâse sotto Antandro' ('This is he who by Antandros wept'), a reference to Aeneas' mourning for his wife Creusa, lost in the flight from Troy.[99] Xanto's design was based on an engraving after Raphael's *Fire in the Borgo* that had reversed the direction the figures are facing. Such engravings after works of well-known painters were a common source of inspiration for maiolica designers.[100]

Raphael's Trojan trio remained an artistic touchstone for centuries to come, and well beyond Italy. An example is a colour woodcut created shortly before 1630 in Paris by German wood-engraver Ludolph Büsinck (1599/1602–1669), after a design by Georges Lallemand (Fig. 222).[101] The bold *chiaroscuro* image reveals the mental and physical strain on Aeneas as he presses on, leaving behind his burning home. On his back, his old father Anchises raises his hand in a gesture that appears to bless their journey and clutches the household gods that embody the family's past, as Ascanius, the family's future, charges forward. The boy's cheerful confidence betrays divine guidance, also suggested by the small dove, the sacred bird of Aphrodite/Venus, seated on his hand.[102] In the sixteenth and seventeenth centuries, paintings of blazing cities or villages on fire and other effects of light were seen as a

LEFT
Fig. 220*
Maiolica plate painted with an image of Aeneas fleeing Troy

1531
Urbino, Italy, Francesco
Xanto Avelli
Tin-glazed earthenware
Diam. 376 mm
British Museum
1855,1201.45

BELOW
Fig. 221*
The Fall of Troy as the Greeks rush in, while Aeneas, protected by Venus, escapes with Anchises and Ascanius

1540–50
Giorgio Ghisi, after
Giovanni Battista Scultori
Engraving
H. 225 mm | W. 350 mm
British Museum
1856,0712.1050

ABOVE LEFT
Fig. 222*
Aeneas Saving His Father Anchises from the Burning Troy

1620–40
Ludolph Büsinck, after
Georges Lallemand
Colour woodcut
H. 500 mm | W. 383 mm
British Museum
W,5.53

ABOVE RIGHT
Fig. 223*
Aeneas and His Family Fleeing Burning Troy

1654
Henry Gibbs
Oil on canvas
H. 155 cm | W. 159.8 cm
Tate
T06782

particular challenge for the expressive ability of artists, some of whom specialized in scenes such as the burning of Troy.[103] But an image's subject matter might also carry contemporary or personal meaning. Büsinck was working for a collector's market, and the composition and link to Raphael undoubtedly constituted the image's main appeal. Nonetheless, it was created during the time of the Thirty Years War (1618–48), which devastated whole regions in central Europe, costing the lives of some eight million people, and so could hardly have failed also to evoke contemporary tragedies.

In 1654 British artist Henry Gibbs (1631–1713) completed his painting *Aeneas and His Family Fleeing Burning Troy* (Fig. 223), featuring the now standard group of Aeneas, Anchises clutching the household gods, and Ascanius.[104] The burning city of Troy forms the background; the Trojan Horse still stands in the town's square, now emptied of its Greek warriors. What is unusual, however, is the inclusion of Aeneas' wife Creusa. In Virgil's text she follows at some distance and is eventually lost; though mourned, her disappearance is an essential prerequisite for Aeneas forming new alliances in his future home. In art she is represented only occasionally, seen falling behind or appearing to Aeneas as a ghost, absolving him from blame. Here, however, she occupies a prominent position, being pulled back by a Greek soldier who clasps his hand on her shoulder, a dramatic detail that is rare, if not unique, in representations of this scene.[105] Like other artists of the period, Gibbs drew on a variety of different sources when composing his painting, and for this particular detail used a sixteenth-century engraving by Jan Sadeler of a biblical episode in Genesis (6:5–7), titled *Wickedness and Violence on Earth*, a brutal image of murder, rape and destruction in war.[106] The subject of destruction and displacement would have been topical in Britain in the wake of the English Civil War, which resulted in exile for many, perhaps including Gibbs, about whom very little is known.

The role of Aeneas as a moral exemplar, a bringer of civilization and a founder of Europe and its empires overseas had ensured the Trojan hero's popularity until the eighteenth century.[107] The modern era was to recognize itself most readily in a different traveller: Greek Odysseus.

Odysseus: the first modern man?

> He extends a palm calloused by the ropes and the tiller, his
> skin weathered by the dry north wind, by heat and snow.
> It's as if he wants to expel from among us the superhuman
> one-eyed Cyclops, the Sirens who make you forget
> with their song, Scylla and Charybdis:
> so many complex monsters that prevent us from remembering
> that he too was a man. struggling in the world
> with soul and body.
> Georges Seferis, 'Reflections on a Foreign Line of Verse'[108]

Odysseus is perhaps the most complex and multifaceted of the Greek heroes who fought at Troy.[109] For French philosopher Simone Weil (1909–1943), the *Iliad* was a poem about force.[110] The *Odyssey*, in contrast, celebrates the triumph of the mind over force. Already in the Trojan War, Odysseus is the brains behind the operation: it is he who succeeds in enlisting Achilles, luring Iphigenia to Aulis and stealing the Palladium, and it is his idea to build the Trojan Horse and thus bring about the downfall of Troy. It is this craftiness that also, eventually, helps secure his return from ten years of adventures at sea, guided by Athena, goddess of wisdom and partial to cleverness.

Odysseus' adventures were among the first mythical stories to become popular in ancient art, during the period of early Greek expansion of trade and overseas settlement. He has remained the archetypal voyager over the centuries: a trickster and shape-shifter, a morally ambiguous hero, a man in search of himself, an eternal wanderer. Clever, cunning and eloquent, Odysseus had the sympathy of Homer and of many ancient philosophers. The *Odyssey* painted a favourable picture of him as a versatile yet steadfast survivor. The idea of him as the most human, most approachable of all Greek heroes, the one who is most like 'us', a 'common man', has echoed through centuries to the modern day, to the writings of James Joyce or Greek poet George Seferis (as in the quote above). Yet from the fifth century BC, and especially later, in Roman times, Odysseus was also reviled as a ruthless politician and heartless pragmatist, and it was the more straightforwardly brave warriors who made better role models for the young.[111] During the Middle Ages and Renaissance, Odysseus' perseverance was again emphasized, and he came to be admired as a paragon of Christian fortitude and constancy, along with his faithful wife Penelope. From the fifteenth century the story of Odysseus once more became popular in the visual arts. Just as centuries ago the houses of wealthy Romans featured paintings of Odysseus' adventures, these now decorated the walls of fifteenth- and sixteenth-century palaces and castles in Italy (see Fig. 7) or France, alongside similar cycles showing Aeneas' travels or the deeds of other heroes.[112] This was also the time when the travels of Odysseus and Aeneas gained new currency in the context of great sea voyages by European explorers.

Yet it is to the people of more recent times, the modern age, that Odysseus has perhaps spoken most forcefully. For German archaeologist Bernard Andreae, writing in 1982,[113] Odysseus represented the greatest gift of ancient Greek civilization to the world – the first self-determined human being, who is creative and ingenious in his attempts to outwit even the gods, a new hero for a new age. In this Andreae followed in the footsteps of the Romantic writers of the late eighteenth and early nineteenth centuries, such as Henry Nelson Coleridge, nephew of the poet Samuel Taylor Coleridge, who in 1830 professed his preference for Odysseus over Achilles, as Odysseus 'shines by his own light … demolishes all obstacles by his own arm and his own wit … has a passion, a vehement desire.… This brings him at once in contact with the common feelings of every man in the world.'[114]

But as Max Horkheimer and Theodor W. Adorno, German philosophers,[115] argued, there was also a problematic side to Odysseus' independence: by allowing rationality and the pursuit of personal gain to triumph over nature, modern man denies his own humanity. An illustration of just this opposition between man and nature can be seen in J. M. W. Turner's 1829 painting *Ulysses Deriding Polyphemus – Homer's Odyssey* (Fig. 224).[116] Polyphemus, the elemental force of nature, towers awe-inspiringly above the cliffs. Yet he is writhing with pain, defeated by Odysseus' cunning, the hero's prime skill as advertised also on his ship's flag. It shows the Trojan Horse, Odysseus most deceitful invention, which brought about the downfall of Troy. Odysseus' victory over Polyphemus may be read as an allegory for the relentless subjugation of nature by technology in the Industrial Revolution, which dominated Turner's own era as it does our own.

Modern artists have successfully teased out the complexity and ambiguity in Odysseus' character. In 1973 to 1975 British artist Elisabeth Frink (1930–1993), known for her

LEFT
Fig. 225*
Calypso
When published in an
edition by the Folio
Society in 1974, this work
was captioned 'For a long
time Odysseus was kept
under water.'

1973–74
Elisabeth Frink
Lithograph, part of the
series *The Odyssey*
H. 254 mm | W. 164 mm
Tate
P06193

sculptures, lithographs and etchings, created a series of book illustrations for both the *Iliad* and the *Odyssey*, drawing on elements from ancient and medieval art as well as her own reading of the myth.[117] One of her lithographs (Fig. 225), shows the hero shipwrecked upon leaving Calypso, swimming next to his boat, just before he is rescued by yet another sea goddess, Ino-Leucothea. The episode is not depicted in ancient art, but Frink's rendering draws on Italian Renaissance imagery of the same scene.[118] Odysseus here is a man marked by his experiences: his beard and long hair are unkempt, yet his strong, sinuous body still masters the blue Mediterranean seas. In Frink's illustration of the Cyclops episode (Fig. 226) we see Odysseus and his comrades clinging to the bellies of sheep to escape the giant's cave, just as in ancient Greek art (p. 113, Figs 95, 96). Behind them sits blinded Polyphemus, a dishevelled, oversized figure who faces the viewer in all his pained helplessness. Though monstrous in appearance, there is a vulnerability about his ugliness that contrasts with the slick beauty of Odysseus' comrades, with their picture-book 'heroic' nudity and 'Grecian' profiles; again, we wonder if he is not a victim who deserves our sympathies.[119]

It is another image by Frink, though, that provides the most food for thought (Fig. 227). According to the *Odyssey*, after his return to Ithaca and following the slaying of the suitors, Odysseus ordered the killing of twelve slave girls who had slept with them: like doves or

thrushes that had been trapped 'just so the girls, their heads all in a row were strung up with the noose around their necks to make their death an agony' (*Odyssey* 22.471–72). It is this haunting image that Frink, uniquely, chose to illustrate. The maids' dead bodies are lined up as if pegged on a washing line. The *Odyssey* (22.462–64) gives Telemachus' justification for the way the death sentence ordered by Odysseus has been carried out: the girls did not deserve a 'clean death', for they had brought shame on the family when they 'lay beside the suitors'.

The episode underlines the importance of honour in early Greek society, but has resonated with modern audiences as a surprisingly cruel act. In 2005, Margaret Atwood made Odysseus' wife Penelope and the twelve maids the central characters of her novella *The Penelopiad*, which exposes double standards in ancient Greece as much as in contemporary society.[120] Recalling modern victims of rape who are ostracized by their community, Atwood's maids are portrayed as enslaved women who had no choice: they are not traitors but innocent victims. Their fury at being condemned by a man who himself got away with dallying with 'every goddess, queen and bitch' now haunts Odysseus from beyond their graves as they decry the injustice of the harsh judgment of their lesser actions.[121]

Odysseys: migration and displacement

That sail which leans on light,
tired of islands,
a schooner beating up the Caribbean
for home, could be Odysseus,
home-bound on the Aegean.
Derek Walcott, 'Sea Grapes'[122]

The *Odyssey* is often seen as the ancestor of all road novels. Odysseus' travels take him to the ends of the world – and in fact beyond, as he descends into the Underworld to converse with the dead. Transgressing the physical boundaries of the world, he also transgresses the psychological boundaries of knowledge. Already Homer hints that a thirst for knowledge is his true siren call, and it is this that connects him with humans across time and place.[123]

Of course, Odysseus is neither the first nor the last intrepid sea-traveller to make his mark in world history.[124] Leaving home and returning, being waylaid by dangerous monsters or shipwreck, are the stock in trade of folk stories, from the 4,000-year-old Egyptian *Tale of the Shipwrecked Sailor* to the travels of Gulliver, Robinson Crusoe's shipwreck or the adventures of Sinbad the Sailor, who among other fantastic monsters encounters a man-eating giant who must trace his ancestry back to the *Odyssey*'s Cyclops.[125] It is little surprise that Max Slevogt, who illustrated Sinbad's story in 1908, called Sinbad the 'oriental Odysseus' (Fig. 228).[126] Some such stories are obviously fantastic, such as the Roman second-century AD satirist Lucian's *A True Story*, which (like Sinbad's story) in part draws on the *Odyssey*, and which takes the reader as far as the moon. Frequently, though, the borders between fact and fiction are blurred.[127] Thus, Homer's *Odyssey* echoes the realities of Greek (and Phoenician) mariners sailing the Mediterranean, while the tales of Sinbad reflect Arab voyages in the Indian Ocean. With space travel the final modern frontier, more than a nod to Homer can be found in science fiction epics, as exemplified by Stanley Kubrick's *2001: A Space Odyssey* of 1968.[128]

RIGHT
Fig. 228
Sindbad der Seefahrer
(Sinbad the Sailor)
The lithograph illustrates
an episode of Sinbad's
third voyage, from
Baghdad to Basra, when
a storm forced him and
his crew on to an island
inhabited by a huge man-
eating giant. They escape
his castle after they blind
him with a hot stick while
he sleeps.

1908
Max Slevogt
Lithograph
H. 360 mm | W. 270 mm
British Museum
1909,1216.15

Even though Aeneas is the true refugee, who flees war and destruction, it is the story of Odysseus that has most resonated with those experiencing, or reflecting on, migration and displacement in modern times. Jewish migrants to South America and twenty-first-century refugees crossing the Mediterranean have all seen themselves and their experiences mirrored in the *Odyssey*. A set of symptoms resulting from chronic extreme stress felt by displaced people has even become known as 'Ulysses Syndrome'.[129] But it is with the global diaspora of people of African descent that Odysseus appears to have struck a particular chord.

In literature, the most famous exponent of the phenomenon is probably Ralph Ellison (1914–1994), whose 1952 novel *Invisible Man* tells of a black man's journey from the American South to New York. More recently, St Lucian poet and dramatist Derek Walcott (1930–2017) drew freely on Homer and the Troy story for a number of his works.[130] He is best known for his Caribbean epic *Omeros* (1990) and for the play *The Odyssey: A Stage Version* (1993), which retold Odysseus' story in a Caribbean setting. Both address themes of colonization and slavery, migration and identity, and the meaning of home – a complicated concept especially in the Caribbean archipelago, with its multiethnic population displaced by the colonial rupture.[131] Yet Walcott looks beyond the dichotomy of colonizer and colonized. In *Omeros*, Homer is the 'poet of the Seven Seas' and in his *The Odyssey*, the Homer character pronounces 'The sea speaks the same language around the world's shores' (Act II, scene iv). It is this emphasis on the story's universality, and on the universality of human experience, that unites Walcott with African-American artist and blues composer Romare Bearden (1911–1988).

LEFT
Fig. 229*
The Siren's Song

1977
Romare Bearden
Collage
H. 813 mm | W. 1118 mm
The Collection of Alan
and Pat Davidson

OPPOSITE ABOVE
Fig. 230
Circe

1977
Romare Bearden
Collage on paper
mounted to fibreboard
H. 381 mm | W. 238 mm
Chazen Museum of Art,
University of Wisconsin-
Madison
2014.1

In the 1940s Bearden had engaged with the Homeric stories in a series of watercolours and ink drawings based on the *Iliad*. Thirty years later, in 1977, he found in the character of Odysseus an alter ego for himself and for global audiences, in a series of twenty collages based on episodes from the *Odyssey*.[132] The collages set Odysseus' travels in an imaginary world of Caribbean islands and African shores infused with a wide range of cultural connotations. Amidst the rich chromatics of seas, sky and land, strikingly, the human figures are black,[133] thus visually transforming the story into a Black African Odyssey. In *The Siren's Song* (Fig. 229), a lush, possibly Caribbean island is populated by nude women in the company of a musician playing an African arched harp. Odysseus sails past, tied high up on the mast to resist their allure, much as in Italian Renaissance paintings.[134] *The Return of Odysseus (Homage to Pinturicchio and Benin)* (see Fig. 6) draws on a fresco by Italian Renaissance artist Pintoricchio, elements of African Benin sculptures and early twentieth-century Cubist style. Images of Circe (Fig. 230) and of Poseidon recall African or Caribbean spirits, wearing African masks and jewellery.[135] For Bearden, the god Poseidon in particular embodied the link between Greece and Africa, as the first book of the *Odyssey* (1.22–26) has him visiting the Ethiopians.[136] As in Walcott's work, Bearden's Black Odysseus is not so much a victim as a hero. Having made the world his own, his travels become his privilege, and his resourcefulness and tenacity in the face of adversity become a global inspiration.[137]

The eternal traveller

Modern odysseys have had their hero travel through the conflict-ridden Balkans as in Theo Angelopoulos' film *Ulysses' Gaze* of 1995, or rural Mississippi during the Great Depression as in the Coen brothers' *O Brother, Where Art Thou?* of 2000. Yet for all the insights these journeys provide about the wider world, they are also always a hero's journey of self-discovery. In 1914, a play by German playwright Gerhart Hauptmann (1862–1946), *Der Bogen des Odysseus* (The Bow of Odysseus), had portrayed Odysseus as a man transformed, and brutalized, by his experiences both in war and vagrancy.[138] More recently, psychologist Jonathan Shay has pointed to the hero's eventful journey as a mirror image of a veteran's return home, part of a process of coming to terms with deeply troubling experiences.[139] Others have recognized more universal human experiences. In Franco Piavoli's 1989 film *Nostos, il ritorno* (Nostos: The Return), Odysseus' sea voyage turns into a reflection on his whole life.[140] In his 1956 work *Die Arche des Odysseus* (The Ark of Odysseus) (Fig. 231), Austrian fantastic realist painter Rudolf Hausner (1914–1995) depicts Odysseus as a sailor whose journey is his voyage from birth to death, always in search of himself, through a sea of contemporary events comprising war, peace and the whole cosmos of human experience.[141]

Similar ideas underlie the novel *Ulysses* by James Joyce.[142] Startlingly different and of epic proportions, the novel compresses the ten-year wanderings of Odysseus into an ordinary day in the life of the protagonist, Leopold Bloom, as he walks around Dublin accomplishing small tasks. Bloom is both Irish and Jewish by origin, but is something of an outsider in both respects. Each episode in his day is related to the *Odyssey*, but here the Sirens are barmaids and Circe runs a brothel, while the god of the winds becomes a newspaper editor, controlling the winds of popular opinion. The work was considered by many to be disgraceful on its full publication in 1922 because its honest descriptions of the interior worlds of its characters include many physical aspects of their lives that were considered gross and unmentionable. Subsequently, it has gained a revered place in the literary canon as an epic of the mundane that sees the heroic in commonplace human experience.

RIGHT
Fig. 231
***Die Arche des Odysseus* (The Ark of Odysseus)**

1948–56
Rudolf Hausner
Oil on wood
H. 850 mm | W. 1410 mm
Wien Museum
Inv. Nr. 101929

The idea of life itself as an odyssey also transforms the meaning of destination, of homecoming – is not then the journey an end in itself? Many modern writers have found the essence of Odysseus' character in his restlessness.[143] In Book 11 of the *Odyssey* Homer, in a deeply poetic image, hints that a further voyage awaits Odysseus after his return to Ithaca: he needs to placate the wrath of Poseidon by travelling to a place so far from the sea that an oar will be thought to be a winnowing fan. But it is in Dante's *Divine Comedy* that Odysseus most radically renounces domestic bliss: he sails beyond the Pillars of Hercules into the unknown Western Sea, never to return (*Inferno* Canto XXVI). In the 1904 poem 'L'Ultimo viaggio' (The Last Voyage) by Giovanni Pascoli (1855–1912), it takes nine tedious years on Ithaca to prompt Odysseus to set off once more to retrace the steps of his great journey. But one can never go back: finding little to connect with, he dies following shipwreck on Calypso's island. Indeed, Odysseus' ambiguous relationship with his home may be at the very heart of his character, determining his need to wander, as revealed in the poem 'Ithaka' (1911) by Constantine Cavafy:

> Ithaka gave you the marvellous journey.
> Without her you would not have set out.
> She has nothing left to give you now.[144]

It is after just a single night back home that the hero becomes bored with Ithaca in *The Odyssey: A Modern Sequel* (*Odysseia*), an epic poem by Nikos Kazantzakis (1883–1957). An illustration by the Greek artist Nikos Ghika (1906–1994) beautifully captures him sneaking away from his sleeping wife (Fig. 232). In the book, Kazantzakis' semi-autobiographical Odysseus is a deeply human figure driven to become a traveller between continents:

> 'I'm not pure, I'm not strong, I cannot love, I'm afraid!
> I'm choked with mud and shame, I fight but fight in vain
> with cries and gaudy wings, with voyages and wiles
> to choke that quivering mouth within me that cries "Help!"
> A thin, thin crust of laughter, mockery, voices, tears,
> a lying false façade—all this is called Odysseus!'[145]

Temptresses and true loves: Odysseus' women

> What seith Omer of goode Penalopee?
> Al Grece knoweth of hire chastitee.
> Chaucer, *The Franklin's Tale*, 1443–44

Many of the women linked to Aeneas had little luck. His first wife Creusa became separated from him and died at Troy. Dido entered into a love affair with Aeneas, but took her own life in despair as he abandoned her. The females in the story of Odysseus appear more like survivors, and they have certainly proved a source of fascination, debate and artistic inspiration throughout the ages.[146]

One example is the 1909 painting of *Ulysses and the Sirens* by Herbert James Draper (1863–1920), a British classicist painter famous for his detailed mythological-allegorical paintings (Fig. 233).[147] In the ancient Greek story, the Sirens are perched on their rocky lair,

ABOVE
Fig. 232
Penelope's Bed
Study for the illustration of Nikos Kazantzakis' *The Odyssey*. Ghika made some 150 drawings, of which 35 were reproduced in the English translation by Kimon Friar, published in 1958.

1938–58
Nikos Hadjikyriakos-Ghika
Pencil on paper
H. 370 mm | W. 260 mm
Ghika Gallery, Benaki Museum, Athens
PHG621

BELOW
Fig. 233*
Ulysses and the
Sirens

1909
Herbert Draper
Oil on canvas
H. 175.9 cm | W. 210 cm
Ferens Art Gallery
KINCM:2005.4878

trying to lure sailors to be shipwrecked on the cliffs below with their irresistible singing. Draper's Sirens, in contrast, are up close and physical. They are about to climb on to Odysseus' ship, while his men frantically struggle to row out of danger – and there is danger indeed. The Sirens are no longer the female-headed birds of the ancient Greek tradition, they are fish-tailed mermaids, who take on fully human form as they emerge from the sea. Mermaid Sirens, common since the Middle Ages, may have been inspired by other ancient Greek sea monsters, such as Scylla or the Tritons, or perhaps reflect a conflation with other European, pre-Christian water spirits, such as the mermaids of Britain and Ireland, who can bring either doom or salvation to seamen.[148] Whatever their origin, they came with a new emphasis on the Sirens as symbols of bodily desire.[149] In Romare Bearden's collage (above, Fig. 229), which draws on medieval and Renaissance imagery, the mast with a crossbar

recalls precisely this idea of Odysseus clinging to it like the soul adheres to the cross, as the ship of the church provides safety from temptation. Yet Draper's Odysseus displays a very different psychology: half mad with lust he is restrained only by one of his crew, who tightens the ropes. This is no self-possessed, steadfast hero, but a man tormented by his own desires.

Another female to be wary of was Circe. The English painter John William Waterhouse (1849–1947) repeatedly chose Circe as his subject for images that marry a classicist style with Pre-Raphaelite aesthetics.[150] In his *Circe Offering the Cup to Ulysses* of 1891 (Fig. 234), the sorceress is a powerful queen entirely in control of the situation as she holds out her poisoned chalice, already having turned Odysseus' comrades into pigs, one of them lying at her feet. Odysseus himself, visible only in the mirror behind her, approaches with hesitation. In *Circe Invidiosa*, painted a year later, Circe, in a shimmering peacock-feather robe, is a jealous, brooding beauty who empties her magic potion into the sea to poison Scylla, her rival for the love of the sea god Glaucus, thus transforming her into a sailor-devouring

LEFT
Fig. 234
Circe Offering the Cup to Ulysses

1891
John William Waterhouse
Oil on canvas
H. 148 cm | W. 92 cm
Gallery Oldham
3.55/9

ABOVE
Fig. 235*
**Cassone panel
depicting Odysseus
and Penelope**

c. 1475
Sienese artist in the style
of Liberale da Verona
Tempera on poplar panel
H. 56 cm | W. 177.8 cm
Victoria and Albert
Museum
5792-1860

monster. The two paintings draw on different ancient sources, one on the *Odyssey* and the other on Ovid's *Metamorphoses* (14.52–65). Yet both place Circe centre stage. Indeed, looking out of the picture, it is not so much Odysseus to whom Circe offers the cup, but us, the viewer: will we take the poison chalice and succumb to her magic charms?[151]

Circe and the Sirens stand in a long tradition in Western thought that casts women in the role of dangerous temptresses or devious witches, demonizing sexuality as part of man's struggle with the overwhelming power of human nature. It is no coincidence that they, along with other mysterious *femmes fatales,* became a prominent topic in art especially at the turn of the nineteenth and twentieth centuries, a time of redefinition of gender norms and sexual morals and of fascination with the subconscious in the nascent field of psychoanalysis.[152] Just as long-lived is the reaction against this, from the image illustrating Christine de Pizan's works showing a regal Circe (see Fig. 191), to the idea that Circe's drug turning men into pigs merely brings out their true nature, explored both in Katherine Anne Porter's novel *A Defense of Circe* of 1954 and in Madeline Miller's more recent *Circe*.[153]

Penelope, the main female character in Odysseus' story, has always had a special position, both in Homer and in later art and literature. She is the wife for whom Odysseus pines throughout his ten years at sea, and the equal partner who matches him in cleverness and the ability to manipulate others.[154] The *Odyssey* characterizes her as *periphron,* prudent and carefully calculating. Watching her interact with the suitors on his return to Ithaca, Odysseus is happy that she is 'secretly procuring presents, and charming them with pretty words, while her mind moved elsewhere' (*Odyssey,* 18.281–83).

In the Middle Ages and Renaissance, Odysseus and Penelope were hailed as the exemplary faithful couple. Odysseus' reunion with Penelope was celebrated in an early opera by Monteverdi (see p. 196), and his departure and return home were among the images that from around the mid-fifteenth century adorned Tuscan and Umbrian wedding chests, *cassoni*, prestige items commissioned by patrician families for weddings, often in pairs. Painted scenes from classical myth, history and the Bible focused on men's heroic deeds, conjugal love, and female chastity and faithfulness that were intended to serve as examples for the newlywed couple.[155] Penelope proved a popular heroine, as 'a woman of untarnished honour and inviolate chastity, and a holy and eternal example for women', as Boccaccio characterized her in his collection of biographies *De claris mulieribus* (Concerning Famous Women), written in 1361–62.[156]

Inside the illustration panel:

... ÉTAIT-CE DONC LE SOUVENIR DE
CALYPSO QUI LE HANTAIT ? OU CELUI
DE CIRCÉ ? PEUT-ÊTRE AVAIT-IL ENTREVU
TROP DE CHOSES DONT LE SENS NE LUI
PARVENAIT QU'APRÈS COUP ?... ÉTRANGER
PARMI LES SIENS, ULYSSE SE SENTAIT
À PRÉSENT PLUS PROCHE DES DIEUX
QUE DES HOMMES ET TRAÎNAIT AVEC
LUI LA NOSTALGIE DE SES VOYAGES.

LEFT
Fig. 236
One of the final scenes of the graphic novel *Ulysse*, showing the hero tormented by memories
Now feeling estranged from Ithaca's shore, Odysseus recalls (from top to bottom) Zeus, Athena, Circe, Calypso and Poseidon.

2018 (black and white edition; first published in 1968)
Georges Pichard and Jacques Lob; published by Editions Glénat
Graphic novel

On one *cassone* panel we see Penelope and Odysseus as gilded relief figures framed by classical columns (Fig. 235). They are the 'alter egos' of the bride and groom, with Penelope's 'classical' dress contrasting with the knightly figure of Odysseus.[157] In the painted panel between them, Penelope is seated indoors at her loom. On the seashore, Odysseus, leading a horse, steps on to the gangplank of his ship, seemingly about to join the rest of his fleet already at sea. In the grounds of the estate, nude young males are fishing, while an older man walks alongside a youth. They may be Laertes, Odysseus' father, with his grandson Telemachus, though if the scene indeed shows Odysseus' departure for Troy, rather than his return, he should be much younger at this point. The scene may have been composed so as to have special meaning for the family that commissioned the chest.

When in the sixteenth century Francesco Primaticcio (1504–1570) painted a major fresco cycle of the story of Odysseus for King François I in the palace at Fontainebleau, outside Paris (the famed Galerie d'Ulysse, destroyed in 1738–39), he included a panel that showed the faithful couple reunited in the marital bed, Odysseus gazing at Penelope with desire and admiration.[158] Not everyone, however, thought that it all ended so happily: as mentioned earlier, Kazantzakis' Odysseus escapes domestic dullness after a single day, Pascoli's after nine years, and Tennyson's Ulysses, too, plots a speedy departure from his now 'aged wife'. The 1968 graphic novel *Ulysse* by J. Lob and G. Pichard, paints a more complex picture. Odysseus clearly has difficulty getting used to domestic normality, as he is haunted by memories of his exhilarating adventures in a fantastically psychedelic, erotically charged Mediterranean (Fig. 236).[159] His decision to leave comes, however, only after his advances to Penelope have been brushed off, as she, too, struggles to adjust: she simply cannot stop working at her loom, which has dominated her life for the past twenty years.

Indeed, how does all this look from Penelope's perspective? It has often been noted that to modern readers Penelope's role in the story scarcely seems emotionally plausible. In a poem of 1875 Jemimah Makepiece Sturt had Penelope feel estranged and mistrustful of her husband after his long absence, while in 1928 Dorothy Parker painted her domestic routine as heroic in its own right.[160] Both ancient and modern writers, from Douris of Samos to James Joyce, gave her lovers. In Carol Ann Duffy's 1999 poem, Penelope has discovered in her weaving her artistic calling and is self-sufficient and contented. This interesting vision, hinted at also by Lob and Pichard, was suggested already at the end of the nineteenth century by German symbolist sculptor and painter Max Klinger (1857–1920) (Fig. 237). His etching shows Penelope brooding in a pose echoing that of her most famous ancient Greek image (Figs 104, 105) – but here she is more likely pondering her work rather than longing for her absent husband. She is portrayed as an accomplished artist, weaving the story of the world into her tapestry with the same skill a bard would use to weave a story from words.[161]

It is hardly surprising that suggestions that Homer could have been a woman have been attached to the *Odyssey* in particular.[162] The poem's cast of women is exceptionally rich and complex, and this has been translated also on to the screen. Mario Camerini's 1954 cinematic rendering of the story, *Ulysses*, influenced by the experiences of soldiers and their wives in the Second World War, introduces a particularly intriguing concept of female identity into the familiar story. Silvana Mangano is cast opposite Kirk Douglas in a double role as both Penelope and Circe/Calypso.[163] It is she who puts the question to Odysseus: 'Isn't the difference between one woman and another only in the mind of a man?'[164]

RIGHT
Fig. 237
Penelope
Penelope's tapestry depicts early humans in Africa. Klinger's work was a commission to honour the famous Leipzig Darwinian zoologist Rudolf Leuckart.

1896
Max Klinger
Colour etching and aquatint
H. 189 mm | W. 300 mm
Fine Arts Museums of San Francisco
1963.30.1556

HEROES: ACHILLES AND HECTOR

In the huge cast of combatants and participants in the Trojan War, one pre-eminent hero stands out on each side: the Greek Achilles and the Trojan Hector. In Homer's *Iliad*, Achilles is the *aristos Achaion*, 'best of the Achaeans' (Greeks);[165] Hector is the man most vital to the defence of Troy.[166] These two warriors and their intertwined destinies have captured the attention of writers and artists from ancient Greece to the modern day, raising questions about heroism, and violence and its impact upon those who fight and those they leave behind.

Lives cut short

The story of Achilles' life and death carries powerful messages about the idea of a hero. Achilles knew from his goddess mother that he had a choice to make: 'two fates bear me on to the day of death' (*Iliad* 9.411). Continuing to fight at Troy meant he would win eternal glory, but would meet an early death; if instead he returned home, he would have a long

BELOW
Fig. 238*
***Achilles Lamenting
for Patroclus***

1770
Henry Fuseli, after Johan
Tobias Sergel
Pen and brown ink, with
grey wash, over graphite
on paper
H. 195 mm | W. 280 mm
British Museum
1885,0314.254

life but be destined for obscurity. For the ancient Greeks, the idea of *kleos*, glory or renown, was highly significant: without it, one was literally an unsung hero, whose exploits would not be remembered through the singing of epic poems.[167] In the end, the short and glorious life was Achilles' fate, and the *Iliad* is itself the proof of his long-lasting glory. But the Achilles of the *Iliad* does not make a conscious choice to seek glory over a long life. Indeed, as Odysseus, Phoenix and Ajax try to persuade him to rejoin the fighting in Book 9, Achilles seems inclined to reject the typical warrior's ethos – glory at any cost – saying that 'nothing equals the worth of my life' (*Iliad* 9.401).

What ultimately drives Achilles back into battle and seals his fate is his need to avenge the death of Patroclus, at a time when grief renders his own life meaningless to him. Swiss artist Henry Fuseli (Johann Heinrich Füssli, 1741–1825) depicted Achilles mourning Patroclus as part of a collection of drawings now known as the Roman Album (Fig. 238). He made these drawings during the years he studied in Rome, from 1770 to 1778, before settling in England and later becoming Professor of Painting at the Royal Academy Schools.[168] Fuseli had an enduring interest in literary themes and his works also illustrated translations of the *Iliad* and *Odyssey* by Alexander Pope and William Cowper. In Rome he was deeply impressed by the ancient and Renaissance works he encountered, inspired both by Neo-Attic and Roman relief sculpture and by Michelangelo – especially in the treatment of the human body. In responding to the ancient works, he learned from his friend Johan Tobias Sergel (1740–1814), a Swedish sculptor in the same circle of artists in 1770s Rome.[169] Fuseli's drawing of Achilles mourning Patroclus is based on one by Sergel, showing Achilles bent forward, hands clasped, over Patroclus' body.[170] Fuseli adapted the composition of his friend's drawing, setting the two men, alive and dead, face to face. The exact relationship between Achilles and Patroclus has been the topic of much speculation. Were they lovers as, for example, sensitively explored in Madeline Miller's *The Song of Achilles*, in which the story is seen through the eyes of Patroclus?[171] Or is the deep bond between them psychologically plausible as comrades in arms, even without an erotic dimension? Parallels have been drawn between the emotions and actions of Achilles in the *Iliad* and the experiences of veterans of the Vietnam War. Psychiatrist Jonathan Shay famously linked real-life cases with Achilles' berserk rage, prompted by betrayal on the part of his commander and the loss of his closest brother-in-arms.[172] It is this latitude for each generation, culture or individual to discover a new and different meaning in the characters that creates their eternal appeal. What continues to speak across the ages is a heart-rending portrait of a man's grief for a comrade's life cut short.

The brutal consequences of Achilles' vengeance – the killing of Hector and the terrible mistreatment of his body, which offended both gods and men – are emotively confronted by the nineteenth-century British painter Briton Rivière (1840–1920) (Fig. 239). Rivière was best known as a painter of animals, and he often included them in the composition even when painting the biblical and classical themes that were so popular with the Victorian artistic establishment. Here Hector's corpse lies face down, cast in the sand by the vengeful Achilles, while the dogs that circle around it seem more mournful than threatening. Hector's muscular, naked body almost shines from the dark wasteland surrounding it, capturing the tension between heroic perfection and physical vulnerability. It is completely whole and unmarked, despite Achilles' mistreatment, reflecting the supernatural preservation described in the *Iliad*, which also kept the dogs at bay. The relevant lines (*Iliad* 23.182–90) accompanied the painting when it was exhibited at the Royal Academy in 1892, in a translation by Lord Derby:[173]

But Hector, Priam's son …
Not to the fire, but to the dogs I give.
… But him the dogs molested not, for Venus night and day,
Daughter of Jove, the ravening dogs restrained;
Apollo too a cloudy veil from heaven
Spread o'er the plain, and covered all the space
Where lay the dead.

Artists have found in Achilles himself an opportunity to explore the tension between superhuman qualities and vulnerability. The death of Achilles is not described in the *Iliad*, and he was not regarded in the poem as invulnerable. In a later tradition he was famously rendered almost entirely invincible by his mother Thetis. To achieve this she dipped him in the River Styx while holding him by his heel, which was therefore left undipped and consequently his only point of weakness (see p. 92). The neoclassical sculptor Thomas Banks (1735–1805) showed this moment, with Achilles a helpless baby dangling from his mother's grasp (Fig. 241). The *Iliad* movingly conveys Thetis' fears and grief for her son, whom she knows she cannot save from premature death, and this sculpted moment of his early life is similarly charged with pathos. For its original owners, Thomas and Jane Johnes, the sculpture was surely a personal reflection of their desire as parents to protect their child

from harm, for the features of Achilles were modelled on their young daughter, named Mariamne, and Thetis is a portrait of Jane.[174] It was perhaps especially meaningful since they had lost an infant son in 1786, and would have acquired a new poignancy after Mariamne herself died in 1811 at the age of only 27.[175]

Thetis tried to protect her son further by providing him with armour forged by the god Hephaestus, as described in Book 18 of the *Iliad*. Nicolas Poussin (1594–1665) drew this scene in delicate pen and wash (Fig. 240). In his portrayal Thetis and her son tenderly embrace, while Nereids follow behind, carrying the armour. This is an extraordinarily human goddess, despite her divine near-nudity: her demeanour is entirely that of a mother concerned for her grown-up child. The work is one of a series of emotion-filled scenes of classical mythology and history known as the Marino drawings, after the poet Giovanni Battista Marino with whom the artist became acquainted at the court of France at the time he drew them in 1622 to 1623. It was previously thought that they illustrated Marino's poetry, but most of the surviving drawings were more likely intended to accompany a new edition of Ovid's *Metamorphoses* that never came to fruition.[176]

Even Achilles' divine mother, though, could not save him from his mortality. Once Achilles decided to rejoin the fighting at Troy, his own approaching death became inevitable: Paris was destined to complete Achilles' destiny by shooting him with an arrow not long afterwards (see p. 92). One of the most evocative images of wounded Achilles was sculpted by Filippo Albacini (1777–1858) in neoclassical style (Fig. 242). The pose of this Achilles is reminiscent of the famous classical sculpture known as the 'Dying Gaul', but the Gaul's expression of endurance seems to have been replaced in Albacini's Achilles with an almost masochistic abandonment to his fate.[177] When the great nineteenth-century cataloguer of private art collections Gustav Waagen saw the sculpture, he found it too demonstrative for his tastes: 'a well-executed work, but neither the character nor the excessive expression of pain is suited for an Achilles'.[178] It has been argued that the 6th Duke of Devonshire, William Spencer Cavendish, was motivated by the homoerotic appreciation of ancient sculptures, in the mode established by Johann Joachim Winckelmann (see also p. 198), when he chose this work for his sculpture gallery at Chatsworth House.[179] For Winckelmann and his followers, the male nude was the high point of idealized beauty, which the viewer could both desire and strive to emulate.[180] The ancient and classicizing sculptures decorating the homes of the English elites were part of a world view based on admiration of the Greeks.

BELOW
Fig. 242*
The Wounded Achilles

1825
Filippo Albacini
Marble
H. 114 cm | L. 197 cm
The Devonshire
Collections, Chatsworth

The human cost

The tragic human cost of heroism extends beyond the heroes themselves, and nowhere is this clearer than in Hector's relationship with his family. In the Middle Ages, when European dynasties were seeking a Trojan lineage (see p. 188), the popularity of Hector greatly surpassed that of Achilles. The Trojan warrior was seen as an exemplary hero and a pattern for rulers: he became one of the 'Nine Worthies', role models selected from classical antiquity, the Bible and more recent history, who appeared as a common medieval decorative theme across Europe.[181] A double-page spread from the *Florentine Picture-Chronicle* (Fig. 243a, b), an illustrated world history put together by a group of Florentine goldsmiths, brings to life the scene in which Hector says goodbye to his wife Andromache for the last time. The artists were almost certainly following the medieval romances rather than the classical texts: here the couple have the two children of some later accounts instead of the single child in Homer.[182] The stricken Andromache is pleading with Hector not to rejoin the battle. Hector stands bedecked in the finest Renaissance armour: a hero for the *Chronicle*'s own times, the perfect embodiment of a great knight, dutiful ruler and family man.

Hector's parting from his wife and son was equally well suited to the melancholy, intimate mood of Romantic and Victorian art. German poet Friedrich Schiller (1759–1805) wrote a ballad on the theme, as part of his play *Die Räuber* (The Robbers) (1781), which was set to music by Franz Schubert:

> Oh! Hector, wilt thou go for evermore,
> Where fierce Achilles, on the blood-stained shore,
> Heaps countless victims o'er Patroclus' grave?
> Who then thy hapless orphan will rear,
> Teach him to praise the gods and hurl the spear,
> When thou art swallowed up in Xanthus' wave?[183]

The eighteenth-century neoclassical history painter Angelica Kauffman (1741–1807), one of only two women among the founding members of the Royal Academy, often painted scenes of loss and longing, reflecting the sentimental, melancholic view of love and friendship of the period.[184] In her *Hector Taking Leave of Andromache* (Fig. 245), Andromache holds her husband's hand as the couple gaze tenderly at one another. Their son Astyanax, here a baby in the arms of his nurse, does not look at his father, perhaps referencing the boy's fear of Hector's nodding helmet in Homer's description. As well as the ancient text, Kauffman would have drawn inspiration from the recently published handbook by the Comte de Caylus, *Tableaux tirés de l'Iliade, de l'Odyssée d'Homère et de l'Enéide de Vergile* (1757) (see also p. 199).[185] Kauffman's painting was one of a set of four classical scenes probably commissioned for the Grand Saloon at Saltram House in Devon, but which ultimately hung on the main staircase there. Together the paintings contrasted love and war, male and female roles, passion and judgment, representing difficult choices.[186]

In the late nineteenth century, Harry Bates (1850–1899), one of the group of artists collectively described as the New Sculpture movement, showed the same scene of leave-taking in a bronze relief entitled *War* (Fig. 244).[187] His style was characterized by a combination of classical idealism and romantic realism, having been greatly influenced by the French sculptor Auguste Rodin while working in Paris from 1883 to 1885. That this quiet family scene could be chosen to represent the theme of war is an indication of the resonance and

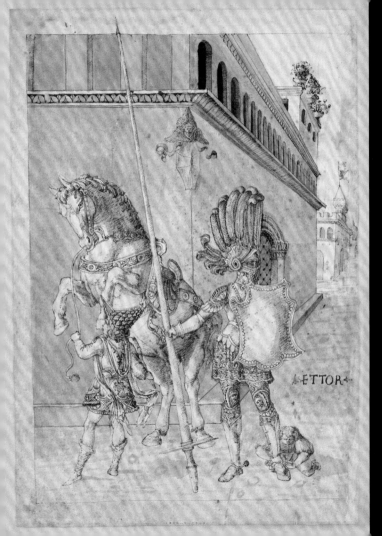

ETTOR

ADROMANGHA· MOGLIE ETOA·

impact that these characters had in an era versed in classical literature. Below the main scene Bates sculpted in miniature the dragging of Hector's body: a poignant reminder that this was to be Hector's fate, and that he would never see his wife and child again.

Kauffman also painted Andromache mourning her husband after his death. The seated, heavily draped, weeping figure in this composition has sometimes been identified as Andromache, making the standing figure a companion, perhaps Helen.[188] However, when the original painting was exhibited at the Royal Academy in 1772, it was catalogued as 'Andromache and Hecuba weeping over the ashes of Hector'.[189] The standing young woman with face visible is therefore surely Andromache and the seated figure must be Hector's mother, Hecuba, comforted by her grandson Astyanax. The scene is set around an urn containing Hector's ashes, inspired perhaps by similar scenes on Roman sarcophagi and a common motif for representing mourning in the classicizing art of the later eighteenth century. Kauffman's rendering differs from representations of the same scene by other neoclassical painters, who, in line with the *Iliad*, represent Hector's corpse. Less stark and dramatic, her version is more focused on female suffering. As with many of Kauffman's works, the painting was much reproduced and circulated in the form of prints, reaching a wide audience (Fig. 246).[190] The central figure of Andromache was rendered in porcelain by both the Derby and Bristol porcelain factories (Fig. 247). The Derby figure was probably modelled by Pierre Stephan, who had purchased a copy of the Kauffman print in 1774.[191]

Hero or brute?

When I think of Troilus, Hector, Paris, my heart bleeds. When I think of Polyxena, I feel like flying into a rage. If only nothing survived me but my hatred. If the hatred sprouted from my grave, a tree of hate that would whisper: 'Achilles the brute'. If they felled the tree it would grow again. If they pinned it down, each blade of grass would take over the message: 'Achilles the brute, Achilles the brute'.

Christa Wolf, *Cassandra*[192]

Just as Hector became the exemplary hero for Europeans in the Middle Ages who traced their descent from his Trojan family, so Achilles became a vilified enemy and the model of how not to behave. While for the lyric poets of Archaic and Classical Greece, Achilles had been a glorious example of greatness to be emulated, as early as the fourth century BC Plato in his *Republic* had denounced his passions and vices.[193] In the medieval romances, which relied on the versions of Dares and Dictys (see p. 186), various changes to the narrative of events at Troy made Achilles into a scoundrel who killed Hector by cowardly means and destroyed himself through his lustful passions, based on an elaboration of his relationships with Deidamia, Briseis and Polyxena.[194]

ABOVE LEFT
Fig. 246*
Andromache Weeping Over the Ashes of Hector

1771
Thomas Burke, after
Angelica Kauffman
Mezzotint
H. 505 mm | W. 335 mm
British Museum
1879,0614.829

ABOVE RIGHT
Fig. 247*
Porcelain figure of Andromache weeping over the ashes of Hector
This figure was based on the Kauffman print in Fig. 246.

c. 1775–85
Derby Porcelain Factory
Porcelain
H. 229 mm | W. 110 mm |
D. 80 mm
British Museum
1905,0318.8

Achilles began to be rehabilitated in the Renaissance with the rediscovery of Greek texts including the *Iliad* and inspiration drawn from Roman relief sculptures. Just as on Roman sarcophagi (see p. 74 and Fig. 55), the focus often fell on his youth and education with the centaur Chiron, and on his time on Skyros. The artist Peter Paul Rubens (1577–1640) was well versed in classical literature and around 1630 to 1635 he designed a series of eight tapestries representing scenes from the life of Achilles.[195] It is not known who commissioned them – one possibility is his father-in-law, merchant Daniel Fourment – but it is likely that Rubens himself was closely involved in the choice of subjects and their treatment. There were a number of precedents for scenes featuring Achilles – for example a series of paintings in the Palace of Fontainebleau (see p. 232) – and Achilles was a popular topic for French and Dutch theatre of the period, but a full series depicting Achilles' life was nonetheless innovative.[196] The eight scenes were: Thetis dipping Achilles in the Styx; Achilles educated by the centaur Chiron; his discovery among the daughters of Lycomedes on Skyros; the wrath of Achilles; the return of Briseis; Thetis receiving the arms of Achilles; the death of Hector; the death of Achilles. For his life of Achilles, Rubens clearly drew not only on Homer, but also on other sources probably including Ovid, Philostratus and Servius, as well as the didactic and moralizing interpretations of classical myths by sixteenth- and seventeenth-century Dutch mythographers, to create something new.[197] He seems deliberately to have chosen episodes that emphasized Achilles' education, humanity and heroism, as well as the role of fate and passion, which may have had particular meaning in the context of neo-Stoicism (a philosophical movement he knew of through his learned brother Philip).[198]

Rubens' process involved initial oil sketches, which were then worked up into larger modelli, with the help of assistants, before finally being scaled up into full-size cartoons on paper for the tapestry makers.[199] The modello and tapestry of *Wrath of Achilles* follow the Homeric account of the quarrel with Agamemnon very closely (Fig. 248). Achilles puts his hand to his sword, intending to attack Agamemnon, who begins to rise from his throne in response. The tension of the moment is brought out through the energetic movement of Achilles' sword arm, and the anxious faces of the onlookers. In the modello, Achilles draws his sword with his left hand, which would be reversed when the tapestries were woven. However, the goddess Athena (Minerva) restrains Achilles by his hair, averting a physical confrontation, exactly as described in the *Iliad*. Rubens' wealthy and royal European patrons were now decorating their homes with scenes from Achilles' life in the same way that Roman elites once chose the theme for the decoration of their sarcophagi.

Pietro Testa (1612–1650) was an Italian High Baroque artist who first specialized in making copies after classical antiquities before becoming an etcher in Rome. He too created a series of images of the life of Achilles, in this case comprising three prints, probably drawing inspiration from the Iliac Tablets (*Tabulae Iliacae*) (see p. 50, Fig. 34), as well as Renaissance mythological compilations. The first print shows Achilles being dipped in the Styx, represented by a vase of Stygian water, the second his education by Chiron and the third the dragging of Hector, with Achilles' chariot angled so that the two heroes, victor and vanquished, dominate the composition (Fig. 249).[200] Testa's Achilles in this final print is a masterpiece of triumphant masculinity, and his brutality in the dragging of Hector's body seems at first glance to reinforce his status as victorious hero, affirmed by the Victory goddess who flies overhead to crown him. But the figure of Victory also links back to a Victory in the first print in the series, which decorates the vase holding the water of the Styx: here she is perhaps to be understood as crowning Achilles with his fate and

foreshadowing his own death. The Trojan figures in the background, including Andromache swooning on the walls of a Troy incorporating Roman buildings, may be intended to encourage sympathy with the Trojans, or to contrast with Achilles' fortitude in facing his fate. While Testa's works were not highly appreciated in his lifetime, he became famous after his death, and his images of Achilles influenced later artists including John Flaxman (see p. 277).

Scenes from Achilles' life were also the subject of a series of six relief tablets produced by Wedgwood, of a type intended to be incorporated into decorative architectural schemes, such as in fireplaces or plinths.[201] The tablets were designed by Camillo Pacetti in 1788[202] – a time when the Grand Tour was at the height of its popularity and British gentlemen flocked to Rome. Classical subjects and motifs began to dominate architecture, interior design and the decorative arts.[203] The final relief in the sequence (see Fig. 199) shows the scene in which King Priam journeys to the Greek camp to meet with Achilles face to face and beg for the return of his son's body. The cart piled with gifts stands on the left-hand side, Hector's chariot is in the centre, and the old king meets with Achilles on the right. Wedgwood designs were commonly directly based on the images on Greek vases and other classical objects.[204] Here the source – as for many artists since the Renaissance – was a Roman sarcophagus, in this case in the Capitoline Museum in Rome, the so-called sarcophagus of Alexander Severus and Julia Mamaea.[205] The encounter shown on the tablet between Priam and the man who brutally slaughtered his son is an extraordinary emotional turning-point in the *Iliad* (see p. 89). The poem ends with reconciliation and resolution, pointing a way forward, where compassion, dialogue and humanity can prevail.[206]

For the age of Romanticism, Achilles was the perfect hero, the embodiment of a life given over to emotion and of beauty doomed to ruin. German romantic poet Friedrich Hölderlin (1770–1843) wrote an elegy, 'Achill', in 1798 and praised Achilles in an unpublished work:

> He is my favourite amongst the heroes, so strong and tender, the most accomplished and most ephemeral bloom on the pantheon of heroes, 'born to live but briefly' according to Homer, precisely because he is so beautiful.[207]

Most of Hölderlin's compatriots shared his view. Goethe also began an epic poem entitled 'Achilleis' but abandoned the project. And in 1809, aged just eleven, the great Italian Romantic poet Giacomo Leopardi (1798–1837) presented both Achilles and Hector as two great, virtuous, tragic heroes in 'La morte di Ettore' (The Death of Hector).[208] Leopardi elsewhere wrote, 'we will always admire more the Achilles described by Homer, with all his defects, than the perfect hero incarnated by the Aeneas of Virgil'.[209]

The fascination with Achilles shows little sign of abating. In the twentieth century and into the twenty-first, a range of artists and writers have explored his character and emotions in all their many-sided complexity and from different perspectives, including authors such as Madeline Miller, mentioned above, Christa Wolf, whose *Cassandra* abandons herself to vehement rage against Achilles 'the brute' in the passage quoted at the beginning of this section, and Pat Barker, whose *The Silence of the Girls* opens with the words:

> Great Achilles. Brilliant Achilles, shining Achilles, godlike Achilles…. How the epithets pile up. We never called him any of those things; we called him 'the butcher'.[210]

Vengeance of Achilles by American artist Cy Twombly (1928–2011) dramatically abstracts Achilles' rage at the killing of his beloved Patroclus into a form that evokes both the initial letter of his name and a bloodied spear (Fig. 250). Twombly's art engaged deeply with Greek mythology over a long period.[211] He also painted an *Achilles Mourning the Death of Patroclus* in the same year, 1962, in which two clouds of painted colour float on the canvas, forever linked together by an unsteady line. Later, he created a series of ten paintings, *Fifty Days at Iliam* (1977–78), based on Alexander Pope's eighteenth-century translation of Homer's *Iliad* (see p. 196), again characteristically bringing together words and images, and including another *Vengeance of Achilles*.[212] In the 1962 version of this subject, the power of Achilles' emotion seems to burn from the huge canvas, and to have inscribed itself into the lines that are scrawled on its surface.

Fig. 250*
*Vengeance
of Achilles*

1962
Cy Twombly
Oil, chalk and graphite
on canvas
H. 300 cm | W. 175 cm
Kunsthaus Zürich
1987/0008

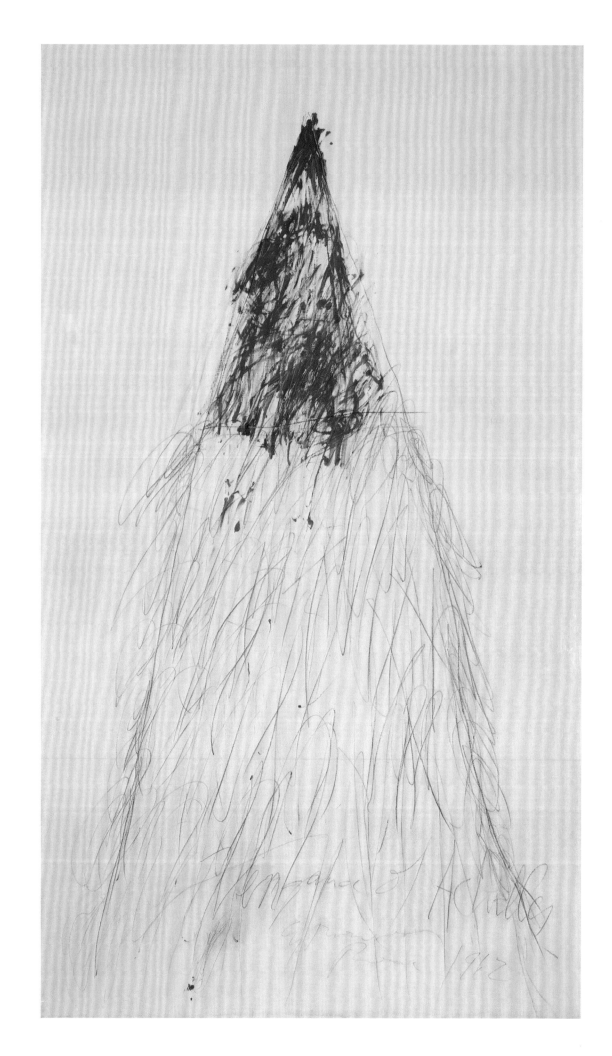

Battle and glory?

The *Iliad*, containing what we would nowadays call 'Despatches from the Siege of Troy', a campaign almost duplicate to ours, although it took place 3,000 years ago. Instead of a wooden horse, we made use of a steel ship, that's about the extent of the difference… Speech by General Sir Ian Hamilton at Anzac Day ceremony in London, 1935[213]

Combat and violence are the hallmarks of a hero and the Trojan War myth has regularly served as a model of heroism and valour in battle. Italian Renaissance painter Biagio d'Antonio (1446–1516) painted two panels featuring the siege of Troy, one of which focused on the death of Hector (Fig. 251) and the other on the sack of Troy and the wooden horse (Fig. 252; see also Fig. 3).[214] They were made for a wedding chest, for the Albizzi family of Florence, and evoke the realities of late fifteenth-century warfare, including the heavy armour and fighting styles of Renaissance knights,[215] while the classical-looking city in the background includes Italian buildings of the period, from Rome, Florence and Venice.[216] Hector and Achilles appear twice in the panel featuring their combat. Near the centre they fight on horseback; at the right-hand side Achilles drags Hector's body behind his horse. That the narrative of the Trojan War, including the story of Achilles and Hector, was chosen to decorate these important family status symbols shows its continuing importance in Renaissance Italy, re-imagined in the visual language of the time.[217]

TOP
Fig. 251*
The Siege of Troy –
The Death of Hector

c. 1490–95
Biagio d'Antonio
Tempera on panel; one of
a pair of *cassone* panels
H. 470 mm | W. 1610 mm
Fitzwilliam Museum,
University of Cambridge
M.44

BELOW
Fig. 252*
The Siege of Troy –
The Wooden Horse

c. 1490–95
Biagio d'Antonio
Tempera on panel; one of
a pair of *cassone* panels
H. 470 mm | W. 1610 mm
Fitzwilliam Museum,
University of Cambridge
M.45

THE TROJAN HORSE: AN UNHEROIC TRICK?

It is ironic that it is not as a result of heroic combat during the ten years of siege that the Trojan War was finally won, but instead through the underhand and unheroic means of the trick of the Trojan Horse. Whereas Hector and Achilles, in the classical tradition, fought in hand-to-hand combat, as warriors should, it was the cunning of Odysseus, a very different kind of hero, that finally won the war. In a *cassone* panel (see Fig. 252), Biagio d'Antonio shows the horse being transported into the city on a wheeled trolley, while Greeks already seem to be attacking, and the walls, partially destroyed, are being set alight.

One etching from a set of six by Jean Mignon (active 1537–1552) representing various episodes from the Trojan War also shows the horse being dragged into Troy (Fig. 253). The original compositions are attributed to Luca Penni (after 1504–1557)[218] and were engraved by Mignon in 1544, at the latest. Their circulation as prints inspired enamellers and makers of helmets and shields to adopt their imagery at a time when scenes of Troy were fashionable among French aristocrats. Both Penni and Mignon were attached to the French royal court of François I at Fontainebleau, which developed as a significant centre of artistic production, including printmaking, in this period.[219] In this print, King Priam kneels, welcoming the horse, while the city walls are being dismantled to allow its passage. The horse looms large, its truncation at the side of the image helping to exaggerate its size, but it is all the same difficult to imagine it concealing more than a very few Greek warriors.

Classical war scenes, including the Trojan War, were also used to commemorate specific contemporary battles, as on a silver dish probably made in Portugal between 1500 and 1520 (Fig. 255). It is crowded with figured scenes in a way that is typical for Portuguese dishes of this period. The town shown is Asilah (Arzila) on the coast of Morocco, which had been captured by the Portuguese in 1471, but it is also Troy, as the artist conflates the recent and the ancient conflict to celebrate heroic victory. Hector and Achilles are in combat, mounted on horseback, to the right of the city walls. The dish may have been made in Oporto, as the arms of the local Pintos da Cunha family were added to the central medallion in the seventeenth century.[220]

Following his Renaissance rehabilitation, Achilles himself could again stand as an exemplar for the modern soldier. The Achilleion in Corfu, a residence originally designed for Empress Elisabeth of Austria, was intended to evoke an ancient palace in Achilles' homeland, in Thessaly. It was decorated with multiple statues and paintings of the hero, including a *Dying Achilles* by German sculptor Ernst Herter (1846–1917). The German Kaiser Wilhelm II bought the palace in 1907 and set up another statue of Achilles there inscribed 'To the Greatest Greek from the Greatest German', thus framing himself as a latter-day version of Homer's hero.[221] The bronze reconstruction made by Georg Römer (1868–1922) of the Classical Doryphoros, or 'Spear-Bearer', by Polykleitos, commonly thought to represent Achilles, was used in a First World War memorial at a university in Munich (Fig. 254).[222]

German Impressionist painter and illustrator Max Slevogt (1868–1932) created a series of lithographs of Achilles and Hector which returned to the literary sources, looking beyond the idealized versions of neoclassical and Romantic art.[223] Even though their creation in 1905 preceded Slevogt's own traumatic experience of German defeat in the First World War, they emphasize the darker side of battle. In Slevogt's version of the dragging of Hector (Fig. 256), based on a drawing by Flaxman, Achilles is still the dominant, victorious protagonist, but the mood is more forbidding, transformed in Slevogt's modernist style. Achilles' back, following Flaxman, is completely turned to the viewer and Slevogt adds an additional figure who hands him the reins, looking down towards the ground. There is a sense that we cannot – and would not wish to – look Achilles in the eyes, consumed as he is by anger and the lust for retribution. Fifteen of the lithographs were chosen for publication under the title *Achilles* in 1907, followed by a further nine on Hector published in 1921.[224] In another of the *Achilles* lithographs, Slevogt chose to focus on the Homeric scene in which Achilles appears at the Greeks' defensive ditch to intimidate the Trojans (Fig. 257). Here Achilles is transformed into a larger-than-life monster who screams his terrifying battle cry over the tangle of men fighting over the corpse of Patroclus, seen slung over a warrior's back in the foreground. The emphasis on brutal violence and anger in these illustrations gave them an obvious resonance once the First World War broke out. Slevogt's *Achilles* series was re-published in a new edition in 1915.[225]

In the poetry of the First World War, the Trojan War is mostly drawn upon as a source of solace and a justification for the soldiers' sacrifice, reinforcing the nobility, validity and courage of their actions.[226] Poems either emphasize the valour of the modern soldiers through comparison with the ancient, or they invoke Homer's heroes, including Achilles, as witnesses.[227] A poem by Patrick Shaw-Stewart, 'I saw a man this morning', refers to the same episode of the *Iliad* as Slevogt's illustration in its famous ending, mirroring the poet's return to combat from a short leave in Imbros in July 1915:[228]

ABOVE
Fig. 254
Reconstruction of the *Doryphoros* or 'Spear-Bearer'

c. 1920, based on an original by Polykleitos of around 440–430 BC
Georg Römer
Bronze
H. 212 cm
Ludwig-Maximilians-Universität, Munich

OPPOSITE
Fig. 255*
Dish with Trojan War imagery, celebrating the capture of the town of Asilah (Arzila) on the Moroccan coast by the Portuguese in 1471

1500–20
Possibly made in Oporto, Portugal
Silver, partially gilded, embossed, chased and engraved
Diam. 301 mm | D. 54 mm
Victoria and Albert Museum
M.2-1938

Fig. 256*
Triumph des Achill
(Triumph of Achilles)

1906
Max Slevogt
Lithograph
H. 268 mm | W. 380 mm
British Museum
1951,0501.110

Fig. 257*
*Achill schreckt
die Troer* (Achilles
Frightens the Trojans)

1905
Max Slevogt
Lithograph
H. 262 mm | W. 371 mm
British Museum
1951,0501.111

I will go back this morning
From Imbros over the sea;
Stand in the trench, Achilles,
Flame-capped, and shout for me.

Shaw-Stewart and his friend the poet Rupert Brooke (see also p. 206) found themselves close to Troy in the Dardanelles Campaign of the First World War. Both classically educated, they were very conscious of following in the footsteps of their ancient predecessors. Shaw-Stewart re-read the *Iliad* on the way to Gallipoli, and wrote: 'It is the luckiest thing and the most romantic. Think of fighting in the Chersonese … or alternatively, if it's the Asiatic side they want us on, on the plains of Troy itself! I am going to take my Herodotus as a guide-book.'[229] 'I saw a man this morning' seems to have been his only war poem. Like Brooke, Shaw-Stewart did not survive the war; he died in France in 1917.

The dreadful toll of death of the world wars of the twentieth century could only put all past wars into a different perspective. A collage made by Eduardo Paolozzi (1924–2005),

RIGHT
Fig. 258*
Homeric Combat and
Hector, Dead Trojan
A train (upper image) and machinery (lower image) are superimposed on photographs of an ancient Greek marble frieze depicting battle scenes from the Trojan War.

1946
Eduardo Paolozzi
Collage of printed material
H. 313 mm | W. 240 mm
British Museum
1981,1107.7

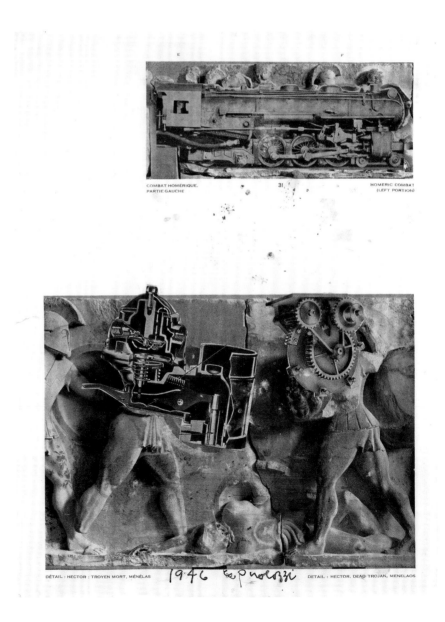

entitled *Homeric Combat and Hector, Dead Trojan*, takes images of reliefs from the east frieze of the sixth-century BC Siphnian Treasury at Delphi depicting the battle between the Greeks, fronted by Achilles, and the Trojans, supported by the Ethiopian Memnon, and transforms them by superimposing images of machinery, including a train (Fig. 258). Paolozzi's work often reflected on the idea of man as an assemblage of parts in a machine, and on the ways individual identity was subsumed by progress and technology. The collage, one of a series incorporating images of classical sculpture torn from books the artist bought from a bookshop near the British Museum, was made in 1946, just after the end of Second World War.[230] The choice of Trojan War imagery for this particular print was surely intended as a comment on the recent conflict that had marked Paolozzi's young life. Born in Scotland to Italian immigrant parents, he had been interned in 1940; his father and grandfather, also detained, had been killed on a boat sunk by a German U-boat on its way to Canada.[231] By 1946 Paolozzi was a student at the Slade School of Fine Art, which had been transferred to Oxford's Ruskin School during the war. Classical reference points were a substantial part of the training provided to artists at that time. Dramatically juxtaposing the 'naturalistically' rendered figures of ancient art with the abstract forms of machinery, Paolozzi's collage literally lays contemporary references over these ancient representations to create a new way of looking at the Trojan War in the context of twentieth-century experiences.

War and peace

Homer's Achilles is a flawed hero whose emotions and actions reveal the cracks in the value systems of his day. Hector is perhaps a less complicated character, but his dedication to duty in fighting to defend his city, and behaving in the way an honourable hero should, paradoxically leaves his family undefended and his city destined to fall. The two heroes' stories prompt reflection on questions which were pressing for ancient society and have remained highly relevant: about the qualities we admire in those who are pre-eminent in society; about tensions between the needs of the individual and those of the community; about reason and debate versus violence and revenge.[232]

Marian Maguire, an artist from New Zealand whose work combines ancient Greek, Māori and colonial European imagery to reflect on the colonization of New Zealand, took the ancient Greek Trojan War image of Ajax and Achilles playing a board game (see Fig. 49) and titled the reworked image *Te Whiti and Titokowaru discuss the question, 'What is Peace?'* (Fig. 259). This is part of a series, *Titokowaru's Dilemma*, in which the protagonist is a Māori leader who fought against settlers in the 1860s (known as Titokowaru's War) but later tried to find a peaceful solution to the conflict.[233] Here he is in conversation with Te Whiti o Rongomai of Parihaka discussing the question 'What is peace?', just as the Greek philosopher Socrates might have debated it. In a peaceful image set in Parihaka, a village on the slopes of Mount Taranaki in New Zealand, the Māori leaders discuss strategy and philosophy, intent on creating a future for their people in a changed world. As Maguire explains:

> In 1881 Parihaka was invaded by colonial forces. The men were imprisoned, the women raped, the village destroyed – mirroring the fate of Troy. Peace is one thing for the victors and another for the losing side, requiring from its leaders a different type of heroism; a more complex one.[234]

RIGHT
Fig. 259*
***Te Whiti and
Titokowaru discuss
the question, 'What
is Peace?'**

2010–11
Marian Maguire
Lithograph, part of the
series *Titokowaru's
Dilemma*
H. 460 mm | W. 655 mm
British Museum
2015,5007.1.10

HELEN AND THE WOMEN OF THE TROJAN WAR

> You think I'm not a goddess?
> Try me.
> This is a torch song.
> Touch me and you'll burn.
> Margaret Atwood, *Helen of Troy Does Counter Dancing*[235]

The figure of Helen, the most beautiful woman in the world, has been the focus of endless fascination and tireless speculation. She was Helen of Sparta, then of Troy, then of Sparta again – unless indeed she was Helen in Egypt for a time, and only her *eidolon*, a strange manufactured double, went to Troy (see p. 262). She was the beautiful bane that would cause the city's downfall, but was she an innocent victim or a guilty seductress? When Troy falls, Helen is the only prominent woman in the story who seemingly finds a happy ending: while Andromache, Hecuba and Cassandra are enslaved to Greek captors, Helen is reunited with her first husband, and the *Odyssey* shows her living apparently contentedly with Menelaus in Sparta. This seems only to compound her guilt, in contrast with the undeserved suffering of other more clearly innocent women, both Trojan and Greek. The stories of Helen and the other women of the Trojan War are powerfully emblematic of the experiences of – and attitudes towards – women, in ancient Greece and beyond.[236]

Beauty, virtue and power: the Judgment of Paris

> Paris judged foolishly: what this shows us is that the sound mind must keep from passing judgment on others …
> Christine de Pizan, *Epistle of Othea to Hector*[237]

BELOW
Fig. 260*
A wedding casket featuring scenes from the life of Paris
Panels on the box depict Paris' infancy and upbringing by a herdsman, the Judgment of Paris, and Paris carrying off Helen. The lid shows the seven Virtues.

c. 1390–1410
Florence or Venice, Italy, made by the workshop of Baldassare Ubriachi
Bone, horn and intarsia (wood inlaying) on a core of poplar
H. 370 mm | W. 335 mm
Victoria and Albert Museum
A.19-1952

Helen first becomes important in the story of Troy in an episode in which she herself takes no part. She is far away in Sparta when the three goddesses, Hera, Athena and Aphrodite, are brought to Mount Ida to be judged by Paris, and is completely unaware of the momentous divine beauty contest.

The Judgment of Paris was often shown in ancient art (see Figs 38, 39) and went on to be the episode that was most frequently represented by later artists in all media. Visually, it appealed because it offered the challenge of portraying the beauty of the three goddesses. Renaissance artists, inspired by classical art, especially sculpture, moved away from the medieval traditions that largely eschewed nudity and so depicted the goddesses naked or only partially clothed. In the sixteenth and seventeenth centuries, naked mythical gods and goddesses in idyllic surroundings offered a vehicle for sensual scenes with powerfully erotic overtones, often involving a titillating element of the dangers of female seduction. Meanwhile, a moralizing rationalization was always close at hand to justify the viewer's pleasure.[238] In the medieval and Renaissance world, the choice offered to Paris was viewed allegorically, as that between different ways of life (see p. 258). This moral dimension joins the scene's more obvious importance as the episode that began the Trojan War, as well as its sensual appeal, in explaining its dominance in the artistic canon.

In the medieval period Paris was seen as a hero, and so could not have acted wrongly in taking Helen from Sparta. Their union represented a virtuous marriage and events from the life of Paris were therefore popular on wedding caskets, such as the bone, horn and intarsia box made by the workshop of Baldassare Ubriachi in either Florence or Venice, in around 1390 to 1410 (Fig. 260).[239] Two of the eight panels show the Judgment. In the first the goddesses are led to Paris by Hermes, in the next they stand naked facing Paris to be judged, while in a further panel we see the result of his choice, as he grasps Helen round the waist and bodily lifts her away to become his wife in Troy. Depicting the goddesses naked in this episode goes back to ancient representations of female nudes such as the Three Graces, but not actually to the predominant classical tradition of Judgment scenes, in which the goddesses were shown clothed. The story that Paris asked them to disrobe is, though, found in ancient literature, and indeed they are shown naked in some Roman works. The idea became embedded in romance literature, particularly following the thirteenth-century work of Guido delle Colonne (see p. 192), and soon became the norm.

The allegorical element of the Judgment of Paris is to the fore in a painting by Lucas Cranach the Elder (1472–1553), which shows Paris looking dazed and moonstruck as he awakes from a dream (Fig. 261).[240] He is dressed in the dark, heavy armour of Cranach's time, in contrast with the three goddesses. They have white skin, elaborate hairstyles, jewellery and wisps of diaphanous drapery – clearly inhabitants of another world. Cranach seems again to follow the story as told by delle Colonne, based on Dares. In this version Paris is a knight who falls asleep exhausted when hunting and dreams that Hermes presents the three goddesses to him, asking him to award the apple (here represented by a crystal orb) to the fairest. After requesting that they disrobe, Paris chooses Aphrodite and is then released from sleep.

Cranach's goddesses stand in a pose analogous to that of the Three Graces in ancient art. In the Hellenistic period, it became canonical to show the Graces with the central figure seen from the back, flanked by the front view of her two sisters, and variants on this were frequently applied to the three goddesses in the Judgment of Paris from the Renaissance onwards. It allowed artists to show the female form from different angles, as Cranach does, but the creation of such a compositional whole makes it harder to draw any distinctions between the three figures, all of outwardly equal appeal. They represent the life of the senses (Aphrodite), the politically active life (Hera) and the contemplative life (Athena). This allegory, a modified version of the bribes offered by the goddesses in antiquity and a dilemma central to Christian theology, was firmly rooted in the humanist thinking of Cranach's time. His even-handed rendering may imply that the perfect life should be a balance of all three aspects in due measure, rather than offering a more conventional condemnation of the sensual.[241]

Indeed, a straightforward moral message is undermined even further. Aphrodite is clearly identified as the winner, as Eros' arrow points at her, while she turns her head to look seductively at the viewer. Her beauty is perhaps irresistible to us, as it was to Paris, and we are invited to question whether it (or she) should therefore be blamed. Yet according to the medieval version of the story, Paris' choice was made only in a dream, so perhaps the real danger is not the seductive powers of women, but male fantasy.[242]

The modern world has become uneasy with the parading of female beauty for judgment under male scrutiny. It is thus all the more pleasing to see the gender reversal in a painting by Hans Eworth (d. 1574) of 1569, in which Queen Elizabeth I of England plays the role of Paris (Fig. 262).[243] Here the goddesses are subjected not to the male gaze, but rather are

LEFT
Fig. 262*
Elizabeth I and the
Three Goddesses

1569
Hans Eworth
Oil on panel
H. 629 mm | W. 844 mm
Royal Collection Trust
RCIN 403446

judged, and indeed routed, by the queen. A Latin inscription on the frame explains how the entrance of the Queen overwhelms the goddesses: 'Queen Juno took flight; Pallas was silenced; Venus blushed for shame'. Elizabeth chooses to retain the 'apple' herself, though in fact what she holds is the golden orb of power. She has no need of the goddesses' proffered gifts, because she already combines and uses them all in her role as beautiful, wise and powerful monarch. The painting also represents a further twist in the story: the effect of the Judgment of Paris would be reversed. The result is now not a long and destructive war, but the promise of peace and plenty during the reign of this all-gifted queen.

A later artist, William Blake (1757–1827), imagined the moment when Paris, languid and apparently mesmerised by Aphrodite, hands her the golden apple (Fig. 263). Athena, to the right of Aphrodite and holding her helmet, looks on with a stern and fixed expression in reaction to his choice, while Hera, to the left, clearly shows her dismay. The winged Eros begins to swoop away from the scene, presumably taking his arrow of love to Sparta, and to Helen, and an unperturbed Hermes flies above the main figures. Yet in the top left-hand corner, a contorted, demonic figure grimaces and wields flaming torches, presaging the disaster and destruction that this moment sets in motion. With figures recalling the work of Michelangelo, the scene is typical of the art of William Blake, who drew on classical and Renaissance imagery, and the products of his own visionary imagination.[244]

At the turn of the twentieth century, when interest in the human psyche and sexuality was growing, the three goddesses increasingly came to embody not sensual, moral or intellectual beauty, but three types of femininity. The unmarried woman was seen reflected in the virgin goddess Athena; the mother and wife in Zeus' consort Hera; and the lover or

RIGHT
Fig. 263*
The Judgment of Paris

1806–17
William Blake
Pen, grey ink and
watercolour over graphite
on paper
H. 389 mm | W. 476 mm
British Museum
1949,1112.4

prostitute in Aphrodite, all of them defined in relation to men.[245] A contemporary imagining of the Judgment of Paris takes this idea one step further, subverting the archetypes with humorous effect. In Eleanor Antin's version (Fig. 264),[246] Athena is a khaki-clad and black-booted gun-slinger, Aphrodite, in long gloves and evening dress, looks as though she has just left a party, while Hera, in the garb of a 1950s housewife, wields a vacuum-cleaner. A disconsolate Helen sits to one side of the judgment scene, ignoring the foppish and faintly ridiculous figures of Hermes and Paris, but still engaging our sympathy because she so clearly has no part to play or power to take the slightest responsibility for her own future. She is objectified as the prize in the beauty contest, waiting to be awarded to the male who wins her. She has had no agency throughout the process, and is both angry and sad as a result.

Antin's *Judgment of Paris* is based on a 1638 painting of the same name by Rubens, who revisited the subject several times. In Rubens' painting Helen is not present and his main focus is the ideal naked bodies of the goddesses; the left-hand side of his composition only shows Paris' dog. It is of course unusual to find Helen represented in this scene, except in ancient works that show successive elements of the story simultaneously, as in an Etruscan wall-painting featured earlier (see Fig. 38). Yet Antin's focus is Helen, and in two different versions of this work she uses both the dark-haired model shown here and a light-haired alternative. She explains that in the series of works to which these images belong she felt the need to create two Helens: a flirtatious Helen who uses her blonde beauty and her wiles to navigate through the world of men, and the dark-haired Helen, who is brooding and angry.[247]

BELOW
Fig. 264*
***Judgment of Paris
(after Rubens)***

2007
Eleanor Antin
Chromogenic print
H. 935 mm | W. 1622 mm
Ronald Feldman Fine Arts

The face that launched a thousand ships: beauty and responsibility

Was this the face that launched a thousand ships
And burnt the topless towers of Ilium?
Christopher Marlowe, *Doctor Faustus*[248]

The judgment of Paris in many ways segued seamlessly into the judgment of Helen.
Ever since the fifth century BC, the jury has been out on whether to exonerate or condemn
her. She has been seen as a lascivious mischief-maker of lax morals who deserves opprobrium;
a pawn in the gods' game who had no powers to resist; a creature of flesh and blood fatally
burdened by men's responses to her unasked-for beauty; a royal lady commanding respect,
whether in Sparta or Troy; or a goddess to be worshipped, as she was in ancient Sparta.
No other single character in the story of Troy has cast such a spell and elicited such a
range of responses.

In the ancient story, Helen's beauty was an irrefutable absolute, as irresistible as it was
destructive. Fighting men, enduring great hardships and risking their lives, could scarcely
fail to question whether war over a woman, however beautiful, could ever make sense.
It was easy, perhaps natural, to blame Helen. In Dante's *Inferno*, we meet Helen, alongside
Paris (and also Dido and Achilles), in the section of the Underworld for those whose sin
was lust. In Goethe's *Faust Part Two*, a clear-sighted Helen introduces herself as 'so much
admired and so much censured'.

But did she deserve censure? Her defenders would say that she was simply the plaything
of the gods. Indeed, some ancient tales allege she was conceived by Zeus precisely for the
purpose of wreaking destruction, while others say her mother was the goddess Nemesis,
personification of retribution (see also p. 60). Viewing Helen as a 'beautiful evil' and
a mechanism for disaster aligns her with Greek mythology's Pandora, the first woman,
as well as with biblical Eve and a long line of female temptresses. The stereotype panders
to a widespread misogynistic trope in which the 'blame' for male desire is projected on
to the woman desired. Yet the Greeks themselves did not take quite so simple a view,
recognizing the irresolvable tension between personal responsibility and the will of the
gods, or fate (see p. 59).

The Helen of the *Iliad* is a flesh and blood character who has an uncomfortable and
ambiguous life in Troy. This is not physical discomfort – like other royal princesses she
lives in the royal apartments, filling her days with weaving and virtuous womanly pursuits.
Yet she is unhappy. She plays a relatively small but very important role in the poem, and
certainly speaks more often than the other female characters, so we gain unusual insight
into her state of mind. She knows that the Trojans, and particularly the Trojan women,
have come to hate her, and she is pathetically grateful to King Priam and to Hector as
the only two Trojans who show her kindness. She regrets her past actions, and ultimately
blames herself as much as she blames Aphrodite, frequently berating herself, most memorably
as a 'chilling, evil-devising bitch' (*Iliad* 6.344).[249]

We have no sense that Homer's Helen is self-serving, but nonetheless she is a great survivor.
When we meet her again in the *Odyssey*, she receives her guests in Menelaus' palace in
Sparta in a queenly and hospitable way. She mixes herbs to make them forget their sorrows,
perhaps here demonstrating her semi-divine status. This is one of the ways in which she is
not quite like the other women in the story. Andromache, Penelope or Hecuba, the strong
and loyal wives, remain flesh and blood in a way that Helen sometimes transcends.

The fifth-century BC tragedian Euripides, always interested in strong female characters and women who transgress the social norms, used this contrast to present a view of Helen that put her in the most excoriating light. *The Trojan Women* contrasts Helen with Andromache and Hecuba and the other Trojan captive women, with whom she occupies the stage. She is beautifully dressed, while the other women are in rags, with shorn hair and faces torn with lamentation. Their grief is honest and all-consuming, while Helen is a vicious, cunning and sly defender of her own role in the war, blaming the gods and all the other human players – everyone apart from herself. We hate Helen in this play, even as we weep with the women of Troy.

Interestingly, Euripides, in another tragedy, *Helen*, also presents her in the most positive light possible, as a virtuous, tragic victim. Helen regrets her ill-fated beauty; she wishes she could wipe it off, as if wiping paint from a coloured statue. This play retells the version of the story in which it was not Helen but a lookalike double (*eidolon*) who was abducted by Paris. In the Greek mind this *eidolon* was a seemingly real presence that deceived everyone, yet to the modern mind it recalls the phantasm of Helen that Mephistopheles conjures to tempt Doctor Faustus in Marlowe's play (see p. 196). The audience knows this phantasm comes from no good place: it is Helen as a beautiful evil that, at the devil's behest, will help lure Faustus' soul to eternal damnation.

It is not surprising to find that Helen, in all her complexity, became a favourite not just of poets but also of artists. In confronting the challenge to depict perfect female beauty, their images also chart the changing tastes of their times. The fifth-century BC Greek artist Zeuxis made a famous painting of Helen of Troy, now lost, for which we are told he chose five beautiful female models from many contenders, then incorporated the best features of each to create what he hoped would be an incomparable whole.[250]

Antonio Canova certainly strove for an ideal Helen in his bust carved around 1812 (Fig. 265).[251] She is serene in white marble, according to the taste of the day, with classically inspired features and abundant curls beneath her plain cap. The poet Byron felt that Canova had indeed surpassed nature and captured the essence of the beautiful when he wrote:

> In this beloved marble view,
> Above the works and thoughts of man,
> What Nature *could*, but *would not*, do,
> And Beauty and Canova *can*!
> Beyond Imagination's power,
> Beyond the bard's defeated art,
> With immortality her dower,
> Behold the *Helen* of the *heart*![252]

For the poet W. B. Yeats (1865–1939), it was this beauty that formed Helen's destiny. In his poem 'No Second Troy' his own, latter-day Helen was Maud Gonne (1866–1953), an actress and revolutionary who incited violence against the British in Ireland, and who rejected the poet's love. He speaks of her 'beauty like a tightened bow' that is 'high and solitary and most stern' and concludes with the rhetorical question:[253]

> Why, what could she have done, being what she is?
> Was there another Troy for her to burn?

ABOVE LEFT
Fig. 265*
Helen of Troy

c. 1812
Antonio Canova
Marble
H. 640 mm | W. 300 mm
Victoria and Albert
Museum
A.46-1930

ABOVE RIGHT
Fig. 266
Helen of Troy

1863
Dante Gabriel Rossetti
Oil on mahogany
H. 328 mm | W. 277 mm
Hamburger Kunsthalle
HK-2469

This both squarely holds Helen responsible for the burning of Troy, and yet exonerates her. She acted according to her essential nature, which was defined by her beauty. It has agency that is both separate from and dominates her own will.

The enigma of Helen's power also drew the Pre-Raphaelite painters of the nineteenth century as part of their wider fascination with themes of sensual women as sirens. Dante Gabriel Rossetti (1828–1882) painted her in 1863, using Annie Miller (1835–1925) as his model (Fig. 266).[254] His Helen is a beauty who looks pensively into the distance while touching the flaming torch that is part of her necklace, prefiguring the burning of Troy. On the back of the painting is a Greek inscription which is a quotation from the *Agamemnon* of Aeschylus, which describes Helen as 'destroyer of ships, destroyer of men, destroyer of cities'. Each of the three Greek words (ἑλένας, ἕλανδρος, ἑλέπτολις) begins with the syllable 'hel', meaning 'destroying' and echoing the first syllable of Helen's name. Rossetti also considers the character of Helen in his poem 'Troy Town' (1869), in which Helen prays to Venus for love with erotic fervour, characterizing her breasts as apples and reminding Venus of the apple that Paris gave her. The repeated refrain of 'Oh Troy's down, Tall Troy's on fire' makes Helen's agency unmistakeable: she, and specifically her erotic desire, is responsible for the fall of Troy.[255] Rossetti's affair with Annie Miller, the mistress of his friend Holman Hunt, had spelled trouble for all three of them, and Rossetti may have been thinking of her when he pondered the dangers of beautiful women.

Evelyn De Morgan (1855–1919) painted her full-length portrait *Helen of Troy* (Fig. 267) to form a pair with her depiction of Cassandra, both of 1898 (Fig. 268).[256] Here, Helen seems to be gazing into her mirror, admiring her flowing blonde tresses. She is apparently self-absorbed, even self-satisfied: a vision in pink drapery against a calm background with white doves. Yet in fact she looks not at but beyond the mirror, into the distance. She shares this elusive gaze with the portrait by Rossetti, indicating the difficulty of knowing the person behind the beautiful face. This tendency to elusiveness, even blankness, in portraits of Helen is also markedly present in the works of Gustave Moreau (1826–1898), and this is not only because some are unfinished. Moreau painted Helen repeatedly and she is always a pale, statue-like figure who stands apart from the carnage she has caused. She is inscrutable and unknowable: there is an absence at the heart of her beauty.[257]

Between 1882 and his death, Edward Burne-Jones (1833–1898) painted a series of small watercolours based on the traditional names of flowers, which were published posthumously in facsimile by his wife in *The Flower Book* (1905). The small roundel *Helen's Tears* (Fig. 269) was inspired by a flower known as elecampane (*Inula helenium*), which in folklore was said to have sprung from the spot where Helen's tears fell. This Helen remains statuesque, but holds her hands to her head in horror as Troy burns behind her.[258] Burne-Jones' friend and fellow artist William Morris (1834–1896) created a medieval-looking Helen in around 1860 as a design for an embroidered panel (Fig. 270).[259] It was part of a series of twelve panels

intended to decorate the dining room in the poet's new marital home, Red House in Bexleyheath, southeast London, all depicting legendary and mythical queens, goddesses, saints and mythological heroines, probably intended to represent different facets of love, from carnal desire through romantic love to religious worship. Looking pensively downwards, Helen holds a large burning torch with a banner wrapped around it reading 'Flamma Troiae', 'the flame of Troy', a reference both to the burning of the city and also perhaps to the passions she ignites.

Like Zeuxis or Canova, many artists attempted to create a perfect Helen whose ideal beauty transcended that of any living person. Others used models who in their day were considered outstandingly beautiful. Indeed, some artists and writers felt they had met their own Helen, as W. B. Yeats did in the poem quoted above. This was certainly Oscar Wilde's view of the actress Lillie Langtry (1853–1929). She was the subject of 'The New Helen', his poem of 1879. He sent her a copy of this paean of praise to her beauty, inscribed 'To Helen, formerly of Troy, now London.' Langtry was well-known in Victorian society and widely viewed as the most beautiful woman of her day. She was also famous for a number of love-affairs, most notably with the Prince of Wales, later Edward VII. In 1881, Sir Edward John Poynter (1836–1919) painted Helen of Troy using Lillie Langtry as his model (Fig. 271).[260]

In the contemporary world, we have perhaps learnt more compassion for Helen, viewing her as she is shown in Eleanor Antin's Judgment of Paris – a sad and isolated figure (see Fig. 264). Seeing her as a product of Greek male imagination, and as a focus for male anxieties

BELOW LEFT
Fig. 270*
Helen (Flamma Troiae)

c. 1860
William Morris
Pencil and watercolour
on paper
H. 124.7 cm | W. 62.4 cm
Victoria and Albert
Museum
E.571-1940

BELOW RIGHT
Fig. 271*
Helen

This watercolour was
created six years after
Poynter painted a larger
version of the same
portrait in oil.

1887
Edward John Poynter
Watercolour and
bodycolour
H. 288 mm | W. 213 mm
Royal Collection Trust
RCIN 913534

about female beauty and sexuality, makes her no less sympathetic if we think of her as a real person with human feelings. This is often the modern approach, which is personal and individual, though it picks up on the strand of thought already present in ancient Greece, where the tendency to objectify Helen as a desirable woman was sometimes balanced with recognition of the fact of her humanity.

Women in war: victims and vengeance

We have no chance against a time that needs heroes.
Christa Wolf, *Cassandra*[261]

Helen relates directly to the other women in the story of Troy in a variety of ways. Sister of Clytemnestra, aunt of Iphigenia and cousin of Penelope, her blood-ties are naturally on the Greek side, while Hecuba, Andromache, Cassandra and Polyxena become her relatives by marriage when Paris takes her to Troy. Yet it is at once apparent that these relationships are in no sense happy. All of these women are, to a greater or lesser extent, badly affected by Helen's history and her role as the cause of the Trojan War. Even Penelope, far away in Ithaca, must endure twenty years of waiting for her husband to return. The Trojan royal women will be enslaved, two innocent virgin princesses, Iphigenia and Polyxena, will be cruelly sacrificed, and Clytemnestra will take bloody revenge for the death of her daughter, for which she will then pay with her own life. While the men in the story may view Helen as a beautiful evil, the women could be forgiven for regarding her simply as evil. Yet it is not just Helen, but the state of war itself that brings about these tragic fates.

The story of Iphigenia has resonated down the ages: Agamemnon's plight as he must sacrifice what he loves, the ennobling of the girl as she becomes, in some versions at least, a willing victim, and the 'happy ending' that sees her not dead but whisked away to the land of the Taureans, are just some of the aspects of the story that have evoked strong responses. One example is the painting by Edward Henry Corbould (1815–1905), which unusually shows Helen and Iphigenia together (Fig. 272).[262] It is based on Tennyson's poem 'A Dream of Fair Women', in which Helen says of herself, 'Wher'er I came I brought calamity' and expresses her deep regret to Iphigenia, but the girl is immovable. '"My youth", she said, "was blasted with a curse. This woman was the cause."' Tennyson's works were favourites of Prince Albert, and Queen Victoria gave this painting to him at Christmas in 1859. Iphigenia's role as victim is mirrored by that of Polyxena, so the whole story of the Trojan War is framed by the sacrifice of innocents.

Yet not all the women in the story are equally helpless. In Mycenae, Clytemnestra plots her revenge against Agamemnon for the death of their daughter, murdering him after his triumphant return home. The strength of Clytemnestra is manifest in the painting by John Collier (1850–1934), which shows her as a vivid and commanding figure (Fig. 273).[263] Fierce, pale and stern, she still holds the axe with which she has killed her husband. This painting is notable for its response to the archaeology of both Troy and Mycenae. Clytemnestra wears a diadem closely based on the large one from Schliemann's 'Jewels of Helen', while the architectural setting contains Mycenaean decorative motifs.[264] Her presence seems androgynous, appropriately for a woman who has acted with the violence usually reserved for warriors. In fact, the painting was probably inspired by a contemporary production of Aeschylus' Classical Greek tragedy *Agamemnon* which followed the ancient convention and used male actors for all roles.

LEFT
Fig. 272*
Helena and Iphigenia

1859
Edward Henry Corbould
Watercolour and
bodycolour with gum
arabic
H. 770 mm | W. 615 mm
Royal Collection Trust
RCIN 451115

The figure of Cassandra occupies a particularly interesting position in this range of active or passive women who may be victims or perpetrators. She has a great power – that of true prophecy – yet she is fated by the god Apollo never to be believed. Because she is an ecstatic prophetess, possessed of the god when she makes her predictions, it is too easy to see her simply as mad. This possession bordering on madness is captured by George Romney (1734–1802) in a fine portrait oil sketch of 1785–86, where she is wide-eyed and clawing wildly at her hair (Fig. 274).[265] The model here was Emma Hart (1765–1815), later Lady Hamilton and mistress of Lord Nelson, an acknowledged beauty of the day, known for her ability to bring classical figures to life through her 'Attitudes'. A hundred years later, in 1898, Evelyn De Morgan also painted Cassandra (see Fig. 268), the companion piece to her portrait of Helen (see Fig. 267). Here, too, Cassandra tears her hair, but unlike the peaceful backdrop for Helen, behind Cassandra the city of Troy is in flames.

This is consonant with depictions of Cassandra in ancient art, where she is particularly associated with her futile attempt to warn the Trojans that the Trojan Horse will bring disaster and that Troy is doomed to fall (see Figs 80 and 81). In the *Iliad* she is simply a marriageable daughter (13.365) and a sister mourning her brother Hector (24.699), though in Greek tragedy she is the virgin priestess and prophetess who suffers not just physical anguish when she is raped as Troy falls (see Fig. 83), but also mental anguish because of her gift.

Fig. 273*
Clytemnestra

1882
John Collier
Oil on canvas
H. 239 cm | W. 174 cm
Guildhall Art Gallery
577

As time went on, Cassandra the prophetess became a foil for various social and individual concerns. In the medieval period she foretold the coming of Christ and the Day of Judgment, while for Friedrich Schiller she embodied the lonely melancholy of knowledge. Yet, unlike Laocoön, who also warned against the wooden horse and became one of the Trojan War's most well-known figures, not least because of the famous sculpture (see p. 194), Cassandra long remained in the shadows.[266] The twentieth century, however, responded particularly to Cassandra, the prophetess giving voice to existential fears at a time of global catastrophes – clear-sighted but unheeded in the face of human folly. This was her role in the play by Giraudoux discussed above (p. 207) and is the focus, too, of American Robinson Jeffers' (1887–1962) poem 'Cassandra':

> The storm-wrack hair and screeching mouth: does it matter, Cassandra,
> Whether the people believe
> Your bitter fountain? Truly men hate the truth…[267]

Cassandra is ultimately powerless, and for this reason she embodies a modern, cynical view of the world. Perhaps because Cassandra's medium is above all the spoken word and not the image, she is relatively rarely represented in art. Exceptions include a 1936 painting by Karl Hofer (1878–1955), in which her presence is stark and foreboding.[268] This is Cassandra as the prophetess of death and destruction on the eve of global war. As ever, her efforts to warn will be futile and in vain.

Humanity has learnt much from engagement with the characters in the story of Troy, but has not yet learnt to heed Cassandra's warning. War remains as much a part of the human condition as it did when the armies met and clashed outside the walls of Troy.

LEFT
Fig. 274*
***Lady Hamilton
as Cassandra***

c. 1785–86
George Romney
Oil on canvas
Diam. 460 mm
Tate
No1668

HELEN'S JEWELS

The story of the jewellery in Edward John Poynter's portrait of Helen is interesting. The London goldsmith Carlo Giuliano (1831–1895) was famous for the 'archaeological' style of the jewellery he created, which became extremely fashionable in the latter part of the nineteenth century. Heinrich Schliemann invited him to see the pieces that he had found at Troy (see p. 150) in Priam's Treasure, which he liked to think had belonged to Helen. The well-known photograph of his wife Sophia wearing the so-called 'Jewels of Helen', taken around 1874 (see Fig. 135), had in fact helped to fuel the vogue for jewellery in the archaeological style. Yet the pieces Giuliano made (Figs 275, 276) were based not on Schliemann's finds but on the necklaces and earrings worn by Helen in Poynter's portraits, the first of which was exhibited at the Royal Academy in 1881, the year it was painted (see Fig. 271).[270] The Trojan finds actually had remarkably little impact on jewellery design, perhaps because the pieces, particularly the large and elaborate diadems, did not easily translate into 'wearable' items. It was not until the twentieth century that Greek goldsmith Ilias Lalaounis (1920–2013) based many of his most striking designs on the jewellery found at Troy.[271] Exact replicas of the jewellery from Schliemann's collection have been made (Fig. 277), usually either for museum display or for use as film props.

TOP
Fig. 275*
'Helen of Troy'
necklace

c. 1881
Carlo Giuliano
Silver-gilt and bowenite
D. 15 mm (bead);
L. 79 mm (central plaque)
Victoria and Albert
Museum
M.9:1,2-2011

ABOVE
Fig. 276*
Necklace and earrings
This necklace is based on
that in Edward Poynter's
paintings of Helen of Troy.

c. 1881
Carlo Giuliano
Gold, mottled jasper,
chalcedony and
bloodstone

L. 430 mm (necklace);
L. 27 mm (earrings, each)
Victoria and Albert
Museum
M.10:1 to 4-2011

RIGHT
Fig. 277*
**Replicas of the 'great
diadem' and earrings
from Priam's Treasure**

2006; 1980s; based
on gold originals of
c. 2550–2300 BC
Germany (diadem);
Wolfgang Kuckenberg,
Germany (earrings)
Brass, gilded (diadem);
silver-gilt (earrings)
L. 522 mm | H. 300 mm;
H. 93 mm | W. 50 mm
(each earring)
Museum für Vor- und
Frühgeschichte, Berlin
VIIa 2355; VIIa 1425, 1426

EPILOGUE
THE SHIELD OF ACHILLES

ALEXANDRA VILLING AND J. LESLEY FITTON

THE SHIELD OF ACHILLES AS A DEPICTION OF THE *KOSMOS*

And first Hephaestus makes a great and massive shield,
[…]
and across its vast expanse with all his craft and cunning
the god creates a world of gorgeous immortal work.
Iliad 18.478–82

Homer's description of the Shield of Achilles in Book 18 of the *Iliad* (18.474–608) is one of the most remarkable and fascinating passages in the entire poem.[1] According to the story, Achilles needed new armour to replace that borrowed by Patroclus, which Hector had stripped from him when he killed him. Thetis, Achilles' divine mother, asks the smith god Hephaestus to make a new set (see pp. 74–83). With the help of fire, wind and his tools, the god uses his matchless skills to fashion a new 'great and massive' shield from four metals – copper (or bronze), tin, gold and silver – in five layers (474–81). Having set the scene by fashioning the earth, the sky, the sea, the moon, the sun and the constellations of the stars (483–89) as decoration on the shield, Hephaestus proceeds to make images of 'two noble cities filled with mortal men'. One is a city at peace, with scenes of weddings, dancing and a lawsuit in the market place, representing a well-ordered urban community and its joyful celebrations. The other is at war, besieged by an army and characterized by strife, treachery and violent suffering. This is followed by scenes of the cultivation of fertile land; a king's domain with fields being harvested while a meal is prepared for the workers; young men and women joyfully harvesting in a lush vineyard; a herd of cattle being attacked by a lion; a peaceful sheep pasture and a circle of dancing boys and girls. The shield's outer rim, finally, is formed by the great stream of Ocean, which encompasses all within (607–8).

ABOVE
Fig. 278
Babylonian map of the world showing it as a disc surrounded by a ring of water called the 'Bitter River'
'Babylon' is marked as a rectangle at the right end of the Euphrates.

700–500 BC
Probably from Sippar, Iraq
Clay tablet with cuneiform inscription
H. 122 mm | W. 82 mm
British Museum
1882,0714.509

The Shield of Achilles is a highly symbolic work of art. Within the context of the *Iliad*, it is often seen as a commentary on the central themes of the poem. It evokes the brutal nature of war and its poignant contrast to times of peace, and highlights the key role played not just by individual people but also by the wider community.[2] Reflecting the extremes of human existence between joy and despair, life and death, it nonetheless reverses the general balance of the *Iliad*, where war predominates, and for the most part shows peace and the achievements of human civilization.[3] Yet the decoration is a synopsis not just of the inhabited world (the Greek concept of the *oikoumene*), but a microcosm of the whole world through space and time, while its materials and construction echo early Greek ideas of the succession of the ages, from the golden age, to the silver age, the bronze age, the age of heroes and the iron age of Homer's own time.[4] It is the first Greek abstract model of the *kosmos*, the existing world in its given order and in some sense the first Greek map of the world. Envisaging the earth as essentially a disc surrounded by an ocean river, it mirrors the earliest known of all pictorial world maps, preserved on a Babylonian cuneiform tablet dating from not long after the composition of the Homeric epics (Fig. 278).[5]

The conception of the earth as circular was, of course, well-suited to the shape of the round and slightly vaulted shields carried by Greek soldiers from about the later eighth century BC (see, for example, Fig. 58), which differed substantially from their Bronze Age predecessors. At first they would have been the preserve of the aristocratic leaders fighting in the front line of battle, as described in the *Iliad*. They became more common from the later sixth century BC, when growing wealth and redistribution of political power saw an increase in armed *hoplites* (foot soldiers) forming a heavy infantry.[6] Both actual shields and those described in literature commonly bore fierce imagery intended to strike fear in the enemy, such as the shield of Agamemnon:

> at the heart a boss of bulging blue steel
> and there like a crown the Gorgon's grim mask –
> the burning eyes, the stark transfixing horror –
> and round her strode the shapes of Rout and Fear.
> *Iliad* 11.35–37

The more complex and subtly meaningful decoration of the Shield of Achilles, with its kaleidoscope of perspectives, would have confounded expectations.

RECREATING THE SHIELD OF ACHILLES

> Of the twelve wondrous scenes which adorn the shield,
> there is not one which is not replete with beauty of its own.
> Allan Cunningham on John Flaxman's *Shield of Achilles*, 1830[7]

The passage in the *Iliad* that describes the Shield of Achilles is very long, occupying 134 lines of the poem. It is an early example of *ekphrasis*, the description of a visual work of art as a rhetorical device, but in fact it is not so much a description of the finished Shield as an account of its making: Hephaestus forges, hammers and shapes it, stage by stage. The god's strenuous activity creates equally dynamic scenes filled with life and movement, and even with sounds – of music, singing, the crash of battle or the voices in a court of law. This is god-made magic, imagined by a poet, and not truly a description of an object that could ever have existed. Indeed, although the scenes on the Shield are fully described, the passage does not actually tell us anything precise about their placement or form.[8] Homer's readers have therefore long debated not just the meaning but also the exact composition and arrangement of the shield's imagery, and attempts to physically reconstruct or recreate the Shield date back to antiquity.

The earliest surviving visualizations form part of the group of so-called Iliac Tablets (*Tabulae Iliacae*), miniature marble reliefs showing episodes from the *Iliad* (see pp. 49–50 and Fig. 34). These were created for the educated elites of the Roman Empire, for whom a sophisticated engagement with Greek culture became a competitive intellectual game.[9] Most of the tablets were rectangular, but those used to reimagine the Shield were round. Of the two extant round examples, both found in Rome, one is just a small fragment while about half of the other is preserved, allowing us to get a clear sense of its decoration (Fig. 279). In the restricted space afforded by a diameter of less than 18 centimetres (7 inches) were once crammed all the elements of Homer's description. A central zone, which contains the scenes of human life from a bird's-eye perspective, is framed by a circular band with the zodiac and another band with images of the sun and the moon. These are interspersed with carved lines of minuscule Greek text that both evoked the Ocean River and provided the viewer with the whole of the Homeric description of the Shield. Another inscription, carved in Greek letters on a band that divides the central field in two, labels the artwork and gives the name of its maker: 'The shield of Achilles, the art of Theodoros.' It is not clear whether Theodoros, who is also named on other Iliac Tablets, was an actual artist, or whether this is a kind of pun: Theodoros literally means 'gift of god', so could refer to Homer's perceived divine nature or indeed to the god-created shield specifically.[10]

Fascination with the shield has continued into modern times. Literary scholars, archaeologists and artists have all tried to imagine and recreate the physical shield behind

BELOW LEFT
Fig. 279
Fragment of a Roman Iliac Tablet in the form of the Shield of Achilles

c. 5 BC – AD 15
Rome
Giallo antico marble
Diam. 178 mm | D. 42 mm
Musei Capitolini, Rome
IMC 344/S

BELOW RIGHT
Fig. 280*
A sketch of the Shield of Achilles in the manuscript draft of Alexander Pope's translation of the *Iliad*

1712–24
Alexander Pope
Manuscript
H. 260 mm | W. 220 mm
The British Library
Add MS 4808

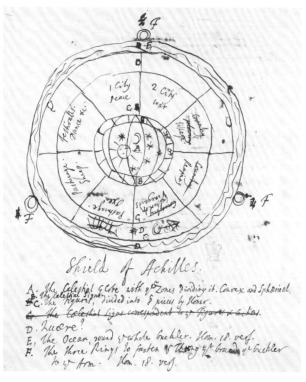

Homer's description, whether on paper or in three dimensions.[11] As early as 1715, the French scholar and translator Jean Boivin de Villeneuve (1663–1726) included an engraving of a reconstruction in his *Apologie d'Homere et bouclier d'Achille* (A Defence of Homer and the Shield of Achilles). Based on a drawing by French painter Nicolas Vleughels (1668–1737), this was an element of an argument within a scholarly debate on Homer's text. Alexander Pope reproduced the engraving in his famous translation of the *Iliad* (see p. 196), though his manuscript notes show that he had considered modifying the design by reducing the number of figured scenes in the main zone from twelve to eight (Fig. 280).[12] Unlike the Roman Iliac Tablet versions, these reconstructions largely arranged the scenes in concentric zones, as have most other modern commentators, in an arrangement corresponding to the concentric circles often found on Greek shields of the period.

The style of the scenes, too, has been a matter of debate. By the nineteenth century the lively, rather baroque figures of Vleughels' shield had become untenable as knowledge of

Figs 281 and 282
Two studies for the
Shield of Achilles
The study for the battle scene (above) shows foot soldiers and cavalrymen fighting while women look on from behind. The study for the wedding scene (below) shows a procession emerging from a doorway. Women follow the bride and groom. The dancing youths and musicians who precede them are inspired by ancient reliefs.

1818
John Flaxman
Pen and grey ink with brown wash on paper
H. 162 mm | W. 391 mm;
H. 178 mm | W. 357 mm
British Museum
1862,0308.5; 1862,0308.6

BELOW
Fig. 283*
Shield of Achilles

1822
Phillip Rundell, from a
design by John Flaxman
Silver-gilt
Diam. 970 mm | D. 180 mm
National Trust, Anglesey
Abbey
NT 516395

ancient art was enhanced by study of actual Greek masterpieces, from the Parthenon sculptures to Greek vase-paintings. A reconstruction by A. Chr. Quatremère de Quincey (1755–1849), completed in 1809 and published in 1817, owes much to Roman art.[13] It was John Flaxman, however, who was responsible for what is the best known of all the Shield's artistic interpretations, not just drawing it but actually recreating it. This revived the Renaissance tradition of display chargers, large circular dishes, or shields decorated with scenes celebrating military triumphs, an example of which is the fine silver dish with Homeric associations that was made in Portugal in around 1500 to commemorate a Portuguese military victory (see Fig. 255).

Flaxman worked on his *Shield of Achilles* between 1810 and 1817, commissioned by the London jewellers and goldsmiths Rundell, Bridge & Rundell. Taking inspiration from ancient works of art, he created numerous delicate drawings to form the basis for the individual scenes (Figs 281 and 282).[14] When the Shield was finally completed in 1818, it was widely considered a masterpiece, and one of his most successful works. Flaxman carefully controlled the whole process, first modelling the shield from clay, casting this in plaster, reworking it and then casting multiple versions. Five shields were cast in silver-gilt (Fig. 283) and three or more in bronze.[15] The first of the gilded silver versions was prominently displayed at the coronation banquet of King George IV in 1821. Much later, electrotype copies were made for the Great Exhibition of 1851 in London, the first of a long and still continuing series of World Fairs.

In Flaxman's magnificent composition (Fig. 284) the scenes arranged within the shield's diameter of almost 1 metre (39 inches) are centred on a depiction of Apollo, shown in his

RIGHT
Fig. 284
Graphic arrangement of scenes on Flaxman's shield

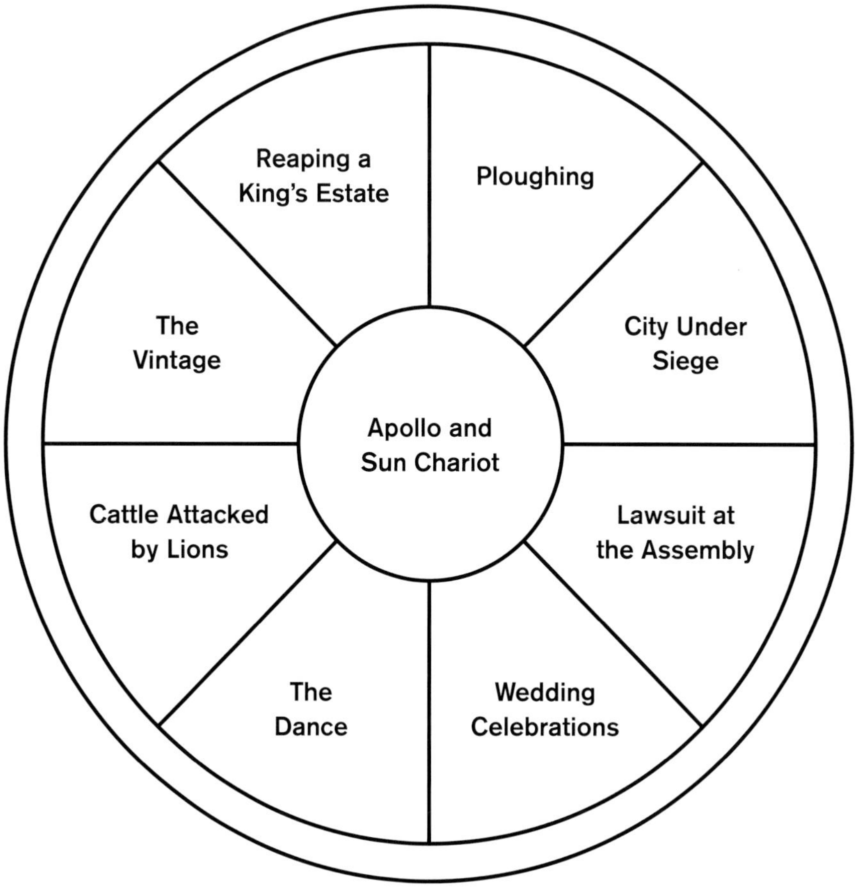

guise as the sun god in his chariot, set against the heavenly backdrop of moon, stars and constellations. This image is encircled by a frieze arranged as one continuous narrative. In Homeric order it depicts (anticlockwise) a wedding procession and banquet, a quarrel and a lawsuit, a town under siege, ploughing and reaping, the vintage with a boy singing, herdsmen defending their flock from lions, and a Cretan dance. The great river Oceanus encircles the rim of the shield. As well as being deeply immersed in classical literature and art, Flaxman drew from life, particularly during the time he spent in Rome in 1787–94. He viewed these studies as a resource to be drawn on in his later career, and his lively figures for the *Shield of Achilles* probably combine inspiration from both art and life.

THE ETERNAL LIGHT OF TROY

> As Dawn rose up in her golden robe from Ocean's tides,
> Bringing light to immortal gods and mortal men
> *Iliad* 19.1–2

As a weapon of war but decorated with scenes of peace, the Shield is like many of the similes in the *Iliad*. Even when describing battle, the poet draws on images from nature – the flights of birds or crashing waves – or of human beings engaged in everyday tasks. Homer tells of war, but that it is only one aspect of life, and is not in fact the dominant element of human experience.

Writers and artists through the ages have reacted to the powerful symbolism of the Shield and have teased out new and diverse meanings. The ancient tradition tells us that after the death of Achilles and the dispute over his armour, Odysseus inherited the Shield. In Derek Walcott's play *The Odyssey*, Odysseus carries it throughout his long journey home; it covers him like a turtle shell, giving him a sense of 'at-homeness' wherever he goes.[16] For the eternal traveller, this shield – which is the world – becomes his home.

Perhaps the best-known twentieth-century response is the poem 'The Shield of Achilles' (1952) by W. H. Auden. Auden creates a desolate atmosphere. He repeats the line 'She looked over his shoulder …' as Thetis watches Hephaestus at work. She expects to see the pleasant and lively scenes of peace described by Homer, but instead is greeted by bleak horrors:

> She looked over his shoulder
>   For vines and olive trees,
>   Marble well-governed cities
>   And ships upon untamed seas,
>   But there on the shining metal
>   His hands had put instead
>   An artificial wilderness
>   And a sky like lead.[17]

Auden seems to have in mind not just the Second World War, but also the fears of depersonalized and dehumanized further wars in this Cold War period of anxiety and tension. The poem goes on to evoke a faceless and multitudinous army and nameless victims in a grim world where there can be no room for heroes. Finally, Thetis is dismayed by the work of the god, who in this poem is cruel:

The thin-lipped armorer,
 Hephaestos, hobbled away,
 Thetis of the shining breasts
 Cried out in dismay
 At what the god had wrought
 To please her son, the strong
 Iron-hearted man-slaying Achilles
 Who would not live long.[18]

In the *Iliad*, we have no sense that Thetis 'commissions' Hephaestus to decorate the Shield with specific scenes. But we know that she always wanted Achilles to choose peace and a long life, rather than war, death and eternal fame. Auden's poem reminds us of her maternal feelings: the scenes she expects to see are those described by Homer, but they are also ones that can only remind Achilles of what he is giving up.

We know Achilles is mythical, but we relate to him as though he were real, and this is important to contemporary American artist Spencer Finch, who created his work *Shield of Achilles (Dawn, Troy, 10/27/02)* after a visit to Troy (Fig. 285).[19] Inspired by the *Iliad*, he was motivated by the idea of seeing for himself what Achilles saw more than three thousand years ago, and then sharing the experience with people who would view the resulting artwork in other places and times. Finch has often been drawn to the idea of experiencing what certain historical or mythical figures may have seen, and imagined that the light of the sun is perhaps the only phenomenon that may not have changed over thousands of years. His method, characteristically, was scientific, even though this is an intensely romantic notion. Using equipment to measure the colour and intensity of ambient light, he took multiple readings of the quality of the light at dawn on the plain of Troy. Dawn is frequently described by Homer, and the expression 'rosy-fingered dawn' (ῥοδοδάκτυλος Ἠώς) is of course one of the most famous of the Homeric epithets. Finch then recreated, with carefully calibrated precision, the morning light of Troy using fluorescent lamps. He has reworked the piece on a number of occasions, at first using tubes filtered with blue, violet, pink and green theatre lighting gels; this is the version illustrated here. In a new version, made specifically for the *Troy* exhibition, he has adopted a colour palette based on the description of the shield in the *Iliad*, resulting in a work that differs substantially in appearance, but draws on identical themes.

In his installation of the work, Finch arranges the fluorescent tubes in a radiating circle, referring both to the sun and to the legendary Shield created by Hephaestus. The Shield encapsulated the world, but Finch conflates it with the sun, the all-encompassing subject of his own artistic pursuits. There is here, too, an unconscious echo of Flaxman's *Shield*, in which the sun god dominates the composition. Finch himself is influenced by the work of J. M. W. Turner, whose final words are said to have been 'The sun is God.'

In this attempt to capture and recreate something eternal about Troy, Finch also responds to the sense of continuity and eternity that is part of Homer's description of the Shield of Achilles. This is not only because of its cosmological elements, but also because the human actions are frozen in time and uncompleted as they circle around it, while the ceaseless stream of Ocean runs endlessly around its edge. In our modern world, the city of Troy lies in ruins, but its story has the same eternal quality as the light that dawns each day over the mythical battlefield.

Spencer Finch is not the first artist to have responded to the sense of Troy as a physical place. The poet Byron visited and explored the plain of Troy, and was passionately convinced

OPPOSITE
Fig. 285
***Shield of Achilles
(Dawn, Troy, 10/27/02)***
A new version of this
work has been created
specifically for the *Troy*
exhibition.

2013
Spencer Finch
Fluorescent fixtures
and filters
Dimensions variable

that here was the scene of heroic endeavour. In his poetry, he reflected on the transience of such deeds and the way that nature had re-established peace over the scene of conflict:

> High barrows, without marble, or a name,
>   A vast, untill'd, and mountain-skirted plain,
>   And Ida in the distance, still the same,
>   And old Scamander (if 'tis he) remain;
>   The situation seems still form'd for fame—
>   A hundred thousand men might fight again,
>   With ease; but where I sought for Ilion's walls,
>   The quiet sheep feeds, and the tortoise crawls.
> *Don Juan*, Canto 4, 77

This Troy of the poetic imagination, the once-great city brought low, would frequently be seen as a suitable subject for musings on the evanescence of human affairs, as it had been in antiquity: the poet Ovid wrote, 'Iam seges est ubi Troia fuit' (Now corn grows where Troy once stood).[20] Yet the tragic fate of individual characters would continue to speak to people across time and place. Shakespeare's Hamlet famously asked the rhetorical question, 'What's Hecuba to him or he to Hecuba, that he should weep for her?' But in truth both he and we know the answer.

Fig. 286
Map showing the
location of Troy and
other significant sites
in the Mediterranean

ITALY

● Rome

Cumae ● Naples
●●
Pithecusae ●

SICILY

Carthage ●

ADRIATIC SEA

*ION
SE*

MEDITERRANEAN SEA

0   500 m

0   800 k

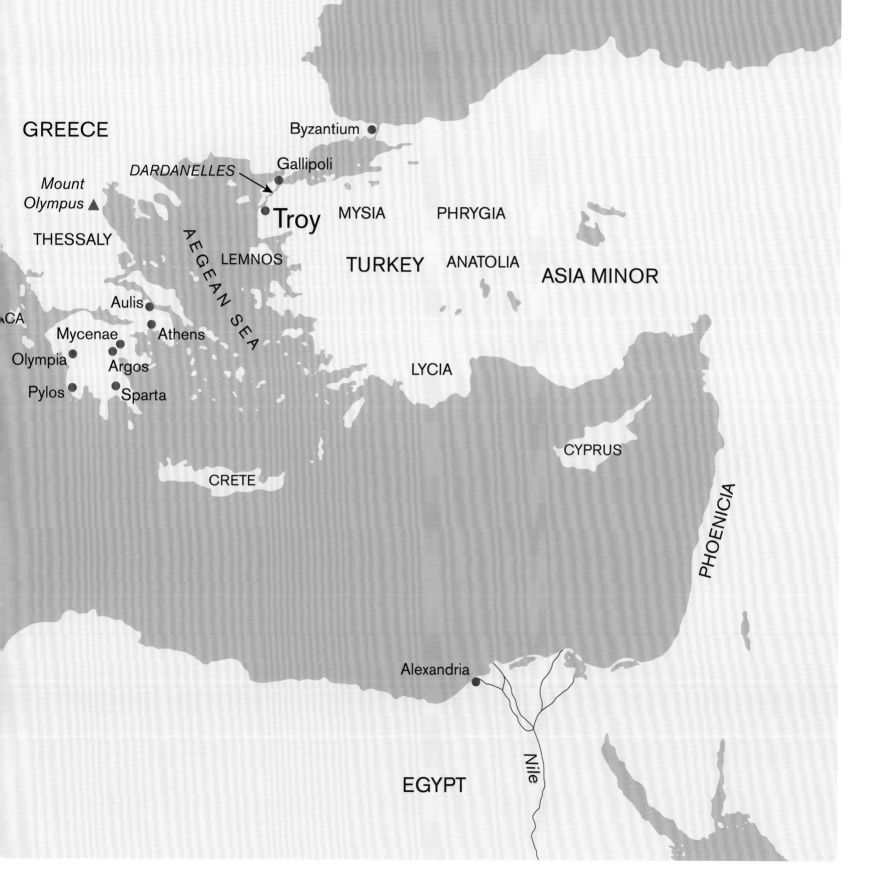

BLACK SEA

GREECE

Byzantium

DARDANELLES Gallipoli

Mount Olympus ▲

Troy

MYSIA PHRYGIA

THESSALY

AEGEAN SEA LEMNOS

TURKEY ANATOLIA ASIA MINOR

Aulis

CA

Mycenae Athens

Olympia

Argos LYCIA

Pylos Sparta

CYPRUS

CRETE

PHOENICIA

Alexandria

Nile

EGYPT

NOTES

Abbreviations
BAPD = Beazley Archive Pottery Database
LIMC = Lexicon Iconographicum Mythologiae Classicae. Artemis & Winkler Verlag, Zurich, Munich, Dusseldorf

INTRODUCTION: TROY – FALL OF A CITY, RISE OF A LEGEND (pp. 8–15)

1. On sources of translation. This and all other English extracts from the *Odyssey* are from *The Odyssey. Homer*, translated by Emily Wilson. Copyright © 2018 by Emily Wilson. Used by permission of W. W. Norton & Company, Inc.

   Excerpts from THE ILIAD by Homer, translated by Robert Fagles, translation copyright © 1990 by Robert Fagles. Used by permission of Viking Books, an imprint of Penguin Publishing Group, a division of Penguin Random House LLC. All rights reserved.

   Extracts from the *Aeneid* are from *The Aeneid. Virgil*, translated by Sarah Ruden. Copyright © 2008 by Yale University. Reproduced by permission of Yale University Press.

2. For an earlier, similar collage Paolozzi drew on a related Trojan theme, the ancient sculptural group of Laocoön, which also features in other works by Paolozzi: Spencer 2000, 102–3 (cf. pp. 2, 31, 316).

3. Schliemann 1880, 3.

4. On the history of Priam's Treasure, see

G. Korff in Latacz et al. 2001, 455–61. On the mythical quality of Schliemann – himself the subject of a 1995 French opera – and his work, see Zintzen 1998; 2001; Cobet 2006.

5. Walcott 1993, p. 13. *The Odyssey: A Stage Version*, Derek Walcott, published by Farrar, Straus & Giroux, 1993. © 1993 by Derek Walcott. Used by permission of Farrar, Straus & Giroux.

6. The story of the Trojan War has been successfully applied in therapy work with soldiers returning from recent conflicts, see Shay 1994 and 2002; Meineck and Konstan 2014.

7. https://www.barbican.org.uk/whats-on/2018/event/brink-productions-memorial [accessed 31.8.2019]

8. *Queens of Syria*, 2014, director Yasmin Fedda. Tell Brak Films; https://www.youngvic.org/whats-on/queens-of-syria [accessed 31.8.2019]

9. Queens of Syria fundraising video. https://www.developingartists.org.uk/queens-of-syria [accessed 31.8.2019]

10. On Romare Bearden, see pp. 225–25. On the Pintoricchio fresco, see Scherer 1963, 69–70; Hagen and Hagen 2005, 118–23.

11. Spurling and Bryant 1994.

12. Quoted in Spurling and Bryant 1994, 10.

1 STORYTELLERS (pp. 16–51)

1. Translation Paton 1917.

2. Translation Usher 1985.

3. Scholarly literature on Homer, the *Iliad* and the *Odyssey* is vast and there is a lively debate on nearly every aspect of the topic. More details and further references on the various issues touched on in this brief summary can be found in Graziosi 2016; Nicolson 2014; West 2011a, b; 2017; Nagy 2009; Graziosi and Greenwood 2007; Fowler 2004; Graziosi 2002; West 2001; Morris and Powell 1997; Janko 1992. On the reception of Homer's epics by Greek philosophers, see H. Flashar in Latacz et al. 2008, 215–20; cf. also Montiglio 2011.

4. Athenaeus, *The Learned Banqueters* 8.347e.

5. On the Epic Cycle see Fantuzzi and Tsagalis 2015; West 2013; Burgess 2001.

6. P. Higgs in Picón and Hemingway 2016, 137 no. 44; Stewart 2014, 135–36, 139 fig. 75.

7. On the so-called Homeromanteion (Homer-oracle), see Chaniotis 2010, 258.

8. On P.Lond.Lit. 30 see McNamee 2007, 276–81, no. 1039; on the transmission of the epic texts, West 2001.

9. Farnoux 2019; Spivey 2016; Graziosi 2002, 126–32; Richter 1965, 45–56. As noted by Morris 2014, 8, it is peculiar that the cities and regions that claimed a particular link with Homer are absent from the *Iliad* and even from the Catalogue of Ships in *Iliad* Book 2.

10. Sheedy 2009.

11. P. Higgs in Picón and Hemingway 2016, 135 no. 42; cf. L. Lougier in Farnoux et al. 2019, 88–89.

12. BAPD no. 201668. The verse is probably

a hexameter (C. Tsagalis in Ready and Tsagalis 2018, 73 note 38) or a lyric dactylo-epitrite (Sider 2010, 549 note 31). The pipe player (*aulete*) on the other side of the vase suggests the performance of an elegy (Bowie 1986). On epic performance see Ready and Tsagalis 2018.

13. Bourogiannis 2018.

14. BAPD no. 215997.

15. Cribiore 1996, 249 no. 310; 1993; on Homer in ancient education, see also Chaniotis 2010, 264–67; Cribiore 2001.

16. Etman 2011. A Syriac translation is said to have been completed as early as the eighth century AD.

17. West 2001, 141–52. In total, the *Iliad* is preserved in some one and a half thousand ancient manuscripts and at least two hundred medieval ones.

18. West 2011b.

19. Translation Susan Woodford. The original is quoted in Graziosi 2016, 12–13: 'Der Wolfische Homer. Sieben Städte zankten sich drum, ihn geboren zu haben; nun da der Wolf ihn zerriß, nehme sich jede ihr Stück.' On Goethe and Homer see Riedel 1999.

20. Butler 1897.

21. Staal 2010.

22. On oral poetry and music in the Greek Bronze Age see the essays by S. Deger-Jalkotzy and S. Hagel in Latacz et al. 2008, 99–105 and 106–12. For different views on orality and the transmission of the epic, see Nagy 2009; West 2001.

23. Burgess 2009a; Lane-Fox 2008, 34; Luce 1998; cf. Kolb 2014–15.

24. See e.g. Bachvarova 2016; Haubold

2013; Morris 1997. On itinerant bards and poets, see the essays in Hunter and Rutherford 2009.

25. Węcowski 2014, 127–34; Jeffery 1990, 236–37, 239, pl. 47.1. The translation given here for the Greek inscription is by Alan Johnston (pers. comm.). For the cup's production at Teos, see Kerschner 2014, 109–10. On the wider cultural context, now redefined by recent finds at Methone in northern Greece, see Janko 2017; Węcowski 2017.

26. Plutarch, *Life of Alexander* 8.2.

27. Adapted from the translation by Green 2005.

28. See e.g. Hunter 2014; A. Bierl in Latacz et al. 2008, 208–14; Pallantza 2005; Anderson 1997.

29. Anderson 1997, 105. On Euripides' *The Trojan Women*, see Haywood and Mac Sweeney 2018, 76-92.

30. Phillips 1959.

31. Hart 2010, 93 no. 43; Touchefeu 1992a, 957 no. 93.

32. Hornblower 2015.

33. Burgersdijk 2012; Harich-Schwarzbauer 2008; Farrell 2004.

34. See e.g. Hopkinson 2018; James 2004.

35. Quintus of Smyrna, *Posthomerica*, 13. 334–41. Translation James 2004.

36. There is much scholarly literature on Virgil and his work. For discussion of the topics covered here, see esp. Martindale 1997; cf. also Hardie 2014. On images of Virgil including the Hadrumetum mosaic, see Joyner 2014; Dunbabin 1978, 131, 242, pl. 131.

37. The *Aeneid* remained in circulation in Europe throughout Late Antiquity and the Middle Ages, including in some richly illuminated manuscripts: Wright 2001.

38. *Iliad* 20.292–309.

39. Erskine 2001, 16.

40. Canciani 1981, 301 no. 168.

41. Scappaticcio 2013, 109–11 no. 14. On the reverse of Papyrus P. Hawara 24, apparently the same writer wrote seven repetitions of another line, *Aeneid* 4.I74, of which only ']iut velocius' is preserved, as well as traces of a third word, perhaps from a line of Horace.

42. Hardie 2014, 5.

43. There are numerous publications on the myth of Troy in the visual arts and its relation to poetry, see e.g. Morris 2014; Lowenstam 2008; Blome 2008b; 2001; Wünsche 2006; Muth 2006; Recke 2002, 7–98; Hedreen 2001; Stansbury-O'Donnell 1999; Snodgrass 1998; Shapiro 1994; Woodford 1993; Schefold 1966. On images of the fall of Troy in South Italian pottery, see Moret 1975. On the link between images and texts in general, see also Giuliani 2013; Chaniotis 2010.

44. Pausanias 1.15.1–3; Plutarch, *Life of Cimon* 4.5–6; cf. Dué 2006.

45. Snodgrass 1998; cf. Blome 2008a; Schefold 1966.

46. Giuliani 2013, 32–34; Snodgrass 1998, 33–35. The identification of the scene remains disputed, but as already noted by Hampe and Krauskopf 1981, 508–9 no. 56, and Kahil 1988b, 532 no. 180, most

alternative suggestions to that of Paris and Helen involve couples where the woman is left behind (such as Theseus and Ariadne or Hector and Andromache), which is, however, contradicted by the hand-on-wrist gesture.

47. Sparkes 1971.

48. Carpenter 2015; Giuliani 2013.

49. Snodgrass 1998, 140–44. Popular are, for example, Achilles' ambush of the Trojan prince Troilus, the rape of the Trojan princess Cassandra, and the flight from Troy of Aeneas with Anchises.

50. Muth 2006, with reference to Athenian pottery.

51. Blome 2008b, 204–5; on the bronze figure see Jenkins 2002.

52. Hausmann 1994, 292 no. 6.

53. BAPD no. 200108.

54. On the art of Exekias see Mackay 2010.

55. Lowenstam 2008, 47.

56. Giuliani 2013, esp. 195–205; Hedreen 2001, 10–12.

57. Louvre G146: BAPD no. 204682; Villa Giulia 121110: BAPD no. 13363.

58. As discussed in detail by Shapiro 1994, 11–15.

59. Meyer 2012; Muth 2006; von den Hoff 2005; Recke 2002; Mangold 2000; Knittlmayer 1997.

60. Osborne 2018; Meyer 2012; Recke 2002.

61. Though the episode appears in art already earlier: Morris 2014, 7; Recke 2002; Kron 1981a, b; cf. Shapiro 1994, 152–54. The episode is alluded to in the *Iliou Persis*, though details and context are unclear; see also Burgess 2001, 152; Anderson

1997, 100.

62. BAPD no. 202164; Kron 1981a, no. 66.

63. Translation James 2004.

64. Shapiro 1994, 165; Castriota 1992. Cf. also McHardy and Deacy 2015, 258–59, on the popularity of depictions of Ajax and Cassandra in the period.

65. Cf. Recke 2002, 163–210.

66. Chaniotis 2010, 270–72.

67. Giuliani 2013, 225–42; Squire 2011, 62–63.

68. Athenaeus, *The Learned Banqueters*, 5.207c.

69. Pliny, *Natural History*, 35.144.

70. F. W. von Hase in Latacz et al. 2008, 221–31; Bonfante and Swaddling 2006, 11–20.

71. Parker 2017.

72. Sgubini Moretti 2004; Camporeale 1981, 206 no. 87.

73. Walter 2006; Harich-Schwarzbauer 2008.

74. Burgersdijk 2012; Simon 2008; 2001; Sinn 2006.

75. Andreae 1999.

76. Canciani 1981, 391 no. 174.

77. Petrain 2014; Squire 2011.

78. Weis 2000; cf. Andreae 1999; and see p. 276, Fig. 279.

2 THE MYTH OF THE TROJAN WAR (pp. 52–123)

1. A wide range of ancient and modern literature is drawn on in this chapter and we have necessarily had to be selective. For Greek written sources, besides the

references given in Chapter 1, see esp. Gantz 1993. Pictorial renderings of the story are surveyed in Woodford 1993; Schefold 1993; 1992; 1966; Schefold and Jung 1989, and in the various chapters and entries in *LIMC* and Wünsche 2006; cf. also Scherer 1963.

2. *Cypria* lines 1–7, West 2003. GREEK EPIC FRAGMENTS, translated by Martin L. West, Loeb Classical Library Volume 497, Cambridge, Mass.: Harvard University Press, Copyright © 2003 by the President and Fellows of Harvard College. Loeb Classical Library ® is a registered trademark of the President and Fellows of Harvard College.

3. Translation Coleridge 1938 [1891].

4. Translation Nagy 2013, 12§25.

5. West 2003, 64–107. It remains disputed when the narrative of this 'plan of Zeus' was first devised. See esp. Fantuzzi and Tsagalis 2015 and West 2013; cf. also Barker 2008; Scodel 2008; B. Kaeser in Wünsche 2006, 62–73; Burgess 2001.

6. B. Kaeser in Wünsche 2006, 87–100.

7. Williams 1983; BAPD no. 350099.

8. BAPD no. 207; Giroux 1986, 850 no. 1.

9. As discussed by Stinton 1965.

10. Translation Coleridge 1938 [1891].

11. BAPD no. 205649.

12. B. Kaeser in Wünsche 2006, 106–19; Kossatz-Deissmann 1994. Boccanera plaques: Bonfante and Swaddling 2006, 12–13; Kossatz-Deissmann 1994, 180 no. 41.

13. Schmitt 2008; Janko 1992, 1–7; cf. also Graf 2002; Burkert 1991.

14. Translation Grube 1957.

15. E.g. Schmitt 2008.

16. Woodford 1993, 12–13 fig. 1; Kahil 1988b, 504 no. 8.

17. On Helen, see Edmunds 2015; B. Kaeser in Wünsche 2006, 7–86; on Helen in ancient art, esp. Kahil 1955; 1988b.

18. *Iliad* 3.156–57.

19. On different renderings of Helen's abduction, see F. Knauß in Wünsche 2006, 120–27; Kahil 1955; on the moral dimension, see Edmunds 2015; Blondell 2013; Hughes 2005.

20. Euripides, *The Trojan Women* 987–96, translation Coleridge 1938 [1891].

21. Euripides, *Helen* 237–38, 249; cf. *Odyssey* 4.260–64; *Iliad* 3.399–412.

22. Plato, *Republic* 586c and *Phaedrus* 244. Cf. Scodel 2008, 220; B. Kaeser in Wünsche 2006, 66–69; Austin 1994. On Stesichorus see also Noussia-Fantuzzi 2015.

23. Froning 1981, 63–71; Kahil 1988b, 526 no. 146. Kolb 2014–15 argues for the origins of the 'Trojan War' in a conflict between different tribes of Late Bronze Age Greeks on the Greek mainland that was only later attached to the northwestern Anatolian region.

24. Kahil 1988b, 515–16, no. 74.

25. BAPD no. 231037; Kahil 1988b, 517 no. 86.

26. Krauskopf 1988, 264–65; Massa-Pairault 1972, 156–62; Kahil 1955, 274–79.

27. The identification as Helen has been disputed (e.g. Simon 2008, 241 fig. 14) but remains widely accepted: e.g. Newby 2016, 195–96, fig. 4.20; Hodske 2007, 267 no. 220, pl. 185.2; Bergmann 1994, 232 with note 25; Kahil 1988b, 532 no. 176.

28. Shapiro 1994, 165; Castriota 1992.

29. Mac Sweeney 2018, 80–82; Harrison 2000; Hall 1989; Said 1978.

30. Dué 2006, though this was balanced by a general notion of Athenian virtues trumping Persian vices: Harrison 2000, 848.

31. Fragment 282 lines 25–31, adapted from the translation by West 1993.

32. For ancient Greek literary and artistic renderings of this early stage of the Trojan War, see F. Knauß in Wünsche 2006, 128–39.

33. F. Knauß in Wünsche 2006, 132–35; Woodford 1993, 52–54.

34. F. Knauß in Wünsche 2006, 136–37; Woodford 1993, 34–38.

35. A. Villing in Stampolidis and Oikonomou 2014, 54–55 no. 1.

36. Mangieri 2018.

37. Translation Frazer 1921.

38. Canciani 1994.

39. B. Kaeser in Wünsche 2006, 41–46; F. Knauß in Wünsche 2006, 154–61.

40. BAPD no. 302224. On this episode in ancient art, see Lowenstam 2008, 39–43; F. Knauß in Wünsche 2006, 172–79; Hedreen 2001, 91–119; Woodford 1993, 59–64.

41. The rather different story of Troilus and Cressida is a much later, medieval creation (see p. 192).

42. BAPD no. 301518 and BAPD no. 302023. On the episode in ancient art, see F. Knauß in Wünsche 2006, 162–71; von den Hoff 2005; Hedreen 2001, 120–81; Woodford 1993, 55–59.

43. B. Kaeser in Wünsche 2006, 52–55; F. Knauß in Wünsche 2006, 141–51; Anderson 1997, 92–97; Woodford 1993, 45–48.

44. Hedreen 2011.

45. This detail may be no earlier than Roman times, being mentioned by Virgil and Valerius Flaccus, though Jason and the Argonauts as such appear already in the *Odyssey* (12.69–72); cf. West 2005.

46. The narrative in this section is based on the *Iliad*, except where alternative sources are specified.

47. BAPD no. 204400; V. Brinkmann in Wünsche 2006, 181–82; Hedreen 2001, 10; Williams 1993, 65–66 no. 50, pls (GB 848–49) 72–73; Woodford 1993, 68; Kossatz-Deissmann 1986, 158 no. 1 and 160 no. 14. Shapiro 1994, 13–14, draws attention to the parallel with wedding scenes.

48. Muellner 2012.

49. Smith (1904, 437–38 no. 2670) suggested that this relief is a modern copy of a nineteenth-century relief by the sculptor Bertel Thorvaldsen, but this seems unlikely on grounds of style. It appears to be Roman, probably reworked in the late eighteenth or early nineteenth century.

50. A major source for the early life of Achilles is the unfinished *Achilleid* of Papinius Publius Statius (*c.* AD 45–96). González González 2018, 59–60 summarizes sources for the Skyros episode.

51. On the nature of their relationship see González González 2018, 62–69.

52. Touchefeu-Meynier 1997, 949 no. 4.

53. Zanker and Ewald 2012, 229–30, 283–94.

54. On this sarcophagus: Grassinger 1999, 199 no. 13; Walker 1990, 39–40 no. 44a. On the Chiron scene: Kossatz-Deissmann 1981, 62 no. 138.

55. Döhle (1967, esp. 125) suggested that the vase depictions draw on both Homer and Aeschylus. On embassy scenes, see also Woodford 1993, 73–74; Schefold and Jung 1989, 196–200; Kossatz-Deissmann 1981, 113–14.

56. BAPD no. 205225.

57. See also pp. 71–73.

58. Williams 1993, 43–44 no. 28, pls. (GB 817–818) 41–42; Kossatz-Deissmann 1981, 109 no. 444.

59. Herda 2012. The temple of Hera at Argos also claimed possession of Euphorbus' shield. For the plate see also Giuliani 2013, 98–102; Burgess 2001, 77–81; Snodgrass 1998, 105–9; Kahil 1988a, 69 no. 1; Touchefeu 1988, 487 no. 35.

60. Bragantini and Sampaolo 2009, 350–51 no. 161; Borriello 1986, 136 no. 98.

61. Grassinger 1999, 202–3 no. 24; Angelicoussis 1992, 82; Kossatz-Deissmann 1981, 117 no. 477.

62. González González 2018, 30–39.

63. BAPD no. 206766; Woodford 1993, 80; Carpenter 1991, 203–4; Kossatz-Deissmann 1981, 124 no. 515.

64. Grassinger 1999, 199 no. 13; Vollkommer 1997, 10 no. 33; Walker 1990, 39 no. 44a.

65. BAPD no. 201941; F. Knauß in Wünsche 2006, 230–31; Woodford 1993, 82–83; Schefold and Jung 1989, 226–27; Kossatz-Deissmann 1981, 134 no. 565.

66. In Homer's version, there is no mention of the body being dragged three times around the walls of Troy; Virgil's *Aeneid* (1.483–84) gives this detail.

67. Shapiro 1994, 27–32 (Greek vases); Zanker and Ewald 2012, 283–84 (sarcophagi); Kossatz-Deissmann 1981, 143 no. 624 (on the dragging scene in Fig. 79).

68. BAPD no. 206109. Identified as Hector, Andromache and Astyanax in Birch and Newton 1851, 253 no. 810. See Touchefeu-Meynier (1981, 769 no. 19) for the modern interpretation.

69. Lowenstam 2008, 93–98, 157–65; Bonfante and Swaddling 2006, 55–57.

70. BAPD no. 302142; Kossatz-Deissmann 1981, 140 no. 593. On compressing different parts of the narrative into one image see Woodford 1993, 84.

71. Woodford 1993, 86; Kossatz-Deissmann 1981, 154 no. 687.

72. Grassinger 1999, 202–3 no. 24; Angelicoussis 1992, 81; Kossatz-Deissmann 1981, 156 no. 706.

73. Most of the events in this section were told in detail in the lost epic poems, the *Aethiopis*, the *Little Iliad* and the *Iliou Persis* (see p. 32). Many are also recounted – some in passing and some in full – in Virgil's *Aeneid* and the fourth-century AD *Posthomerica* of Quintus of Smyrna.

74. The earliest source for the stories of the Amazons and Memnon at Troy is the *Aethiopis*. The Memnon episode was the topic of two lost tragedies by Aeschylus.

75. F. Knauß in Wünsche 2006, 247–49; Woodford 1993, 89–91.

76. BAPD no. 310389; Mackay 2010, 315–26; Carpenter 1991, 205; Kossatz-Deissmann 1981, 163 no. 723.

77. Woodford 1993, 92; Kossatz-Deissmann 1981, 179 no. 837.

78. The earliest extant author who records this version is Publius Papinius Statius in the first century AD. See González González 2018, 20–21.

79. Translation Kline 2000.

80. For the version featuring Polyxena, given by Servius and Dictys, see Touchefeu-Meynier 1994, 431. For the illustrated scarab see Camporeale 1981, 208 no. 130.

81. R. Wünsche in Wünsche 2006, 258–69; Woodford 1993, 94–96; Woodford and Loudon 1980.

82. On this episode in art see Woodford 1993, 96–99; Carpenter 1991, 207; Schefold and Jung 1989, 259–61. On the cup see BAPD no. 203901; Williams 1993, 56–58 no. 44; Touchefeu 1981a, 325 no. 73, 326 no. 84.

83. Brommer 1973, 419–23 provides examples. On the *hydria* see BAPD no. 302033.

84. Touchefeu 1981a, 325.

85. Translation Moore 1957.

86. Shapiro 1994, 149–55; Woodford 1993, 99–101; Schefold and Jung 1989, 261–65; Touchefeu 1981a, 328–32 nos 103–41 (330 no. 117 for the illustrated vessel). For the bronze see Jenkins 2002.

87. Translated by Richard Woff.

88. That there are three preconditions goes back to the *Little Iliad*; a further one, that the bones of Pelops, a long-dead Greek hero, must be secured, appears to be a

later addition (Parke 1933).

89. For sources for the story of Philoctetes see Pipili 1994, 376–77.

90. Pipili (1994, 383 no. 74 and 384) lists this scene under the category of the healing of Philoctetes but suggests it may in fact be the wounding, whereas e.g. Schefold and Jung (1989, 270–72) interpret it as the healing in the camp of Troy. On the pair of cups (Figs 66 and 76) see also Squire 2011, 293–95; S. Klingenberg in Latacz et al. 2008, 385 no. 127; Simon 2008, 236; V. Brinkmann in Wünsche 2006, 284–87; Blome 2001, 144; Simon 2001, 163–64.

91. It was also – like the story of Ajax – covered in the *Little Iliad*. According to Proclus' summary, in that version it is Diomedes who brings back Philoctetes, while Odysseus fetches Neoptolemus, the son of Achilles.

92. Pipili 1994, 383 no. 69.

93. Castiglione 2015; Letoublon 2014; Demargne 1984, 965–69 nos 67–117. For the coins of Ilion, see Ellis-Evans 2016.

94. Carpenter 1991, 208; Boardman and Vafopoulou-Richardson 1986, 401–6 nos 23–105 and 397 for literary sources. On the Argive coin type: Demargne 1984, 968 no. 108.

95. Henig and MacGregor 2004, 104 no. 10.20; Simon 2001, 165; Schefold and Jung 1989, 274–75; Boardman and Vafopoulou-Richardson 1986, 402 no. 42.

96. The version of the sack and fall of Troy that is followed here is Virgil's. These events were told in the *Iliou Persis*, and parts of the story also in the *Little Iliad*, which Virgil must have drawn on, though there are variations in the details as conveyed in the summary which survives. The story of the wooden horse is also mentioned in Book 8 of the *Odyssey*.

97. Perhaps only to increase the height of the main gate. See Ward Jones Jr 2011.

98. Sparkes 1971.

99. Vickers 2006, 20–21; Grassinger 1999, 206 no. 31; Sadurska 1986, 814 no. 13.

100. Stewart 2016; Sadurska 1986, 814 no. 15.

101. Bragantini and Sampaolo 2009, 344 no. 157; Sadurska 1986, 814 no. 8; Woodford 1993, 106–7.

102. Translation Kline 2000.

103. BAPD no. 301625; A. Bignasca in Latacz et al. 2008, 396 no. 142; Sadurska 1986, 815 no. 18. Schefold (1992, 283–84) instead interprets the warriors as climbing in.

104. Anderson 1997, 182–91; Sadurska 1986, 815 no. 23; Woodford 1993, 107–8.

105. The episode is described in *Aeneid*, 2.403–4. He is also sometimes referred to as Locrian Ajax or son of Oileus.

106. *Iliou Persis*, according to Proclus' summary; Quintus Smyrnaeus, *Posthomerica*. For discussion of the attack on Cassandra see McHardy and Deacy

2015 (stressing that the offence is against the goddess); Anderson 1997, 49–51 and 199–202.

107. BAPD no. 411069; Kaltsas and Shapiro 2008, 194–95 no. 78; Woodford 1993, 110; Carpenter 1991, 209.

108. Delivorrias et al. 1984, 142 no. 1487.

109. Touchefeu 1981b, 343 no. 58.

110. For the recovery of Helen see S. Lorenz in Wünsche 2006, 327–32; Anderson 1997, 202–6; Kahil 1988b, 559–61.

111. Stansbury-O'Donnell 2009, 359–60.

112. BAPD no. 202723; Woodford 1993, 112; Kahil 1988b, 541 no. 248.

113. Bonfante and Swaddling 2006, 20.

114. *Aeneid* 2.506–58.

115. BAPD no. 310315; J. L. Fitton in Latacz et al. 2008, 354–55 no. 90; Touchefeu 1984, 932 no. 11; Neils 1994, 518 no. 116.

116. The *Iliou Persis* had Odysseus kill the boy instead.

117. Carpenter 1991, 20–21.

118. On the scene in art see also Giuliani 2013, 171–76; F. Knauß in Wünsche 2006, 310–16; Anderson 1997, 192–99; Woodford 1993, 108–10.

119. S. Lorenz in Wünsche 2006, 333–37; Woodford 1993, 114; Carpenter 1991, 209; Canciani 1981, 386–90 nos 59–194; Woodford and Loudon 1980. For the illustrated amphora, see BAPD no. 331258; Woodford and Loudon 1980, 39 no. VI.5.

120. Mac Sweeney 2018, 103; S. Lorenz in Wünsche 2006, 338–39; Galinsky 1969, 8–9. For the illustrated lamp see Bailey 1988, 413 no. Q3287.

121. Summaries in S. Lorenz in Wünsche 2006, 338–39; Walter 2006; Canciani 1981.

122. Anderson 1997, 59–61.

123. The story was told in the *Iliou Persis*, in Euripides *The Trojan Women* and in Euripides *Hecuba*.

124. Translation Coleridge 1938 [1891].

125. F. Knauß in Wünsche 2006, 323–25.

126. BAPD no. 310027; J. L. Fitton in Latacz et al. 2008, 405 no. 156; Blome 2001, 139–40; Touchefeu-Meynier 1994, 433 no. 26.

127. Rose 2014, 72–103, esp. 79–87; Blome 2001, 139–41.

128. Translation Kovacs 1999.

129. On the topic of *nostoi*, see Hornblower and Biffis 2018.

130. Apollodorus, *Library* Epitome 6.2–6.

131. Lane-Fox 2008; Dougherty 2001; Malkin 1998; see also the various contributions in Hornblower and Biffis 2018.

132. Letoubloun 2014.

133. On various ancient and modern interpretations of Odysseus see e.g. Montiglio 2011; Hall 2008; Andreae 1999; see also Wilson 2017, 1–79 and below, Chapter 4. On Wilson's (2017) and others' translations of *polytropos*, see W. Mason,

The first woman to translate the 'Odyssey' into English, *The New York Times* 2.11.2017, https://www.nytimes.com/2017/11/02/magazine/the-first-woman-to-translate-the-odyssey-into-english.html [accessed 10.8.2019].

134. Phillips 1959.

135. On Homer's *Odyssey*, see Wilson 2017, 1–79; West 2017; S. West in Latacz et al. 2008, 139–50.

136. Lane Fox 2008; Dougherty 2001; Malkin 1998.

137. Images of Odysseus and his adventures are discussed by A. Bierl in Latacz et al. 2008, 117–19; Schmidlin in Wünsche 2006, 346–77; Schmidlin and Knauß in Wünsche 2006, 342–45; Shapiro 1994, 46–63; Buitron 1992a; Touchefeu 1992a; Andreae 1999; 1982; Schefold and Jung 1989, 315–60; Brommer 1983; Schefold 1978, 262–70; Schefold 1966; Touchefeu-Meynier 1968; cf. also Farnoux and Estaquet-Legrand 2019; Pomarède 2019; Scherer 1963, 141–70, for images of the Odyssey through the ages. The role of women in the *Odyssey* is the focus of essays in Cohen 1995.

138. Weis 2000; Andreae 1999, 188–205; Andreae 1982, 152–54.

139. C. Braun in Latacz et al. 2008, 408–9 no. 160.

140. Translation Kovacs 1994.

141. *Odyssey* Book 9; the episode was also treated in a satyr play by Euripides, first staged in 408 BC. For representations in art see Giuliani 2013, 70–88; Schmidlin in Wünsche 2006, 353–59; Shapiro 1994, 49–55; Andreae 1999; 1982, 41–48.

142. British Museum 1837,0609.72: BAPD no. 4950.

143. Hall 2008, 78; Andreae 1982.

144. P. Liverani in Andreae and Parisi Presicce 1996, 332–41; Andreae 1982, 216–20.

145. The marble group is signed by the Rhodian sculptors Athanadoros, Hagesandros and Polydoros, who were also responsible for the famous copy of the sculptural group of Laocoön: T. Lochmann in Latacz et al. 2008, 414–15 no. 168. On the identification, meaning and problematic dating of the sculptures, see Weis 2000; Andreae 1999, 177–223; 1982. A further group of Odysseus and Polyphemus was set up in a nymphaeum at Baiae, probably of the time of Claudius: Andreae 1999, 225–41.

146. *Odyssey* Book 10; Circe features also in several Classical Athenian theatre plays now lost. On the episode of Circe in ancient art see Shapiro 1994, 55–59; Canciani 1992; Andreae 1999, 257–67.

147. Sabetai and Avronidaki 2018, 356–59; Mitchell 2009, 272–76; Walsh 2009, 197–201; Wannagat 1999; Touchefeu, 1992a, 964–65.

148. *Odyssey* Book 11; cf. La Rocca 1999.

149. BAPD no. 202628. Lowenstam 2008,

47–51, links the theme of dangerous erotic appeal with the three flying figures of Eros on the back of the vase. The Sirens episode is recounted in *Odyssey* Book 12. On the Sirens in ancient art see Andreae 1999, 288–301; Hofstetter 1997; S. Ensoli in Andreae and Parisi Presicce 1996, 96–107.

150. Montiglio 2011.

151. Wall-painting: Touchefeu 1992a, 962 no. 159. Urn: Camporeale 1992, 975 no. 93; cf. C. Cianferoni in Latacz et al. 2008, 427; Cohen 1992, 108–11. For both Roman and Etruscan images it has been argued that part of the attraction of the motif was the suspected location of the episode in the region of Italy.

152. The episode with Scylla is described in *Odyssey* Book 12. For treatments in ancient art and literature see also Hopman 2012; Andreae 1999, 303–19; 1982, 49–54; Jentel 1997; G. B. Waywell in Andreae and Parisi Presicce 1996, 108–19; Buitron 1992b.

153. Andreae 1999, 205–15; 1982, 221–44, esp. 236–40; Jentel 1997, 1141 no. 41; Andreae and Parisi Presicce 1996, 152–53 no. 2.67. The myth was also represented in monumental sculptural groups at Tivoli and Sperlonga.

154. *Odyssey* Books 5, 7 and 12. According to Hesiod, *Theogony* 1017–20, three sons were the results of this liaison, while Odysseus had two sons already with Circe; the passage, though, could be a later interpolation, see the discussion in Malkin 1998, 180–90.

155. BAPD no. 216268; Shapiro 1994, 46–49; Touchefeu 1992b, 713, no. 4 (suggesting the figure might not be Nausicaa as she seems too 'undignified'). Nausicaa is rare in art, see Andreae 1999, 327–33; Touchefeu 1992b. The episode is described in *Odyssey* Books 7, 8 and 13, and was the topic of a (now lost) play by Sophocles.

156. Translation Frazer 1921.

157. Research history is summarized in Wolf and Wolf 1983; see also Burgess n.d.; Ballabriga 1998; Luce 1998; Stanford and Luce 1974. Even the location of Ithaca has been doubted, see e.g. Bittlestone 2005. Sailing journeys include those of Severin 1987 and Bradford 2004.

158. For further supposed links with the British Isles see Wolf and Wolf 1983, 155, 171, 175–76, 187–89, 193–200.

159. Malkin 1998; Ballabriga 1998; Lane Fox 2008.

160. *Odyssey* Book 1. Some later authors questioned Penelope's fidelity: Douris of Samos, for example, writing in the early Hellenistic period (*FGrHist* F21) proposed that she slept with all of the suitors, thus conceiving the god Pan.

161. Backe-Dahmen n.d.; Kader 2006; C. Parisi Presicce in Andreae and Parisi

Presicce 1996, 378–94; Hausmann 1994, 292 no. 2 d-1. On the Campana relief, Siebert 2011, 40–42. The same figural type was also used to represent other female characters.

162. BAPD no. 216788. Odysseus' return to Ithaca is described in *Odyssey* Books 13 to 24. For a survey of ancient treatments of this scene see A. Pasquier in Andreae and Parisi Presicce 1996, 396–431; Touchefeu 1992c.

3 ARCHAEOLOGICAL TROY
(pp. 124–81)

1. Rose 2014, 271.
2. Lucan, *Pharsalia* 9. 969.
3. Xerxes' visit: Herodotus *Histories* 7.42–43; Alexander the Great's visit: Plutarch, *Life of Alexander* 15.7–9.
4. Strabo, *Geography* 13.1.31.
5. Allen 1999, 40.
6. Cook 1973, 17.
7. Nagy 2009, chapter 7; Allen 1999, 40; Easton 1991, 112; Cook 1973, 156–59.
8. Wood 1775, 338, 341.
9. Chevalier 1791.
10. Allen 1999, 42; Cook 1973, 46.
11. Choiseul-Gouffier 1809, pl. 19. On the coins of Ilion, see Ellis-Evans 2016 (p. 117 for the illustrated coin).
12. Clarke 1816, 151.
13. Gell 1804. On Gell see Gaschke 2006; Clay 1976.
14. From the 'Ravenna Journal' 11 January 1821: Marchand 1978, 21–22.
15. Maclaren 1863, viii.
16. Frisch 1975, 234–36, no. 142. Inscription translated by Alan Johnston.
17. Allen 1999, 42; cf. Nagy 2009, chapter 7. The drawing possibly by Préaulx is part of the British Museum's Elgin drawings, see Gallo 2009; on Préaulx, see Hasluck 1911/1912.
18. Allen 1999, 16.
19. Allen 1999, 42–44; cf. Lascarides 1977.
20. Frisch 1975, 251–52 no. 174.
21. Newton 1865, 125.
22. Fitton 1995, 52.
23. Allen 1999, 94.
24. Allen 1999, 95.
25. Allen 1999, 74.
26. Allen 1995, 384–87.
27. Fitton 1995, 52.
28. Newton 1865, 134.
29. Calvert 1859, 6.
30. Silver 2007.
31. Brunton 1939, 68.
32. Allen 1999, 77–79. Allen points out that Frank Calvert never mentioned this work and concludes that he must have been opposed to it. It is possible that he used Brunton's labour force without feeling the need to distinguish it from other labour he used.
33. Brunton 1939, 68–70.
34. Rose 2014, 267.

35. Silver 2007, 156–57.
36. Easton 1991, 120.
37. Calvert 1864.
38. Calvert to Newton, 24 September 1863. BM Central Archive Officers' Reports.
39. Report from Newton to British Museum Trustees, 6 October 1863; British Museum Trustees' Minutes 17 October 1863. British Museum Central Archive Trustees' Minutes.
40. Newton to Calvert, 8 October 1863 and 3 February 1864. British Museum Department of Greece and Rome Letterbook.
41. Easton 1991, 124.
42. Meeting of the Royal Archaeological Institute in London on 7 July 1865, reported in *Archaeological Journal* 22 (1865), 337.
43. Schliemann 1880, 3.
44. Schliemann 1880, 7.
45. Schliemann 1880, 41.
46. Wood 1985; Calder and Traill 1986.
47. Traill 1995, 9–12.
48. Traill 1995, 302.
49. Schliemann 1867; Traill 1995, 29.
50. David Traill's careful comparison of the diaries and published work has revealed these discrepancies. Traill 1995, 46.
51. Schliemann 1869, 32.
52. Calvert 1874.
53. Schliemann 1880, 19.
54. Traill 1995, 55–57. As Allen 1999, 7, notes, Schliemann suddenly double dates his diary entries in the Gregorian and Julian calendar after 12 August, rather than when he entered Greece, where the shift to the Julian calendar would naturally have occurred. This allowed him to backdate some of the entries.
55. Traill 1995, 56; Schliemann 1869, 175.
56. Anderson 2015.
57. Schliemann 1875, 80.
58. Schliemann 1875, 348.
59. Schliemann 1875, 99. At other times Schliemann gives the figure as 16 metres (52 feet) because he was using a different datum (Easton 2002, 34).
60. Easton 2002. Easton also provides a concordance of Schliemann's published finds, building on Schmidt's (1902) catalogue and concordance.
61. Schliemann 1875, 34.
62. Schliemann 1880, 232.
63. Schliemann 1875, 13.
64. Schliemann 1880, 299–302.
65. Schliemann 1880, 354–56.
66. Schliemann 1875, 302–7.
67. Schliemann 1875, 19–20.
68. Schliemann 1880, 41.
69. Easton 1998; 1984.
70. Fitton 1991, 24.
71. Traill 1984; 2000.
72. Easton 1998; 1984.
73. Hänsel 2009, 54.
74. Easton 1994; Moorehead 1994; Antonova et al. 1996.

75. Piotrovskii 2013; A. Rinke, 21 June 2013, 'Merkel tells Putin Germany wants looted art returned', Reuters. https://www.reuters.com/article/us-germany-russia-merkel-art/merkel-tells-putin-germany-wants-looted-art-returned-idUSBRE95K0OG20130621 [accessed 26.8.2019].
76. O. Erbil, 13 June 2018, 'Troy treasures to be displayed in new museum', Hürriyet Daily News. http://www.hurriyetdailynews.com/troy-treasures-to-be-displayed-in-new-museum-133232. See http://www.troya2018.com/en/museum-of-troy/ [both accessed 26.8.2019].
77. Demakopoulou 1990, 149–52.
78. Allen 1999, 169.
79. Allen 1999, 177.
80. Schliemann 1874a, b.
81. Schliemann 1875.
82. Dickinson 2005.
83. Traill 1995, 167–72.
84. Dickinson et al. 2012.
85. Schliemann 1878, 65–66; Newton 1880, 283–94.
86. Baker 2019. Abigail Baker has reconstructed the London exhibition from contemporary press reports and archival sources.
87. Traill 1995, 205–11.
88. British Museum registration number for the inscription: 1877,0815.1.
89. Rose 2014, 186–88.
90. Pearsall 2008, 157–58.
91. H. Schliemann, 'The Tomb of Agamemnon', *The Times*, 12 January 1877, p. 7.
92. Pavúk 2002.
93. Schliemann 1881, 154.
94. Schliemann 1875, 232, fig. 162; Schliemann 1880, 616.
95. Schliemann 1880, 614.
96. Schliemann 1884, 216. These sherds were included in the first survey of Mycenaean pottery by Furtwängler and Loeschcke (1886, 33).
97. Traill 1995, 220–23.
98. Schliemann 1884, 279.
99. Traill 1995, 280–81.
100. *The Times*, 8 April 1890, p. 5
101. Schliemann and Dörpfeld 1891, 331.
102. Schliemann and Dörpfeld 1891, 349.
103. Easton 1991, 125.
104. Easton 2002, 311; Blegen 1963, 113.
105. Schmidt 1902.
106. Published in four volumes: Blegen 1950–58.
107. Blegen 1950, Vol. 1, 6.
108. The results from this project have been published in its own journal and monograph series, *Studia Troica*, since 1991. The numerous contributors often revisit earlier excavations at Troy in the light of recent findings. For a synthesis see Korfmann 2006, Pernicka et al. 2014 and Rose 2014. See also Mac Sweeney 2018.
109. Rose 2014, 44–57.

110. Rose 2014, 255–57.
111. Rose 2014.
112. Mountjoy 2017.
113. Rose 2014, 9–10, 22–23, pl. 5.
114. Böhlendorf-Arslan 2008; Rose 2014, 271–76.
115. Latacz et al. 2001.
116. Easton et al. 2002; Hertel and Kolb 2003; for a more recent contribution to the debate see Kolb 2014–15.
117. Although scholars have debated more recently whether a small number of the spindle whorls are indeed inscribed in the undeciphered Linear A script of Bronze Age Crete. Waal 2017.
118. Virchow 1884, 680.
119. Hawkins and Easton 1996.
120. Güterbock 1986.
121. Hawkins 1998.
122. Latacz 2004, 57.
123. Latacz 2004, 112–13.
124. Cline 2014.
125. Schofield and Parkinson 1994.
126. Sherratt 1990.

4 TROY: ENDURING STORIES
(pp. 182–271)

1. Modern responses, like ancient ones, to the Troy story are countless and our references here are necessarily selective. For surveys see e.g. Mac Sweeney 2018; Thompson 2013; Manguel 2007; Scherer 1963, and the essays in Farnoux et al. 2019; Simms 2018; Goldwyn 2015a; Kelder et al. 2012; Colpo et al. 2007; Latacz et al. 2001; 2008; Zimmermann 2006. Cf. also Baier 2017; Brandt 2006.
2. C. Cupane in Latacz et al. 2008, 251–58; Aerts 2012.
3. For summaries of the medieval European reception of Troy see Montanari 2008; Wilson 2004 and the essays in Latacz et al. 2001; cf. also Brescia et al. 2018; Shepard and Powell 2004.
4. Early Greek authors, in contrast, sometimes hinted at a love interest of Achilles in Polyxena's young brother, Troilus: Noussia-Fantuzzi 2015, 445–46.
5. H. Cancik in Latacz et al. 2001, 174–79.
6. Brunner 2001. Cf. also Haywood and Mac Sweeney 2018, 114–28.
7. See the surveys by Mac Sweeney 2018, 114–25; M. Borgolte and H. Kugler in Latacz et al. 2001, 190–203 and 226–38; and the more detailed studies of e.g. Wolf 2009; Tanner 1993; Borst 1957–63.
8. Posselt 2015; Brunner 2001, 220–21.
9. In German 'also enden sich menschliche ding'; Luckhardt 2001, 245.
10. Adolf 2015; Wolf 2009, 184–85; Clark 1981.
11. On the European dimension of Troy, see Baier 2017; Brandt 2006.

12. On Troy Town mazes, see Higgins 2018, 83–87; Matthews 1922, 156–63. On the Pace Egg play see John Priestnall and William Mitchell, *The Play of St George, the knights and the dragon, being a mumming play for pace-eggers*, compiled for private circulation, Rochdale, 1930.

13. Mac Sweeney 2018, 121; Thompson 2013, 112–13.

14. D. Rijser in Kelder et al. 2012, 105–8; G. Uslu in Kelder et al. 2012, 106–11; Kreiser 2001.

15. Michael Kritoboulos, *History of Mehmed the Conqueror*, § 73. Translation Riggs 1954.

16. Mac Sweeney 2018, 123–24.

17. Mac Sweeney 2018, 122–25; Baier 2017, 51–53; B. Ayavazoğlu in Kelder et al. 2012, 150–54; Ö. F. Şerifoğlu in Kelder et al. 2012, 160–61; Kreiser 2001.

18. Montanari 2008; Görich 2006; Müller 2004; Lienert 2001; Brunner 2001; Tanner 1993; cf. also Brescia et al. 2018; Lavagnini 2016; Wolf 2009; Shepard and Powell 2004.

19. Greub 2008, 266–68.

20. Jason and the Argonauts had sailed to Colchis in the Black Sea to recover the Golden Fleece and, as emphasized and embellished by medieval writers, destroyed Troy on their voyage home: Tanner 1993; cf. Colavito 2014.

21. Lienert 1996; 2001. Cf. also Moormann 2000, esp. 20–21, for the Trojan story in the Dutch Middle Ages.

22. Moennig 2018; Lavagnini 2016; Aerts 2012.

23. See e.g. Edwards 1998.

24. Luckhardt 2001, 246–47.

25. Cf. Desmond and Sheingorn 2003, 142–45.

26. Aerts 2012.

27. Graziosi 2016, 1.

28. T. Bartsch, in *Hochrenaissance im Vatikan. Kunst und Kultur im Rom der Päpste I. 1503–1534*, Bonn 1999, 516, no. 236. On the Laocoön group, see Brilliant 2000; cf. Luckhardt 2001, 252–55; Haskell and Penny 1982, 243.

29. Alternative identifications include Ajax and Achilles or Aeneas and Lausus: Weis 2000.

30. Greub 2008, 269; Büttner 2001, 270; B. Franke in Latacz et al. 2001, 239–44; Moormann 2000, 29–30.

31. Haywood and Mac Sweeney 2018, 93–106; Pearsall 2015; Palmer 1982, 22–30.

32. R. Glitz in Kelder et al. 2012, 118–21.

33. Brunner 2001, 220–24.

34. Monteverdi: Rosand 1991. Purcell: Harris 1990.

35. From Jonson's poem prefixed to the First Folio edition of Shakespeare's plays.

36. On translations of Homer see Young 2003; cf. also Greub 2008, 268 (German translations); Büttner 2001, 272 (French); Moormann 2000, 28 (Dutch). On Chapman and Pope see also Wilson 2004.

37. John Keats, *The Complete Poems*, ed. by J. Barnard, 3rd edn, London: Penguin Books, 1988, 72.

38. Samuel Johnson, 'The Life of Pope', in *Lives of the English Poets*, ed. by G. B. Hill (Oxford: Clarendon Press, 1905), Vol. III, 119. The quotation from Bentley is footnoted on p. 126 of *The Works of Samuel Johnson, LL.D. in Eleven Volumes* by John Hawkins, Vol. IV (1787), *The Lives of the Most Eminent English Poets*, 'Life of Pope'.

39. Childs 2007. On translations of Virgil, see Braund and Martirosova Torlone 2018.

40. The reach of the phenomenon is exemplified by eighteenth-century Portuguese neoclassical poet Cruz e Silva, whose Pindaric odes liken modern Portuguese to ancient Greek and Trojan heroes: Fonseca 2015.

41. Potts 1994.

42. On Caylus, see Rees 1999.

43. Coltman 2006; Opper 2003; Scott 2003.

44. On the Tischbein drawing, see Bartrum 2011, 134–35 no. 33; Griffiths and Carey 1994, no. 85; cf. also P. Betthausen in Kunze 1999, 119–20, no. IV.13a and b. Here and in another drawing (P. Betthausen in Kunze 1999, 118 no. IV.11) Tischbein used as the model a Roman marble 'portrait' of Odysseus then in the collection of Lord Bristol and now in Mougins (Fig. 198): Pollini 2011, 87 fig. 26; S. Albersmeier in Albersmeier 2009, 194–95, no. 18.

45. Bindman 2013; 1979.

46. Trusted 2008.

47. de Smaele 2016.

48. Kunze 1999, esp. 109, 125–28. Similar competitions also took place e.g. in France: Schwartz 2004.

49. Gladstone 1858 [2010], 535.

50. Eskilson 2007, 27, fig. 20.

51. Lovatt 2013.

52. On the work of Messel, see Messel 2012.

53. Barrow 2007.

54. E. F. Prettejohn in Becker et al. 1996, 231–32.

55. Hammerschlag 2015, 37–39; Asleson 1999.

56. On Gillray see Godfrey 2001. Cf. also Hardie 2014, 173–88, on comical and satirical treatments of the *Aeneid*.

57. Greub 2008, 270.

58. E.g. P. Den Boer in Kelder et al. 2012, 114–17.

59. Grote 1880 [1846], 44.

60. A commemorative book of the 'sonnets', with 82 lithographs by Walter Crane, was published in London in 1887: Warr 1887. Cf. Richards 1999.

61. Kohl and Fawcett 1996; cf. Kolb 2010 and G. Weber in Zimmerman 2006, pp. 165–78 on current debates about Troy in particular.

62. On Troy in the twentieth century, see Biegel 2001; cf. also Farnoux et al. 2019; Goldwyn 2015a; Latacz et al. 2008.

63. Translation Sachperoglou 2007. Bertold Brecht based one of his poems on Cavafy's 'Trojans': Fiedler 1973.

64. Mac Sweeney 2018, 137–46.

65. Brooke died on the journey and was buried in 'some corner of a foreign field', though not a battlefield – rather his grave lies among olive groves on the island of Skyros. On Trojan War themes in British war poetry see Vandiver 2010; 2008; see also p. 253.

66. Brooke notebooks, quoted after Mac Sweeney 2018, 141.

67. Mac Sweeney 2018, 141–43; Rose 2014, 284–87; R. Aslan and M. Atabay in Kelder et al. 2012, 155–59; Midford 2011 and 2013; E. Eickhoff in Latacz et al. 2001, 292–99. For Nolan's drawing, see https://www.awm.gov.au/collection/ART91209 [accessed 11.8.2019].

68. Mac Sweeney 2018, 147–49; Manguel 2007, 206–8; Biegel 2001, 443–44. For links between the Trojan War and the Vietnam and Iraq wars see Goldwyn 2015b; Shay 1994; 2002; Tuchman 1984.

69. Republished with permission of Oxford University Press, *The Collected Poems*, by C. P. Cavafy, translated by Evangelos Sachperoglou, 2008; permission conveyed through Copyright Clearance Center, Inc.

70. Power 2018; Greenwood 2007.

71. *War Music: An Account of Homer's Iliad*, Christopher Logue, Faber and Faber Ltd. Used by permission of Faber and Faber Ltd.

72. The parallel with Northern Ireland was drawn already in *The Cure at Troy*, a 1991 play in verse by Irish poet Seamus Heaney, see Mac Sweeney 2018, 151–52.

73. See Introduction, notes 8 and 9.

74. Wolf 1983; cf. Michaels 2015; Biegel 2001, 447–48.

75. Tziovas, D. 2014. The wound of history. Ritsos and the reception of Philoctetes. In D. Tziovas (ed.), *Re-imagining the Past. Antiquity and Modern Greek Culture*. Oxford, pp. 297–317.

76. Troy-related examples include McHardy and Deacy 2015; von den Hoff 2005; Recke 2002.

77. On Troy in graphic novels, see e.g. H. Verreth in Kelder et al. 2012, 174; Jenkins 2011; cf. Lochmann 1999. On manga see Theisen 2011.

78. On Troy in film, see esp. Winkler 2015; 2007; Salvador Ventura 2015; Salvadori 2007.

79. Burgess 2009b; Fitton 2007, 99–106 and note 7; Shanower 2013.

80. *Collected Poems, 1948–1984*, Derek Walcott, published by Farrar, Straus and Giroux, 1987 © 1986 by Derek Walcott. Used by permission of Farrar, Straus & Giroux.

81. Quoted after Hall 2008, 46.

82. Quoted after Hall 2008, 46.

83. On Lovis Corinth and the Trojan War myth, see Biegel 2001, 449–50. On Claude's painting, see Hardie 2014, 204; Langdon 1999, 148–150; Kitson 1960.

84. Authors' own translation.

85. Rennie 1995, 88; cf. Romm 1992.

86. On Odysseus and the New World, see Boitani 1994; on Aeneas, cf. Hardie 2014; Tanner 1993.

87. Hardie 2014, 154–59, 166–70; cf. also Hall 2008, 78–79 (*Lusiads*); Shields 2001 (Aeneas in America, esp. p. 188 for George Washington's bronze sculpture of Aeneas' flight from Troy with Anchises, Ascanius and Creusa). Colavito 2014 and Tanner 1993 discuss the related appropriation of the Argonauts myth.

88. Hardie 2014, 196–97. The episode was especially popular in the seventeenth and eighteenth centuries.

89. Langdon 1999, 148–50; Nicholson 1990, 276–91. Turner was heavily influenced by Dryden's translation of the *Aeneid*, which was also the source for the quotation with which the painting was first displayed in 1814.

90. Blayney Brown 2012.

91. Hardie 2014, 206–7; Finley 1999, 61–81.

92. Kitson 1960.

93. The reception of Aeneas is reviewed in Hardie 2014. For Aeneas in post-ancient art, see also Houghton 1994; Scherer 1963, 192–215.

94. Reilly 2010; cf. Verstegen 2015, 401–3; Hardie 2014, 198; D. Rijser in Latacz et al. 2012, 108.

95. Hardie 2014, 193; Büttner 2001, 259–64.

96. Bellini, 1998, 55–57 no. 9; Boorsch, Lewis and Lewis 1985, 51–52 no. 8.1.

97. Thornton and Wilson 2009, 268–70 no. 160; cf. Boutin Vitela 2018; Syson and Thornton 2001, 250–61.

98. Syson and Thornton 2001, 200–28.

99. Cf. Holcroft 1988.

100. Syson and Thornton 2001, 246–54.

101. Dencher 2015, 183–84; Strauss 1973, 94; Stechow 1938. Amidst numerous religious and some genre images this is the only classical subject depicted by Büsinck.

102. Already in Virgil, Ascanius sometimes has the role of Venus' agent, Cupid, as was well known in the Renaissance: Boutin Vitela 2018.

103. S. Paarlberg and P. Schoon, in Schoon and Paarlberg 2000, 220–21 no. 32.

104. Hearn 1998.

105. Verstegen 2015; Gillgren 2011, 162–67, 253–54, on the painting by Barocci that provided inspiration for Gibbs. For Creusa in Virgil, see Grillo 2010.

106. Hearn 1998, 100–1, fig. 27 (cf. also British Museum 1959,0221.11.10). The central scene is a woman grasped by a soldier; all is watched from above by God, grieving and resolving to wipe mankind from the face of the earth.

107. Hardie 2014, 12–14, 90–92.
108. Reproduced with permission of Princeton University Press, *George Seferis: Collected Poems*, translated, edited and introduced by Edmund Keeley and Philip Sherrard, revised edition, Copyright © 1995 by Princeton University Press; permission conveyed through Copyright Clearance Center, Inc.
109. The reception of Odysseus through the ages is discussed in numerous publications, such as Hall 2008; Costantino 2007; Boitani 1994; Rubens and Taplin 1989; Stanford 1963; and the essays in Boitani and Ambrosini 1998 and Doherty 2009; cf. also, on imagery, Farnoux and Estaquet-Legrand 2019; Pomarède 2019; Scherer 1963, 142–80, and for a wider Mediterranean perspective Rovira Guardiola 2018.
110. Holoka 2006.
111. Montiglio 2011.
112. See the essays by Fortunati, Capodieci, Conticelli and Fiorenza in Capodieci and Ford 2011; Stoschek 1999; Lorandi 1996; Béguin, Guillaume and Roy 1985; cf. also Büttner 2001, 270.
113. Andreae 1982.
114. Coleridge 1830, 155.
115. Horkheimer and Adorno 1988 [1944], 50–87; cf. Hall 2008, 94–95.
116. Hall 2008, 98; Finley 1999, 61–63. On Turner and the Industrial Revolution, see Rodner 1997.
117. Homer, *The Odyssey*, translated by E. V. Rieu, lithographs by Elisabeth Frink, London: The Folio Society, 1974. The prints were also published as a separate folio by Leslie Waddington Prints; it is these versions, which differ in colour scheme, that are illustrated here; see Wiseman 1998, 170–73 nos. 95, 97, 98.
118. Miziołek 2006.
119. Hall 2008, 93–94; cf. also below.
120. Akgün 2018; Hall 2008, 132–36; Manguel 2007, 189–90.
121. Atwood 2005, 5.
122. *Collected Poems, 1948–1984*, Derek Walcott, published by Farrar, Straus and Giroux, 1987 © 1986 by Derek Walcott. Used by permission of Farrar, Straus & Giroux.
123. See esp. Boitiani 1994.
124. Foulke 1997.
125. Manguel 2007, 83–85; Stanford 1963, 175–210.
126. Löschenberger 2012, 47–48. The volume with Slevogt's illustrations was published by Bruno Cassirer in 1908.
127. Rennie 1995.
128. Hall 2008, 82–86.
129. Ulysses syndrome: Achotegui Loizate 2002. Migrants: Fornaro 2018; Hall 2008, 172.
130. Hall 2008, 53–55.
131. Walcott 1993; 1990. Cf. McConnell 2013; Tynan 2011; Hall 2008, 170–71; Friedman

2007; Manguel 2007, 208–13; Martyniuk 2005.
132. O'Meally 2007; cf. also Dawes 2017.
133. A scheme that also, as noted by Walcott, recalls the silhouettes of black-figure pottery: Price and Price 2006, 94–96; O'Meally 2007, 20.
134. For related fifteenth-century Italian imagery, see e.g. Miziołek 2006. For equations between the mast and the cross, see Ambrosius of Milan, *Expositio Evangelii secundum Lucam* IV.2 (fourth century AD).
135. Price and Price 2006, 94–96.
136. O'Meally 2007, 11–14, 78–81.
137. Tynan 2011, xiv; O'Meally 2007, 10, 16.
138. See Hall 2008, 41, 182.
139. Shay 2002; cf. Meineck and Konstan 2014.
140. Lapeña Marchena 2018; Salvadori 2007.
141. Biegel 2001, 451.
142. Joyce 1922; cf. Stanford 1963, 211–22.
143. Rubens and Taplin 1989, 162–63.
144. Republished with permission of Oxford University Press, *The Collected Poems*, by C. P. Cavafy, translated by Evangelos Sachperoglou, 2008; permission conveyed through Copyright Clearance Center, Inc.
145. Kazantzakis 1958 [1938], 424, translation K. Friar. The poem, begun in 1924 and published in 1938, consists of 24 poetic rhapsodies containing 33,333 17-syllable verses. Cf. Klironomos 2018; Stanford 1963, 222–40. *The Odyssey: A Modern Sequel*, by Nikos Kazantzakis. Translated with intro by Kimon Friar. English language translation © 1958 by Simon & Schuster, Inc. Renewed 1986 by Simon & Schuster, Inc. Reprinted with the permission of Touchstone, a division of Simon & Schuster, Inc. All rights reserved.
146. On the women in Odysseus' story see Piralla-Heng Vong 2019; Cohen 1995.
147. Renger 1999, 283.
148. On medieval sirens, see Berti and Carlà-Uhink 2018, 205–13. Fish-shaped sirens are first attested in the *Liber Monstrorum* of the late seventh or early eighth century.
149. Moraw 2018; Leclercq-Marx 1997; Rahner 1963.
150. E. Prettejohn in Prettejohn et al. 2008, 31, 114–15 no. 21, 120–21 no. 31, 182–83 nos. 56–57; Piralla-Heng Vong, 2019, 227–29; A. Estaquet-Legrand in Farnoux et al. 2019, 242–43 no. 130.
151. Max Beckmann used much the same ploy in his *Odysseus and the Sirens* of 1933, putting the viewer in Odysseus' position as he faces the Sirens over Odysseus' shoulder: Biegel 2001, 450.
152. Karentzos 2005; Renger 1999.
153. Hall 2008, 121; Miller 2018.
154. Piralla-Heng Vong 2019, 229–31.
155. Miziołek 2006; see also note 134.
156. Translation Guarino 1963.
157. Kauffmann 1973, 265, no. 328. The

cassone's iconography is difficult to decipher, not least because *cassone* painters often had to make up new iconographies, drawing inspiration from other contemporary art as well as classical antiquity. Schubring (1923, 224 no. 26), interpreted the scene as generic, but there can be no doubt as to its mythological nature. Compare, e.g., the similar composition of the *cassone* panel by Guidoccio Cozzarelle, *The Departure of Ulysses*, 1480–81, Écouen, Musée National de la Renaissance.
158. Béguin, Guillaume and Roy 1985, 305–7 no. 48. In 1668 a Dutch couple chose to be portrayed by artist Jan de Bray as Odysseus and Penelope, see Sluijter 2000; M. van Soest in Schoon and Parlberg 2000, 184–85 no. 14.
159. Jenkins 2011. On ancient myths in graphic novels see Kovacs and Marshall 2016; 2011; Lochman 1999.
160. Hall 2008, 121.
161. Morton 2014, 94–95. The pose of Penelope was inspired by the Classical type of the 'mourning Penelope' (see p. 121), cf. also the image on a mid-fifth-century BC Athenian *skyphos* (BAPD no. 216789).
162. Butler 1897; cf. Hall 2008, 116–17.
163. Paul 2013.
164. Quoted after Paul 2013, 155.
165. Nagy 1999, esp. Chapter 2; King 1987, 2–13.
166. E.g. *Iliad* 24.728–30.
167. On *kleos* as glory and also the poem or song which confers it, see Nagy 2013, 25–47.
168. For Fuseli, see Lentzsch et al. 2005, especially von Waldkirch's chapter on the early drawings (pp. 33–83).
169. On this circle of artists see Pressly 1979.
170. For the drawing and influence of Sergel, see Schiff 1973, 77, 86 and 441 no. 383.
171. Miller 2011.
172. Shay 1994.
173. The painting is discussed and the lines cited in Barrow 2007, 174.
174. Trusted 2008, 21 no. 3; Bilbey and Trusted 2002, 49 no. 71.
175. For the biography of the Johnes family, see Inglis-Jones 1950.
176. Costello 1955, especially 307–8 (on the connection with Ovid) and 315 (on the depiction of Thetis and Achilles); Blunt 1945, 33–36.
177. On the sculpture in the context of the Chatsworth collection, see Kenworthy-Browne 1972. On Albacini, see Pepe 2019. Felleman (2015, 167) draws attention to Achilles' expression of abandonment.
178. Waagen 1854, 367.
179. Ferrari 2017.
180. Potts 1994, 5.
181. Moorman 2000, 22; Scherer 1963, 63–65.

182. Whitaker 1986, 161–64; Scherer 1963, 82.
183. Bohn 1849.
184. Baumgärtel 1990, 229–37.
185. Roworth 1992, 45.
186. Ibid., 42–51.
187. On Bates, see Beattie 1983, esp. 53 and 155. The relief was paired with a second entitled *Peace*. Bates later used the same family scene with only minor modifications to represent Harvest.
188. P. Keller in Kunze 1999, 61–62 no. II.1.
189. *The exhibition of the Royal Academy, MDCCLXXII. The fourth*, 13 no. 128. https://www.royalacademy.org.uk/art-artists/exhibition-catalogue/ra-sec-vol4-1772 [accessed 22.4.2019].
190. On Kauffman's paintings as prints, see Alexander 1992.
191. Young 2000, 84.
192. Quotes from *Cassandra* by Christa Wolf, translated by Jan van Huerck (Daunt Books, 2013) Copyright © Christa Wolf 1983. Van Heurck, 116.
193. King 1987, xvi–xvii.
194. Ibid., xviii.
195. On the tapestries see Nativel 2011; Lammertse and Vergara 2003; de Poorter 2000 (who dates them to 1630 to 1632).
196. Nativel 2011, 400–1; Healy 2003, 45.
197. See especially Nativel 2011.
198. Ibid., 413–16.
199. On the process see Lammertse 2003.
200. See Büttner 2001, 271; P. Keller in Kunze 1999, 42–43 no. I.27; Cropper 1988, 262, cat. 121 (on the print) and 257 (on the series).
201. Reilly 1995, 411.
202. Ibid., 303.
203. See for example Coltman 2006.
204. On Wedgwood's use of the publications of William Hamilton's vase collection, see Coltman 2006, 85–96.
205. Reilly 1995, 12.
206. Katz Anhalt 2017, 80–114.
207. Harris 2008.
208. Rigoni 2007.
209. Cited by Manguel 2007, 57.
210. Barker 2018, 3.
211. Stampolidis and Storsve 2017.
212. Basualdo 2018; Latacz 2014; Greub 2008, 272–75.
213. Cited in Midford 2010, 9.
214. Goodison and Robertson 1967, 17–18 nos M44–45.
215. Lee 2013, 601–2.
216. Bartoli 1999, 166–68.
217. On the significance of *cassoni* in fifteenth-century Florence, see Syson and Thornton 2001, 70–73; and see p. 231.
218. On Penni's Trojan War series and its diffusion in the form of prints see Cordellier 2012, 47–59.
219. On the printmakers at Fontainebleau see Jenkins 2017, esp. Vol. I 29–30 (Mignon), 64–67 (Penni); Vol. II, 307–15 nos JM 40–45 (Trojan War etchings).

220. Oman 1968, xxv and 30 no. 81.
221. On the Achilleion see Haderer 2019; 2018.
222. Schneider 2004.
223. Löschenberger 2012, esp. 47–126.; T. Greub, in Latacz et al. 2008, 464–65 no. 227; Suhr 1992, 79–80.
224. 1907 series published by Albert Langen; 1921 series by Paul Cassirer (Löschenberger 2012, 47–49).
225. Published by Bruno Cassirer. Klarmann 2015; Löschenberger 2012, 49.
226. Vandiver 2010, 228, 232.
227. Ibid., 245.
228. For the dating of the poem, probably written on 13 July 1915, see Vandiver 2010, 273.
229. Letter to Lady Desborough, 24 February 1915, cited in Vandiver 2010, 245.
230. For other works in this series see Spencer 2000, 14–15.
231. Spencer 2000, 9.
232. Mac Sweeney 2018, 12–14; Katz Anhalt 2017, especially Chapters 1 and 3.
233. Maguire 2011.
234. Marian Maguire, pers. comm.
235. M. Atwood, *Morning in the Burned House* (Toronto: McClelland & Stewart, 1995), 33–36. Reproduced with permission from Curtis Brown Group Ltd, London, on behalf of Margaret Atwood. Copyright © Margaret Atwood 1995.
236. Recent studies of Helen include Blondell 2013; Maguire 2009; Hughes 2005.
237. Authors' own translation.
238. Sluijter 2000; cf. also de Poorter 2000, 84.
239. Williamson and Davies 2014, 814–17, no. 267; cf. Syson and Thornton 2001, 58–56, on the significance and imagery of such caskets.
240. Heard and Whitaker 2011, 136–37, no. 59. For Cranach's various renderings of the Judgment of Paris, see M. W. Ainsworth in Ainsworth and Waterman 2013, 5, 54–58, 286–87, no. 11; cf. Scherer 1963, 10–23 for images of the Judgment through the ages.
241. Luckhardt 2001, 247–53.
242. Damisch 1996, 163 –81, pointing to Cranach's 'imagery rich in proto-feminist messages'; cf. also ibid. p. 188 for parallels drawn at the time between the Judgment of Paris and another fateful decision, original sin.
243. Hackett 2014; Reynolds 2013, 218–81; Millar 1963, 59 no. 58.
244. Butlin 1981, 486–87 no. 675, with further references. On Blake and classical antiquity, see Manguel 2007, 139–41; Bindman 1977, 208.
245. Karentzos 2005, 75–79.
246. Bloom 2009.
247. https://art21.org/watch/extended-play/eleanor-antin-helens-odyssey-short/ [accessed 15.8.2019].
248. C. Marlowe, *The Tragical History of Dr. Faustus*. Vol. XIX, Part 2 (New York: P. F. Collier: 1909–14 [1604]).
249. Cf. also *Iliad* 3.180; 6.356; *Odyssey* 4.145.
250. Mansfield 2007.
251. Pope-Hennessy 1964, cat. no. 704.
252. Cited after the poem's first publication, in T. Moore (ed.), *Letters and Journals of Lord Byron: with notices of his life*, Vol. 2 (New York: J. & J. Harper, 1830–31), p. 44.
253. 'No Second Troy', first published in W. B. Yeats, *Responsibilities and Other Poems* (New York: Macmillan, 1916). On Maud Gonne, see Pratt 1983.
254. Haywood and Mac Sweeney 2018, 58–74; Treuherz, Prettejohn and Becker 2003, 187 no. 99; R. Upstone in Wilton and Upstone 1997, 98 no. 3.
255. Published in D. G. Rossetti, *Poems. A New Edition* (London: Ellis & White, 1881), p. 77.
256. Smith 2002, 92–96, 100.
257. Maguire 2009, 81.
258. On *The Flower Book*, see Lady Burne-Jones' introduction to the 1905 Fine Art Society edition. Burne-Jones also began a Troy polyptych in 1872, but this remained unfinished; it is now in the collection of Birmingham Museums and Art Gallery (1922P178).
259. Dudkiewicz 2016; Fagence Cooper 2003, 87. The completed embroidery is today in the Castle Howard Collection. Themes from the Trojan legend were present also elsewhere in Morris' house. For the scheme, compare also Edward Burne-Jones' *Flamma Vestalis* of 1896.
260. Millar 1995, no. 4409. Wilde published 'The New Helen' first in *Time* magazine. He then revised it for his *Poems* of 1881.
261. Quotes from *Cassandra* by Christa Wolf, translated by Jan van Huerck (Daunt Books, 2013) Copyright © Christa Wolf 1983. Van Heurck, 200.
262. Millar 1995, no. 1237.
263. https://artsandculture.google.com/exhibit/RAIi4MO8WEE_Lg [accessed 16.8.2019].
264. Barrow 2007, 73.
265. Kidson 2015, 675–77 no. 1488; on Emma Hart see Colville and Williams 2016. The oil sketch was made for a full-length painting.
266. See the historical overview of Cassandra's perception through the ages in Falke 2006.
267. 'Cassandra' in Jeffers 1965. Permission granted by Jeffers Literary Properties.
268. Biegel 2001, 449. Cf. also Heckmann and Ottomeyer 2009.
269. See Gere and Rudoe 2010, 302 and fig. 254 for the jewellery in this painting.
270. See Chacour-Sampson and Lalaounis-Tsoukopoulou 1998, esp. 74–91 (chapter by E. Hamaldi, I. Lalaounis-Tsoukopoulo and D. Plantzos). Examples are displayed in the Ilias Lalaounis Jewelry Museum, Athens

EPILOGUE: THE SHIELD OF ACHILLES (pp. 272–83)

1. See the discussion with further literature by Lecoq 2010; cf. also Squire 2013; Herda 2012.
2. Mac Sweeney 2018, 14–15; Scully 2003.
3. Taplin 1980, 12.
4. Hesiod, *Works and Days* 106–200.
5. Finkel and Seymour 2008, 16–17; Horowitz 1998, 20–42; cf. Michalowski 2010 for earlier Mesopotamian cosmologies. On the ancient view of the world, see also Cole 2010; Couprie 2003 (on links with Near Eastern maps); Romm 1992.
6. Van Wees 2004.
7. Cunningham 1830, 365.
8. Lecoq 2010, 13.
9. Squire 2011, 303–70, 393–95 no. 4N; on the Iliac Tablets see also, pp. 50–51, Fig. 34.
10. Discussed by Squire 2011, 368–70.
11. See the surveys by Lecoq 2004; Fittschen 1973; cf. also Farnoux et al. 2019, 340–41 no. 199; Squire 2011, 344–45; J. Rees in Kunze 1999, 89–91.
12. Lecoq 2004, 31–33, fig. 4.
13. Lecoq 2004; A. Rügler in Kunze 1999, 91–93.
14. For Flaxman's working practices, see Bindman 1979, particularly the essays by S. Bury (pp. 140–48) and M. Snodin (pp. 149–51).
15. Hartop 2005, 99–118; Bury and Snodin 1984; Bindman 1979, 140–42, 145–47.
16. Cf. Friedman 2007, 467–68.
17. 'The Shield of Achilles', in W. H. Auden, *The Shield of Achilles* (London: Faber & Faber, 1955). Copyright © 1955 by W. H. Auden, renewed. Reprinted by permission of Curtis Brown, Ltd.
18. 'The Shield of Achilles', in W. H. Auden, *The Shield of Achilles* (London: Faber & Faber, 1955). Copyright © 1955 by W. H. Auden, renewed. Reprinted by permission of Curtis Brown, Ltd.
19. Cross 2016, 20–21.
20. Penelope to Ulysses in Ovid, *Heroides*, 53.

BIBLIOGRAPHY

Achotegui Loizate, J. 2002. *La depresión en los inmigrantes: Una perspectiva transcultural.* Barcelona.

Adolf, A. 2015. *Brutus of Troy, and the Quest for the Ancestry of the British.* Barnsley.

Aerts, W. J. 2012. Troy in Byzantium. In Kelder et al. 2012, pp. 98–104.

Ainsworth, M. W. and Waterman, J. 2013. *German Paintings in the Metropolitan Museum of Art, 1350–1600.* New York; New Haven.

Akgün, B. 2018. Spinning a Thread of One's Own from Homer to Atwood. In Simms 2018, pp. 206–23.

Albersmeier, S. (ed.) *Heroes: Mortals and Myths in Ancient Greece.* Baltimore; New Haven.

Alexander, D. 1992. Kauffman and the Print Market in 18th-century England. In Roworth 1992, pp. 141–78.

Allen, S. 1995. 'Finding the Walls of Troy': Frank Calvert, Excavator. *American Journal of Archaeology* 99, pp. 379–407.

Allen, S. H. 1999. *Finding the Walls of Troy: Frank Calvert and Heinrich Schliemann at Hisarlık.* Berkeley.

Anderson, B. 2015. 'An alternative discourse': Local interpreters of antiquities in the Ottoman empire. *Journal of Field Archaeology* 40(4), pp. 450–60.

Anderson, M. J. 1997. *The Fall of Troy in Early Greek Poetry and Art.* Oxford.

Andreae B. 1982. *Odysseus. Archäologie des europäischen Menschenbildes.* Frankfurt.

Andreae, B. (ed.) 1999. *Odysseus: Mythos und Erinnerung.* Mainz.

Andreae, B. and Parisi Presicce, C. (eds) 1996. *Ulisse: Il mito e la memoria.* Rome.

Angelicoussis, E. 1992. *The Woburn Abbey Collection of Classical Antiquities.* Mainz.

Antonova, I. A., Tolstikov, V., Treister, M. and Easton, D. F. 1996. *The Gold of Troy: Searching for Homer's Fabled City.* London.

Asleson, R. 1999. On translating Homer: Prehistory and the limits of classicism. In E. F. Prettejohn and T. J. Barringer 1999 (eds) *Frederic Leighton: Antiquity, Renaissance, Modernity.* London, pp. 67–86.

Atwood, M. 1997. *Morning in the Burned House.* Toronto.

Atwood, M. 2005. *The Penelopiad.* Edinburgh.

Austin, N. 1994. *Helen of Troy and Her Shameless Phantom.* Ithaca.

Bachvarova, M. R. 2016. *From Hittite to Homer: The Anatolian Background of Ancient Greek Epic.* Cambridge.

Backe-Dahmen, A. n.d. Kopf der Penelope (SK 2270). In Antikensammlung, Berlin (ed.) *Gesamtkatalog der Skulpturen* (Cologne 2013–) http://arachne.uni-koeln.de/item/objekt/2270 [accessed 14.8.2019].

Baier, C. 2017. Homer's Cultural Children. The Myth of Troy and European Identity. *History & Memory* 29(2), pp. 35–62.

Bailey, D. M. 1988. *A Catalogue of the Lamps in the British Museum II: Roman Provincial Lamps.* London.

Baker, A. 2019. *Troy on Display: Scepticism and Wonder at Schliemann's First Exhibition.* London.

Ballabriga, A. 1998. *Les fictions d'Homère. L'invention mythologique et cosmographique dans l'Odyssée.* Paris.

Barker, E. T. E. 2008. Momos advises Zeus: Changing representations of 'Cypria' fragment 1. In E. Cingano and L. Milano (eds) *Papers on Ancient Literatures: Greece, Rome and the Near East.* Padua, pp. 33–73.

Barker, P. 2018. *The Silence of the Girls.* London.

Barrow, R. 2007. *The Use of Classical Art and Literature by Victorian Painters 1860–1912: Creating Continuity with the Traditions of High Art.* Lewiston, NY.

Bartoli, R. 1999. *Biagio d'Antonio.* Milan.

Bartrum, G. (ed.) 2011. *German Romantic Prints and Drawings from an English Private Collection.* London.

Basualdo, C. (ed.) 2018. *Cy Twombly: Fifty Days at Iliam.* New Haven.

Baumgärtel, B. 1990. *Angelika Kauffmann (1741–1807). Bedingungen weiblicher Kreativität in der Malerei des 18. Jahrhunderts.* Weinheim.

Beattie, S. 1983. *The New Sculpture.* New Haven; London.

Becker, E. et al. (eds) 1996. *Sir Lawrence Alma-Tadema.* Zwolle.

Béguin, S., Guillaume, J. and Roy, A. 1985. *La Galerie d'Ulysse à Fontainebleau.* Paris.

Bellini, P. 1998. *L'opera incisa di Giorgio Ghisi.* Bassano del Grappa.

Bergmann, B. 1994. The Roman House as Memory Theater: The House of the Tragic Poet in Pompeii. *The Art Bulletin* 76(2), pp. 225–26.

Berti, I. and Carlà-Uhink, F. 2018. Mixanthropoi. Die mittelalterliche Rezeption antiker hybrider Kreaturen. In Rehm 2018, pp. 193–222.

Biegel, G. 2001. Mythenwandel. In Latacz et al. 2001, pp. 440–54.

Bilbey, D. and Trusted, M. 2002. *British Sculpture 1470 to 2000: A Concise Catalogue of the Collection at the Victoria and Albert Museum.* London.

Bindman, D. 1977. *Blake as an Artist.* Oxford; New York.

Bindman, D. (ed.) 1979. *John Flaxman.* London.

Bindman, D. 2013. *John Flaxman: Line into Contour.* Birmingham.

Birch, S. and Newton, C. T. 1851. *A Catalogue of the Greek and Etruscan Vases in the British Museum.* London.

Bittlestone, R. 2005. *Odysseus Unbound: The Search for Homer's Ithaca.* Cambridge.

Blayney Brown, D. 2012. Studies for Pictures: Isleworth sketchbook c. 1804–7. In D. Blayney Brown(ed.) *J. M. W. Turner: Sketchbooks, Drawings and Watercolours.* https://www.tate.org.uk/art/research-publications/jmw-turner/studies-for-pictures-isleworth-sketchbook-r1129800 [accessed 24.4.2019].

Blegen, C. et al. 1950–58. *Troy, Excavations Conducted by the University of Cincinnati 1932–1938,* Princeton.

Blegen, C. W. 1963. *Troy and the Trojans.* London.

Blome, P. 2001. Der Mythos in der griechischen Kunst. In Latacz et al. 2001, pp. 118–53.

Blome, P. 2008a. Die Bildkunst in der Zeit Homers. In Latacz et al. 2008, pp. 56–61.

Blome, P. 2008b. Die Rezeption der Homerischen Dichtung in der griechischen Bildkunst. In Latacz et al. 2008, pp. 196–207.

Bloom, L. E. 2009. Tableaux Vivants, Dying Empires: Eleanor Antin's *The Last Days of Pompeii, Roman Allegories* and *Helen's Odyssey*. *n.paradoxa*. 24, pp. 13–21.

Blondell, R. 2013. *Helen of Troy: Beauty, Myth, Devastation*. Oxford.

Blunt, A. F. 1945. *The French Drawings in the Collection of His Majesty The King at Windsor Castle*. Oxford; London.

Boardman, J. and Vafopoulou-Richardson, C. E. 1986. Diomedes I. In *LIMC* III, pp. 396–409.

Böhlendorf-Arslan, B. 2008. Die Funde der byzantinischen Zeit. In *Heinrich Schliemanns Sammlung Trojanischer Altertümer, Neuvorlage*, Band 1. Berlin, pp. 177–82.

Bohn, H. G. 1849. *The Works of Frederick Schiller. Early Dramas and Romances*. London.

Boitani, P. 1994. *The Shadow of Ulysses: Figures of a Myth*. Oxford.

Boitani, P. and Ambrosini, R. (eds) 1998. *Ulisse: archeologia dell'uomo moderno. Atti del Convegno Internazionale 29–31 maggio 1996*. Rome.

Bonfante, L. and Swaddling, J. 2006. *Etruscan Myths*. London; Austin.

Boorsch, S., Lewis, M. and Lewis, R. E. 1985. *The Engravings of Giorgio Ghisi*. New York.

Borriello, M. R. 1986, *Le collezioni del Museo Nazionale di Napoli*, Vol. 1 (*I mosaici, le pitture, gli oggetti di uso quotidiano, gli argenti, le terracotte invetriate, i vetri, i cristalli, gli avori*). Rome.

Borst, A. 1957–63. *Der Turmbau von Babel. Geschichte der Meinungen über Ursprung und Vielfalt der Sprachen und Völker*. Stuttgart.

Bourogiannis, G. 2018. The transmission of the alphabet to the Aegean. In Ł. Niesiołowski-Spanò and M. Węcowski (eds) *Change, Continuity and Connectivity: North-Eastern Mediterranean at the Turn of the Bronze Age and in the Early Iron Age*. Wiesbaden, pp. 235–57.

Boutin Vitela, L. 2018. Virgilian Imagery and the Maiolica of the Mantuan Court. In L. B. T. Houghton and M. Sgarbi (eds) *Virgil and Renaissance Culture*. Turnhout, pp. 49–62.

Bowie, E. 1986. Early Greek elegy, symposium and public festival. *Journal of Hellenic Studies* 106, pp. 13–35.

Bradford, E. 2004. *Ulysses Found*. London.

Bragantini, I. and Sampaolo, V. (eds) 2009. *La Pittura Pompeiana*. Naples.

Brandt, H. 2006. Europa und der Mythos von Troia. In Zimmermann 2006, pp. 26–39.

Braund, S. and Martirosova Torlone, Z. (eds) 2018. *Virgil and His Translators*. Oxford.

Brescia, G., Lentano, M., Scafoglio, G. and Zanusso, V. (eds) 2018. *Revival and Revision of the Trojan Myth. Studies on Dictys Cretensis and Dares Phrygius*. Hildesheim.

Brilliant, R. 2000. *My Laocoön: Alternative Claims in the Interpretation of Artworks*. Berkeley.

Brommer, F. 1983. *Odysseus. Die Taten und Leiden des Helden in antiker Kunst und Literatur*. Darmstadt.

Brommer, F. 1973. *Vasenlisten zur griechischen Heldensage*. 3rd edn, Marburg.

Brunner, H. 2001. Die in jeder Hinsicht schönste und beste Stadt. In Latacz et al. 2001, pp. 212–25.

Brunton, J. 1939. *John Brunton's Book: Being the Memories of John Brunton, Engineer, from a Manuscript in His Own Hand Written for His Grandchildren and Now First Printed*. Cambridge.

Bryant, J. 1994. Caro's Trojan War. In Spurling and Bryant 1994, pp. 3–10.

Buitron, D. (ed.) 1992a. *The Odyssey and Ancient Art: An Epic in Word and Image*. New York.

Buitron, D. 1992b. Skylla. In Buitron 1992a, pp. 136–39.

Burgersdijk, D. 2012. The Troy game: The Trojan heritage in the Julio-Claudian house. In Kelder et al. 2012, pp. 90–97.

Burgess, J. S. 2001. *The Tradition of the Trojan War in Homer and the Epic Cycle*. Baltimore.

Burgess, J. S. 2009a. *The Death and Afterlife of Achilles*. Baltimore.

Burgess, J. S. 2009b. Achilles' heel: The historicism of Troy the movie. In K. Mysiades (ed.) *Reading Homer: Film and Text*. Madison, pp. 163–85.

Burgess, J. S. (ed.) n.d. *Wake of Odysseus* http://wakeofodysseus.com/ [accessed 25.8.2019].

Burkert, W. 1991. Homer's Anthropomorphism: Narrative and Ritual. In D. Buitron-Oliver (ed.) *New Perspectives in Early Greek Art*. Washington, pp. 181–91.

Bury, S. and Snodin, M. 1984. The *Shield of Achilles* by John Flaxman R.A. In *Sotheby's Art at Auction, 1983–4*. London, pp. 274–83.

Butler, S. 1897. *The Authoress of the Odyssey*. London.

Butlin, M. 1981. *The Paintings and Drawings of William Blake*. New Haven; London.

Büttner, N. 2001. Für die homerischen Helden begeistert – ohne Homer zu lesen. In Latacz et al. 2001, pp. 257–79.

Calder, W. and Traill, D. (eds) 1986. *Myth, Scandal and History: The Heinrich Schliemann Controversy*. Detroit.

Calvert, F. 1859. The tumulus of Hanai Tepeh in the Troad. *Archaeological Journal* 16, pp. 1–6.

Calvert, F. 1864. Contributions towards the ancient geography of the Troad. On the site of Gergithe. *Archaeological Journal* 21, pp. 48–53.

Calvert, F. 1874. Trojan Antiquities. *The Athenaeum* 2454, pp. 610–11.

Camporeale, G. 1981. Achle. In *LIMC* I, pp. 200–14.

Camporeale, G. 1992. Odysseus/Uthuze. In *LIMC* VI, pp. 970–83.

Canciani, F. 1981. Aineias. In *LIMC* I, pp. 381–96.

Canciani, F. 1992. Kirke. In *LIMC* VI, pp. 48–59.

Canciani, F. 1994. Protesilaos. In *LIMC* VII, pp. 554–60.

Capodieci, L. and Ford, P. (eds) 2011. *Homère à la Renaissance: Mythe et transfigurations*. Paris.

Carpenter, T. 1991. *Art and Myth in Ancient Greece: A Handbook*. London.

Carpenter, T. 2015. The Trojan War in early Greek art. In Fantuzzi and Tsagalis 2015, pp. 178–96.

Castiglione, M. P. 2015. Il Palladion e la statua di Atena a Troia: riflessioni su due temi iconografici e sulla loro fusion. *Gaia: revue interdisciplinaire sur la Grèce Archaïque* 18, pp. 435–54.

Castriota, D. 1992. *Myth, Ethos, and Actuality: Official Art in Fifth Century B.C. Athens*. Madison.

Cavafy, C. P. 2008. *The Collected Poems*, translated by Evangelos Sachperoglou. Oxford.

Chadour-Sampson, A.B. and Lalaounis-Tsoukopoulou, I. (eds) 1998. *Ilias Lalaounis: Modern Revival of Ancient Gold*. Athens.

Chaniotis, A. 2010. 'The Best of Homer'. Homeric Texts, Performances, and Images in the Hellenistic World and Beyond: The Contribution of Inscriptions. In E. Walter-Karydi (ed.) *Homer: Myths, Texts, Images: Homeric Epics and Ancient Greek Art*. Ithaca, pp. 257–78.

Chevalier, J.-B. 1791. *Description of the Plain of Troy: with a Map of that Region, Delineated from an Actual Survey*. Edinburgh.

Childs, J. 2007. *Henry VIII's Last Victim: The Life and Times of Henry Howard, Earl of Surrey*. New York.

Choiseul-Gouffier, M.-G.-A.-F. 1809. *Voyage pittoresque de la Grèce*, Vol. 2. Paris.

Clark, J. 1981. Trinovantum — the evolution of a legend. *Journal of Medieval History* 7(2), pp. 135–51

Clarke, E. D. 1816. *Travels in Various Countries of Europe, Asia and Africa*. London.

Clay, E. 1976. *Sir William Gell in Italy: Letters to the Society of Dilettanti, 1831–1835*. London.

Cline, E. H. 2014. *1177 B.C.: The Year Civilization Collapsed*. Princeton.

Cobet, J. 2006. Schliemanns Troia. In Zimmermann 2006, pp. 149–64.

Cohen, B. 1992. The Sirens. In Buitron 1992, pp. 108–11.

Cohen, B. (ed.) 1995. *The Distaff Side: Representing the Female in Homer's Odyssey*. Oxford; New York.

Colavito, J. 2014. *Jason and the Argonauts through the Ages*. Jefferson.

Cole, S. G. 2010. 'I Know the Number of the Sand and the Measure of the Sea': Geography and Difference in the Early Greek World. In K. A. Raaflaub and R. J. A. Talbert (eds) *Geography and Ethnography: Perceptions of the World in Pre-Modern Societies*. Chichester, pp. 197–214.

Coleridge, E. P., 1938 [1891] *Euripides. The Complete Greek Drama*. New York.

Coleridge, H. N. 1830. *Introductions to the Study of the Greek Classic Poets: Designed Principally for the Use of Young Persons at School or College*. London.

Colpo, I. et al. (eds) 2007. *Iconografia 2006. Gli eroi di Omero*. Rome.

Coltman, V. 2006. *Fabricating the Antique: Neoclassicism in Britain, 1760–1800*. Chicago.

Colville, Q. and Williams, K. 2016. *Emma Hamilton: Seduction and Celebrity*. London

Cook, J. M. 1973. *The Troad: An Archaeological and Topographical Study*. Oxford.

Cordellier, D. 2012. *Luca Penni: un disciple de Raphaël à Fontainebleau*. Paris.

Costantino, D. 2007. *Ulisse e l'altro. Itinerari della Differenza nell'Odissea*. Milan

Costello, J. 1955. Poussin's Drawings for Marino and the New Classicism: I: Ovid's *Metamorphoses. Journal of the Warburg and Courtauld Institutes* 18, No. 3/4, pp. 296–317.

Couprie, D. 2003. The Discovery of Space: Anaximander's Astronomy. In D. L. Couprie, R. Hahn and G. Naddaf (eds) *Anaximander in Context: New Studies in the Origins of Greek Philosophy*. New York, pp. 165–254.

Cribiore, R. 1993. A Homeric Exercise from the Byzantine Schoolroom. *Chronique d'Égypte* 68, pp. 145–54.

Cribiore, R. 1996. *Writing, Teachers, and Students in Graeco-Roman Egypt. American Studies in Papyrology* 36. Atlanta.

Cribiore, R. 2001. *Gymnastics of the Mind: Greek Education in Hellenistic and Roman Egypt*. Princeton.

Cropper, E. (ed.) 1988. *Pietro Testa, 1612–1650*. Aldershot.

Cross, S. (ed.) 2016. *Spencer Finch: The Brain is Wider than the Sky*. Munich.

Cunningham, A. 1830. *The Lives of the Most Eminent British Painters, Sculptors, and Architects*, Vol. III. London.

Damisch, H. 1996. *The Judgement of Paris*. Chicago.

Dawes, K. et al. (eds) 2017. *Bearden's Odyssey: Poets Respond to the Art of Romare Bearden*. Evanston.

Delivorrias, A., Berger-Doer, G. and Kossatz-Deissmann, A. 1984. Aphrodite. In *LIMC* II, pp. 2–151.

Demakopoulou, K. (ed.) 1990. *Troy, Mycenae, Tiryns, Orchomenos. Heinrich Schliemann: The 100th Anniversary of his Death*. Athens.

Demargne, P. 1984. Athena. In *LIMC* II, pp. 955–1044.

Dencher, A. 2015. The 'Camaïeu' print in seventeenth-century Paris: On the origins of multi-tonal printmaking in France. In A. Stijnman and E. Savage (eds) *Printing Colour 1400–1700: History, Techniques, Functions and Receptions*. Leiden; Boston, pp. 180–86.

De Poorter, N. 2000. Of Olympian gods, Homeric heroes and an Antwerp Apelles. Observations on the function and 'meaning' of mythological themes in the age of Rubens (1600–1650). In Schoon and Paarlberg 2000, pp. 65–85.

de Smaele, H. 2016. Achilles or Adonis: Controversies surrounding the male body as national symbol in Georgian England. *Gender & History* 25(1), pp. 77–101.

Desmond, M. and Sheingorn, P. 2003. *Myth, Montage, & Visuality in Late Medieval Manuscript Culture: Christine de Pizan's Epistre Othea*. Ann Arbor.

Dickinson, O. T. P. K. 2005. The 'Face of Agamemnon'. *Hesperia* 74(3), pp. 299–308.

Dickinson, O. T .P. K., Papazoglou-Manioudaki, L, Nafplioti, A. and Prag, A. J. N. W. 2012. Mycenae Revisited Part 4: Assessing the New Data. *Annual of the British School at Athens* 107, pp. 161–88.

Doherty, L. E. (ed.) 2009. *Homer's Odyssey. Oxford Readings in Classical Studies*. Oxford.

Döhle, B. 1967. Die Achilleis des Aischylos in ihrer Auswirkung auf die attische Vasenmalerei des 5. Jahrhunderts. *Klio* 49, pp. 63–149.

Dougherty, C. 2001. *The Raft of Odysseus: The Ethnographic Imagination of Homer's Odyssey*. New York.

Dudkiewicz, J. 2016. The Kelmscott Manor *Venus* and Morris's Idea for a 'House of Love' at Red House. *Useful and Beautiful. The Newsletter of the William Morris Society in the United States* 2016(1), pp. 3–18.

Dué, C. 2006. *The Captive Woman's Lament in Greek Tragedy*. Austin. http://nrs.harvard.edu/urn-3:hul.ebook:CHS_Due.The_Captive_Womans_Lament_in_Greek_Tragedy.2006 [accessed 25.8.2019].

Dunbabin, K. M. D. 1978. *The Mosaics of Roman North Africa: Studies in Iconography and Patronage*. Oxford.

Easton, D. M. 1984. Priam's Treasure. *Anatolian Studies* 34, pp. 141–69.

Easton, D. M. 1991. Troy before Schliemann. In *Studia Troica* 1, pp. 111–29.

Easton, D. M. 1994. Priam's Gold: The Full Story. *Anatolian Studies* 44, pp. 221–43.

Easton, D. M. 1998. Heinrich Schliemann: Hero or Fraud? *Classical World* 91, pp. 335–43.

Easton, D. M. 2002. *Schliemann's Excavations at Troia 1870–1873. Studia Troica* 2. Mainz.

Easton, D. M. et al. 2002. Troy in Recent Perspective. *Anatolian Studies* 52, pp. 75–109.

Edmunds, L. 2015. *Stealing Helen: The Myth of the Abducted Wife in Comparative Perspective*. Princeton; Oxford.

Edwards, R. R. 1998. Troy Book: Introduction. In R. R. Edwards (ed.) *John Lydgate, Troy Book: Selections*. Kalamazoo. https://d.lib.rochester.edu/teams/text/edwards-lydgate-troy-book-introduction [accessed 18.8.2019].

Ellis-Evans, A. 2016. The Koinon of Athena Ilias and its Coinage. *American Journal of Numismatics* 28, pp. 105–58.

Erskine, A. 2001. *Troy Between Greece and Rome. Local Tradition and Imperial Power*. Oxford; New York.

Eskilson, S. J. 2007. *Graphic Design: A New History*. New Haven.

Etman, A. M. 2011. Homer in the Arab World. In J. Nelis (ed.) *Receptions of Antiquity*. Gent, pp. 69–79.

Fagence Cooper, S. 2003. *Pre-Raphaelite Art in the Victoria & Albert Museum*. London.

Fagles, R. 1998. *The Iliad*. London

Falke, M. 2006. *Mythos Kassandra. Texte von Aischylos bis Christa Wolf*. Leipzig.

Fantuzzi, M. and Tsagalis, C. (eds) 2015. *The Greek Epic Cycle and Its Ancient Reception: A Companion*. Cambridge.

Farnoux, A. 2019. Homère et son image. In Farnoux et al. 2019, pp. 82–103.

Farnoux, A. and Estaquet-Legrand, A. 2019. III. L'Odyssée. In Farnoux et al. 2019, pp. 184 221.

Farnoux, A., Jaubert, A., Piralla, L. and Pomarède, V. 2019. *Homère*. Paris.

Farrell, J. 2004. Roman Homer. In Fowler 2004, pp. 254–71.

Felleman, S. 2015. *Real Objects in Unreal Situations: Modern Art in Fiction Films*. Bristol; Chicago.

Ferrari, R. C., 2017. The Sculptor, the Duke, and Queer Art Patronage: John Gibson's *Mars Restrained by Cupid* and Winckelmannian Aesthetics. In T. Macsotay (ed.) *Rome, Travel and the Sculpture Capital, c. 1770–1825*. London; New York, pp. 225–47.

Fiedler, T. 1973. Brecht and Cavafy. *Comparative Literature* 25(3), pp. 240–46.

Finkel, I. and Seymour, M. J. 2008. *Babylon: Myth and Reality*. London.

Finley, G. 1999. *Angel in the Sun. Turner's Vision of History*. Montreal.

Fitton, J. L. 1991. *Heinrich Schliemann and the British Museum*. London.

Fitton, J. L. 1995. *The Discovery of the Greek Bronze Age*. London.

Fitton, J. L. 2007. Troy and the role of the historical advisor. In Winkler 2007, pp. 99–106.

Fittschen, K. 1973. *Der Schild des Achilleus. Archaeologia Homerica* II.N.1. Göttingen.

Fonseca, R. C. 2015. The Pindaric poetry of Cruz e Silva and the Neoclassical revival among Lusitanian national heroes. In Goldwyn 2015, pp. 111–27.

Fornaro, S. 2018. A Sea of Metal Plates: Images of the Mediterranean from the Eighteenth Century until Post-modern Theatre. In Rovira Guardiola 2018, pp. 109–20.

Foulke, R. 1997. *The Sea Voyage Narrative*. New York.

Fowler, B. (ed.) 2004. *The Cambridge Companion to Homer*. Cambridge.

Frazer, J. G. 1921. *Apollodorus, The Library*. Loeb Classical Library. Cambridge, MA; London.

Friedman, R. 2007. Derek Walcott's Odysseys. *International Journal of the Classical Tradition* 14(3/4), pp. 455–80.

Frisch, P. 1975. *Die Inschriften von Ilion. Inschriften griechischer Städte aus Kleinasien*, 3. Bonn.

Froning, H. 1981. *Marmor-Schmuckreliefs mit griechischen Mythen im 1. Jahrhundert V. Chr.: Untersuchungen zu Chronologie und Funktion*. Mainz.

Furtwängler, A. and Loeschcke, G. 1886. *Mykenische Vasen: vorhellenische Thongefässe aus dem Gebiete des Mittelmeeres*. Berlin.

Galinsky, K. 1969. *Aeneas, Sicily and Rome*. Princeton.

Gallo, L. 2009. *Lord Elgin and Ancient Greek Architecture: The Elgin Drawings at the British Museum*. Cambridge.

Gantz, T. 1993. *Early Greek Myth*. Baltimore.

Gaschke, J. 2006. *Hellas ... in one living picture: Britische Reisende und die visuelle Aneignung Griechenlands im frühen 19. Jahrhundert*. Frankfurt; New York.

Gell, W. 1804. *The Topography of Troy*. London.

Gere, C. and Rudoe, J. 2010. *Jewellery in the Age of Queen Victoria: A Mirror to the World*. London.

Gillgren, P. 2011. *Siting Federico Barocci and the Renaissance Aesthetic*. Farnham.

Giroux, H. 1986. Eris. In *LIMC* III, pp. 846–50.

Giuliani, L. 2013. *Image and Myth: A History of Pictorial Narration in Greek Art*. Chicago; London.

Gladstone W. E. 1858 [2010]. *Studies on Homer and the Homeric Age*, Vol. III. Cambridge.

Godfrey, R. T. 2001. *James Gillray: The Art of Caricature*. London.

Goldwyn, A. J. (ed.) 2015a. *The Trojan Wars and the Making of the Modern World*. Uppsala.

Goldwyn, A. J. 2015b. Achaeans, Athenians and Americans in the Post-9/11 Era. Comparing empires in *The New York Times*. In Goldwyn 2015a, pp. 245–58.

González González, M. 2018. *Achilles. Gods and Heroes of the Ancient World*. London; New York.

Goodison, J. W. and Robertson, G. H. 1967. *Catalogue of Paintings in the Fitzwilliam Museum, Cambridge. Italian School*. Cambridge.

Görich, K. 2006. Troia im Mittelalter – der Mythos als politische Legitimation. In Zimmermann 2006, pp. 120–34.

Graf, F. 2002. Zum Figurenbestand der Ilias: Götter. In J. Latacz (ed.) *Homers Ilias. Gesamtkommentar. Prolegomena*. Munich; Leipzig, pp. 115–32.

Grassinger, D. 1999. *Die mythologischen Sarkophage Teil I, Achill, Adonis, Aeneas, Aktaion, Alkestis, Amazonen. Die antiken Sarkophagreliefs* 12.1. Berlin.

Graziosi, B. 2002. *Inventing Homer: The Early Reception of Epic*. Cambridge.

Graziosi, B. 2016. *Homer*. Oxford.

Graziosi, B. and Greenwood, E. (eds) 2007. *Homer and the Twentieth Century: Between World Literature and the Western Canon*. Oxford.

Green, P. 2005. *The Poems of Catullus*. Berkeley.

Greenwood, E. 2007. Logue's Tele-Vision: Reading Homer from a Distance. In Graziosi and Greenwood 2017, pp. 145–76.

Greub, T. 2008. Nähe und Ferne zu Homer: Die künstlerische Rezeption Homers in der Neuzeit. In Latacz et al. 2008, pp. 265–75.

Griffiths, A. and Carey, F. 1994. *German Printmaking in the Age of Goethe*. London.

Grillo, L. 2010. Leaving Troy and Creusa: Reflections on Aeneas' flight. *The Classical Journal* 106(1), pp. 43–68.

Grote, G. 1880 [1846]. *History of Greece*, Vol. 1. 2nd edn, New York.

Grube, G. M. A. 1957. *Longinus, On Great Writing (On the Sublime)*. New York.

Guarino, G. A. 1963. *Boccaccio, Concerning Famous Women*. New Brunswick, NJ.

Güterbock, H. G. 1986. Troy in Hittite texts? Wilusa, Ahhiyawa, and Hittite history. In J. M. Machteld (ed.) *Troy and the Trojan War*. Bryn Mawr, pp. 33–44.

Hackett, H. 2014. A new image of Elizabeth I: The three goddesses theme in art and literature. *Huntington Library Quarterly* 77(3), pp. 225– 56.

Haderer, S. 2018. A fairytale palace on Corfu I: The Achilleion and Empress Elisabeth of Austria. *Royalty Digest Quarterly* 4(2018), pp. 56–61.

Haderer, S. 2019. A fairytale palace on Corfu II: The Achilleion and German Emperor Wilhelm II. *Royalty Digest Quarterly* 1(2019), pp. 48–54.

Hagen, R.-M. and Hagen, R. 2005. *What Great Paintings Say: From the Bayeux Tapestry to Diego Rivera*. Vol. 2. Cologne.

Hall, E. 1989. *Inventing the Barbarian: Greek Self-definition through Tragedy*. Oxford.

Hall, E. 2008. *The Return of Ulysses. A Cultural History of Homer's Odyssey*. London; New York.

Hammerschlag, K. R. 2015. *Frederic Leighton: Death, Mortality, Resurrection*. Aldershot.

Hampe, R. and Krauskopf, R. 1981. Alexandros. In *LIMC* I, pp. 494–529.

Hänsel, A. 2009. *Schliemann und Troja*. Berlin.

Hardie, P. 2014. *The Last Trojan Hero: A Cultural History of Virgil's Aeneid*. New York.

Harich-Schwarzbauer, H. 2008. Homer in der römischen Literatur. In Latacz et al. 2008, pp. 245–59.

Harris, E. T. 1990. *Henry Purcell's Dido and Aeneas*. Oxford.

Harris, S. 2008. Friedrich Hoelderlin: Ueber Achill (1799). In J. Morrison and F. Krobb (eds) *Prose Pieces, Germanistik in Ireland*. Konstanz, pp. 39–46.

Harrison, T. 2000. *The Emptiness of Asia: Aeschylus' Persians and the History of the Fifth Century*. London.

Hart, M. L. 2010. *The Art of Ancient Greek Theater. Exhibition Catalogue*. Los Angeles.

Hartop, C. 2005. *Royal Goldsmiths: The Art of Rundell & Bridge 1797–1843*. Cambridge.

Haskell, F. and Penny, N. 1982. *Taste and the Antique*. New Haven; London.

Hasluck, F. W. 1911/1912. Topographical Drawings in the British Museum illustrating Classical Sites and Remains in Greece and Rome. *The Annual of the British School at Athens* 18, pp. 270–81.

Haubold, J. 2013. *Greece and Mesopotamia: Dialogues in Literature*. Cambridge.

Hausmann, C. 1994. Penelope. In *LIMC* VII, pp. 290–95.

Hawkins, J. D. 1998, Tarkasnawa King of Mira 'Tarkondemos', Boğazköy Sealings and Karabel, *Anatolian Studies* 48, pp. 1–31.

Hawkins, J. D. and Easton, D. M. 1996. A hieroglyphic seal from Troia. In *Studia Troica* 6, pp. 111–18.

Haynes, N. 2019. *A Thousand Ships*. London.

Haywood, J. and Mac Sweeney, N. 2018. *Homer's Iliad and the Trojan War: Dialogues on Tradition*. London.

Healy, F. 2003. 'This is Homer and more than Homer'. Rubens' depiction of the Life of Achilles. In Lammertse and Vergara (eds) 2003, pp. 43–55.

Heard, K. and Whitaker, L. 2011. *The Northern Renaissance: From Dürer to Holbein*. London.

Hearn, K. 1998. An English gentleman painter, Henry Gibbs. *Burlington Magazine* 140(1139), pp. 99–101.

Heckmann, S. and Ottomeyer, H. 2009. *Kassandra: Visionen des Unheils 1914–1945*. Berlin.

Hedreen, G. 2001. *Capturing Troy: The Narrative Functions of Landscape in Archaic and Early Classical Greek Art*. Ann Arbor.

Hedreen, G. 2011. The Trojan War, theoxenia, and Aegina in Pindar's *Paean* 6 and the Aphaia sculptures. In D. Fearn (ed.) *Aegina: Contexts for Choral Lyric Poetry*. Oxford, pp. 323–69.

Henig, M. and MacGregor, A. 2004. *Catalogue of the Engraved Gems and Finger-Rings in the Ashmolean Museum. II. Roman*. Oxford.

Herda, A. 2012. Soul and *Kosmos*. Menelaos and the Shield of Euphorbos in Didyma. In V. Bers, D. Elmer, D. Frame and L. Muellner (eds) *Donum natalicium digitaliter confectum Gregorio Nagy septuagenario a discipulis collegis familiaribus oblatum. A virtual birthday gift presented to Gregory Nagy on turning seventy by his students, colleagues, and friends*. http://chs.harvard.edu/wa/pageR?tn=ArticleWrapper&bdc=12&mn=4804 [accessed 25.8.2019].

Hertel, D. and Kolb, F. 2003. Troy in clearer perspective. *Anatolian Studies* 53, pp. 71–88.

Higgins, C. 2018. *Red Thread. On Mazes and Labyrinths*. London.

Hodske, J. 2007. *Mythologische Bildthemen in den Häusern Pompejis: Die Bedeutung der zentralen Mythenbilder für die Bewohner Pompejis*. Ruhpolding.

Hofstetter, E. 1997. Seirenes. In *LIMC* VIII, pp. 1097–104.

Holcroft, A. 1988. Francesco Xanto Avelli and Petrarch. *Journal of the Warburg and Courtauld Institutes* 51, pp. 225–34.

Holoka, J. P. 2006. *Simone Weil's the Iliad or Poem of Force: A Critical Edition*. Frankfurt.

Hopkinson, N. 2018. *Quintus Smyrnaeus, Posthomerica*. Loeb Classical Library 19. Harvard.

Hopman, M. G. 2012. *Scylla: Myth, Metaphor, Paradox*. Cambridge; New York.

Horkheimer, M. and Adorno, T. W. 1988 [1944]. *Dialektik der Aufklärung*. Frankfurt.

Hornblower, S. 2015. *Lykophron: Alexandra*. Oxford; New York.

Hornblower, S. and Biffis, G. 2018. *The Returning Hero: Nostoi and Traditions of Mediterranean Settlement*. Oxford.

Horowitz, W. 1998. *Mesopotamian Cosmic Geography*. Winona Lake.

Houghton, L. 1994. Virgil in Art. In Martindale 1994, pp. 141–70.

Hughes, B. 2005. *Helen of Troy, Goddess, Princess, Whore*. New York.

Hunter, R. 2014. Homer and Greek literature. In Fowler 2004, pp. 235–53.

Hunter, R. and Rutherford, I. (eds) 2009. *Wandering Poets in Ancient Greek Culture: Travel, Locality and Pan-Hellenism*. Cambridge; New York.

Inglis-Jones, E. 1950. *Peacocks in Paradise*. London.

James, A. 2004. *Quintus of Smyrna. The Trojan Epic. Posthomerica*. Baltimore; London.

Janko, R. 1992. *The Iliad: A Commentary*. Vol. IV, books 13–16. Cambridge.

Janko, R. 2017. From Gabii and Gordion to Eretria and Methone: The Rise of the Greek Alphabet. In J. Strauss Clay, I. Malkin and Y. Z. Tzifopoulos (eds) *Panhellenes at Methone. Graphê in Late Geometric and Protoarchaic Methone, Macedonia (ca. 700 BCE)*. Berlin; New York, pp. 135–64.

Jeffers, R. 1965. *Selected Poems*. New York.

Jeffery, L. H. 1990, *The Local Scripts of Archaic Greece*. Revised with a supplement by A. W. Johnston, Oxford.

Jenkins, C. 2017. *Prints at the Court of Fontainebleau, c. 1542–47*. Ouderkerk aan den Ijssel.

Jenkins, I. 2002. The earliest representation in Greek art of the death of Ajax. In A. Clark et al. (eds) *Essays in Honour of Dietrich von Bothmer*. Amsterdam, pp. 153–56.

Jenkins, T. E. 2011. Heavy Metal Homer. Countercultural Appropriations of the *Odyssey* in Graphic Novels. In Kovacs and Marshall 2011, pp. 221–35.

Jentel, M.-O. 1997. Skylla I. In *LIMC* VIII Suppl., pp. 1137–45.

Joyce, J. 1922. *Ulysses*. Paris.

Joyner, D. B. 2014. Virgil, portraits of. In R. F. Thomas and J. M. Ziolkowski (eds) *The Virgil Encyclopedia*. Malden, MA; Oxford.

Kader, I. 2006. *Penelope rekonstruiert. Geschichte und Deutung einer Frauenfigur*. Munich.

Kahil, L. 1955. *Les enlèvements et le retour d'Hélène dans les texte et les documents figurés*. Paris.

Kahil, L. 1988a. Euphorbos I. In *LIMC* IV, p. 69.

Kahil, L. 1988b. Helene. In *LIMC* IV, pp. 498–572.

Kaltsas, N. and Shapiro, A. (eds) 2008. *Worshiping Women: Ritual and Reality in Classical Athens*. New York.

Karentzos, A. 2005. *Kunstgöttinnen: mythische Weiblichkeit zwischen Historismus und Secessionen*. Marburg.

Katz Anhalt, E. 2017. *Enraged: Why Violent Times Need Ancient Greek Myths*. New Haven; London.

Kauffmann, C. M. 1973. *Catalogue of Foreign Paintings, I. Before 1800*. London.

Kazantzakis, N. 1958 [1938]. *The Odyssey: A Modern Sequel*. Translated by Kimon Friar. London; New York.

Keeley, E. and Sherrard, P. 1995. *Collected Poems (George Seferis)*. Princeton.

Kelder, J. et al. (eds) 2012. *Troy: City, Homer, Turkey*. Zwolle.

Kenworthy-Browne, J. 1972. A Ducal Patron of Sculptors. *Apollo* 96(128), pp. 322–31.

Kerschner, M. 2014. Euboean Imports to the East Aegean and East Aegean Productions of Pottery in Euboean Style: New Evidence from Neutron Activation Analyses. In M. Kerschner and I. S. Lemos (eds) *Archaeometric Analyses of Euboean and Euboean Related Pottery: New Results and Their Interpretations*. Vienna, pp. 109–40.

Kidson, A. 2015. *George Romney: A Complete Catalogue of His Paintings*. New Haven.

King, K. C. 1987. *Achilles. Paradigms of a War Hero from Homer to the Middle Ages*. Berkeley; Los Angeles; London.

Kitson, M. 1960. The 'Altieri Claudes' and Virgil. *The Burlington Magazine* 102(688), pp. 312–18.

Klarmann, J. 2015. Max Slevogt als Illustrator – die Folge 'Achill' aus Homers 'Ilias'. http://blog.liebermann-villa.de/max-slevogt-als-illustrator-die-folge-achill-aus-homers-ilias/ [accessed 27.4.2019].

Kline, A. S. 2000. *Ovid: The Metamorphoses. A Complete Translation and Mythological Index*. www.poetryintranslation.com/PITBR/Latin/Ovhome.php [accessed 8.8.2019].

Klironomos, M. 2018. Nikos Kazantzakis' *Odysseia*: The Epic Sequel in Modern Greek Poetry and Classical Reception. In Simms 2008, pp. 189–205.

Knittlmayer, B. 1997. *Die Attische Demokratie und ihre Helden, Darstellungen des trojanischen Sagenkreises im 6. und frühen 5. Jh.v.Chr.* Heidelberg.

Kohl, P. and Fawcett, C. (eds) 1996. *Nationalism, Politics and the Practice of Archaeology*. Cambridge.

Kolb, F. 2010. *Tatort 'Troia': Geschichte, Mythen, Politik*. Paderborn.

Kolb, F. 2014–15. Phantom Trojans at the Dardanelles?, *Talanta* 46–47, pp. 27–50.

Korfmann, M. (ed.) 2006. *Troia: Archäologie eines Siedlunghügels und seiner Landschaft*. Mainz.

Kossatz-Deissmann, A. 1981. Achilleus. In *LIMC* I, pp. 37–200.

Kossatz-Deissmann, A. 1986. Briseis. In *LIMC* III, pp. 157–67.

Kossatz-Deissmann, A. 1994. Paridis Iudicium. In *LIMC* VII, pp. 176–88.

Kovacs, D. (ed.) 1994. *Euripides: Cyclops, Alcestis, Medea*. Loeb Classical Library 12. Cambridge, MA.

Kovacs, D. (ed.) 1999. *Euripides: Trojan Women, Iphigenia among the Taurians, Ion*. Loeb Classical Library 10. Cambridge, MA.

Kovacs, G. and Marshall, C. W. (eds) 2011. *Classics and Comics. Classical Presences*. Oxford; New York.

Kovacs, G. and Marshall, C. W. (eds) 2016. *Son of Classics and Comics*. Oxford.

Krauskopf, I. 1988. Helene/Elina. In *LIMC* IV, pp. 563–72.

Kreiser, K. 2001. Troia und die homerischen Epen. Von Mehmet II. bis İsmet İnönü. In Latacz et al. 2001, pp. 282–91.

Kron, U. 1981a. Aithra. In *LIMC* I, pp. 420–37.

Kron, U. 1981b. Akamas et Demophon. In *LIMC* I, pp. 435–46.

Kunze, M. (ed.) 1999. *Wiedergeburt griechischer Götter und Helden: Homer in der Kunst der Goethezeit*. Mainz.

Lammertse, F. 2003. Small, larger, largest: the making of Peter Paul Rubens' 'Life of Achilles'. In Lammertse and Vergara 2003, pp. 11–31.

Lammertse, F. and Vergara, A. (eds) 2003. *Peter Paul Rubens: The Life of Achilles*. Rotterdam; Madrid.

Lane Fox, R. 2008. *Travelling Heroes: Greeks and Their Myths in the Epic Age of Homer*. London.

Langdon, H. 1999. *Claude Lorrain*. 2nd edn, London.

Lapeña Marchena, Ó. 2018. Ulysses in the cinema: the example of *Nostos, il ritorno* (Franco Piavoli, Italy 1990). In Rovira Guardiola 2018, pp. 93–107.

La Rocca, E. 1999. Odysseus in der Unterwelt. In Andreae 1999, pp. 269–88.

Lascarides, A. C. 1977. *The Search for Troy: 1553–1874*. Bloomington.

Latacz, J. 2004. *Troy and Homer: Towards a Solution of an Old Mystery*. Oxford.

Latacz, J. 2014. Cy Twombly mit Achill vor Troia. In T. Greub (ed.) *Cy Twombly Bild, Text, Paratext*. Paderborn, pp. 116–66.

Latacz, J. et al. (eds) 2001. *Troia: Traum und Wirklichkeit*. Stuttgart.

Latacz, J. et al. (eds) 2008. *Homer. Der Mythos von Troia in Dichtung und Kunst*. Munich.

Lavagnini, R. 2016. Tales of the Trojan War: Achilles and Paris in Medieval Greek Literature. In C. Cupane and B. Krönung (eds) *Fictional Storytelling in the Medieval Eastern Mediterranean and Beyond*. Leiden, pp. 234–59.

Leclercq-Marx, J. 1997. *La sirène dans la pensée et dans l'art de l'Antiquité et du Moyen Âge. Du mythe païen au symbole chrétien*. Brussels.

Lecoq, A.-M. 2004. Poésie et peinture: le bouclier d'Achille, *Comptes rendus des séances de l'Académie des Inscriptions et Belles-Lettres* 148(1), pp. 11–42.

Lecoq, A.-M. 2010. *Le bouclier d'Achille: Un tableau qui bouge*. Paris.

Lee, A. 2013. *The Ugly Renaissance*. London.

Lentzsch, F. et al. 2005. *Fuseli: The Wild Swiss*. Zurich.

Letoublon, F. 2014. Le Palladion dans la guerre de Troie: un talisman du cycle épique, un tabou de l'*Iliade*. In G. Scafoglio and E. Lelle (eds) *Studies on the Greek Epic Cycle* (*Philologia Antiqua* 7–8), pp. 61–84.

Lienert, E. 1996. *Geschichte und Erzählen. Studien zu Konrads von Würzburg, Trojanerkrieg*. Wiesbaden.

Lienert, E. 2001. Ein mittelalterlicher Mythos. In Latacz et al. 2001, pp. 204–11.

Lochman, T. (ed.) 1999. *"Antico-mix". Antike in Comics*. Basel.

Lorandi, M. 1996. *Il mito di Ulisse nella pittura a fresco del Cinquecento italiano*. Milan.

Löschenberger, N. 2012. Held und Antiheld: Leitfiguren antiker Autoren in Grafikzyklen von Max Slevogt und Lovis Corinth. Aachen, PhD Diss. http://publications.rwth-aachen.de/record/51090/files/4334.pdf [accessed 25.8.2019].

Lovatt, H. 2013. Operatic Visions: Berlioz stages Virgil. In H. Lovatt and C. Vout (eds) *Epic Visions: Visuality in Greek and Latin Epic and Its Reception*. Cambridge; New York, pp. 60–77.

Lowenstam, S. 2008. *As Witnessed by Images: The Trojan War Tradition in Greek and Etruscan Art*. Baltimore

Luce, J. V. 1998. *Celebrating Homer's Landscapes: Troy and Ithaca Revisited*. New Haven.

Luckhardt, J. 2001. Moralische Bilder und antike Gestalt. In Latacz et al. 2001, pp. 245–56.

McConnell, J. 2013. *Black Odysseys: The Homeric Odyssey in the African Diaspora Since 1939*. Oxford.

McHardy, F. and Deacy, S. 2015. Ajax, Cassandra and Athena: Retaliatory warfare and gender violence at the sack of Troy. In G. Lee, H. Whittaker and G. Wrightson (eds) *Ancient Warfare: Introducing Current Research*. Vol. 1. Cambridge, pp. 252–72.

Mackay, E. A. 2010. *Tradition and Originality. A Study of Exekias*. Oxford.

Maclaren, C. 1863. *The Plain of Troy Described and the Identity of the Ilium of Homer with the Ilium Novum of Strabo Proved*. Edinburgh.

McNamee, K. 2007. *Annotations in Greek and Latin texts from Egypt*. Oakville.

Mac Sweeney, N. 2018. *Troy: Myth, City, Icon*. London.

Maguire, L. 2009. *Helen of Troy: From Homer to Hollywood*. Oxford.

Maguire, M. (ed.) 2011. *Titokowaru's Dilemma*. Christchurch.

Malkin, I. 1998. *The Returns of Odysseus: Colonization and Ethnicity*. Berkeley.

Mangieri, A. F. 2018. *Virgin Sacrifice in Classical Art: Women, Agency, and the Trojan War*. London.

Mangold, M. 2000. *Kassandra in Athen. Die Eroberung Trojas auf attischen Vasenbildern*. Berlin.

Manguel, A. 2007. *Homer's the* Iliad *and the* Odyssey*: A Biography*. London.

Mansfield, E. 2007. *Too Beautiful to Picture: Zeuxis, Myth and Mimesis*. Minneapolis.

Marchand, L. A. (ed.) 1978. *Byron's Letters and Journals*, Vol. VIII: 'Born for opposition', 1821, Harvard.

Martindale, C. (ed.) 1997. *The Cambridge Companion to Virgil*. Cambridge.

Martyniuk, I. 2005. Playing with Europe: Derek Walcott's Retelling of Homer's *Odyssey. Callaloo* 28(1), pp. 188–99.

Massa-Pairault, F. H. 1972. *Recherches sur quelques séries d'urnes de Volterra*. Rome.

Matthews, W. H. 1922. *Mazes and Labyrinths. A General Account of Their History and Development*. London.

Meineck, P. and Konstan, D. (eds) 2014. *Combat Trauma and the Ancient Greeks*. The New Antiquity. New York.

Messel, T. 2012. *Oliver Messel: In the Theatre of Design*. New York.

Meyer, M. 2012. Der Heros als Alter Ego des Kriegers in archaischer und klassischer Zeit. Bilder im Wandel. *Antike Kunst* 55, pp. 25–51.

Michaels, J. E. 2015. The Trojan War as a warning for her time: Christa Wolf 's depiction of feminism and the Cold War in her Cassandra project. In Goldwyn 2015, pp. 203–22.

Michalowski, P. 2010. Matters for the Four Corners of the Heavens: Views of the Universe in Early Mesopotamian Writings. In K. A. Raaflaub and R. J. A. Talbert (eds) *Geography and Ethnography: Perceptions of the World in Pre-Modern Societies*. Chichester, pp. 147–68.

Midford, S. 2010. From Achilles to Anzac: Heroism in the Dardanelles from Antiquity to the Great War. *Australasian Society for Classical Studies* 31, pp. 1–12.

Midford, S. 2011. Constructing the 'Australian *Iliad*': Ancient Heroes and Anzac Diggers in the Dardanelles. *Melbourne Historical Journal* 39(2), pp. 59–79.

Midford, S. 2013. Anzacs and the Heroes of Troy: Exploring the Universality of War in Sidney Nolan's 'Gallipoli Series'. In I. Güran Yumsak and M. Mehdi Ilhan (eds) *Gelibolou: Tarih, Esfane ve Ani (Gallipoli: History, Legend and Memory)*. Istanbul, pp. 303–12.

Millar, D., 1995. *The Victorian Watercolours in the Collection of Her Majesty The Queen*. London.

Millar, O. 1963. *The Tudor, Stuart and Early Georgian Pictures in the Collection of Her Majesty The Queen*. London.

Miller, M. 2011. *The Song of Achilles*. London.

Miller, M. 2018. *Circe*. London.

Mitchell, A. G. 2009. *Greek Vase Painting and the Origins of Visual Humour*. Cambridge.

Miziołek, J. 2006. The 'Odyssey' *Cassone* Panels from the Lanckoroński Collection: On the Origins of Depicting Homer's Epic in the Art of the Italian Renaissance. *Artibus et Historiae* 27(53), pp. 57–88.

Moennig, U. 2018. Intertextuality in the Late Byzantine Romance Tale of Troy. In T. Shawcross and I. Toth (eds) *Reading in the Byzantine Empire and Beyond*. Cambridge, pp. 351–72.

Montanari, F. 2008. Die Rezeption der Homerischen Dichtung im lateinischen Mittelalter. In Latacz et al. 2008, pp. 259–64.

Montiglio, S. 2011. *From Villain to Hero: Odysseus in Ancient Thought*. Michigan.

Moore, J. 1957. *The Complete Greek Tragedies. Sophocles II*. Chicago.

Moorehead, C. 1994. *The Lost Treasures of Troy*. London.

Moormann, E. M. 2000. Between Olympus and Merwede. Greek gods and heroes in Dutch culture in the late Middle Ages and the Renaissance. In Schoon and Paarlberg 2000, pp. 15–33.

Moraw, S. 2018. Der miles Christianus als Sirenen- und Skyllatöter. Die Odyssee in den monastischen Diskursen des Mittelalters. In Rehm 2018, pp. 105–25.

Moret, J. M. 1975. *L'Ilioupersis dans la ceramique italiote*. Rome.

Morris, I. and Powell, B. (eds) 1997. *A New Companion to Homer*. Leiden.

Morris, S. P. 1997. Homer and the Near East. In Morris and Powell 1997, pp. 599–623.

Morris, S. P. 2014. Helen Re-Claimed, Troy Re-Visited: Scenes of Troy in Archaic Greek Art. In A. Avramidou and D. Demetriou (eds) *Approaching the Ancient Artifact: Representation, Narrative, and Function. A Festschrift in Honor of H. Alan Shapiro*. Berlin, pp. 3–14.

Morton, M. 2014. *Max Klinger and Wilhelmine Culture: On the Threshold of German Modernism*. Farnham.

Mountjoy, P. A. 2017. *Troy VI Middle, VI Late and VII. The Mycenaean Pottery. Studia Troica* 9. Bonn.

Muellner, L. 2012. Grieving Achilles. In F. Montanari, A. Rengakos and C. Tsagalis (eds) *Homeric Contexts: Neoanalysis and the Interpretation of Oral Poetry*. Berlin; Boston, pp. 197–220.

Müller, J.-D. 2004. Das höfische Troia des deutschen Mittelalters. In H. Hofmann (ed.) *Troia: von Homer bis heute*. Tübingen, pp. 119–41.

Muth, S. 2006. Bilder des Troias-Mythos in der griechischen Kunst. In Zimmermann 2006, pp. 71–88.

Nagy, G. 1999. *The Best of the Achaeans: Concepts of the Hero in Archaic Greek Poetry*. Revised edn. Harvard University: Centre for Hellenic Studies. http://nrs.harvard.edu/urn-3:hul.ebook:CHS_NagyG.The_Best_of_the_Achaeans.1999 [accessed 18.4.2019].

Nagy, G. 2010. *Homer the Preclassic*. Harvard. https://chs.harvard.edu/CHS/article/display/4377.gregory-nagy-homer-the-preclassic [accessed 25.8.2019].

Nagy, G. 2013. *The Ancient Greek Hero in 24 Hours*. Cambridge, MA. http://nrs.harvard.edu/urn-3:hul.ebook:CHS_NagyG.The_Ancient_Greek_Hero_in_24_Hours.2013 [accessed 2.5.2019].

Nativel, C. 2011. Peter Paul Rubens, 'L'Homère de la peinture'? In L. Capodieci and P. Ford (eds) *Homère à la Renaissance: Mythe et transfigurations*. Paris, pp. 399–422.

Neils, J. 1994. Priamos. In *LIMC* VII, pp. 507–22.

Newby, Z. 2016. *Greek Myths in Roman Art and Culture: Imagery, values and Identity in Italy. 50 BC – AD 150*. Cambridge.

Newton, C. T. 1880. *Essays on Art and Archaeology*. London.

Newton, C. T. 1865. *Travels & Discoveries in the Levant*. London.

Nicholson, K. 1990. *Turner's Classical Landscapes: Myth and Meaning*. Princeton.

Nicolson, A. 2014. *The Mighty Dead*. London.

Noussia-Fantuzzi, M. 2015. The Epic Cycle, Stesichorus, and Ibycus. In Fantuzzi and Tsagalis 2015, pp. 430–49.

Oman, C. 1968. *The Golden Age of Hispanic Silver 1400–1665*. London.

O'Meally, R. G. 2007. *Romare Bearden: A Black Odyssey*. New York.

Opper, T. 2003. Ancient glory and modern learning: The sculpture-decorated library. In K. Sloan (ed.) *Enlightenment, Discovering the World in the Eighteenth century*. London, pp. 58–67.

Osborne, R. 2018. *The Transformation of Athens: Painted Pottery and the Creation of Classical Greece*. Princeton.

Pallantza, E. 2005. *Der troische Krieg in der nachhomerischen Literatur bis zum 5. Jahrhundert v. Chr*. Stuttgart.

Palmer, K. (ed.) 1982. *Troilus and Cressida*. Arden Shakespeare. London.

Parke, H. 1933. The bones of Pelops and the siege of Troy. *Hermathena* 23(48), pp. 153–62.

Parker, R. 2017. *Greek Gods Abroad: Names, Natures, and Transformations. Sather Classical Lectures* 72. Oakland.

Paton, W. R. 1917. *The Greek Anthology III. Book 9: The Declamatory Epigrams*. Cambridge, MA.

Paul, J. 2013. Madonna and whore: The many faces of Penelope in *Ulisse*. In K. Nikoloutsos (ed.) *Ancient Greek Women in Film*. Oxford, pp. 139–61.

Pavúk, P. 2002. Troia VI and VIIa. The Blegen Pottery Shapes: Towards a Typology. In *Studia Troica* 12, Mainz, pp. 35–71.

Pearsall, C. D. J. 2008. *Tennyson's Rapture: Transformation in the Victorian Dramatic Monologue*. Oxford.

Pearsall, D. 2015. Chaucer's Criseyde and Shakespeare's Cressida: Transformations in the reception history of the Troy story. In Goldwyn 2015, pp. 35–50.

Pepe, M. 2019. Filippo Albacini. *Dizionario Biografico degli Italiani*. http://www.treccani.it/biografie/ [accessed 23.4.2019].

Pernicka, E., Rose, C. B. and Jablonka, P. (eds) 2014. *Troia 1987–2012: Grabungen und Forschungen I. Forschungeschichte, Methoden und Landschift. Studia Troica* 5. Bonn.

Petrain, D. 2014. *Homer in Stone: The Tabulae Iliacae in their Roman Context. Greek Culture in the Roman World*. Cambridge; New York.

Phillips, E. D. 1959. The Comic Odysseus. *Greece & Rome* 6(1), pp. 58–67.

Picón, C. A. and Hemingway, S. (eds) 2016. *Pergamon and the Hellenistic Kingdoms of the Ancient World*. New York.

Piotrovskii, Y. 2013. *Bronzovii Vek: Evropa bez Granits* (Bronze Age: Europe Without Borders). St Petersburg.

Pipili, M. 1994. Philoktetes. In *LIMC* VII, pp. 376–85.

Piralla-Heng Vong, L. 2019. Figures féminines. In Farnoux et al. 2019, pp. 222–49.

Pollini, J. 2011. Roman marble sculpture. In M. Merrony (ed.) *Mougins Museum of Classical Art*. Mougins, pp. 73–110.

Pomarède, V. 2019. Le poème du retour: Ithaque. In Farnoux et al. 2019, pp. 250–71.

Pope-Hennessy, J. 1964. *Catalogue of Italian Sculpture in the Victoria and Albert Museum*. London.

Posselt, B. 2015. *Konzeption und Kompilation der Schedelschen Weltchronik* (= *Monumenta Germaniae historica*, Schriften, Band 71). Wiesbaden.

Potts, A. 1994. *Flesh and the Ideal: Winckelmann and the Origins of Art History*. New Haven; London.

Power, H. 2018. Christopher Logue, Alexander Pope and the Making of *War Music*. *The Review of English Studies* 69(291), pp. 747–66.

Pratt, L. R. 1983. Maud Gonne: 'Strange Harmonies Amid Discord'. *Biography* 6(3), pp. 189–208.

Pressly, N. 1979. *The Fuseli Circle in Rome: Early Romantic Art of the 1770s*. New Haven.

Prettejohn, E., Trippi, P., Upston, R. and Wageman, P. 2008. *J. W. Waterhouse: The modern Pre-Raphaelite*. London.

Price, S. and Price, R. 2006. *Romare Bearden: The Caribbean Dimension*. Philadelphia.

Rahner, H. 1963. *Greek Myths and Christian Mystery*. London.

Ready, J. L. and Tsagalis, C. C. (eds) 2018. *Homer in Performance. Rhapsodes, Narrators, and Characters*. Texas.

Recke, M. 2002. *Gewalt und Leid, Das Bild des Krieges bei den Athenern im 6. und 5. Jh. v. Chr*. Istanbul.

Rees, J. 1999. 'Der weitläufigste Maler, den die Natur hervorgebracht hat': mediale Aspekte der Homerrezeption des Comte de Caylus. In Kunze 1999, pp. 220–36.

Rehm, U. (ed.) 2018. *Mittelalterliche Mythenrezeption. Paradigmen und Paradigmenwechsel*. Weimar.

Reilly, P. 2010. Raphael's 'Fire in the Borgo' and the Italian Pictorial Vernacular. *The Art Bulletin* 92(4), pp. 308–25.

Reilly, R. 1995. *Wedgwood: The New Illustrated Dictionary*. Woodbridge.

Renger, A.-B. 1999. Imagination gefährlicher Liebschaften: Die Sirenen in der Malerei des europäischen Spätsymbolismus. In Kunze 1999, pp. 277–93.

Rennie, N. 1995. *Far-Fetched Facts: The Literature of Travel and the Idea of the South Seas*. Oxford.

Reynolds, A. 2013. *In Fine Style: The Art of Tudor and Stuart Fashion*. London.

Richards, J. 2009. John Ruskin, the Olympian painters and the amateur stage. In A. Heinrich, K. Newey and J. Richards (eds) *Ruskin, the Theatre and Victorian Visual Culture*. Basingstoke, pp. 19–41.

Richter, G. M. A. 1965. *The Portraits of the Greeks*. London.

Riedel, V. 1999. Goethe und Homer. In Kunze 1999, pp. 243–59.

Riggs, C. T. 1954. *History of Mehmed the Conqueror, by Kritovoulos*. Princeton.

Rigoni, M. A. 2007. Ettore, Achille e Ulisse nell'interpretazione di Leopardi. In Colpo et al. 2007, pp. 163–66.

Rodner, W. S. 1997. *J. M. W. Turner: Romantic Painter of the Industrial Revolution*. Berkeley.

Romm, J. S. 1992. *The Edges of the Earth in Ancient Thought: Geography, Exploration, and Fiction*. Princeton.

Rosand, W. 1991. *Opera in Seventeenth-Century Venice: The Creation of a Genre*. Berkeley.

Rose, C. B. 2014. *The Archaeology of Greek and Roman Troy*. Cambridge.

Rovira Guardiola, R. (ed.) 2018. *The Ancient Mediterranean Sea in Modern Visual and Performing Arts: Sailing in Troubled Waters*. Imagines: Classical Receptions in the Visual and Performing Arts. London.

Roworth, W. W. 1992. Kauffman and the Art of Painting in England. In W. W. Roworth (ed.) *Angelica Kauffman: A Continental Artist in Georgian England*. London, pp. 11–95.

Rubens, B. and Taplin, O. 1989. *An Odyssey Round Odysseus*. London.

Ruden, S. 2008. *The Aeneid*. New Haven.

Sabetai, V. and Avronidaki, C. 2018. The Six's Technique in Boiotia: Regional Experiments in Technique and Iconography. *Hesperia* 87, pp. 311–85.

Sadurska, A. 1986. Equus Troianus. In *LIMC* III, pp. 813–17.

Said, E. 1978. *Orientalism*. New York.

Salvador Ventura, F. 2015. *From Ithaca to Troy: The Homeric City in Cinema and Television*. London.

Salvadori, M. 2007. Riflessi dell'epos omerico nel cinema: i 'ritorni' di Ulisse. In Colpo et al. 2007, pp. 185–96.

Scappaticcio, M. C. 2013. *Papyri Vergilianae: l'apporto della Papirologia alla Storia della Tradizionee virgiliana (I-VI d.C.)*. Liege.

Schefold, K. 1966. *Myth and Legend in Early Greek Art*. London.

Schefold, K. 1978. *Götter- und Heldensagen der Griechen in der spätarchaischen Kunst*. Munich.

Schefold, K. 1992. *Gods and Heroes in Late Archaic Greek Art*. London.

Schefold, K. 1993. *Götter- und Heldensagen der Griechen in der früh- und hocharchaischen Kunst*. Munich.

Schefold, K. and Jung, F. 1989. *Die Sagen von den Argonauten, von Theben und Troia in der klassischen und hellenistischen Kunst*. Munich.

Scherer, M. 1963. *The Legends of Troy in Art and Literature*. New York.

Schiff, G. 1973. *Johann Heinrich Füssli 1741–1825*. Zurich.

Schliemann, H. 1867. *La Chine et le Japon au temps présent*. Paris.

Schliemann, H. 1869. *Ithaque, le Péloponnèse, Troie, recherches archéologiques*. Paris.

Schliemann, H. 1874a. *Trojanische Alterthümer: Bericht über die Ausgrabungen in Troja*. Leipzig.

Schliemann, H. 1874b. *Atlas trojanischer Alterthümer: Photographische Berichte über die Ausgrabungen in Troja*. Leipzig.

Schliemann, H. 1875. *Troy and Its Remains*. London.

Schliemann, H. 1878. *Mycenae: A Narrative of Researches and Discoveries at Mycenae and Tiryns*. London.

Schliemann, H. 1880. *Ilios: The City and Country of the Trojans*. London.

Schliemann, H. 1881. Exploration of the Boeotian Orchomenus. *Journal of Hellenic Studies* 2, pp. 122–63.

Schliemann, H. 1884. *Troja: results of the latest researches and discoveries on the site of Homer's Troy and in the heroic tumuli and other sites, made in the year 1882 and a narrative of a journey in the Troad in 1881*. London.

Schliemann, H. and Dörpfeld, W. 1891. Report on the Excavations at Troy in 1890. In K. Schuchhardt *Schliemann's Excavations: An Archaeological and Historical Study*. London, pp. 323–49.

Schmidl, H. 1902. *Heinrich Schliemann's Sammlung Trojanischer Altertümer*. Berlin.

Schmitt, A. 2008. Gott und Mensch bei Homer. In Latacz et al. 2008, pp. 164–70.

Schneider, R. M. 2004. Verehrt – verdrängt – vergessen? Der 'Speerträger' der Münchner Universität. *Aviso: Zeitschrift für Wissenschaft und Kunst in Bayern* 3, pp. 10–17.

Schofield, L. and Parkinson, R. 1994. Of helmets and heretics: A possible Egyptian representation of Mycenaean warriors on a papyrus from El-Amarna. *The Annual of the British School at Athens* 89, pp. 157–70.

Schoon, P. and Paarlberg, S. (eds) 2000. *Greek Gods and Heroes in the Age of Rubens and Rembrandt*. Athens; Dordrecht.

Schubring, P. 1923. *Cassoni: Truhen und Truhenbilder der italienischen Frührenaissance: ein Beitrag zur Profanmalerei im Quattrocento*. Leipzig.

Schwartz, E. 2004. *The Legacy of Homer: Four Centuries of Art from the École Nationale Supérieure des Beaux-Arts*. Paris.

Scodel, R. 2008. Stupid, Pointless Wars. *Transactions of the American Philological Association* 138(2), pp. 219–35.

Scott, J. 2003. *The Pleasures of Antiquity: British Collections of Greece and Rome*. Yale.

Scully, S. 2003. Reading the Shield of Achilles: Terror, anger, delight. *Harvard Studies in Classical Philology* 101, pp. 29–47.

Seferis, G. 1976. *Collected Poems, 1924–1955*. Translated by Edmund Keeley. Princeton.

Severin, T. 1987. *The Ulysses Voyage*. London.

Sgubini Moretti, A. M. 2004. *Eroi etruschi e miti greci: gli affreschi della Tomba François tornano a Vulci*. Calenzano.

Shanower, E. 2013. Trojan Lovers and Warriors: The Power of Seduction in *Age of Bronze*. In S. Knippschild and M. G. Morcillo (eds) *Seduction and Power: Antiquity in the Visual and Performing Arts*. London; New York, pp. 57–70.

Shapiro, H. A. 1994. *Myth into Art: Poet and Painter in Classical Greece*. New York; London.

Shay, J. 1994. *Achilles in Vietnam: Combat Trauma and the Undoing of Character*. New York.

Shay, J. 2002. *Odysseus in America: Combat Trauma and the Trials of Homecoming*. New York.

Sheedy, K. 2009. Ios and Syros. Studies in the Hellenistic Coinages of the Cyclades. In S. Drougou et al., *Kermatia philias: timētikos tomos gia ton Iōannē Touratsoglou* (Coins of Friendship:

Festschrift for Ioannis Touratsoglou), Athens, pp. 263–69.

Shepard, A. and Powell, S. D. (eds) 2004. *Fantasies of Troy. Classical Tales and the Social Imaginary in Medieval and Early Modern Europe*. Toronto.

Sherratt, E. S. 1990. 'Reading the texts': archaeology and the Homeric question. *Antiquity* 64, pp. 807–24.

Shields, J. C. 2001. *The American Aeneas: Classical Origins of the American Self*. Knoxville.

Sider, D. 2010. Greek verse on a vase by Douris. *Hesperia* 79, pp. 541–54.

Siebert, A. V. 2011. *Geschichte(n) in Ton. Römische Architekturterrakotten*. Regensburg.

Silver, C. 2007. *Renkioi: Brunel's Forgotten Crimean War Hospital*. Sevenoaks.

Simms, R. (ed.) 2018. *Brill's Companion to Prequels, Sequels, and Retellings of Classical Epic*. Leiden.

Simon, E. 2001. Rom und Troia. In Latacz et al. 2001, pp. 154–73.

Simon, E. 2008. Homer in der römischen Bildkunst. In Latacz et al. 2008, pp. 232–44.

Sinn, U. 2006. Der Troia-Mythos in der römischen Kunst. In Zimmermann 2006, pp. 104–19.

Sluijter, E. J. 2000. Prestige and emulation, eroticism and morality: Mythology and the nude in Dutch painting of the 16th and 17th century. In Schoon and Paarlberg 2000, pp. 35–63.

Smith, A. H. 1904. *A Catalogue of Sculpture in the Department of Greek and Roman Antiquities*, Vol. III. London.

Smith, E. L. 2002. *Evelyn Pickering De Morgan and the Allegorical Body*. Madison; London.

Snodgrass, A. 1998. *Homer and the Artists: Text and Picture in Early Greek Art*. Cambridge.

Sparkes, B. A. 1971. The Trojan Horse in Classical Art. *Greece & Rome* 18(1), pp. 54–70.

Spencer, R. 2000. 'Introduction'. In R. Spencer (ed.) *Eduardo Paolozzi: Writings and Interviews*. Oxford, pp. 1–43.

Spivey, N. 2016. Homer and the Sculptors. In J. Bintliff and K. Rutter (eds) *The Archaeology of Greece and Rome: Studies in Honour of Anthony Snodgrass*. Edinburgh, pp. 113–52.

Spurling, J. and Bryant, J. 1994. *The Trojan War: Sculptures by Anthony Caro*. London.

Squire, M. 2011. *The Iliad in a Nutshell: Visualizing Epic on the Tabulae Iliacae*. Oxford.

Squire, M. 2013. Ekphrasis at the forge and the forging of ekphrasis: the 'Shield of Achilles' in Graeco-Roman word and image. *Word & Image* 29(2), pp. 157–91.

Staal, F. 2008. *Discovering the Vedas: Origins, Mantras, Rituals, Insights*. New Delhi.

Stampolidis, N. Ch. and Oikonomou, S. (eds) 2014. *Beyond. Death and Afterlife in Ancient Greece*. Athens.

Stampolidis, N. Ch. and Storsve, J. 2017. *Divine Dialogues: Cy Twombly and Greek Antiquity*. Athens.

Stanford, W. B. 1963. *The Ulysses Theme*. 2nd edn, Oxford.

Stanford, W. B. and Luce, J. V. 1974. *The Quest for Odysseus*. New York.

Stansbury-O'Donnell, M. 1999. *Pictorial Narrative in Ancient Greek Art*. Cambridge.

Stansbury-O'Donnell, M. D. 2009. The Structural Differentiation of Pursuit Scenes. In D. Yatromanolakis (ed.) *An Archaeology of Representations: Ancient Greek Vase-Painting and Contemporary Methodologies*. Athens.

Stechow, W. 1938. Ludolph Buesinck: A German Chiaroscuro master of the seventeenth century. *Print Collectors' Quarterly* 25, pp. 393–419.

Stewart, A. 2014. *Art in the Hellenistic World: An Introduction*. New York.

Stewart, P. 2016. The Provenance of the Gandharan 'Trojan Horse' Relief in the British Museum. *Arts Asiatiques* 71, pp. 3–12.

Stinton, T. C. W. 1965. *Euripides and the Judgement of Paris*. London.

Stoschek, J. 1999. Themen der Odyssee in der italienischen Malerei des 15. und 16. Jahrhunderts. In Kunze 1999, pp. 195–203.

Strauss, W. L. 1973. *Chiaroscuro: The Clair-Obscur Woodcuts by the German and Netherlandish Masters of the XVI and XVII Centuries*. London.

Suhr, N. 1992. Max Slevogt als Graphiker. In E.-G. Gäse, H.-J. Imiela and B. Roland (eds) *Max Slevogt. Gemälde, Aquarelle, Zeichnungen*. Stuttgart, pp. 75–93.

Syson, L. and Thornton, D. 2001. *Objects of Virtue. Art in Renaissance Italy*. London.

Tanner, M. 1993. *The Last Descendant of Aeneas: The Hapsburgs and the Mythic Image of the Emperor*. New Haven.

Taplin, O. 1980. The Shield of Achilles within the *Iliad*. *Greece & Rome* 27(1), pp. 1–21.

Theisen, N. 2011. Declassicizing the Classical in Japanese Comics. In Kovacs and Marshall, 2011, pp. 59–72.

Thompson, D. 2013. *The Trojan War: Literature and Legends from the Bronze Age to the Present*. 2nd edn, Jefferson; London.

Thornton, D. and Wilson, T. 2009. *Italian Renaissance Ceramics: A Catalogue of the British Museum Collection*. London.

Touchefeu, O. 1981a. Aias I. In *LIMC* I, pp. 312–36.

Touchefeu, O. 1981b. Aias II. In *LIMC* I, pp. 336–51.

Touchefeu, O. 1984. Astyanax I. In *LIMC* II, pp. 929–37.

Touchefeu, O. 1988. Hektor. In *LIMC* IV, pp. 482–98.

Touchefeu, O. 1992a. Odysseus. In *LIMC* VI pp. 943–70.

Touchefeu, O. 1992b. Nausicaa. In *LIMC* VI, pp. 712–14.

Touchefeu, O. 1992c. Mnesteres II. In *LIMC* VI, pp. 631–34

Touchefeu-Meynier, O. 1968. *Thèmes Odysséens dans l'Art Antique*. Paris.

Touchefeu-Meynier, O. 1981. Andromache I. In *LIMC* I, pp. 767–74.

Touchefeu-Meynier, O. 1994. Polyxène. In *LIMC* VII, pp. 431–35.

Touchefeu-Meynier, O. 1997. Patroklos. In *LIMC* VIII, pp. 948–52.

Traill, D. 1984. Schliemann's discovery of 'Priam's treasure': a re-examination of the evidence. *Journal of Hellenic Studies* 104, pp. 96–115.

Traill, D. 1995. *Schliemann of Troy: Treasure and Deceit*. Harmondsworth.

Traill, D. 2000. 'Priam's Treasure': Clearly a Composite. *Anatolian Studies* 50, pp. 17–35.

Treuherz, J., Prettejohn, E. and Becker, E. 2003. *Dante Gabriel Rossetti*. London.

Trusted, M. 2008. *The Return of the Gods: Neoclassical Sculpture in Britain*. London.

Tuchman, B. 1984. *The March of Folly: From Troy to Vietnam*. New York.

Tynan, M. 2011. *Postcolonial Odysseys: Derek Walcott's Voyages of Homecoming*. Newcastle.

Usher, S. 1985. *Dionysius of Halicarnassus. Critical Essays*, Volume II: *On Literary Composition. Dinarchus. Letters to Ammaeus and Pompeius*. Loeb Classical Library 466. Cambridge, MA.

Vandiver, E. 2008. Homer in British World War One Poetry. In L. Hardwick and C. Stray (eds) *A Companion to Classical Receptions*. Oxford, pp. 452–65.

Vandiver, E. 2010. *Stand in the Trench, Achilles: Classical Receptions in British Poetry of the Great War*. Oxford.

Van Heurck, J. 2013. *Cassandra*. Christa Wolf. Translated from the German by Jan Van Heurck. London.

van Wees, H. 2004. *Greek Warfare. Myths and Realities*. London.

Verstegen, I. 2015. Conjugal Piety: Creusa in Barocci's *Aeneas' Flight from Troy*. In A. Poe and M. Rose (eds) *Receptions of Antiquity, Constructions of Gender in European Art, 1300–1600*. Leiden, pp. 393–417.

Vickers, M. 2006. *The Arundel and Pomfret Marbles*. Oxford.

Virchow, R. 1884. Troy and Hissarlik. In Schliemann 1884, pp. 673–85.

Volkommer, R. 1997. Thetis. In *LIMC* VIII, pp. 6–14.

Von den Hoff, R. 2005. Achill, das Vieh? Zur Problematisierung transgressiver Gewalt in klassischen Vasenbildern. In S. Moraw and G. Fischer (eds) *Die andere Seite der Klassik: Gewalt im 5. und 4. Jahrhundert. v. Chr.* Stuttgart, pp. 225–46.

Waagen, G. 1854. *Treasures of Art in Great Britain*, Vol. III. London.

Waal, W. 2017. How to read the signs: The use of symbols, markings and pictographs in Bronze Age Anatolia. In A.-M. Jasink, J. Weingarten and S. Ferrara (eds) *Non-scribal Communication Media in the Bronze Age Aegean and Surrounding Areas*. Florence.

Walcott, D. 1987. *Collected Poems, 1948–1984*. New York.

Walcott, D. 1990. *Omeros*. New York.

Walcott, D. 1993. *The Odyssey: A Stage Version*. New York.

Walker, S. 1990. *Catalogue of Roman Sarcophagi in the British Museum*. London.

Walsh, D. 2009. *Distorted Ideals in Greek Vase-Painting: The World of Mythological Burlesque*. Cambridge.

Walter, U. 2006. Die Rache der Priamos-Enkel? Troia und Rom. In Zimmermann 2006, pp. 89–103.

Wannagat, D. 1999. Die 'Bostoner Kirkeschale': Homerische Mythen in dionysischer Deutung? *Antike Kunst* 42, pp. 9–20.

Ward Jones Jr., J. 2011. *Aeneid* 2: Sizing up Vergil's horse. *The Classical Outlook* 89(1), pp. 6–9.

Warr, G. C. 1887. *Echoes of Hellas*. London.

Węcowski, M. 2014. *The Rise of the Greek Aristocratic Banquet*. Oxford.

Węcowski, M. 2017. Wine and the Early History of the Greek Alphabet. Early Greek Vase-Inscriptions and the Symposion. In J. Strauss Clay, I. Malkin and Y. Z. Tzifopoulos (eds) *Panhellenes at Methone. Graphê in Late Geometric and Protoarchaic Methone, Macedonia (ca. 700 BCE)*. Berlin; New York, pp. 309–28.

Weis, H. A. 2000. Odysseus at Sperlonga. In N. T. de Grummond and B. S. Ridgway (eds) *From Pergamon to Sperlonga: Sculpture and Context*. Berkeley, pp. 111–65.

West, M. L. 2001. *Studies in the Text and Transmission of the* Iliad. Munich; Leipzig.

West, M. L. 2003. *Greek Epic Fragments*. Loeb Classical Library 497. Cambridge MA; London.

West, M. L. 2005. *Odyssey* and *Argonautica*. *The Classical Quarterly* 55(1), pp. 39–64.

West, M. L. 2011a. *The Making of the* Iliad: *Disquisition and Analytical Commentary*. Oxford.

West, M. L. 2011b. The Homeric Question Today. *Proceedings of the American Philosophical Society* 155(4), pp. 383–93.

West, M. L. 2013. *The Epic Cycle. A Commentary on the Lost Troy Epics*. Oxford.

West, M. L. 2017. *The Making of the Odyssey*. Oxford; New York.

Whitaker, C. L. 1986. *The Florentine Picture Chronicle: A Reappraisal*. Unpublished PhD dissertation, Courtauld Institute of Art.

Williams, D. 1983. Sophilos in the British Museum. In *Greek Vases in the J. Paul Getty Museum* 1. Malibu, pp. 9–34.

Williams, D. 1993. *Corpus Vasorum Antiquorum* (Great Britain, 17; The British Museum, 9). London.

Williamson, P. and Davies, G. 2014. *Medieval Ivory Carvings, 1200–1500*. London.

Wilson, E. 2017, *Homer. The Odyssey*. New York.

Wilson, P. 2004. Homer and the English epic. In Fowler 2004, pp. 272–86.

Wilton, A. and Upstone, R. 1997. *The Age of Rossetti, Burne-Jones & Watts: Symbolism in Britain 1860–1910*. London.

Winkler, M. M. 2007. *Troy. From Homer's* Iliad *to Hollywood Epic*. Malden; Oxford.

Winkler, M. M. 2015. *Return to Troy. New Essays on the Hollywood Epic*. Leiden.

Wiseman, C. 1998. *Elisabeth Frink: Original Prints: Catalogue Raisonné*. London.

Wolf, A. and Wolf, H.-H. 1983. *Die wirkliche Reise des Odysseus. Zur Rekonstruktion des Homerischen Weltbildes*. Munich; Vienna.

Wolf, C. 1983. *Kassandra*. Darmstadt.

Wolf, K. 2009. *Troja – Metamorphosen eines Mythos. Französische, englische und italienische Überlieferungen des 12. Jahrhunderts im Vergleich*. Berlin.

Wood, M. 1985. *In Search of the Trojan War*. London.

Wood, R. 1775. *An Essay on the Original Genius of Homer*. London.

Woodford, S. 1993. *The Trojan War in Ancient Art*. London; New York.

Woodford, S. and Loudon, M. 1980. Two Trojan themes: The iconography of Ajax carrying the body of Achilles and of Aeneas carrying Anchises in black figure vase painting. *American Journal of Archaeology* 84(1), pp. 25–40.

Wright, D. H. 2001. *The Roman Vergil and the Origins of Medieval Book Design*. London.

Wünsche, R. (ed.) 2006. *Mythos Troja*. Munich.

Young, H. 2000. Pierre Stephan: The Career of a Derby Modeller Reviewed. *Derby Porcelain International Society* 4, pp. 83–93.

Young, P. H. 2003. *The Printed Homer: A 3,000 Year Publishing and Translation History of the* Iliad *and the* Odyssey. Jefferson.

Zanker, P. and Ewald, B. 2012. *Living with Myths: The Imagery of Roman Sarcophagi*. Oxford.

Zimmermann, M. (ed.) 2006. *Der Traum von Troia. Geschichte und Mythos einer ewigen Stadt*. Munich.

Zintzen, C. 1998. *Von Pompeji nach Troja. Archäologische Literatur und Öffentlichkeit*. Vienna.

Zintzen, C. 2001. Ich taufe sie mit den Namen Troia und Ilium…. In Latacz et al. 2001, pp. 430–39.

PICTURE CREDITS

Fig. 1 akg-images/Pietro Baguzzi
Fig. 2 © Trustees of the Paolozzi Foundation, Licensed by DACS 2019. Purchased 1982 © Tate, London 2019
Fig. 3 (detail of Fig. 252) © The Fitzwilliam Museum, Cambridge
Fig. 4 Images & Stories/Alamy Stock Photo
Fig. 5 © Christoph Haußner, München
Fig. 6 © Romare Bearden Foundation/VAGA at ARS, NY and DACS, London 2019.

Mary and Leigh Block Fund (1977.127), Art Institute of Chicago. Image: © 2019. The Art Institute of Chicago/Art Resource, NY/Scala, Florence
Fig. 7 © The National Gallery, London
Fig. 8 © Barford Sculptures Ltd. Photo: Christopher Cunningham
Fig. 10 © The British Library Board (Papyrus 271 (2) f002r)
Fig. 15 Donated by the British School of Archaeology, Egypt
Fig. 16 © The British Library Board (Burney MS 86 f240v)
Fig. 17 Courtesy the Department of Classics, University of Cincinnati
Fig. 18 With permission of the Soprintendenza Archeologia Belle Arti e Paesaggio per l'area metropolitana di Napoli. Museo Archeologico di Pithecusae, Villa Arbusto, Lacco Ameno.
Fig. 21 © 2019. Photo Scala, Florence
Fig. 22 With permission of the Ministero per i Beni e le Attività Culturali – Museo Archeologico Nazionale di Napoli. Photo: Patrizio Lamagna/Giorgio Albano
Fig. 24 On loan from University College London, Institute of Archaeology. Image © The Trustees of the British Museum
Fig. 28 © Antikensammlung, Staatliche Museen zu Berlin, Preussischer Kulturbesitz. Photo: Johannes Laurentius
Fig. 29 Photo © RMN-Grand Palais (musée du Louvre)/Hervé Lewandowski
Fig. 32 © 2019. DeAgostini Picture Library/ Scala, Florence
Fig. 33 With permission of the Ministero per i Beni e le Attività Culturali – Museo

Archeologico Nazionale di Napoli. Photo: Luigi Spina
Fig. 34 Rome, Musei Capitolini, Sala delle Colombe – Archivio Fotografico dei Musei Capitolini, foto Vasari © Roma, Sovrintendenza Capitolina ai Beni Culturali
Fig. 37 © Antikensammlung, Staatliche Museen zu Berlin, Preussischer Kulturbesitz. Photo: Christa Begall
Fig. 40 With permission of the Ministero per i Beni e le Attività Culturali – Museo Archeologico Nazionale di Napoli. Photo: Patrizio Lamagna/Giorgio Albano
Fig. 41 With permission of the Ministero per i Beni e le Attività Culturali – Museo Archeologico Nazionale di Napoli.
Fig. 44 With permission of the Ministero per i Beni e le Attività Culturali – Museo Archeologico Nazionale di Napoli. Photo: Luigi Spina
Fig. 45 © Antikensammlung, Staatliche Museen zu Berlin, Preussischer Kulturbesitz. Photo: Johannes Laurentius
Fig. 46 Map: Kate Morton
Fig. 48 Hewitt Fund, 1925. Metropolitan Museum of Art, New York
Fig. 50 Donated by C. W. Scott
Fig. 52a, b Staatliche Antikensammlungen und Glyptothek München. Photograph by Renate Kühling
Fig. 54 Bequeathed by Sir William Temple
Fig. 57 Granger/Bridgeman Images
Fig. 59 With permission of the Ministero per i Beni e le Attività Culturali – Museo Archeologico Nazionale di Napoli. Photo: Giorgio Albano
Fig. 60 From the Woburn Abbey Collection.

Photo: Joanna Fernandes and Kevin Lovelock
Fig. 64 b Line drawing: Kate Morton
Fig. 66a, b The National Museum of Denmark. Photo: Roberto Fortuna and Kira Ursem
Fig. 67 From the Woburn Abbey Collection. Photo: Joanna Fernandes and Kevin Lovelock
Fig. 71 © 2019. Photo Scala, Florence – courtesy of the Ministero Beni e Att. Culturali e del Turismo
Fig. 74 Bequeathed through Dr George Witt
Fig. 76a, b The National Museum of Denmark. Photo: Roberto Fortuna and Kira Ursem
Figs 78, 79 © Ashmolean Museum, University of Oxford
Fig. 80 Funded by Brooke Sewell Permanent Fund
Fig. 81 With permission of the Ministero per i Beni e le Attività Culturali – Museo Archeologico Nazionale di Napoli. Photo: Luigi Spina
Fig. 82 © Antikensammlung, Staatliche Museen zu Berlin. Preussischer Kulturbesitz. Photo: Ingrid Geske
Fig. 83 Bequeathed by Richard Payne Knight
Fig. 85 Illustration: Kate Morton
Fig. 89 Courtesy The David Rumsey Map Collection, David Rumsey Map Center, Stanford Libraries. https://purl.stanford. edu/jm802mt4110
Fig. 91 Image courtesy the Museum of Troy
Fig. 92 © 2019. DeAgostini Picture Library/ Scala, Florence
Fig. 93 © Antikensammlung, Staatliche Museen zu Berlin. Preussischer Kulturbesitz. Photo: Ingrid Geske

LIST OF LENDERS

Antikensammlung, Staatliche Museen zu
    Berlin
The Ashmolean Museum, University of Oxford
Barford Sculptures
The British Library
The Courtauld Institute of Art
The Collection of Alan and Pat Davidson
De Morgan Foundation
The Devonshire Collections, Chatsworth
The Duke of Bedford, the Trustees of the
    Bedford Estates and Woburn Abbey and
    Gardens
Ferens Art Gallery
Fitzwilliam Museum, University of Cambridge
Guildhall Art Gallery
Her Majesty the Queen, Royal Collection Trust
Imperial War Museum
Kunsthaus Zürich
Lisson Gallery
Manchester Art Gallery
Musée d'Art Classique de Mougins
Museo Archeologico di Pithecusae
Museo Archeologico Nazionale di Napoli
Museum für Vor- und Frühgeschichte,
    Staatliche Museen zu Berlin
National Trust
Nationalmuseet, Denmark
The Provost and Fellows of Eton College
Ronald Feldman Fine Arts
Tate
University College London
Victoria and Albert Museum

ACKNOWLEDGMENTS

Many people have been involved in the making of this book and the exhibition it accompanies, and those named below are but some of the many colleagues, friends and collaborators to whom we are deeply grateful.

We are indebted first of all to the individuals and institutions who lent objects to the exhibition and whose works form the core of this book: Museum für Vor- und Frühgeschichte, Staatliche Museen zu Berlin (Marion Bertram, Bernhard Heeb, Susanne Anger and Ramona Föllmer); Antikensammlung, Staatliche Museen zu Berlin (Agnes Schwarzmaier, Nina Zimmermann); Ashmolean Museum, University of Oxford (Paul Roberts, Sophie Evans); Barford Sculptures (Paul Caro, Patrick Cunningham); The British Library (Peter Toth, Claire Breay, Julian Harrison, Hazel Shorland); Courtauld Institute of Art (Karen Serres, Alexandra Gerstein, Julia Blanks); De Morgan Foundation (Sarah Hardy, Sacha Springthorpe); Devonshire Collections, Chatsworth (Charles Noble, Alice Martin, Diane Naylor, Martha Marriott); the Duke of Bedford, the Trustees of the Bedford Estates and Woburn Abbey and Gardens (Matthew Hirst, Victoria Poulton); the Collection of Alan and Pat Davidson (via Edward De Luca, DC Moore Gallery); Ferens Art Gallery (Kirsten Simister, Simon Braithwaite); Fitzwilliam Museum, University of Cambridge (Jane Munro, David Packer, Elena Saggers); Guildhall Art Gallery (Jeremy Johnson, Katherine Pearce); Her Majesty the Queen, Royal Collection Trust (Desmond Shawe-Taylor, Kathryn Jones, Emma Stuart, Carly Collier, Samantha Johnson); Imperial War Museums (Alexandra Walton, Alan Wakefield, Maria Rollo); Kunsthaus

Zürich (Christoph Becker, Karin Marti); Spencer Finch and Lisson Gallery; Manchester Art Gallery (Natasha Howes, Hannah Williamson, David Carden); Christian and Florence Levett and the Musée d'Art Classique de Mougins (Leisa Paoli); Museo Archeologico di Pithecusae (Teresa Elena Cinquantaquattro, Maria Luisa Tardugno); Museo Archeologico Nazionale di Napoli (Paola Rubino de Ritis); National Trust (Susan Paisley, Fernanda Torrente, Phoebe Meiklejohn-McLaughlin); Nationalmuseet, Denmark (Peter Pentz, Lasse Sørensen, Barbara Berlowicz); Provost and Fellows of Eton College (Stephanie Coane, Lucy Cordingley); Eleanor Antin and Ronald Feldman Fine Arts (Peggy Kaplan, Marco Nocella); Tate (Andrew Wilson, Sarah Jane Stockings); University College London (Nikolaos Gonis); Victoria and Albert Museum (Ruth Hibbard, Hannah Kauffman, Kirstin Kennedy, Michaela Zoschg, Andrew Kirk, Richard Edgcumbe, Helen Dawson).

The project has received consistent encouragement from the Museum's Director, Hartwig Fischer, and Deputy Directors, notably Jonathan Williams and Joanna Mackle. Particular thanks go to our Project Manager, Holly Wright, and Interpretation Officer, Rebecca Penrose.

Thanks are also due to many curatorial colleagues, academic collaborators, volunteers and others within the British Museum as well as outside, who generously contributed their expertise and time: Camille Acosta, Richard Abdy, Ellen Adams, Madeleine Allen, Charles Arnold, Abigail Baker, Giulia Bartrum, Lloyd de Beer, Lois Bird, Dirk Booms, Hugo Chapman,

Jessica Clarke, Stephen Coppel, Matteo D'Acunto, Amelia Dowler, Patricia Ferguson, Alexandra Fletcher, Giulietta Guerini, Bernhard Heeb (who also deserves credit for the original idea for the exhibition), Peter Higgs, Francesca Hillier, Olenka Horbatsch, Sushma Jansari, Ian Jenkins, Alan Johnston, Thomas Kiely, Naiose Mac Sweeney, Nico Momigliano and her colleagues at the University of Bristol, Thorsten Opper, Brian Rose, Nicole Coolidge Rousmaniere, Charo Rovira, Nicholas Salmon, Jan Sienkiewicz, Kim Sloan, Neal Spencer, Michael Squire, Judith Swaddling, Ross Thomas, Sarah Vowles, Jonathan Williams, Richard Woff, Susan Woodford. We would like to thank Kate Morton for preparing maps and charts; Kate Brangan for the chapter opening drawings; and John Williams and colleagues in the British Museum's photographic department.

We are grateful to all the core team members: Sandra Smith, Karen Birkhoelzer, Celeste Farge, Hannah James, Philip Jell, Thomas Matthews, Ana Muñoz, Christopher Stewart; Keeley Wilson (Collection Care); Callum Shaw, Samuel Waizeneker (Development); Jill Maggs, Guy Carr, Deklan Kilfeather, Nicola Mayer, Hannah Scully (Exhibitions); Sarah Saunders, Katharine Hoare, Katharine Kelland, Freddie Matthews, Michelle McGrath, Kayte McSweeney, Martin Payne, Sophie Wills (Learning and National Partnerships); Ella Lewis-Collins, Nicola Elvin (Press and Marketing); Carlos Austin-Gonzalez, Clara Potter, Angela Pountney (British Museum Company); Tess Sanders (Information Services). We are enormously grateful to the hard work of their wider teams, which has made

the exhibition possible. Special thanks also to Natalie Buy, Duygu Camurcuoglu, Stuart Frost, Nick Harris, Ann Lumley, Fiona Slater, Vicci Ward and Hilary Williams.

Our external collaborators are also owed a debt of gratitude, even if not all can be named here. The team at Ralph Appelbaum Associates, notably Philip Tefft, Vassiliki Holeva, Mat Mason and Lily Lesser, designed the exhibition. The exhibition interpretation was enhanced by partnerships with two community organizations, whose members brought their own perspectives and insights to the objects and content. They were: Robert Cummings, Moi Watson, Cassandra Gleeson, Tim Jones, John Bryant, Sean Douglas, Mark Evans and Rodney Eldridge from Waterloo Uncovered, a charity supporting veterans through archaeology, and TS Bernard, Carine Zeka, Abdulali Khademi, Adar Adapwa Owuna and Fabiana De Lazzer from Crisis, a national charity for homeless people.

The exhibition would not have been possible without the support of our sponsors, BP, and we are very grateful to Jennifer Suggitt and Des Violaris for making this happen. We are also grateful for the support of the Troy Curator's Circle.

Finally, we want to thank Susanna Ingram at Thames & Hudson, Dan Kosta and Richard Deal at Dexter PreMedia, and Alice Kennedy-Owen and Peter Dawson at Grade Design. Special thanks go to Kathleen Bloomfield, Bethany Holmes and Sarah Vernon-Hunt, our editors at the British Museum and Thames & Hudson, for patiently and skilfully seeing this book through to publication.

INDEX